Davidson
1952

MOCK KINGS IN
MEDIEVAL SOCIETY AND
RENAISSANCE DRAMA

A King and no King.

Acted at the *Globe*, by his Maiesties Seruants.

Written by *Francis Beamount*, and *Iohn Flecher*.

AT LONDON
Printed for *Thomas Walkley*, and are to bee sold
at his shoppe at the Eagle and Childe in
Brittans-Burffe. 1619.

MOCK KINGS IN MEDIEVAL SOCIETY AND RENAISSANCE DRAMA

SANDRA BILLINGTON

CLARENDON PRESS · OXFORD
1991

Oxford University Press, Walton Street, Oxford OX2 6DP

Oxford New York Toronto
Delhi Bombay Calcutta Madras Karachi
Petaling Jaya Singapore Hong Kong Tokyo
Nairobi Dar es Salaam Cape Town
Melbourne Auckland
and associated companies in
Berlin Ibadan

Oxford is a trade mark of Oxford University Press

Published in the United States
by Oxford University Press, New York

© *Sandra Billington 1991*

All rights reserved. No part of this publication may be reproduced,
stored in a retrieval system, or transmitted, in any form or by any means,
electronic, mechanical, photocopying, recording, or otherwise, without
the prior permission of Oxford University Press

British Library Cataloguing in Publication Data
Billington, Sandra
Mock Kings in medieval society and Renaissance drama.
1. Drama in English, 1558–1625. England. Society
I. Title
822.308
ISBN 0-19-811967-4

Library of Congress Cataloging in Publication Data
Billington, Sandra
Mock kings in medieval society and Renaissance drama/Sandra
Billington.
p. cm.
Includes bibliographical references (p.) and index.
1. English drama—Early modern and Elizabethan, 1500–1600—History
and criticism. 2. England—Social life and customs—Medieval
period, 1066–1485. 3. English drama—17th century—History and
criticism. 4. Folk drama, English—History and criticism.
5. Literature and folklore—England. 6. Kings and rulers in
literature. 7. Festivals—England—History. 8. Festivals in
literature. 9. Folklore in literature. 10. Folklore—England.
I. Title.
PR658.K54B55 1991
822'.309—dc20   90-14204
ISBN 0-19-811967-4

Typeset by Rowland Phototypesetting Ltd
Bury St Edmunds, Suffolk

Printed and bound in
Great Britain by Bookcraft Ltd
Midsomer Norton, Bath

To Dorothy and Peter French

Preface

On a term's sabbatical in 1984, one of those conversations beginning, 'Have you read . . . ?' led to my awareness of the possible potential of this subject, and I am grateful to Malcolm Underwood for pointing out to me E. L. G. Stones's article. For further early encouragement and information, I would like to thank Bridget Henisch, Emily Lyle, and Jill Mann; and I am deeply grateful for the interest and enlightened suggestions of Marie and Richard Axton and of Hilda Ellis Davidson during the successive years of work. Further timely interventions, corrections, and nuggets of information came from Sydney Anglo, Alasdair Cameron, Greg Giesekam, Brian Hayward, Kristen Lippincott and other members of the Warburg Institute; Alan Nelson, and Victor Skretkowicz, to all of whom I would like to express my gratitude. I am further grateful to Kenneth Varty and Alison Rawles, for checking my translations of Old French, and to Claude Schumacher for speedily solving many a problem.

Library staff have been invariably helpful and courteous, and I would like to thank all the staff at the Glasgow and Cambridge University Libraries, the National Library of Scotland, and at the British Library—particularly Eve Johanssen; also Elizabeth Arkell at the Bodleian for her informative correspondence. My warm thanks particularly go to Nigel Thorp, Elizabeth Watson, and David Weston for their guidance through the Stirling Maxwell Collection, Glasgow University, and to Trevor Graham for his patience over my search for the ideal print.

I am further grateful to the OUP readers for their helpful comments, to Tom Pettitt for his encouragement of, and corrections to, Chapter 3, and I am especially grateful to Russell Jackson and Peter Thomson, who, despite crowded schedules, found time for detailed, critical reading of the completed typescript. While warmly thanking them all for their guidance, responsibility for errors, omissions, or stubbornness in sometimes going my own way falls solely upon my own head.

Without financial assistance all may well have foundered, and I would like to thank the Carnegie Trust for the Universities of Scotland, for supporting my early research in the libraries at

viii   *Preface*

Cambridge and London, and for help with reproduction fees. I am also most grateful to the Leverhulme Trust for financing a year without teaching, to enable me to complete my research and to write up, without which this book would not yet be finished. I would finally like to thank Jan McDonald and Roy Porter for their repeated support of applications for funding.

University of Glasgow   S.B.

Contents

List of illustrations	xi
Abbreviations	xiii
Introduction	1

PART I

1. Outlaws, Rebels, and Civil War	9
2. Kings of Winter Festive Groups	30
3. Summer Kings and Queens, and Kings of Fortune	55
4. The Role of the Sovereign	86

PART II

A Critical Introduction	117
5. Summer Kings in Conflict: The Popular Perspective in *The Troublesome Raigne of King John*, and *The Misfortunes of Arthur*	123
6. Kings, Princes, and Lords in Shakespeare's Plantagenet Plays	139
7. *Tamburlaine* and *Timon*: Paradigm and Parable	159
8. Comedy	181
9. Festive Tragedy: *Troilus and Cressida*, *King Lear*, and *Antony and Cleopatra*	198
10. Political Dissent and Drama	218
11. Moral Political Criticism through Saturnalia in Jacobean Drama	238
Conclusion	253
Appendices	265
I. *Timon, a play*	265

II. Ben Jonson and 'The War of the Theatres'	272
III. Ben Jonson and *Vetus Comoedia*	273
Select Bibliography	275
Index	283

List of Illustrations

Frontispiece: title-page to Beaumont and Fletcher's *A King and No King*, printed 1619. Variorum edition, ed. R. W. Bond (London, 1904), Glasgow University Library. ii

1. Syons Calamitye, 1643, Thomason Collection, BL 669, fo. 8(17), British Library. 24

2. Costume of 1539 Nuremberg Schembart Festival: *Schönbartbuch*, Fitzwilliam Museum, Cambridge, MS 382, fo. 63. 41

3. *Desert of Religion*, c.1450, BL MS Add. 37049, fo. 80^v, British Library. 61

4. Statutes, St John's College, Oxford, 1562. 62

5. *Le Roman de la rose*, early 15th century, Bodley Douce 371, fo. 40^v, Bodleian Library, Oxford. 66

6. Edmund Spenser, 'Iulye—The Shepheardes Calendar', *Spenser: Poetical Works*, Oxford University Press, 1912. 68

7. Jean Cousin, *Le Livre de fortune*, 1568, reprinted 1883, plate 39, Glasgow University Library. 70

8. *Le Livre de fortune*, plate 181. 70

9. Frontispiece, Robert Recorde's *Castle of Knowledge*, London, 1556, Cambridge University Library. 78

10. *The Mirrour of Maiestie*, 1618, illustration to emblem 28, Glasgow University Library. 81

11. Frontispiece, *Annalia Dubrensia*, 1636, BL B (630)1, British Library. 82

12. Desiderius Erasmus, *Moriae Encomium*, with cartoons by Holbein, Basle 1515, fo. R 1^v, Cambridge University Library. 89

13. The Toison d'or, from Claude Paradin's *Devises heroiques*, 1567, Glasgow University Library. 90

14. The Golden Fleece Inn, Thirsk, Yorkshire. Ray Atkins Photography. 90

15. Holbein's cartoon, 'David Praying' *Moriae Encomium*, fo. V. 4^v, Cambridge University Library. 92

xii   *List of Illustrations*

16. Holbein's cartoon, 'Cardinals', *Moriae Encomium*, fo.
    R. 1ᵛ, Cambridge University Library.   92
17. *Romance of Alexander*, executed in England, *c.*1338,
    Bodley MS 264, fo. 74ʳ, Bodleian Library.   94
18. Thomas Palmer, *Two Hundred Poosees*, 1564–6,
    emblem 5, BL MS Sloane 3794, British Library.   105
19. Frontispiece, *Eikon Basilike*, 1649 edition, Glasgow
    University Library.   259

Abbreviations

AKANK	*A King and No King*
BL	British Library
EETS	Early English Text Society
EHR	*English Historical Review*
HJ	*Historical Journal*
KJ	*King John* (Shakespeare's)
MP	*Modern Philology*
REED	*Records of Early English Drama*
RES	*Review of English Studies*
SP	*Studies in Philology*
SPD	*State Papers Domestic*
SQ	*Shakespeare Quarterly*
SS	*Shakespeare Survey*
STS	Scottish Text Society
TR	*The Troublesome Raigne of King John*
TRHS	*Transactions of the Royal Historical Society*

Play texts used are the Arden editions for all Shakespeare quotations, and where a good modern text is not available for other plays, facsimile reprints are used. I have, however, modernized the titles of Greene's *Frier Bacon and Frier Bongay* and Marston's *Iack Drvms Entertainment* in repeated references to them.

Introduction

The last fifteen years have seen a fruitful investigation into the symbiotic relationship between seasonal festivity and peasant rebels who adopted mock king titles, organizing their defiance of government into festive patterns.[1] The questions and answers which have resulted have radically altered critical views as to the 'safety valve' theory of festive games. The other well-known way of looking at these customs is in the tradition of Mikhail Bahktin, in which the mock king is seen as part of a saturnalian impulse, the *roi pour rire* in medieval carnival who, in Rabelais, was the essence of the indestructible world of folk humour,[2] and who, C. L. Barber perceived, was part of a ritualized disorder which led to social regeneration in some Shakespearean comedy.[3]

The two areas of study are concerned with mock kings as they appear either in festive games or as leaders of peasant rebellions. However, E. L. G. Stones's article on fourteenth-century robber barons makes clear that they too adopted a mock king style.[4] These were men from a different social class, and it seems as improbable that they copied their inferiors as that the association was pure coincidence. Further investigation reveals that real kings, particularly those claiming divine right, might also be given the dubious mock honour, and that as well as the direct analogy there was a further oblique one in which the rise and fall of kings was played out in king games. All but the festive examples were leaders of disorder in the actual fabric of society, therefore it would appear possible that the title bore a relation to real social organization, and the proposition which I am putting forward is that misrule was thought to be allied to rule as an interrelated opposite.

[1] See N. Z. Davis, *Society and Culture in Early Modern France* (London, 1975); Y.-M. Bercé, *Fête et révolte: des mentalités populaires du XVIeme au XVIIIeme siècle* (Paris, 1976); E. le Roy Ladurie, *Carnival in Romans: A People's Uprising at Romans, 1579–80*, trans. M. Feeney (Harmondsworth, 1979); E. J. Hobsbawm and G. Rude, *Captain Swing* (Harmondsworth, 1969); N. Simms, 'Ned Ludd's Mummers Play', *Folklore*, 89 (1978); and T. Pettitt, 'Here Comes I, Jack Straw', *Folklore*, 95 (1984).
[2] M. Bakhtin, *Rabelais and his World*, trans. C. Emerson (Manchester, 1984), p. 5. Cf. M. Bristol, *Carnival and Theater* (London, 1985), pp. 27, 52–3.
[3] C. L. Barber, *Shakespeare's Festive Comedy* (Princeton, 1959), *passim*.
[4] E. L. G. Stones, 'The Folvilles of Ashby-Folville, Leicestershire, and their Associates in Crime 1326–1347', *TRHS* 7 (1957).

2 *Introduction*

Peter Elbow, in *Oppositions in Chaucer*, writes:

In the medieval period more than in most other periods, thinkers took it for granted that conflicting and even contradictory ideas might both be true. It was a time when, presented with an opposition, one might be instinctively more interested in showing how both sides were true than by how one of them was false.[5]

Concordia discors, or the reconciliation of opposites, was a familiar concept. Elbow, in the above quotation, is necessarily speaking about literary dialectic but William Langland, in *Piers Plowman*, argues its relevance to human experience. The eventual salvation of Adam and Eve is presented in terms of oppositions:

> For hadde thei wist of no wo .' wele hadde thei nat knowe.
> For wot no wight what wele is .' that neuere wo suffrede,
> Ho couthe kyndeliche .' with colour discriue,
> Yf alle the worlde were whit . . .
> Yf no nyght ne were .' no man, as ich leyue,
> Sholde wite witerly .' what day were to mene . . .
> For-thi god of hus goodnesse .' the furst man Adam,
> He sette hym in solace furst .' and in souerayne murthe;
> And sutthe suffrede hym to synege .' sorwe to fele,
> To wite ther-thorw what wele was.[6]

This argument is more than literary. It posits a near Manichaean belief that the experience of good, or happiness, cannot be understood without knowledge of evil.[7] In the case of Adam and Eve, the promise of their ultimate salvation is found in the enlightenment given to them by their initial baptism in sin. Langland goes on to draw a parallel between them and the destiny of folk in the troubled society of the 1380s:

> So shal hit fare by this folke .' here folie and here synne
> Shal lere hem what loue is .' and lisse with-outen ende.
>
> (ll. 236–7)

---

[5] P. Elbow, *Oppositions in Chaucer* (Middleton, Conn., 1975), p. 15.

[6] W. Langland, *The Vision of Piers the Plowman in three Parallel Texts*, ed. W. W. Skeat (Oxford, 1886), C XXI. 211–31.

[7] 'The only part of the Manichaean mythology that became popular [in the West] was the crude . . . dualism.' *Encyclopaedia Britannica* (Cambridge, 1911), xvii. 577. Cf. S. Radhakrishnan, *Eastern Religions and Western Thought* (Oxford, 1939), p. 237.

Introduction

I would argue that a similar perspective clarifies much mock king and misrule terminology. Since rule and rulers were fundamental to the cosmic scheme then, necessarily, misrule and mock rulers also had their place. Just as one cannot understand daylight, white, and happiness without the contrast of night, black, and sorrow, so too the boundaries of rule were defined by the existence of its opposite, and it could be said that one did not exist without the other. Rioters in 1452–3 and 1517 were described as 'mysrewled' which suggests that they manifested the essentials of the inverse of rule, and misbehaving kings could be seen satirically as prime examples of lords of misrule since they were intended to epitomize order. Outlaws, who adopted royal titles and behaviour, presented a mirror image of the organization of rule and, for a more temporary period, so too did peasant uprisings; while festive misrule celebrated the concept of disorder itself. In sophisticated environments, such as the universities and inns of court of the sixteenth century, the mirror image was articulated with some exactness. Christmas lords adopted the ceremonies and disciplines of the masters they replaced, and the light–dark parallel for order and disorder was actively included. According to John Stow, lords of misrule were elected on the night that disruptive elements were believed to be at large, 31 October, and they celebrated the forces of misrule during the appropriate dark months of the year, ending their winter reign after the festival of light on 2 February.[8] And, within their season, they frequently gave way to order during the daylight hours.

The purpose of the first part of this book is to examine the evidence for calling men mock kings, or lords of misrule, in the disparate sources, and to clarify in four separate essays the different contexts to which they relate; while the second part is a fresh look at Renaissance drama in the light of the evidence. In writing about disorder, there is the paradox that one needs to impose an order on it so as not to be overwhelmed by its volatility. With regard to outlaws and university entertainments, it becomes clear that it was the participants who imposed the pattern, but popular festivity is more complex and no one analytical pattern can be said to tell the whole truth. For example, I organize my material into winter and summer seasons, but it is essential to note at the outset that the riotous behaviour led

---

[8] J. Stow, *A Survey of London*, ed. C. L. Kingsford (Oxford, 1908; repr. 1971), i. 97. Successful Christmases might return at Shrovetide, as at Gray's Inn in 1594–5.

4   *Introduction*

by winter and summer kings might, in many cases, have been
identical. Thomas Kirchmaier's observation:

> Here sundrie friendes togither come, and meete in companie
> And make a king amongst themselues by voyce or destinie:[9]

summarizes the only essentials for any time of the year. Out of a
group of men, and sometimes women, one was appointed king
and/or queen, either by election or by chance. There is one scripted,
sixteenth-century play, the anonymous farce, *Timon*, which has very
few virtues other than that it plays out the likely activities of either
winter or summer bacchanals, and I have included parts of it in an
appendix as a touchstone. Not only is the season unspecified in the
text, but the king title passes from one participant to another as
different men surpass each other in absurd contribution to the
communal games. The importance they give to nonsense brings to
mind other lines of Kirchmaier's about Shrovetide:

> The chiefest man is he . . .
> Among the rest that can find out the fondest [most foolish] kind of playes,
> On him they looke and gaze upon, and laugh with lustie cheare,
> Whom boyes do follow, crying foole, and such like other geare.

$$\text{(ll. 289-92)}$$

If absurdity is the qualification for being made king of the inverse of
order, then the fool is the most likely contender, as is suggested in the
early poem, 'Thomas of Ercledowne's Prophecy',[10] and in the *Timon*
comedy, where the title alternates between host and fool, and
subsequently, it is suggested, the accolade for being greatest fool is
passed from lover to philosopher. However, in the interests of sanity
I will simply draw on fool implications where relevant, particularly
in relation to the perception of kings. My division into winter and
summer seasons is a further attempt at lucidity by separating customs according to the season in which they are usually recorded, and
acknowledging exceptions such as at York, where the customary
May election of a king and queen appears at Yule.[11]

---

[9] T. Kirchmaier, 'The Popishe Kingdom', ll. 133–4, in P. Stubbes, *Anatomie of
Abuses* (London, 1877–82).
[10] 'When man is mad a kyng of a capped man', in R. H. Robbins (ed.), *Historical
Poems of the XIV and XV Centuries* (New York, 1959), p. 29.
[11] A. F. Johnston (gen. ed.), *Records of Early English Drama*, ed. A. F. Johnston and
M. Rogerson (Toronto and Manchester, 1979), i. 361–2, 369.

Introduction 5

It does appear that there was a *customary* rationale for certain activities at certain seasons but no hard and fast rule, and a popular game in one area might oust the traditional one for that season. Also, the format might change from year to year. My objective, particularly in the first half of the book, is to make the subject coherent, but also to keep alive its variety: therefore, the patterns I am interested in are not claimed as exclusive or comprehensive. The closer one looks at seasonal practices the more one sees variations and changes. Any law which might be said to govern their pattern has more to do with mathematical chaos than literary application and, for this reason, I do not draw comparisons with evidence from outside Britain. For example, the wealth of apparently parallel examples of 'reynages' in Ladurie's *Carnival in Romans* suggests similarities. Yet, as Ladurie shows, the combination of king election and revolt by the lower classes, in contrast to similar elections and defence of the bourgeoisie by the citizens, related to the specific situation in Dauphiné in 1579–80. And the sporting contests to decide the king leader, which in England took place at midsummer, in the gentler climate took place between Christmas and Shrovetide.[12]

The time span covered for both social and seasonal king-led disorders, from the fourteenth to the early seventeenth century, is a long one; but the identification and study of mock kings and their activities has not yet been thoroughly pursued, and the need to concentrate on them provides my focus. In reassessing the Renaissance drama in the light of the complex and interrelated material, I shall be arguing that there is a coherence in some Elizabethan dramas, such as Shakespeare's and Middleton's *Timon of Athens*, and Marston's *Jack Drum's Entertainment*, which needs an understanding of the unscripted, popular plays to perceive. Also, very few staged Princes, particularly in the Elizabethan period, were models of true kingship. Even Henry V casts doubt on his own right to the throne. The hypothesis I shall be putting forward is that most of the corpus of Renaissance drama uses the festive impulse of saturnalian experience for the participants. They experience disorders under the auspices of a mock king who finally resigns (in comedy) or is otherwise disposed of. The plays then end with the restoration of order, the promise of such a restoration, or, in the history trilogies, the continuation of disorder through a further false king coming to power.

[12] Ladurie, *Carnival in Romans*, *passim*.

6   *Introduction*

Although in my argument I maintain that seasonal ritual features as a source for dramatic structures and characterization in plays, this is not a ritualistic study in the anthropological sense. I am not attempting to theorize about the sociological meaning or purpose behind such incorporation. Nor do I intend to add to theories about carnival, though the evidence contributes to some already extant. Rather, it is the entertainment value and, particularly, the satiric potential of ritual which interests me: how such ideas, received from the mass of the people, and from more theoretical concepts of kingship, could contribute to the warp and weft of crafted drama.

For the custom of electing a mock king was inherently questioning and subversive, and this inevitably transferred to the professional theatre. The very act of a player putting a crown on his head to represent a historical figure turned him, and, by association, the character he portrayed, into a mock king even before the text gave greater definition as to the type he portrayed. The iconography inevitably provided a certain freedom from censorship which could not be entirely eliminated, and might help explain the relative freedom play texts were allowed over printed texts. King James, for one, was very aware of dramatic analogies and drawbacks inherent in even a real monarch's public appearances. He wrote to Prince Henry that kings 'are as it were set . . . vpon a publicke stage . . . where all the beholders eyes are attentiuely bent, to look and pry in the least circumstance of their secreatist driftes':[13] in other words to suspect them of not being what they claim; the political possibilities for kings in drama will demand special consideration.

The use of misrule lord and mock king titles was, as has been established, a useful screen for peasant rebels because of a similarity between festive and real riot, but also the titles were used by them, by other outlaws, and by festive lords because the title was absolutely appropriate to all three. The leaders were, in all cases, temporary lords of the permanent antithesis to rule, and this oppositional meaning continued into the Renaissance drama.

[13] James I, *Basilicon Doron*, ed. J. Craigie (Edinburgh, 1944–50), i. 12.

PART I

I

Outlaws, Rebels, and Civil War

Hell itself could not subsist without some good order; and the
very devils are divided into Legions, and have their chieftains.

James I, *Basilicon Doron*

In the society Langland wrote for and about, disorder was endemic.
The background to a complex use of mock king titles and name
calling was one where the forces of disorder, or misrule, were more
effectively in control than were those of rule. The impression of
near-mayhem is confirmed by John Bellamy in the opening chapter of
Crime and Public Order in the Middle Ages: 'In the England of the
later middle ages the preservation of public order was very often the
biggest problem the king had to face. It was not just a police matter.
At heart were the crucial issues of royal authority and the structure of
the state.' Bellamy refers to wilful flouting of authority rather than to
the more justified peasant rebellions, and he finds the problem
extensive. Out of localized studies of different areas at different
periods 'not one investigator has been able to indicate even a few
years of effective policing in the period 1290–1485'.[1] The point at
which the law broke down was at the top. Justices of the peace and
sheriffs were dependent on lordly patrons who, more frequently than
not, applied the law according to their own vested interests. It was
not until the gentry broke free of patronage in the mid-sixteenth
century that open crime decreased and was, perhaps, replaced by
subtler forms of corruption. According to Anna P. Baldwin, the
wages sheriffs earned in the Middle Ages were paid for out of the
fines and bribes exacted from prisoners, who expected to be able to
buy their way out of custody. When one knight 'called Thomas
Ougtred was actually imprisoned for highway robbery by an unusually honest Sheriff of York in 1361, he was so appalled that the
sheriff had not accepted his "gold and grotes" that he got him

---

[1] J. Bellamy, *Crime and Public Order in England in the Later Middle Ages*
(London, 1973), p. 1.

10   *Outlaws, Rebels, and Civil War*

dismissed in disgrace'.[2] There was confusion between what was
expected of criminal and legal behaviour. Interpretation of events
differed. Upholders of the law might behave outside the law and, as
one might expect, outlaws' acts could be seen by the perpetrators as
acts of justice. But the same conclusion might also be reached by
impartial observers. As R. B. Dobson and J. Taylor have observed,
the very 'imposition of outlawry . . . was bound to be an admission of
governmental failure'.[3] The existence of outlaws and public sympathy for them are not surprising under the circumstances; what is
surprising is that, in their attempts to counter alleged injustice by
violence, they frequently imitated the procedures of the king's
justice. As E. L. G. Stones wrote, 'there were people who could not
only persuade themselves that they were the innocent victims of the
law . . . but could go on to represent crime . . . as acts of a rival system
of justice'.[4] A tendency developed in the fourteenth century for
outlaws to organize themselves into groups which were mirror
images of the king's court; brotherhoods with a mock king as leader.

   Most evidence comes from the fourteenth century, when criminal
bands dominated the Midlands during Edward III's periodic absences from the country. The king's constable of Rockingham Castle,
Sir Robert de Vere, turned his curatorship into protection for
outlaws, and Rockingham castle became a safe house for fugitives
from three counties. In one of those counties, Leicestershire, the de
Folville family earned its own notoriety from the activities of six of its
seven sons. All but the eldest turned to outlawry in 1326 after
murdering one of the king's men, an 'unpopular neighbour, Roger
Bellers, a baron of the exchequer'.[5] Sir Roger had fifty men with him
at the time of the ambush, and R. H. Bowers describes the encounter
as 'between two private armies'.[6] The leader of the assassins, Eustace
de Folville, evaded capture for over twenty years, and is believed to
have eventually died peacefully in his bed in 1347. The Folville gang
joined up with one led by James Coterel when they embarked on
other large crimes, such as the kidnapping in 1332 of Sir Richard

   [2] A. P. Baldwin, *The Theme of Government in Piers Plowman* (Bury St Edmunds,
1981), p. 29.
   [3] R. B. Dobson and J. Taylor, *The Rhymes of Robin Hood: An Introduction to the
English Outlaw* (London, 1976), p. 29.
   [4] E. L. G. Stones, 'The Folvilles of Ashby-Folville', *TRHS* 7 (1957) p. 135.
   [5] Bellamy, *Crime and Public Order*, p. 74.
   [6] R. H. Bowers, '"Foleuyles Lawes" ("Piers Plowman", C XXII. 247)', *Notes and
Queries*, 206 (1961), p. 328.

Outlaws, Rebels, and Civil War

Willoughby, justice of the king's bench, for ransom. And, a few weeks before the Willoughby affair, Robert de Vere had harangued another of the king's travelling judiciaries, William la Zouche, in a way which showed that the royal constable was not in fact working for the king, nor did he acknowledge the king's authority. His public challenge to de Vere was:

You wish to destroy me . . . but before I am destroyed I shall destroy all those who intend to destroy me, whatever their rank or estate may be.[7]

This series of attacks was countered at Westminster, and in trailbaston commissions, with peculiar seriousness because the law-breakers began to adopt royal expressions. The trailbaston commission of 1332 reported that there were criminals who had been writing letters 'as if in a royal style (*quasi sub stilo regio*)'.[8] And, later in the century, some parliamentarians were to blame such criminals for the Peasants' Revolt, which they chose to interpret as a protest against 'the grievous oppressions committed in the country by the outrageous numbers of men who take up and maintain quarrels, and are as kings in the country, so that right and law are almost set at nothing'.[9]

The one extant example of an outlaw setting himself up as such a king comes from a Yorkshire case of 1336. The parson of Huntington, Richard de Snaweshill, thought fit to bring a legal action after receiving a letter which ran:

Lionel, king of the rout of raveners, to our false and disloyal Richard de Snaweshill, greeting without love. We command you, on pain of the wrong you can do to us and our laws, that, on reading this letter, you do entirely remove the man you maintain in the vicarage at Burton Anneys and you give the abbot of Notre Dame de Bouthum his liberty and election to the said vicarage . . . If you do not do this we give our oath, first to the king of heaven, then to the king of England, and to our crown, that you will receive the same fate as the Bishop of Exestre en Cheep [Bishop Stapledon, murdered 1326] wherever you may be found . . . And show this letter to your sovereign and tell him he should leave off from false machinations and conspiracies, and let him suffer justice to be done . . . or by the aforesaid vows he will receive £1,000 of damages from us and ours. And if you ignore our demand we will order the Viscount of the North to bring great suffering to you as already said.

---

[7] Stones, 'The Folvilles of Ashby-Folville', p. 124.   [8] Ibid. 134.
[9] Baldwin, *The Theme of Government*, p. 39.

12   *Outlaws, Rebels, and Civil War*

Issued from our castle of the North Wind, within the Green Tower in the first year of our reign.[10]

In this letter, Lionel writes as though he were rightful administrator of Yorkshire, and as though de Snaweshill had insinuated a treacherous alliance with a foreign king by carrying out Edward's appointment. Lionel's vision of himself and his allies is based on a kingly fellowship, as found in the Arthurian legend, and which Stones refers to in the phrase 'allusions drawn from romance'.[11] The outlaws' kingdom both apes and opposes the organization of Edward's and, although the title 'rout of raveners' has a festive ring to it, it also has satiric bite since there was real violence behind Lionel's threats. An ironic festive bluntness is uneasily combined with Arthurian touches, and they convey a heroic rather than a criminal stand against authority.

By contrast, the crowning of Robert the Bruce at Scone in 1306 defied Edward I's control of Scotland, and the well-known festive analogy for the coronation came from English propaganda intended to belittle it. The chronicler made out that Isabella, Bruce's wife, was a lady of easy virtue and invented the following conversation between them. Bruce was alleged to have repeated the crowning ceremony himself saying '"Yesterday you and I were called followers. Today truly I am called king and you queen." Then she said, "I believe you are a summer king, perhaps you will not be winter king . . . just like the flower in the field which is today and tomorrow is returned to the earth".'[12] And, in the ballad on the execution of Sir Simon Frazer, the coronation is again likened to the crowning of a summer king who made a good show with his red-gold or brass crown.[13] Perhaps because in reality the threat from Bruce had been great, and he was in fact a credible king of Scotland—in 1577 Holinshed was to call him one of the 'most valiant' of princes—an attempt was made at the time to diminish his stature. A similar

---

[10] Stones, 'The Folvilles of Ashby-Folville', pp. 134–5.   [11] Ibid. 124.

[12] '"Heri vocabamur ego comes et tu comitissa; hodie vero ego rex et tu regina [vocamur]". Cui illa "Aestimo quod rex aestivalis sis; forsitan hyemalis non eris . . . tanquam flos agri qui hodie est et cras in clibanum mittitur".' H. R. Luard (ed.), *Flores Historiarum*, Rolls Series, iii (London, 1890), p. 130.

[13] 'hii þat him crounede proude were ant bolde; | hii maden kyng of somere, so hii ner ne sholde; | hii setten on ys heuede a croune of rede golde, | And token a kyne-ȝerde (so me kyng sholde) to deme.' R. H. Robbins (ed.), *Historical Poems of the XIV and XV Centuries* (New York, 1959), p. 16.

Outlaws, Rebels, and Civil War

reductive technique was used at the end of the fourteenth century by English satirists against Richard II and his agents. His purveyors were mocked for riding 'On a courser, as it were a king; | With saddle of gold glittering' in 'The Peasants' Complaint'.[14] And, in *Richard the Redeles*, Richard himself was compared with a mock king or lord of misrule, overseeing the disorder in his house:

> For where was euere ony Christen kynge .' that ȝe euere knewe
> That held swiche an household .' be the half-delle [by half]
> As Richard in this rewme .' thoru myserule of other . . .[15]
>
> IV. 1–3

Men ostensibly holding official power were reduced by such comparisons whereas, for outlaws, the comparison was a complimentary reflection of their actual power. It indicated that, locally, their forces were stronger than the official government, and the daring of some men was remembered even after their death.

Bellamy thinks outlaws were not the stuff of folk myth, that they were themselves too aristocratic, unconcerned with the life of the poor, and only involved in feuds with their neighbours: nevertheless it becomes appropriate to consider the actions of the Folvilles in relation to the legend of Robin Hood, since of the various hypotheses about its origin the one which still carries most weight is that it developed out of accumulated tales about outlaws.[16] The first reference to the mythical character comes from William Langland in about 1380 when, in *Piers Plowman*, B, Passus VIII, line 11, Sloth says: 'Ich can rymes of robyn hode .' and of Randolf, erl of chestre', though he cannot repeat his paternoster. A century later Robin Hood had become one of the most popular names for the summer festive king,[17] and, difficult as it may seem to equate Lionel, the Folvilles, Coterel, and Robert de Vere with the sympathetic legends handed

---

[14] 'The Complaint of the Ploughman', *Political Poems and Songs*, Rolls Series (London, 1857), i. 3082.

[15] W. Langland, *The Vision of Piers Plowman . . . together with Richard the Redeles*, ed. W. W. Skeat (Oxford, 1886), i. 626.

[16] See R. H. Hilton, 'The Origins of Robin Hood', *Past and Present*, 13 (1958), pp. 30–44; R. B. Dobson and J. Taylor, *The Rhymes of Robin Hood* (London, 1976), pp. 26–30; and D. Wiles, *The Early Plays of Robin Hood* (Woodbridge, 1981), p. 2.

[17] These outlaw games accidentally received encouragement from government when in 1365 Edward III gave an order that games involving archery should be played, and other games were banned. See A. Highmore, *The History of the Right Honourable Artillery Company of the City of London* (London, 1804), p. 38.

14   *Outlaws, Rebels, and Civil War*

down from the sixteenth century, it seems that Eustace de Folville in particular made just such a contribution, which was disseminated or mediated by a more literate class than the peasants themselves.

To begin with no stigma was attached to having been an outlaw. According to Bellamy:

... to have feuded, used violence, to have poached or pillaged, was not at this time held to debar any man from local or even national office ... there were a considerable number of 'seeming crooks and bandits', guilty of homicides and housebreaking, who were elected to parliament in the early fourteenth century.[18]

Eustace was pardoned in 1333 for services rendered in the Scottish war; then, in 1346, taking further advantage of the king's absence he resorted once more to violence, and yet despite this died a hero. The late fourteenth-century chronicler, Henry Knighton, considered his murder of Bellers in 1326 a courageous act, and saw fit to recall it as an event of national importance. While relating the momentous events of 1347 he wrote: 'In this year died Eustace de Folville who killed Robert Bellers.'[19] Even more surprising is a tribute paid by Langland (again in *Piers Plowman*), and it is this fuller recollection which suggests that, forty years after his death, Eustace and his brothers were slipping into legend. In a vision of the future, Langland describes the new society reorganized by Grace. Among tilers, tillers, and other men of craft, Langland adds men who were taught by Grace:

> ... to ryde and recoeure .' that vnriȝtfully was wonne;
> He wissed hem wynne it aȝeyne .' thorw wightnesse of handes,
> And fecchen it fro fals men .' with Foluyles lawes.

> B, xix. 239–41

The lawlessness of the well-born Folvilles was justified in the moral tract which was to be a source of inspiration to some participants in the 1381 uprising.[20] The ethics Langland voices can be compared

---

[18] Bellamy, *Crime and Public Order*, p. 82.

[19] 'Eodem anno obiit Eustachius de Folvyle qui Robertum Bellere interfecerat.' H. Knighton, *Chronicon Henrici Knighton*, ed. J. R. Lumby (London, 1890), ii. 46.

[20] 'Iohan schep, som-tyme seynte marie prest of ȝork, and now of colchestre, Greteth wel Iohan nameles & Iohn þe mullere and Iohon cartere, and biddeþ hem þei bee war of gyle in borugh, and stondeth to-gidere in godes name, and biddeþ Pers plouȝman | go to his werk and chastise wel hobbe þe robbere ... littera Iohannis balle missa communibus Estsexie.' BM Royal MS 13. E. ix. Robbins, *Historical Poems*, p. 55.

Outlaws, Rebels, and Civil War

with present-day notions of Robin Hood and there is no doubt that even during their lifetime the Folvilles and their like had many supporters. They felt justified in what they did to the extent of consciously appropriating any accusation of disorder against the state and turning it on to their attackers. William Beckwith's Yorkshire gang satirically elected a mock Parliament called Dodelowe, for 'the subversion of the law, oppression of the people, disinherison of the Duke [of Lancaster] and the loss of his ministers lives'.[21] The law itself at this time was frequently subverted by the king's ministers, who also oppressed the people, and there is in Beckwith's inversion a reflection of the real state of government.[22] While such men played on the meanings of government and kingship, the problem they raised for the king was the crucial one of his own position. In a situation where abduction and murder of his men could be seen by educated observers as acts of justice, kingship in practice had little to do with divine authority, but was rather an elaborate, shadowy chess game with opposing kings adopting his style, and imposing their men on his territory.

If outlaws could create an opposition to the king by direct imitation, peasant rebellions more frequently borrowed all the customs associated with periods of festive misrule. Demands for wages could be expressed in terms of a *quête*; the alehouse was frequently the meeting-place both for festive and for rebel groups, and sometimes a livery was worn by each.[23] And it seems to have been of equal importance to each that the leader was a mock king. The name which had developed among observers to describe the leader or head of such unruly groups was captain, from the Latin, *caput*. However, although captain was often used by those involved, it was usually in conjunction with the mock king name. Captain is quite adequate to identify a leader, so it would seem that more specific, parodic elevation was wanted, and that oppositional leadership was bound up with the ideology of kingship. Tudor chroniclers remembered the 1381 rebellion by the festive title of Jack Straw, adopted by its leader,

---

[21] Bellamy, *Crime and Public Order*, p. 76.

[22] Political satire more usually associated with medieval Italy.

[23] See T. Pettitt, 'Jack Straw', *Folklore*, 95 (1984), and N. Simms, 'Ned Ludd's Mummers Play', *Folklore*, 89 (1978), *passim*, and E. J. Hobsbawm and G. Rude, *Captain Swing* (Harmondsworth, 1969), pp. 38–9.

Outlaws, Rebels, and Civil War

rather than as Wat Tyler's uprising,[24] and other anonymous, agrarian titles such as John Sheep, Deer, and Earl of the Plough were given to men accused of the murder of Archbishop Sudbury.[25] In 1450 the Kentish rebel leader, Jack Cade, was known by three titles. One, that of the Yorkist claimant, Mortimer, can be viewed as the name of the opposing, alternative king; Captain is the name used by John Paston in his letters, and it is said that Cade's propaganda name, John Amend-Alle, was the one he preferred.[26] This last was remembered by other men who had a vested interest in justifying an uprising two years after Cade's revolt. In 1452 a band of robbers operating in Norfolk went through the greenwood ritual of electing a leader. No political grievance can be found for this gang, whose activities seem to have been purely criminal. They functioned as the Duke of Norfolk's men in his quarrels with neighbours. However, they followed the recognized custom and their leader adopted for himself Cade's 'favourite' name. It was reported that:

... Roger Cherche ... was at a gaderyng ... of xv persones in a feleshep vnder a wode in the town of Possewyke ... which feleshep, as it is said ... was procured and gaderyd be the seid Rogere Cherche and be his councelores, the same Rogere seyng ... he had remembred a gode name for here capteyn that shuld be John A-mend Alle.[27]

There was no connection between the followers of Cade and these men. The disturbance caused by the peasant uprising was of a short duration and, once the revolt was over, the men did not take to a life of crime. Cherche's adoption of Cade's title seems to have been a confused attempt to add lustre to his motives. For, while he and his

[24] Henry Knighton wrote of the rebels, 'Cui appropinquavit ductor eorum proprio nomine Watte Tyler, sed jam nomine mutato vocatus est Jakke Strawe' (*Chronicon*, ii. 137). Holinshed followed this; see *Chronicles of England, Scotland and Ireland*, ed. J. Hooker *et al.* (London, 1807–8), ii. 736–8. By the 17th cent. the 1 man with 2 names had, in popular belief, become 2 men. Sir Richard Baker, in *A Chronicle of the Kings of England* (London, 1643), pp. 5–6, named the leaders as Watt Tyler and John Ball but included Jack Straw as one of the rebels executed. And an anonymous pamphlet of 1642, 'The iust reward of Rebels', is subtitled 'The life and death of *Iack Straw* and *Wat Tyler*', BL E. 136(1). The belief that Straw was the name of a rebel remains. See F. W. D. Brie, 'Wat Tyler and Jack Straw', *The English Historical Review*, 21 (1906), pp. 106–11, and Robbins, *Historical Poems*, p. 276 n. 25.

[25] Pettitt, 'Jack Straw', p. 9.

[26] H. Lyle, *The Rebellion of Jack Cade 1450*, Historical Association Pamphlet (London, 1950), p. 18.

[27] J. Paston, *The Paston Letters and Papers*, ed. N. Davis (Oxford, 1971–6), i. 62–3.

Outlaws, Rebels, and Civil War

men terrorized the county under the leadership of a man with a famous rebel's title, they claimed that they were putting down rebellion.[28] His gang was a large and vicious one. In 1452 Paston reported that sixty of them threatened the congregation at White Friars Church in Norwich until they were dispersed by the Mayor and a 'gret multitud of people'.[29] For about ten years they controlled the county outside the city, robbing and waging war against up-holders of the king's law. Several squires were captured and held at the gang's pleasure. In 1452 Philip Berney was ambushed and held under the accusation of being a 'traytour'.[30] In context, this appears to be another expression of the outlaws' rule, alternative to that of the king. Berney was not a notable force in the county but he was representative of the dominant order and, as such, an affront and traitor to their own.

The main difference between the Norfolk gang and that of the Folvilles is that, today, we sympathize with Cherche's victims; particularly John Paston the elder, a justice of the peace, responsible to the Sheriff of Norfolk, until the Duke of Norfolk succeeded in ruining him. It is Paston's letters which provide the evidence that Berney died soon after his ill-treatment and that John Paston himself was unjustly hounded by the Duke of Norfolk's fifth column. In 1449 and 1460 Paston appealed directly to Henry VI.[31] Such an action is explained by Baldwin as the last resort of the citizen: the king could intercede outside the law if a citizen failed to obtain justice within it. Again this illustrates the imbalances and ambiguities of the system. On the one hand, focus concentrated on the king as figure-head, and any law-breakers were inevitably opposed to him in person rather than to an impersonal government. Adopting a kingly title in opposition was almost a logical consequence. And, on the other, as Machiavelli observed,[32] the king was himself outside the law, and the justice of his interventions depended on his innate sense of morality, or knowledge of the facts. Any mistakes turned him into an agent of injustice, and the mock king allusion to Richard II does not appear so outrageous (see Chapter 4). Finally, in view of John Paston's ill-treatment at the hands of outlaws, resulting in himself being imprisoned and outlawed in 1464, it is perhaps ironic that a letter, from one of his sons to another, provides an early piece of

---

[28] Ibid. 61.   [29] Ibid. 60.   [30] Ibid. 59.   [31] Ibid. 51, 93.
[32] N. Machiavelli, *The Prince*, trans. G. Bull (Harmondsworth, 1961), p. 99.

18   *Outlaws, Rebels, and Civil War*

evidence for the popularity of Robin Hood plays. The well-known jocular observation from John II speaks of his losing a horseman he had kept 'thys iij yere to pleye seynt Jorge and Robynhod and the shryff off Notyngham, and now when I wolde haue good horse he is goon in-to Bernysdale, and I without a kepere'.[33]

In 1437 a sarcastic swipe was made at another gang of criminal outlaws who had adopted a kingly style. Piers Venables was said to have gathered round him a great number of 'misdoers "beynge of his clothinge, and in manere of insurrection wente into the wodes . . . like it hadde be Robyn Hode and his meynee"'.[34] The contrast implied between the impression Venables created and his real activities suggests that by the 1430s a romanticized Robin Hood legend was already well advanced.[35] A further development appears in 1469 when Robin Hood titles were used by leaders in the Yorkshire rebellion. The rioters against Edward IV were first headed by Robert Hillyard, under the name of Robin of Holderness, until he was beheaded by the Earl of Northumberland. His place was then taken by one of the Conyers family, who took the name Robin of Redesdale. It seems that the borrowing could be either way. Outlaws influenced games and legends, which in turn fed back into revolt, while at the same time the established festive customs continued. The younger John Paston's letter was written only four years after the Yorkshire rebellion.

What appears as the common denominator in all the disparate examples of planned disorder is evidence that 'captain' was not thought of as a sufficient title for the leader and that the instinct was to elect a mock king to govern the retinues, or miniature kingdoms, and to organize them into effective opposition against authority. As James I was to declare, even the devil and his accomplices could not be conceived of without a social structure imitative of the dominant order.

Ten years before the Mayor and citizens of Norwich frightened off Cherche's gang, they themselves had risen in rebellion as a result of a

---

[33] 16 Apr. 1473, Paston, *Paston Letters*, i. 461. Dobson and Taylor (p. 18) argue that by 1429 Barnsdale in Yorkshire had come to be the legendary home of Robin Hood, and both the 1469 Yorkshire rebel titles and Paston's joke could have been affected by this.

[34] Bellamy, *Crime and Public Order*, p. 70.

[35] The first known game of Robin Hood was in 1427 at Exeter when 20d. was 'dato lusoribus ludentibus lusum Robyn Hood'. *REED, Devon*, ed. J. M. Wasson (Toronto, 1986), p. 89. Payment is unusual. See Ch. 3.

Outlaws, Rebels, and Civil War

forty-year dispute over land rights. The uprising on either 24 or 25 January 1443 involved citizens instead of barons or peasants and this third estate also followed the pattern of electing an ostensible[36] leader in the form of a mock king. In the charges brought against them, the display of the mock king was interpreted as a deliberate challenge to Henry VI's authority, similar to the accusation of 1332. But instead of writing letters in a regal style, the citizens were charged with presenting an iconographic threat when John Gladman rode through the city

as a King with a crown and sceptre and sword carried before him by 3 men unknown . . . and others to the number of 24 persons [rode] there in like manner before John Gladman with a crown upon their arms and with bows and arrows as valets of the crown of the Lord King; and ordered 100 other persons now unknown with swords bows and arrows as well on foot as on horseback then and there to follow John Gladman.[37]

The focal point for their aggression was the Prior, whose priory was in a disputed suburb and who also claimed jurisdiction over other disputed suburbs. After attacking the priory, the rebels held out in Norwich for about a week before the Duke of Norfolk and the Earl of Oxford entered the city. In 1448, after Norwich had been restored to the king's good graces, the Mayor and Aldermen brought a counter-charge against the clerk at the previous trial. In their statement they tried to rewrite the events of January 1443, reinterpreting the icons of their procession. Despite the fact that Shrove Tuesday that year fell on 5 March, it was said that John Gladman 'on fastyngong tuesday made a disporte w^t his neighbours having his hors trapped with tyneseyle and otherwyse dysgysyn things crowned as King of Kristmesse in token that all merthe shuld end with ye twelve monthes of ye yer, afore hym eche moneth disgysd after ye seson yerof'.[38] Without trying to judge the rights and wrongs of the conflict, one can see here two quite distinct readings of what was claimed to be the same procession. To begin with, the fact that it mattered enough to the defendants to reconstruct this part of the events, instead of simply denying it as they did much of the rest, is illuminating. It shows how much importance was placed on visual metaphors in an age of low literacy, and the citizens' reconstruction

---

[36] During the trial the Mayor was addressed as real leader.
[37] Trans. from the Latin by W. Hudson and U. J. C. Tingay (eds.), *Selected Records of the City of Norwich* (Norwich, 1906), i. 340. [38] Ibid. 345.

20   *Outlaws, Rebels, and Civil War*

reveals their awareness of variations in misrule display. There was an intrinsic volatility of possibilities which allowed for exploitation; the disallowed insignia, the crown, symbolic of rebellion, and claimed by the court to have been worn by Gladman's men, was countered with an innocent icon of the month. The importance of signs appears in other rebellions, where they also help identify the kind of king leader. In the 1536 Yorkshire rebellion against the dissolution of the monasteries, the insignia was of the five wounds of Christ and the rising was a peaceful one;[39] while Warwick's ragged staff flying over Norwich in 1549, after his suppression of Kett's rebellion, prompted the suggestion that one rebel, rival king was being replaced with another. The laconic remark was made that 'it was not mete to haue any more KYNGS than one'.[40]

During the 1450s, rebel opposition to authority became subordinated to the power struggle between the Houses of Lancaster and York. Rebellion from the lower classes was seen in terms of support for one side or the other and, though mock king analogy was part of the propaganda, subtle resonances were increasingly lost in the confusion. The Lancastrian and Yorkist houses outlawed each other in 1459, 1461, 1470, and 1471 and, when the Lancastrian Bill of Attainder was issued against Richard, Duke of York, in 1459, it was claimed that Jack Cade's 1450 uprising had been part of the larger movement to put Richard on the throne. Richard's last gamble for the crown began on 8 September 1459, when it became 'clear that he had renounced his allegiance to Henry VI'. Documents drawn up in his name on 13 September omit any reference to the regnal year, and were dated instead by the year of grace, quite out of conformity with usual practice'.[41] He then marched on London with a full claim expressed iconographically: 'his trumpeters bearing banners charged with arms of England, and with his sword carried upright before him—the very mark and privilege of a king'.[42] Richard miscalculated the mood of his own supporters, and the last error which led to his death came in the first week of January 1460–1, after a Christmas truce. Bitter fighting ensued, in which Richard and many of his supporters were slain or afterwards executed. The heads of the

---

[39] A. Fletcher, *Tudor Rebellions: Seminar Studies in History* (London, 1968), p. 32.
[40] F. Blomefield, *An Essay towards a Topographical History of the Country of Norfolk* (Norwich, 1745), p. 183.
[41] C. Ross, *Edward IV* (Berkeley, Calif., 1974), p. 28.   [42] Ibid.

Outlaws, Rebels, and Civil War 21

two leading rebels, York and Salisbury, were sent as a warning round the chief towns in Yorkshire, and Richard's severed head was decorated with a paper crown. The festive season coincided with the fall of a man with real pretensions to the throne.

However, many of the images presented by those on the throne between 1450 and 1470 outdid outlaws and rebels for bizarre originality as, for example, when an attempt at reconciliation was made in 1458 and

the Kyng in habite royal, and his dyademe on his hedde, kept his estate in procession, before whom, went hand in hand, the duke of Somerset, the erle of Salisbury, the duke of Excester, and ye erle of Warwyke, and so on of the one faccion, and another of the other sect, and behynd the kyng the duke of Yorke ledde the Quene with great familiaritie to all mens sightes.[43]

Or when, in 1469, Warwick took control and 'England exhibited . . . the extraordinary spectacle of a country with two kings, both in prison'.[44] The upside down quality of events was lamented by Edward Hall whose attempt at impartiality towards King Edward and King Henry reads most uncomfortably. The French Chronicler, de Comines, wrote that he first learned of the instability of the world on witnessing the instant changes of loyalty in the city of Calais.[45] By comparison, Richard III's assumption of power in 1483 seems almost orderly. The early Tudor *Great Chronicle of London* reports briefly, 'The which, afftyr his deth was namyd *Kyng In dede* but not of Rygth.'[46]

As hopes for stability at the pinnacle of power returned with Henry VII's marriage to Elizabeth of York, defiance of the monarch was seen once more as insurrection and rebellion from below. The first major upheavals were direct challenges to Henry from Lambert Simnell and Perkyn Warbeck, probably paid to revive the Yorkist claim. Yet neither was called by a mock king title in any contemporary or near contemporary accounts.[47] And, of the many riots and

---

[43] E. Hall, *Chronicle [of the] History of England*, ed. Sir H. Ellis (London, 1809), p. 238.   [44] J. H. Ramsay, *Lancaster and York* (Oxford, 1892), p. 343.

[45] P. de Comines, *Memoirs*, trans. anon. (London, 1823), p. 271.

[46] Attrib. R. Fabyan, *The Great Chronicle of London*, ed. I. Thornley and A. H. Thomas (London, 1808), p. 233.

[47] Not until John Ford's *Perkin Warbeck*, in which Warbeck's 'pageant majesty' is set against Henry VII's position of 'mockery king in state' (i. i. 3–4) and Perkin appears 'more genuinely royal than the legitimate monarch'. A. Barton, 'He that plays the king', *English Drama*, ed. M. Axton and R. Williams (Cambridge, 1977), pp. 79, 80–8. See Conclusion for Ford's final divergence from iconoclasm.

22   Outlaws, Rebels, and Civil War

uprisings during the one and a half centuries up to the civil war of
1643, mock king titles were used only fitfully and never by the
leaders themselves.[48] It was argued that Robert Kett in 1549 did so
title himself, but, in the light of recent evidence,[49] it is quite clear that
both he and his followers retained their allegiance to Edward VI.
Kett's rebellion was a result of a rumour that elsewhere in England
the king's officers were taking action to remove enclosures from
round common land. As this was not happening in Norfolk, local
men used their initiative to restore their rights, and Kett led them in
the same cause. When his followers referred to themselves as friends
of the king, they meant that they were carrying out Edward's
instructions which were being ignored by his agents in Norfolk. But
their statements were taken to mean that Kett had set himself up as
king and, bearing in mind medieval outlaw precedent, there is real
ambiguity in the following warrant issued by Kett's men:

> We the King's Friends and Deputies, do grant Licence to all Men, to provide
> & bring into the Camp at Mousehold, all Manner of Cattel and Provision of
> Vittels . . . commanding all Persons as they tender the King's Honour, and
> roiall Majestie, and the Releefe of the Common Welth, to be obedient to us
> the Governors, and to those whose Names ensue.[50]

Observers interpreted such statements to mean that 'comyns ys
become a kinge',[51] and Edward's letter to Somerset expressed outrage that Kett had 'taken upon hym our royall power and Dignitie,
and calleth hymselfe master and kyng of Norffolk and Suffolk'.[52]
Nicholas Sotherton's eye-witness account of 'the commoyson in
Norfolk' does not attempt to resolve the ambiguity for contemporary readers, yet his statement that the Rebels set 'their face to bee the
Kings ffriends and to defend the Kings Laws soe impudent were they
now become'[53] does affirm that Kett and his companions believed

---

[48] One potential exception was forestalled in 1592 by legislation. After anti-alien
riots in Southwark in May, the midsummer games were banned and apprentices kept
indoors until Sept. See J. R. Dasent (ed.), *Acts of the Privy Council of England*, NS 22,
1591–2 (London, 1901), pp. 549–51. For what might have happened at midsummer
see Ch. 3.

[49] D. MacCulloch, 'Kett's Rebellion in Context', *Past and Present*, 84 (1979),
pp. 36–59.

[50] Blomefield, *Topographical History*, p. 162.

[51] William Paget, SPD, 7 July 1549, quoted F. W. Russell, *Kett's Rebellion in
Norfolk* (London, 1859), pp. 17, 72.

[52] Ibid. 114–15.

[53] BM Harley MS 1576, fo. 252ᵛ.

Outlaws, Rebels, and Civil War   23

they were acting as the king's agents, in defiance of the greed of local gentry.

One other example of one-sided mock king calling comes as late as 1643, when John Pym's effective parliamentary opposition to Charles I controlled the political initiative, and through his influence the army was first used against the king. The royalist outcry was 'Charles is no longer King | King Pym it is, the Round-heads would have him',[54] and more ambitious verses from Oxford set Pym 'i'th kingdoms chair', dispensing diabolical misgovernment.[55] In the same volume (part 17), is an emblematic combination of verse and image called 'Syons Calamitye or Englands Miserye' (Fig. 1). The king is shown chained and beseiged and, outside the castle of state, the law subverted by fools. Another group of images, showing Fantasy Triumphant, have at their centre a badly dressed king and queen saying, 'I shall be King of Jerusalem', 'and I Queen'. The brief mock king and queen dialogue is consistent with the formula interpolated in 1306 into accounts of Bruce's coronation, and seems to have been part of the self-assertion found in some king games. But nowhere is it suggested that John Pym, the lower born man, had himself indulged in such medieval fantasies. Until 1649, when the outcome was decided in Parliament's favour, it was the royalists who invoked the mock king image, for at least three reasons; one, in outrage at the way Charles was treated, the second to attack the adversary, and the third, as a rallying cry.[56]

But, despite the fact that the Tudor and early Stuart periods were full of rebellions, there was a surprising lack of resort to king game images by the common people, and a total lack of planned mirror images of the king's court by rebels and outlaws, as a brief look at the major disturbances will confirm.

The Pilgrimage of Grace, against the dissolution of the monasteries in 1536, began as a peasant rising: 'the first major one in

---

[54] BL 669, f. 8(23).

[55] 'Pym's Juncto', BL 669, f. 8(16).

[56] Sympathy was gained for Charles by invoking the title of Beaumont and Fletcher's Jacobean play, *A King and No King* (see Ch. 8). John Pym is an example of the adversary, and, in 1641, a mock king was used as a royalist rallying-point at Leicester, when John Hastings was elected on the common and all rode towards the town crying 'a KING a KING, others, for the KING, for the KING, in a strange and un heard of manner'. BL E. 154(4), p. B. 3. See Conclusion for Milton's 1649 use of mock king analogy in *Eikonoklastes*.

1 Syons Calamitye, 1643

Outlaws, Rebels, and Civil War

England since Cade's'.[57] Several captains were elected with Robert Aske as chief captain, but no one was exalted to mock king status. Aske conceived of the rebellion as a Pilgrimage, 'for the preservacyon of Crystes churche, of thys realme of England, the kynge our soverayne lord . . . to macke petycion to the kinges highnes for the reformacyon of that whiche is amysse within thys hys realme'.[58] The only claimed bias of the rebels was towards Christ who was their primary leader or king. When the 30,000 rebels were tricked into making peace, 'the pilgrims tore off their badges of the Five wounds saying, "we will all wear no badge nor sign but the badge of our sovereign lord"'.[59] The Pilgrimage of Grace appears as the only time that a further inversion in the panoply of kingship meanings was played out, and gave to Christ, the king of kings, a role usually played by a mock king. This reversed inversion was a popular irony in dramatists' treatment of Christ by Herod in Mystery plays.[60]

None of the other major rebellions, Evil May day, 1517,[61] the Cornish or Western Rebellion, 1549, Thomas Wyatt's, 1554, nor the Northern rebellion of 1569, adopted mock king leaders. Although evidence in the fifteenth century is sketchy, the tradition appears to have been largely abandoned during the Wars of the Roses. And it may be relevant to refer to Fletcher's observation that Tudor kings reinforced the concept of obligation to the king, with the result that, by the mid-sixteenth century, 'Tudor rebels did not dare to challenge the crown directly'.[62] Further, leaders such as Robert Aske and Robert Kett had practical political objectives and a conviction (however misguided) that they could achieve them. There is a difference here from the integral disorder of the medieval system in which any attempts at amelioration had to survive local feuds and the law employed directly for personal profit. There could have been few illusions in the Middle Ages that the disaffected could change the

---

[57] J. Cornwall, *Revolt of the Peasantry, 1549* (London, 1977), p. 3.

[58] Fletcher, *Tudor Rebellions*, p. 24.   [59] Ibid. 32.

[60] In the York play of the *Lytsteres* Herod presumes Christ's title, King of the Jews, means he is a fool king, elected 'in his kith where he comes froo' (l. 224), and in his attempt to make Christ reveal his skills, himself plays the fool. See S. Billington, *A Social History of the Fool* (Brighton, 1984), pp. 18–20.

[61] Despite the riot being remembered by the festive day on which it took place, there was no mock king organization behind it. Trouble had been brewing throughout Apr., and 1 May was the next non-working day. The only known leader was John Lincoln and he seems not even to have been called captain. See Hall, *Chronicle [of the] History of England*, pp. 588–91.

[62] Fletcher, *Tudor Rebellions*, p. 109.

26   *Outlaws, Rebels, and Civil War*

system. However, they could survive indefinitely in opposition in the security of their local habitat. By contrast, Aske and Kett appear to have spoken with Renaissance confidence in their powers to effect an improvement, and to have called themselves kings would have been gratuitously provocative.[63]

On the other hand, to look for a moment at the subject of order from the point of view of the monarch, there appears to have been flagrant disrespect towards kings, exhibited whenever festive licence was invoked. This was experienced personally by Henry VIII and Katherine during the Epiphany festivities in 1510–11 when the gold letters on their masquing costumes were torn off by the watching multitude and they were left in their basic dress. Hall writes:

After the kyng and his compaignions had daunced, he apointed the ladies, gentelwomen and the Ambassadours to take the letters of their garmentes, in token of liberalitie, whiche thing the common people perceyvyng, ranne to the kyng, and striped hym into his hosen and doublet, and all his compaignions in likewyse. Sir Thomas Knevet stode on a stage, and for all his defence he lost his apparell. The ladies likewyse were spoyled, wherfore the kynges garde came sodenly, and put the people backe . . . [I]t appeared that the garmentes were of a great value.[64]

Though, at the time, 'all these hurtes were turned to laughyng and game',[65] only 'honest persones' were later allowed into court.[66] The fact that such extraordinary liberties were taken with the monarch's person shows to what extent disorder was a part of late medieval life. Any king who intended an effective rule would have to emphasize his authority, and the judgement of the 1517 May Day riot shows Henry demonstrating his power over offenders in a way not done pre-

---

[63] The theory, drawn from evidence in France, that elections of mock kings were attempts to change society would seem to apply in England only in a limited way. The original election of Jack Straw and John Amend-All clearly were attempts to bring about change. However, when Jack Straw was elected as the Lincoln's Inn Christmas king he was no longer serving the original function (see end of Ch. 1). And, in the case of medieval outlaws, the election appears to have been an expression of scepticism or cynicism regarding their ability to effect change. The prolific evidence for the election of festive kings in England came later, when such elections might express satiric comments on political events, but were largely divorced from political engagement.

[64] E. Hall, *The Triumphant Reigne of King Henry the VIII* (London, 1550), ed. C. Whibley (London, 1904) i. 27. Earlier, at their marriage on midsummer day, 1509, the 'cloth of Ray' canopy under which they had been carried was 'cut and spoyled, by the rude and common people, immediately after their repaire into the Abbey' (ibid. 7).

[65] Ibid. 27.   [66] Ibid. ii. 88.

Outlaws, Rebels, and Civil War

viously. Instead of automatically pardoning all but the leaders, he kept them all in suspense:

> ... his majesty, being seated on a lofty platform, surrounded by all those lords, who stood, he caused some four hundred of these delinquents, all in their shirts and barefoot, and each with a halter round his neck, to be brought before him ... the Cardinal [Wolsey] implored him aloud to pardon them, which the King said he would not by any means do ... The criminals, on hearing ... fell on their knees, shouting, 'Mercy!' when the cardinal again besought his majesty to grant them grace, some of the chief lords doing the like. So at length the King consented to pardon them ...[67]

The title of Evil given to the day carries an accusatory seriousness quite different from the unrepentant challenge of many of the medieval uprisings, and Henry's prolonged judgment of the offenders enforced the image of power in kingship, while at the same time publicly demonstrating his magnanimity. As the Italian observer, Saguidino, reported, 'it was a very fine spectacle, and well arranged'.[68]

Tudor control can be seen in other ways. The interrelation between different types of mock kings was broken down and, though we have from the sixteenth century many references to festive lords of misrule, paradoxically, the tendency was to limit their unruliness. The festive outlet was prolific but controlled, and unsanctioned eruptions could curtail the licensed season. The Tudor Twelfth Day carol, 'Now have gud day', expresses the hope that the Lord of Christmas will return the following year, 'If rest and pease in Ynglond may fall'.[69] And, conversely, the rebellious expression of misrule became divorced from kingly metaphors.

Whereas, in the Middle Ages, when *general* disorder was endemic, most of the *organized* disorder we know about was expressed through mock king analogy. The evidence further shows that many ordinary citizens in the Middle Ages were at least familiar with 'king' metaphors and perhaps also understood more philosophical arguments. Interrelation between fact and fantasy argues that the 'king' concept was one which the medieval mind enjoyed playing with: the customs of festive kings were embedded in outlawry and rebellion, and festivity was itself influenced by the exploits of outlaws and

---

[67] Saguidino to Foscari, 19 May 1517, *SPD—Henry VIII*, ii, ed. J. S. Brewer (London, 1864), pt. 2, p. 1045.   [68] Ibid.
[69] R. L. Greene (ed.), *Early English Carols* (2nd edn., Oxford, 1977), p. 85.

28   *Outlaws, Rebels, and Civil War*

rebels. And, as a final twist to this interrelationship, as it affected the
Robin Hood legend, riots broke out in Edinburgh in 1561 when the
Robin Hood games were banned.[70]

Another, more striking, example of the interplay between rebellion and game comes from the records of the inns of court. In 1381
the lawyers' Temple was destroyed by Wat Tyler and his followers,
yet some time after that a lord of misrule called Jack Straw was
elected in Lincoln's Inn at Christmas. Record was made of it when
the title was abolished in 1519:

> For Christmas . . .
> Item that Jack Strawe and all his adherentes be from hensforth uttrely
> banyshed and no more to be vsed in Lincolles Inne, uppon peyne to forfeyt
> for euery tyme fiue poundes.[71]

Less dangerous Christmas kings were still allowed; one was 'King
ouer Christmas Day', and the other the 'Kyng of Cokneys', for
Innocents' day. The reason given for banishing Straw was the
damage done in his name, and there is here a remarkable example of
the name of 'a figure from seasonal revelry'[72] having been borrowed
by a rebel leader and then reabsorbed by an institution constitu-
tionally opposed to misrule, as leader of its own seasonal indulgence
in mayhem: thus commemorating the leader of the antithetical forces
which temporarily destroyed them. One wonders whether, some
time in the fifteenth century, there had been a conscious acknowl-
edgement of the counterforce to law and order, and whether the
adoption of the name of a powerful misrule lord was *concordia
discors* in practice; a way of temporarily conceding to those opposite
forces. Alternatively perhaps, the lawyers simply appreciated the
irony. As with the Robin title which transferred to and from festive
game, and the Norwich burghers playing on the same ambivalence,
the shape-shifting nature of these volatile customs is self-evident.[73]

In the sixteenth century, the subtleties and complexities inherent in
outlaws and kings, in mirror image opposition, were absorbed into
literature and the dramatic possibilities emerged in history plays,

---

[70] *The Works of John Knox*, ed. D. Laing (Edinburgh, 1895), ii. 157–60.
[71] J. D. Walker (ed.), *The Black Books of Lincoln's Inn* (London, 1897), i. 189–90.
[72] Pettitt, 'Jack Straw', p. 8.
[73] The interrelation between serious and festive events can be seen as examples of
the 2 lives—the official and the laughing—coexisting in the medieval consciousness.
See M. Bakhtin, *Rabelais and his World*, trans. H. Iswolsky (Cambridge, Mass.,
1965), p. 96.

Outlaws, Rebels, and Civil War

such as *Henry VI*. C. L. Barber noticed that Jack Cade's rebellion, in Part 2, is expressed in terms of mock kingship, and he identified him as modelled on festive customs. And there were other models. The means of expression of both the festive and rebel example of mock king leader were almost identical and, in Cade's promises, in Act IV, scene ii, are vestiges of Beckwith's Dodelowe-style satire. Falstaff's bulk, too, treads a fine line between criminal robber king and festive lord of misrule, while the mirror image inherent in opposing kings is made specific in *Richard II*.

2

Kings of Winter Festive Groups

> . . . men now become bould to abvse ye churche in tyme of
> diuine service, as at christemas last, at bampton . . . where
> ye . . . servantes of ye lord *William* . . . did erect a christemas
> lord, and . . . did most grossely disturb ye minister in tyme of
> prayer.
>
> REED, *Cumberland*

> . . . in the feaste of Christmas, there was in the kinges house,
> where-soeuer hee was lodged, a Lord of Misrule, or Maister
> of merry disports, and the like had yee in the house of euery
> noble man, of honor, or good worshippe, were he spiritual or
> temporall.
>
> John Stow, *Survey*

French medieval society was prolific in producing festive kings,[1] who
were elevated to their temporary eminence according to one of the
two alternative ways that real kings were exalted; either by election
or by fortune. Literary and dramatic confraternities appointed kings
to lead them in both serious, learned debates and satirical *sotties*,
while minstrel brotherhoods were governed by a king appointed
from outside. In the church at New Year, a chief fool was elected as
king, or *rex stultorum*, and, at Twelfth Night in kings' courts, a *rex
fabarum* was selected through the chance portion of cake containing
the bean.[2] Some of these Norman customs took root in the English
court. 1277 is the earliest known date when a king of the minstrels

---

[1] See R. Vaultier, *Le Folklore pendant la guerre de cent ans* (Paris, 1965); P.
Bautier, *Les Reynages* (Gueret, 1945); Y.-M. Bercé, *Fête et révolte* (Paris, 1976), and
E. le R. Ladurie, *Carnival in Romans*, trans. M. Feeney (Harmondsworth, 1979).

[2] See P. de Julleville, *Les Comédiens en France au moyen age* (Paris, 1885), chs.
2–5; J. Strutt, *Sports and Pastimes of the People of England* (London, 1831), pp.
190–1, 343–4; and B. A. Henisch, *Cakes and Characters* (London, 1984), ch. 2. The
significance of the bean was, probably, that it represented the worth of the king. In
1524–5, Henry VIII was asked why his court continued with masques despite the
French skirmishes and Henry replied it was because 'thei set not by the French kyng
one bene'. E. Hall, *The Triumphant Reigne of Kyng Henry the VIII* (London, 1550),
ed. C. Whibley (London, 1904), ii. 24.

Kings of Winter Festive Groups   31

was recorded at the court of Edward I.[3] Letters patent to John of
Gaunt from Richard II in 1380 show that he was chosen by his lord
to control the behaviour of the minstrel fraternity, and to make them
provide their services according to ancient usage.[4] His role was,
therefore, quite opposite to providing any satiric inversion of order.
Rather, he was expected to enforce order against any nonconformist
brethren. According to Joseph Strutt, the 'title was dropped in the
reign of Edward IV [and] marshal became its substitute'.[5]

However, the Christmas custom, with some modifications,
flourished. The French Epiphany king appears, from English records,
to have been the first title for the winter king who was elected rather
than discovered by chance, and who presided during the whole of
Christmas. For example, the gifts which were given in reward to two
gentlemen for their services as king of the bean at the court of
Edward II, during the Christmases of 1315 and 1316, were very
similar to a gift given in January 1551–2 to the elected lord of misrule
at Edward VI's court, which suggests continuity of custom. A
silver-gilt chased basin, with ewer to match, was given to Sir William
de la Bech, king of the bean in 1315; a silver-gilt basin with stand and
cover, and pitcher to match, was given to Thomas de Weston, squire
of the king's household, for the same service in 1316.[6] And in
1551–2 the Lord Mayor gave Ferrers 'a standing cup with a cover of
silver and guilt of the value of ten pounds, for a reward'.[7] Another
early reference to a king of the bean was recorded in 1335 when
payment was made to minstrels by Edward III, 'in nomine Regis de
Faba'.[8] Again orders were carried out in 1551–2 in the name of the

[3] E. K. Chambers, *The Medieval Stage* (Oxford, 1903), ii. 260, and Strutt, *Sports and Pastimes*, p. 191.
[4] 'Carta le roy de Minstralx', *Monasticon Anglicanum*, ed. Sir W. Dugdale (London, 1655), i. 355.   [5] Strutt, *Sports and Pastimes*, p. 192.
[6] T. Stapleton, 'A brief Summary of the Wardrobe Accounts of the tenth, eleventh and fourteenth years of King Edward the Second', *Archaeologia*, 26 (1836), p. 342.
[7] R. Holinshed, *Chronicles of England, Scotland and Ireland*, ed. J. Hooker et al. (London, 1807–8), iii, 1033. The custom seems to be in imitation of the welcome given to kings on their accession. The young Edward V was presented with a gold cup at Coventry in 1474; R. Withington, *English Pageantry*, i (Cambridge, 1918), p. 153. On the accession of James I, during his journey down from Scotland, the Aldermen of Newark presented him with 'a faire gilt cup, manifesting their duties and loving hearts to him', J. G. Nichols (ed.), *Progresses . . . of King James* (London, 1828), i. 89. At York, 'The Lord mayor deliuered the Sword and Keyes to his maiestie, together with a Cup of Gold, filled full of Gold', *REED, York*, ed. A. F. Johnston and M. Rogerson (Toronto and Manchester, 1979), i. 514; and at London, 1603–4, James, Anne, and Prince Henry were each given gold cups as pledges of loyalty, Nichols, *Progresses . . . of King James*, p. 360.   [8] Strutt, *Sports and Pastimes*, p. 344 n. 3.

32 Kings of Winter Festive Groups

Christmas lord of misrule. The title, king of the bean, seems to have been discontinued at the English court, possibly because of the periodic wars with France. And its appearance in the Scottish records is ambiguous. The accounts of the Lord High Treasurer, beginning 1473, record a 'king of Bene' in 1489–90, without indicating whether this was the return of a usual custom (as one might expect in the court of one of France's allies), or the inauguration of a new one. And at the Scottish court, the honour was for Uphaliday, or Twelfth Night, only; sometimes in a year when an abbot of unreason had also been elected for the whole of Christmas.[9] The one place in England where the title remained in use was Merton College, Oxford, and the information states an election not the discovery of the king. According to the records, which began in 1485, one of the bursars, John Person, was elected *rex fabarum* on 18 November, according to ancient usage.[10] Earlier mention is made of kings under different names at other Oxford colleges; Prester John at Canterbury between 1414–30,[11] and a king Balthasar who presided in 1432 at an unspecified college. A letter from him survives, signed in the familiar style: 'Issued from our palace of Hinksey Hall, in our reign, on the 5 December.'[12] Alan Nelson has recently discovered that, in the fourteenth century, 'Cambridge students made a practice of parading through the streets with a captain and a mock chancellor, mock proctors, and mock bedells'. This was prohibited by 1390, and the earliest documented college Christmas lord was at Christ's in 1539–40.[13] Occasionally, English Christmas festivities also included an Epiphany king, as a further Twelfth Day entertainment, as for example in 1564–5 at Elizabeth's court.[14] But the custom more

[9] *Accounts of the Lord High Treasurer of Scotland AD 1473–98*, ed. T. Dickson (Edinburgh, 1877), pp. ccxxxvii–ccxliii, 126–375. Cf. A. J. Mill, *Mediaeval Plays in Scotland* (Edinburgh, 1927), p. 16.

[10] 'Decimo octauo die Nouembris electus est pro rege fabarum in collegio secundum antiquam consuetudinem magister Iohannes Persons', H. E. Salter (ed.), *Registrum Annalium Collegii Mertonensis 1483–1521* (Oxford, 1923), p. 70.

[11] W. A. Pantin, *Canterbury College, Oxford* (Oxford, 1947), iii. 68–72. Cf. *REED, Oxford*, ed. J. Elliott (forthcoming).

[12] 'Datum in palacio nostro de henxihalle regno nostro Baltasie subiecte Decembris quinto', H. E. Salter, *Formularies which bear on the History of Oxford* (Oxford, 1942), ii. 439.

[13] *REED, Cambridge*, ed. A. Nelson (Toronto, 1989), ii. 730–1, 841. No season is mentioned.

[14] *Calendar of State Papers, Venetian*, vii. 1558–1580, ed. R. Brown and G. C. Cavendish Bentinck (London, 1890), p. 374. This king was elected not discovered. See Ch. 4.

Kings of Winter Festive Groups   33

indigenous to England was the lord overseer for the whole of Christmas, and the most popular title became lord of misrule.

As far as the evidence goes, the etymology of the name is reasonably straightforward. Dictionary citations begin in the late fourteenth century. Bad government is one example, as found in the poem *Richard the Redeles*, where the king's poor government is attributed to 'misrewle of other'. However there is already a festive ambiguity, I think, in this example (see Chapter 1) which anticipates later developments. The other meaning, according to dictionaries, was ill government of the individual; and (as mentioned in the Introduction) this was increasingly applied to rioters and rebels during the fifteenth century, with the implication that their behaviour was an alternative to rule. In Paston's letters, Cherche was described as 'a mysse-rewled and encredibull man',[15] and he and Nowell were said to have gathered round them 'gret multitude of mysrewled people'.[16] Edward Hall, in his *Triumphant Reigne of King Henry VIII*, included a description of the rioters on Evil May day, 1517: '. . . all the misruled persons ranne to the doores and wyndowes of saynct Martyn, and spoyled all that they founde' (i. 160). The meaning of lord of misrule would seem to have derived from such examples, and applied to the winter festive king as being appropriate to the disorders which he incited. Stow's *Survey* says that customs associated with the title were known by 1444,[17] but no record of the title exists before Henry VII's reign, although the association is implied between Richard II and his gentlemen wasters. The actual title seems to have developed during the later fifteenth century,[18] after a period when 'misrule' had been used to describe uncontrollable riots and rebellions.

Initially, lords of misrule were as rough as the derivation suggests,[19] and among other things it was their prerogative to

---

[15] J. Paston, *The Paston Letters*, ed. N. Davis (Oxford, 1971–6), i. 63.

[16] Ibid. 59.

[17] J. Stow, *Survey of London*, ed. C. L. Kingsford (Oxford, 1908; repr. 1971), i. 97.

[18] '. . . it is worth noting . . . that if Lords of Misrule did not originate during the fifteenth century, they only seem to have become generally popular towards its end', C. Phythian-Adams, 'Ceremony and the Citizen: The Communal Year at Coventry 1450–1550', in P. Clark and P. Slack (eds.), *Crisis and Order in English Towns 1500–1700* (London, 1972), p. 69.

[19] Condemnatory statements, which provide much of the evidence, were inevitably biased, but these accounts of the roughness of the custom are confirmed by reports sympathetic to it (see below nn. 28, 29, and 30).

34   Kings of Winter Festive Groups

interrupt church services at Christmas.[20] In 1535 a deposition was brought against the curate at Harwich, Thomas Corthorpe, for expressing reformist zeal in hand-to-hand fighting in his attempt to prevent the young men of the parish from entering the church, to 'chuse them a lord of Mysrule for the Cristmas tyme as it is called as they hav don in tymes past'.[21] In 1576–6, at York, more authoritative resistance (which also distinguishes between lords of misrule and summer kings) was made, in response to Archbishop Grindal's enquiry:

Item that the minister and churchewardens shall not suffer any lordes of misrule or somer lordes, or ladyes, or any disguised persone or others in Christmasse or at Maye games or anye minstrels morice dauncers or others at Rishebearinges or at anye other tymes to come unreverentlye into anye churche or chappell or churcheyeard and there daunce or playe anye unseemlye partes with scoffes ieastes wanton gestures or rybaulde talke namelye in the tyme of divine service or of anye sermon.[22]

Though, presumably, they were allowed entry at other times. At York, Yule and Yule's wife had ridden through the city on St Thomas's day, 'very vndecently and vncomely', according to the ban of 1572, drawing great numbers of people away from church.[23] Stubbes's full description was not entirely fanciful,[24] and because the

[20] Interruptions to services, of course, happened long before the 16th cent. See 'The Tale of the Sacrilegious Carollers' in R. of Brunne's *Handlyng Synne*, ed. F. J. Furnivall (London, 1901), and G. R. Owst, *Preaching in Medieval England* (Cambridge, 1926), p. 188.

[21] PRO SP 1. 99, fo. 200. The later disturbance in Westmorland (see ch. opening) is thought to have been reported and perhaps exaggerated as ammunition against a possible recusant: '. . . others of ye lord william owne servantes came in savage manner disguised into ye churche, in ye time of prayer, others with shooting of gunnes, others with flagges, and banners borne entered ye churche, others sported them selves in ye church with pies, and puddings, vsinge them as bowles in ye churche allies, others tooke dogges counterfeitinge ye shepherds part when he fees his shepe, and all there in ye tyme of diuine service', REED, *Cumberland, etc.*, ed. A. Douglas (Toronto, 1986), pp. 218, 241.

[22] J. S. Purvis (ed.), *Tudor Parish Documents of the Diocese of York* (Cambridge, 1948), pp. 160–1. An almost identical enquiry was made at Canterbury in the same year. See *The Remains of Arch-Bishop Grindal*, ed. W. Nicholson, Parker Society, 19 (Cambridge, 1843), p. 175.   [23] REED, York, i. 309.

[24] P. Stubbes, *Anatomie of Abuses in the Kingdom of Ailgna*, ed. F. J. Furnivall (London, 1877–82), p. 147. Stubbes's example of a lord of misrule could have been either a winter or summer leader, and further seasonal interchange appears in the processing Morris dancers who accompanied the two New Year processions through London in 1552–3 (H. Machyn, *Diary of a Resident in London from 1550 to 1563*, ed. J. S. Nichols (London, 1848), p. 289), as well as the midsummer watches from 1525 to 1541. *Collections III*, Malone Society Reprints, ed. J. Robertson and D. J. Gordon (Oxford, 1954).

Kings of Winter Festive Groups

lord of misrule set his face against the forms of religion, Stubbes connects the name with the devil, taking the meaning of misrule beyond the inversion of secular law into a devilish saturnalia: a blasphemous denial of religious rule, abhorrent even to pagan religions. The acolyte, Spudeus, says 'mee thinke the very name itself caryeth a taste of some notorious evil'.[25] Further confirmation of the wildness of provincial lords comes from Thomas Lodge in 1596. When expressing disapproval of the licence of the household fool, he says such jesters have 'all the feats of a Lord of misrule in the countrie'.[26] Other evidence confirms that, in the country, the roles of fool and mock king might be interchangeable.[27]

Yet Christmas lords elected in some households were also intended to behave outrageously. John Evelyn's father, Richard, gave orders for his lord of misrule to act in a way which was to bring the custom at Lincoln's Inn to an end:

I give full power and authority to his lordship to break up all locks, bolts, bars, doors, latches, and to fling up all doors out of hinges, to come at those who presume to disobey his lordship's commands. God save the king![28]

And Thomas Urquhart wrote in 1652 that both the French king of the bean and the English lord of misrule were elected 'to no other end, but to countenance the bacchanalian riots and preposterous disorders of the family where he is installed'.[29] The games associated with such wild releases seem to have included as much mockery of the lord as mockery of the law by him. In 1607, an invitation to the Christmas prince of St John's, Oxford, to visit another college towards the end of the festive season turned out to be an insult not an honour: '. . . the whole play was a medley of Christmas sportes, by wch occasion Christmas Lords were much jested at, and our Prince was soe placed that many thinges were acted vpon him.'[30] The

---

[25] Stubbes, *Anatomie of Abuses*, p. 147.
[26] *The Complete Works of Thomas Lodge*, ed. E. W. Gosse (New York, 1963), iv. 84.
[27] John Cradock, at South Kyme, Lincolnshire, in 1601 wore a piebald coat, or fool's dress, playing the summer lord of Kyme. C. L. Barber, *Shakespeare's Festive Comedy* (Princeton, 1959), p. 42. Cf. App., *Timon, a play*.
[28] R. W. Chambers (ed.), *The Book of Days* (Edinburgh, 1863), ii. 741–2.
[29] *Tracts of the Learned and Celebrated Antiquarian, Sir Thomas Urquhart of Cromarty 1652* (Edinburgh, 1774), pp. 145–6.
[30] *The Christmas Prince*, ed. F. S. Boas (Oxford, 1923), p. 189. Cf. the Wakefield *Buffeting* of Christ and the York play of the *Tyllemakers* for Christ mocked in mock king terms, S. Billington, *Social History of the Fool* (Brighton, 1984), pp. 18–20.

36 *Kings of Winter Festive Groups*

anonymous *Timon* (see Appendix) contains a selection of bacchanalian riots, overseen by Timon and the clown, with the mockery of Timon included in the second half of the play.

Against this all-licensed behaviour, can be set the attempt to reform the custom, which Thomas Lodge may have been familiar with. Stow's title for the lord of misrule, 'Maister of merry disports',[31] which Holinshed also adopted, is altogether more sedate and appropriate to the changes which took place, for example, at Lincoln's Inn in 1519, when breaking of doors was prohibited, and lords of harmless or even educational pastimes were instituted for a year or two, when these too were ended.[32] At the Middle Temple, election of lords of misrule was forbidden in 1580, and when the ban was defied in 1590–1 Richard Martin and others were temporarily discommoned for 'making outcries, forcibly breaking open chambers in the night, [and] levying money as the Lord of Misrule's rent'.[33] In other words, they attempted to revive their pre-Reformation freedoms and 'feast-day privileges'.[34] In the sixteenth century, the inns of court increasingly became places for the gentry to acquire social graces,[35] and aspiring lawyers needed the same graces to fit them for royal council chambers. Accordingly, the Christmas and other seasonal revels became opportunities to practise courtly skills.

Cambridge colleges, founded by the Tudor dynasty, also show the

[31] Stow, *Survey of London*, i. 97.

[32] J. D. Walker (ed.), *The Black Books of Lincoln's Inn* (London, 1897), i. 181–90. Before the customs were reformed, serious business such as admissions to the Society of Lincoln's Inn was conducted by the seasonal officers: ibid. 188.

[33] C. H. Hopwood (ed.), *Middle Temple Records* (London, 1904–5), i. 318. The dates coincide with a period of increased lawlessness among Elizabethan youth. See Ch. 1 n. 48, and Ch. 10 n. 43, and J. R. Dasent (ed.), *Acts of the Privy Council*, NS 21, *1591* (London, 1901), pp. 297, 299.

[34] M. Bakhtin, *Rabelais and his World*, trans. H. Iswolsky (Cambridge, Mass., 1965), p. 83.

[35] 'There is both in the *Inns of Court*, and the *Inns of Chancery*, a sort of an Academy, or Gymnasium, fit for [gentlemen]; where they learn singing, and all kinds of music, dancing and such other accomplishments and diversions (which are called *Revels*) as are suitable to their quality, and such as are usually practised at Court . . . here everything which is good and virtuous is to be learned; all vice is discouraged and banished. So that knights and barons, and the greatest nobility of the kingdom, often place their children in those Inns of Court; not so much to make the laws their study, much less to live by the profession . . . but to form their manners and to preserve them from the contagion of vice.' Sir J. Fortescue, *De Laudibus Legum Angliae 1467–71*, trans. R. Mulcaster (1567), in A. E. Green, *The Inns of Court* (New Haven, 1931), p. 33. Cf. M. Axton, *The Queen's Two Bodies* (London, 1977), pp. 4–6.

Kings of Winter Festive Groups

influence of humanist improvements and a trend towards a new Renaissance aesthetic. At St John's, founded in 1511 by Lady Margaret Beaufort, Henry VIII had written into the Statutes in 1545 what F. S. Boas calls 'a remarkable passage',[36] ordaining that at Christmas honest recreation and literary exercises were to be performed with joy and mirth under the supervision of a *dominus*. At the founding of Trinity College in 1546, the mathematician, John Dee, was instrumental in instituting an Imperator and himself caused 'great wondering' at the stage techniques he used in his production of Aristophanes's *Pax*.[37] At St John's, the position of Dominus was one of considerable responsibility, which every Fellow had to undertake in his turn. The lord was to stage a fresh spectacle each night of the twelve days, and a heavy fine was the penalty for an omission. By 1548, the costumes used were indented to the Dominus whose responsibility was to ensure they were safely passed on to his successor.[38] It is clear from the instructions that, like the king of the minstrels, this lord had nothing to do with inciting disorder, but was rather to keep the scholars usefully occupied during a period when disorder might otherwise have tempted them. For twelve days he was to be in effect a theatre manager, and in Cambridge colleges the plays dominated the proceedings, while the dominus himself receded into the background, divested of his historical violence and lacking a reformed personality. However, at court and the inns of court, the role of the dominus, and the entertainments he offered, were affected by Renaissance cultural values, which gave the misrule lord a new persona.

Sixteenth-century poetic theory was inspired by classical science, occult science, and cosmology, largely drawn from the works of Pythagoras. Sir Philip Sidney's declaration that the poet was a ποιητης or maker is based on 'Plato in his most pythagorean mood',[39] and the concept of maker made the roles of poet and God comparable. In the words of Cristofor Landino (1424–1504), 'God is the supreme poet and the world is His poem'.[40] An extension to this way of thinking came dangerously close to exalting the poet

---

[36] F. S. Boas, *University Drama in the Tudor Age* (Oxford, 1914), p. 8.
[37] *Autobiographical Tracts of Dr. John Dee*, ed. J. Crossley (Manchester, 1851), p. 5. Cf. F. Yates, *Theatre of the World* (London, 1969), chs. 1 and 2.
[38] S. Billington, 'Sixteenth-century Drama in St. John's College, Cambridge', *RES*, NS 29 (1978), p. 2.
[39] S. K. Heninger, *Touches of Sweet Harmony* (San Marino, Calif., 1974), p. 291.   [40] Ibid. 292.

38   *Kings of Winter Festive Groups*

above God. The worlds created and controlled by poets were claimed not to suffer from any fall of Adam, or resulting mutability, and a poem's deliberate artifice could be argued to be an improvement on nature. Sidney wrote, 'with the force of a diuine breath, he [the poet] bringeth things foorth surpassing her [nature's] doings'.[41] This of course conveniently overlooked the fact that, according to the argument, the maker of the poem must also be a part of flawed, sublunary matter. The claim could be seen to be blasphemous, and Sidney was careful to disavow any such intention. But lords of misrule in court also became creators of fantastic worlds, in which elements of classical philosophy can also be found.

For example, in the pre-Copernican cosmos, three-dimensional perfect worlds were thought to exist beyond the earth's atmosphere. In the strife-ridden sixteenth century, belief in the existence of perfect worlds became of some importance: they 'held out hope to the perennial band of those who seek Utopias'.[42] The closest and most visible was the moon, and the notion that there was an ideal existence there led to flights of fancy from poets who wrote as worshippers of Diana, culling much of their information from the ancient world. The following passage from an early seventeenth-century translation of Plutarch is an example of the material at their disposal:

The *Pythagoreans* affirme, that the Moone appeareth terrestriall, for that she is inhabited round about, like as the earth wherein we are, and peopled as it were with the greatest living creatures, and the fairest plants; and those creatures within her, be fifteene times stronger and more puissant than those with us, and the same yeeld foorth no excrements, and the day there, is in that proportion so much longer.[43]

Misrule entertainments began to draw on the possibilities of *alterae terrae* for their settings, and the *mundus inversus* changed from a reductive to an improving concept. Pythagorean qualities can, I think, be found in George Ferrers's imaginative instructions regarding his second appearance as lord of misrule at Edward VI's 1552 celebrations:

. . . ffirst as towching my Introduction where the last yeare my devise was to cum oute of the mone / this yeare I Imagin to cum oute of a place caulled *vastum vacuum*. I. the great waste / asmoche to saie as a place voyde or

[41] Sir P. Sidney, *Defence of Poesie* (London, 1595), fo. C. 1ᵛ.
[42] Heninger, *Touches of Sweet Harmony*, p. 127.   [43] Ibid. 125.

Kings of Winter Festive Groups   39

emptie withoute the worlde where is neither fier ayre water nor earth / and
that I haue been remayning there sins the Last yeare . . . I wolde yf it were
possyble haue all myne apparell blewe the first daie that I present my self to
the kinges Maiestie . . . Againe how I shall cum into the courte whether
vnder a Canepie as the last yeare, or in a chare trivmphall, or vppon some
straunge beast that I reserve to you / But the serpente with sevin heddes
cauled hidra is the chief beast of myne armes. / and the wholie [holly] bushe is
the devise of my Crest / my worde is *semper ferians*. I. alwaies feasting or
keping holie daie.[44]

This description is an intriguing combination of mythology, carnival
(the holly bush was the insignia of the Guild of Butchers),[45] and
scientific fantasy. On first impression, mention of a *vastum vacuum*
might seem to suggest chaos, but on further reading, as it had in it no
mutable elements 'neither fier ayre water nor earth', it is clear that
Ferrers's model was the immutable heavens and appropriately he
asked for a dress of sky blue.[46] It seems that Ferrers leavened the
concept of misrule through a fusion with that of Utopia, and that in
his first entry into court he refined the role of the misrule lord into
king or mythical god of a fantasy world. It would, moreover, have
been more befitting the dignity of the young king for him to step aside
for such a character rather than for a more boisterous conception.
Ferrers's relationship to Edward was that of a king visiting on equal
terms, taking over Edward's functions with all due respect, and
communicating with him by means of an ambassador. The theme of
opposites to Edward's court was maintained through the cacophony
of his heralds and the nonsense the ambassador spoke.[47] And on
Epiphany each year Ferrers progressed through London in full
imitation of Tudor monarchy. Records of both years, 1551–2 and

[44] A. and G. Feuillerat (eds.), *Documents Relating to . . . Edward VI and Queen
Mary* (Louvain, 1914), p. 89. Cf. *The Loseley Manuscripts*, ed. A. J. Kempe (London
1836), pp. 32–3. Kempe removes 'water'.
[45] This sign of the meat-eating season can best be seen in the costumes for the
Nuremberg Schembart festival. See Fig. 2, S. L. Sumberg, *The Nuremberg Schembart
Carnival* (New York, 1941), and S. Billington, 'Butchers and Fishmongers', *Folklore*
101 (1990), pp. 99–100.
[46] 'Touching my suet of blew, I have sent you a pece of velvet which hath a kinde of
powdered ermaines in it, vearie fytt for my wering', *Loseley Manuscripts*, p. 35. There
is evidence to suggest that a tradition developed of using this colour symbol of
authority to present a foolish wise man. See *Processus Noe*, l. 200, in A. W. Cawley
(ed.), *The Wakefield Pageants in the Towneley Cycle* (Manchester, 1958), p. 19; and
The Masque of Owls (1626), in J. G. Nichols (ed.), *The Progress . . . of Queen
Elizabeth* (London, 1904–8), i. 447. I am grateful to Richard Axton for noting this.
[47] *Losely Manuscripts*, p. 33.

40   *Kings of Winter Festive Groups*

1552–3, survive, and these give some indication of Ferrers's characterization and the parodic entertainments put on by him.

   The first year's celebration was a last-minute idea of the Duke of Northumberland to take Edward's mind off the impending execution of his uncle Somerset, the Lord Protector. Preparations only began on 30 December, but Ferrers issued careful instructions. Special costumes made included pages' coats, decorated with red and white silk, and garments for eight counsellors to accompany him on the progress through London. Ferrers sent these back as inadequate to the honour of the young gentlemen wearing them, and therefore to his own honour.[48] He clearly intended to present a convincing image of regality, and not one which would provoke titters from the crowd. According to Holinshed his procession was met by 'Vause, lord of misrule to . . . one of the shiriffes of London',[49] who conducted him to the Lord Mayor, where Ferrers was given his silver-gilt cup in recognition of his kingly status.

   Events for the second year were more ambitious. Ferrers asked for at least five suits of apparel, and was given three very fine sets of clothes. Details given of his Twelfth Day suit for the procession are reminiscent of the elaborations in Schembart festival dress (see nn. 44 and 45 and Fig. 2). His costume was a purple velvet robe, coat and cape, lined with simulated ermine, and with blue and gilt borders. He also had an elaborate velvet hat or headpiece,[50] and pages carried a shield, sword, and axe,[51] and possibly the holly bush. In Ferrers's retinue were representatives of the sciences and arts (lawyers were appropriately absent),[52] and general entertainers followed behind. Ferrers's orders for this second year's followers were:

There maie be no fewer than six counsailors at the least; I must also have a divine, a philosopher, and astronomer, a poet, a phisician, a potecarie, a mr of requests, a sivilian, a disard [fool], John Smyth [court fool], two gentlemen ushers, besides jugglers, tomblers, fooles, friers, and suche other.[53]

The such other included 'gayllers with pelere, stokes, and ys axe, gyffes, and boltes, sum fast by the leges and sum by the nekes',[54] as a

---

[48] *Losely Manuscripts*, pp. 27–8.   [49] Holinshed, *Chronicles*, iii. 1033.
[50] 'Garnished wt purple vellet striped wth thredes of silver', *Loseley Manuscripts*, p. 47.   [51] Ibid. 33.
[52] A 'doctur of the law' was included in the 1551–2 procession, Machyn, *Diary of a Resident*, p. 14.   [53] *Loseley Manuscripts*, p. 34.
[54] Machyn, *Diary of a Resident*, p. 29.

2 Nuremberg Schembart Festival costume, 1539

reminder that the *mundus inversus* also had its penal system. The procession was again met by the Sheriff's lord of misrule who walked in front of Ferrers carrying the symbol of kingship, an upright sword. Before going to dine with the Lord Mayor, the parade went to Cheapside, where Ferrers performed a mock ceremony of knighting the Sheriff's lord, and his treasurer cast (presumably artificial) gold and silver towards the crowd.[55] The ceremonials each year were faithful copies of those of monarchs taking possession of a city and being accepted by the local authorities. Whereas entertainments held at the court appear to have been more parodic versions of courtly activity: hunting and hawking, and a joust with the participants on (or rather wearing) canvas hobby horses.[56] There was also a 'play of execution',[57] and as recent history had demonstrated, this too was a frequent occupation for princes.[58] During the twelve days Ferrers had a guard of honour of seventy men wearing costumes which showed they were mock soldiers. Their armour was 'canvas paynted lyke maylle'. The costume expense account reveals more parody. John Smith, the court fool, wearing the long skirts of the simpleton, played Ferrers's eldest son and heir, while four others also in long coats played the rest of his family, and two bastard sons were presented as artificial fools in parti-colouring.[59] These spectacles presented a through the looking-glass view of court life, and the more serious and self-important Ferrers was, when, for example, jousting on a hobby horse, the more comic the effect. A mock title given to him, 'the Lorde Myserable',[60] does suggest that Ferrers maintained a ridiculously haughty demeanour.[61] The lord of the fantasy world provided satiric but harmless comedy in which the Dominus was the central, quixotic figure, heading motley processions, competing in absurd games, and performing extravagant ceremonies. Ferrers's inversion of the normal world did not threaten it, though like other mock kings including outlaws he necessarily adopted a regal style in

[55] Machyn, *Diary*, 28–9. [56] *Losely Manuscripts*, pp. 36–7. [57] Ibid. 54.
[58] In his excellent book on Tudor courts, *Spectacle, Pageantry, and Early Tudor Policy* (Oxford, 1969), Sydney Anglo calls the mock execution a 'jest in the poorest possible taste at Somerset's expense', p. 308, but the year was 1552/3, not 1551/2; equipment for executions was carried in the processions both years and, bearing in mind the frequency with which men in power ended their lives on the block —Northumberland's father in 1509, and Northumberland himself was to in the same year as this entertainment!—it seems a very legitimate subject for parody.
[59] *Losely Manuscripts*, pp. 47–8. [60] Ibid. 42.
[61] This could have been like the arrogance of summer kings. See Ch. 3.

Kings of Winter Festive Groups   43

letters.[62] And, despite the grandeur of his first entry into court, Ferrers's pomp could not and was not intended to rival Edward's. His mock world complemented and complimented that of the king. *Concordia discors*, which seems always to have been implicit in misrule celebrations, was fully integrated into his ceremonies. The harmony of the universe, maintained through the reconciliation of opposites, became a part of the court play in which the harmony of the court was highlighted by the interplay between rule and misrule. It was Northumberland's purpose the first year to present a united court, and the harmony was expressed the second year by Ferrers in his last letter to Sir Thomas Cawarden, where he referred to the seasonal necessity for his departure: 'And thus commending the furniture of my decaying estate to your good handling, I byd you hartily farewell.'[63]

Pythagorean science expressed in art was more successful than that pursued too closely in life in Elizabethan England, as the careers of Dr John Dee and others show. Dee's recollection of having created a wonder in Trinity College in 1546 came in a letter of 1592 to the Archbishop of Canterbury, in which he pleaded against the general belief that he was a sorcerer. His defence combined Platonic thought with Pythagorean mathematics in a way quite foreign to orthodox theology.[64] Sidney was also suspected of forbidden occult leanings, and both are today associated with Walter Raleigh's School of Night,[65] so-called because of its involvement with the new Copernican astronomy. Despite his interest in modern science, Dee nevertheless expressed himself philosophically according to the pre-Copernican system, and it is important to explain the seeming contradiction since it relates to the continued use of cosmology in misrule entertainments and drama after 1558.

---

[62] *Loseley Manuscripts*, p. 30.   [63] Ibid. 44.

[64] He declared his allegiance to God, saying he had sought God's truth 'by the true philosophicall method [progressing] from thinges visible to consider of thinges invisible . . . from things transitorie to meditate of things permanent'. He continued this safe Platonic exposition with one more directly from Pythagoras, concluding that his purpose had been to see 'the most mervailous frame of the *whole world*, philosophically viewed, and circumspectly wayed, numbred and measured', 'Compendious Rehearsall', *Autobiographical Tracts*, p. 72.

[65] See M. C. Bradbrook, *The School of Night* (Cambridge, 1935); W. Oakshott, *The Queen and the Poet* (London, 1960); E. G. Clark, *Ralegh and Marlowe* (New York, 1965), and E. M. W. Tillyard, *Shakespeare's History Plays* (London, 1944), p. 23.

44   *Kings of Winter Festive Groups*

Copernicus did not think his new cosmology to be the break with ancient method which it later came to be. In his letter to the Pope, explaining the delay in publication, Copernicus refers to his treatise as a philosophy with precedents in the school of Pythagoras. Quoting Plutarch, he wrote:

Some say that the Earth is at rest, but Philolaos the Pythagorean says that it is carried in a circle round the heavenly fire . . . Heraclides of Pontus and Ecphantus the Pythagorean give the Earth motion . . . I therefore took this opportunity and also began to consider the possibility that the Earth moved.[66]

Copernicus did not refute the theory that the heavens were immutable and the earth mutable, rather his conclusions resulted in reinforcing these beliefs. A. M. Duncan writes:

Copernicus' interest is entirely in the mathematical elegance of [his theory], and his reason for adopting it is mainly that he finds the old system breaks some of the ancient principles of harmony and simplicity. To observe fully the most important principles, that the heavenly bodies move in perfect circles with uniform motion, he is willing to abandon the principle that the Earth is motionless at the centre of the universe.[67]

Therefore, initially, Copernican theory strengthened the concept of perfect movement in the heavens at the expense of the earth's importance, and the idealization of heavenly spheres by poets such as Raleigh, Chapman, and Lyly later in the sixteenth century was not in conflict with the new science. Instead, the contemporary astronomy led to a more intense study of the heavens. Those involved created a hermetic academy which drew its inspiration from the stars and exalted its members through their private intellectual pursuits. The dominant theme of their writings, the moon's influence on the poet, developed into compliments to Elizabeth and debates on her multi-faceted nature.[68] The moon was cabalistic centre and source of intellectual life. As for example, in Drayton's 'Endimion and Phoebe':

---

[66] A. M. Duncan, *Copernicus* (Newton Abbot, 1976), p. 26.
[67] Ibid. 14.
[68] 'The moon cult begun by Raleigh in the eighties as a personal, private one, became public in the nineties. That it was in some of its aspects a celebration of Elizabeth . . . there is plenty of evidence', R. Strong, *The Cult of Elizabeth* (London, 1977), p. 48. Cf. M. Axton, *The Queen's Two Bodies* (London, 1977), ch. 5, 'Triumphs of Diana: Court Entertainments 1575–90'.

Kings of Winter Festive Groups   45

> Life of my life, pure image of my hart,
> Impressure of conceit, invention, art,
> My vitall spirit, receves his spirit from thee,
> Thou art that all which ruleth all in me,
> Thou art the sap, and life whereby I live . . .[69]

And Raleigh wrote in more direct praise in 'The Phoenix':

> Praisd be Dianas faire and harmles light . . .
> Praisd be hir knights in whom true honor liues,
> Praisd be that force, by which she moues the floods,
> Let that Diana shine, which all these giues.[70]

Despite the association between the moon and Queen Elizabeth, the sun could still represent governmental, daytime control and authority. It was active, and the moon reflective and intellectual. Drayton wrote, again in 'Endimion and Phoebe':

> And as the sunne unto the day gives light,
> So is she [the moon] onely mistris of the night.

> ll. 410–11

Moon worship taken literally (and even as metaphor for Queen Elizabeth) is either blasphemous or absurd, like the poet's claim to rival God, and Shakespeare rejected such poetic extremes. In Sonnet 14 he wrote, 'Not from the stars do I my judgement pluck', and in *1 Henry IV* he presented the more realistic picture of the honour of Diana's squires. Falstaff in his first scene with Prince Hal says:

Marry then sweet wag, when thou art king let not us that are squires of the night's body be called thieves of the day's beauty: let us be Diana's foresters, gentlemen of the shade, minions of the moon; . . . of good government, being governed as the sea is, by our noble and chaste mistress the moon, under whose countenance we steal. (I. ii. 23–9)

Words with a moon prefix still convey a sense of Diana worship. Some tongue-in-cheek collusion or sympathy is implied by terms such as moonlighting, moonshine, or a moonlight flit. The excuse is offered that those involved necessarily break the earth's laws, which govern in daylight, because they are obeying those of another sphere

---

[69] *Poems of Michael Drayton*, ed. J. Buxton (London, 1953), i. 36. 571–5.
[70] *The Poems of Sir Walter Raleigh*, ed. A. M. C. Latham (London, 1951), p. 10.

46 *Kings of Winter Festive Groups*

over the hours of darkness. In Falstaff (who has often been described as a lord of misrule) Diana worship is put firmly into the parodic perspective. And some of the thinking which was to emerge in more intense studies of astronomy does seem to have been applied in the second half of the sixteenth century to courtly lord of misrule celebrations, whether parodying inherent excesses or seriously using the ideas for an ambitious programme.[71] Christmas celebrations at court, the inns of court, and at Oxford between 1560 and 1610, provide a panorama of ideas and developments from aesthetic thinking.

There was, in particular, greater refinement for misrule lords, which reached an apotheosis early in Elizabeth's reign, when at the Inner Temple in 1561 Robert Dudley accepted election to the festive post of Constable Marshall or lord of misrule. He was also given a third title, relating to the queen, Pallaphilos. The extant records were compiled by Sir William Dugdale in 1666, and as the original documents have since been lost, we do not know whether some of the description relates to the usual behaviour of Inner Temple misrule lords, and whether Dudley had a deputy to perform the more boisterous for him. But, according to the records, the lord's reign began in the evening before supper on St Stephen's day (26 December). The Constable Marshall entered in full carnival dress, as elaborate as Ferrers's and again bearing some relation to the Guild of Butchers: white and gilt harness, many coloured feathers 'upon his Crest or Helm, and a gilt Pole-axe in his hand'. After a fifteen-minute declaration of allegiance by the Constable Marshall, the Revels Chancellor vacated his seat, and the twelve-day rule began, but each morning after breakfast the authority of the Revels Chancellor was restored, and that of the alternative lord was 'in suspense, until his personal presence at night; and then his power is most potent'.[72] This is reminiscent of Antonio's lines in Webster's *The Duchess of Malfi* when he wishes to stay overnight, and the Duchess accuses him of being 'a lord of Mis-rule'. He replies, 'Indeed, my rule is only in the

---

[71] Interest in astronomy (probably through the influence of John Dee) found immediate expression on Elizabeth's accession. Eight globes were made for the Maske of Astronomers, 1558/9, and a large quantity of canvas was used to make the microcosmic figure of a man. '1 piece of white normandye canvas 35½ ells in makinge of armes and legges steyned flesshe colour', A. and G. Feuillerat (eds.), *Documents . . . in the Time of Queen Elizabeth* (Louvain, 1908), p. 97. Cf. P. J. French, *John Dee* (London, 1972), pp. 62–3.

[72] Sir W. Dugdale, *Originales Iuridiciales* (London, 1666), p. 156.

Kings of Winter Festive Groups   47

night'.[73] Both comments could be taken to mean that disorder is best carried out at night under cover of darkness. However, riot is no respecter of dawn, as rural records show, whereas Antonio says his rule is *only* in the night. Also, the words 'rule' and 'power' refer to a system of disorder rather than to anything actually disordered, and the stronger possibility, in view of Falstaff's declaration, is that in courtly circles misrule became allied to the nocturnal hours. The concept is succinctly put in Carew's observation of Cornwall's inhabitants who, he said, at harvest time spent 'a great part of the night in Christmas rule'.[74] Such an idea of division between day and night provides for a harmonious reconciliation between order and disorder, as well as allowing the appropriate time of the moon's influence to govern the inverted world.

As with Ferrers's fantasy world, the entertainment provided at the Inner Temple was a parody of normal behaviour, yet the *mundus inversus* had a strong decorum. One of the first things the Marshall did on election was to rename the assembly man by man:

Sir *Francis Flatterer*, of Fowleshurst in the County of Buckingham.
Sir *Randle Rackabite*, of Rascall Hall, in the County of Rakehell.
Sir *Morgan Mumchance*, of Much Monkery, in the County of Mad Mopery.[75]

Members of the misrule fellowship were renamed, as were some protagonists in rebellions, but the titles were abstracted away from actual social conflict. Sir Randell was not Randell Ravener or, more appropriately for the period, Sir Randell Rackrent. The ritual embracing the custom fictionalized anything bordering on real disorder. After the opening ceremonies, supper was served 'in all solempnity, as upon Christmas day' and afterwards there was another ritual left over from factionalism:

... the Constable-Marshall presented himself with Drums afore him, mounted upon a Scaffold, born by four men; and goeth three times round about the Harthe, crying out aloud, *A Lord, A Lord, &c.* Then he descendeth & goeth to dance.[76]

During the Wars of the Roses, acclamation of rival kings appears to have been used as an obvious way of judging the strength of any one

---

[73] III. ii. 7–8.
[74] C. L. Barber, *Shakespeare's Festive Comedy* (Princeton, 1959), p. 25.
[75] Sir W. Dugdale, *Originales Iuridiciales* (London, 1666), p. 156.   [76] Ibid.

Kings of Winter Festive Groups

leader's support,[77] and further evidence suggests that, in the sixteenth century, such acclamation generally shifted to the election of the festive lord.[78] At the Inner Temple, usual entertainments during the twelve days were made up of parodies of normal procedure, with some reminder that the misrule world also had punishments. Dugdale mentions debates in which the authority of the Constable Marshall was questioned and losers were imprisoned in the tower, unless they escaped *en route* and secured the sanctuary of the buttery. And, on the evening of New Year's day, tradition was for the Constable Marshall to open the ceremonies from the back of an ass.

It is not impossible that, like Ferrers, Dudley did carry out all these functions. He is reported to have had a strong sense of humour. Yet the most interesting aspect of his performance is that it related very closely to his personal aims, and so it provides an example of reinterpreted misrule played out in high social circles. His official position in Elizabeth's court, in 1561, was the largely ceremonial one of Master of the Horse. He had not as yet been given any title but, as Elizabeth's favourite, his ambitions were towards the highest title in the land, and between 1559 and 1566 he maintained his suit to her. Comments on him and his family history show he was thought of by some as uncrowned king in the court, and that Dudley himself saw in the mock title the promise of eventually gaining the real one (see Chapter 4). His influence with the queen had made him an effective ally for the Inner Temple in 1561, in their suit against Gray's inn, and the Inner Temple's reward was to pledge 'themselves and their successors to Dudley, offering their legal skills in his service and

---

[77] When Edward IV's forces captured Henry VI in 1461 popular allegiance was sought by staging such an acclamation for him: '. . . the Archbishop of Yorke to the entent that the people myght more fermely stycke on his syde, caused [Henry] to ryde about London, appareled in a gowne of blewe veluet, with a great company cryeng kyng Henry, kyng Henry (whiche sight asmuch pleased the citezens as a fier paynted on the wall, warmed the olde woman)', E. Hall, *Chronicle* (London, 1548), ed. Sir H. Ellis(London, 1809), p. 294. In 1485 Henry VII entered York, his erstwhile enemy's stronghold, as king, and 'the Communaltye of euere craft on þer best array without any staffes bering. With due obeysaunce making vnto [þe k] his grace and crying of King Henry &c.', REED, *York*, i. 154.

[78] In *Mucedorus* the fool, Mouse, precedes the young Prince Mucedorus in his final triumphant entry, crying 'A King, a King, a King'. In Marston's *Jack Drum's Entertainment* the Morris dancers approach their patron with the cry, 'A Lord, a Lord, a Lord, who!' (see Ch. 8). Arbaces, in *A King and No King*, is similarly greeted (see Ch. 8), and at the beginning of the Civil War the acclamation was ambiguously used to rally support for Charles 1 (see Ch. 1 n. 56).

Kings of Winter Festive Groups

promising never to give counsel in a cause against Lord Robert'.[79] Marie Axton has shown that the way in which Dudley was honoured as their lord of misrule, or Christmas prince, supported his suit to Elizabeth. The role of mock prince was transformed into a noble, honourable figure and presented to Elizabeth as a suitable candidate for the real position. The *mundus inversus* over which Dudley presided was an idealized one, based on Arthurian and mythological legend, with ideas taken from the coat of arms and chivalric codes of the Knights Templar. Gerard Legh, in *The Accidens of Armorie* (1562), described his approach to the Inner Temple celebrations as though he were a Gulliver arriving at an ancient but unknown world:

> After I had traueiled through the East part of th'unknowen world, to vnderstand of deedes of armes, & so arriuing in the faire riuer of Thames, I laded within halfe a leage fro the city of London, which was (as I coniecture) in December last. And drawing neere the citie, sodenly hard the shot of double canons in so great a nuber, & so terrible that it darkened the whole aire, wherwith although I was in my natiue coutrie: yet stood I amazed, not knowing what it met. Thus as I abode in dispaire either to returne or cotinue my former purpose, I chaunced to see comming towardes me an honest Citizen, clothed in long garmet, keping the high way, seming to walke for his recreation, which prognosticated rather peace then perill. Of whom I demaunded the cause of this great shot, who frendly answered, It is quoth he warning shot to th'officers of the constable Marshall of the Inner Teple, to prepare to dinner. (fo. 119[r&v])

Legh continues with his wonder at the nobility and dignity of the hall, recreating an image of Arthurian splendour, with Dudley as prince the most wonderful of all. His narrative transforms the Master of the Horse into a second Perseus whose title, Prince Pallaphilos, linked ancient Troy and Troy Nova or London, suggesting that Dudley was defender of both Pallas and Elizabeth.[80] The mythological genealogy effaced Dudley's problematic family history,[81] and reinterpreted a man with a dangerous past, who had aided a rebel mock king (see Chapter 4), changing him into an elevated lord of an ideal world which England could become should Elizabeth choose so wisely. This misrule world was not only re-formed, but was presented as an improvement on, defender of, and

---

[79] M. Axton, 'Robert Dudley and the Inner Temple Revels', *HJ* 13 (1970), p. 365.
[80] Ibid. 368–78.
[81] Axton, *Queen's Two Bodies*, p. 42.

50   *Kings of Winter Festive Groups*

model for the real world. And from this setting Dudley set out to woo Elizabeth with masque and play.[82]

Visual metaphor was less ambitious in the Gray's Inn Grand Christmas of 1594–5: *The Gesta Grayorum*. The world of artifice of the Prince of Purpoole, Henry Helmes, was complementary to Elizabeth's court, but did not attempt to be anything other than a dim reflection of it. Helmes's last speech after the Shrove Tuesday 'Masque of the Adamantine Rock', performed at Elizabeth's court, acknowledged this:

> But now our Principality is determined; which although it shined very bright in ours, and other Darkness; yet, at the Royal Presence of Her Majesty, it appeared as an obscured Shadow: In this, not unlike unto the Morning star, which looketh very chearfully in the World, so long as the Sun looke not on it.[83]

And his crest suggested he was lord of a time when the sun was in decline.[84] *The Gesta Grayorum* was perhaps the least parodic and the most serious imitation of government of all the extant inns of court texts. There was imitation of the Tudor court in progresses through London, as Ferrers had done; an invitation to the Inner Temple's ambassador to honour the prince's court, as Vaus also did with Ferrers and as happened in the universities; and there was imitation of government in the set pieces presented, such as in the speeches of six counsellors advising the prince, and thought to be written by Francis Bacon. The sixth counsellor's speech arguing that the king should spend his time in pastimes, contains interesting double ironies based on Erasmus's *Moriae Encomium*.[85] But whereas Ferrers's assumption of dignity seems to have been for comic effect, there is nothing in the account of Helmes's portrayal to suggest anything other than that it was modelled on true princely behaviour.

---

[82] Axton, 'Robert Dudley', pp. 373–8.

[83] *The Gesta Grayorum*, ed. W. W. Greg (Oxford, 1915), p. 68.

[84] 'In his Crest, his Government for the twelve Days of *Christmas* was resembled to the Sun's passing the twelve Signs, though the prince's Course had some odd degrees beyond that time', ibid. 10.

[85] Erasmus identified the chief folly of kings to be desire for the pleasure with none of the responsibility (see Ch. 4). The 6th counsellor advocates this folly and, as a further twist, gives, for the example of tedious responsibility, the player king on stage. The previous counsellor's advice was: 'so cumbersome, as if they would make you a King in a Play; who when one would think he standeth in great Majesty and Felicity, he is troubled to say his part. What! Nothing but Tasks?', *The Gesta Grayorum*, p. 41.

One difference between the Gray's Inn and earlier revels was that, in 1594, an outside audience was present: 'a great Presence of Lords, Ladies, and worshipful Personages, that did expect some notable Performance'.[86] Theatre-going was by then well established, and the proceedings at Gray's Inn were treated with as much disrespect as were the efforts of professional actors. The one evening of real misrule, caused by the audience, threatened to spoil the good fame the revellers sought. The dignity of the Gray's Inn men and their decorum towards the Inner Temple representative were only re-stored after a semi-serious debate, mocking their own follies, to discover who was responsible for the unruly crowd; whether a magician had caused an illusion or whether trouble had resulted from the perennial problem of the king's officers mismanaging the commonwealth. The quality of courtly ritual, which Helmes's court tried to maintain, was based on real etiquette, intended to display the graces of the gentlemen to the outside world and to Elizabeth, to elicit 'great Honour and Applause, as either the good Reports of our honourable Friends . . . could yield, or we our selves desire'.[87] Necessarily more humble than Dudley, yet the seriousness behind Helmes's performance was comparable.

Greater parody is found in the Middle Temple entertainment of 1597–8, the *Prince d'Amour*, in which the folly of lovers was held up for satiric investigation: both through mocking and advocating excess, as for example offering canonization to those who 'do works of superogation, as to . . . go to the Tailors to kiss the sheers wherewith their Mistris Gown was made'.[88] Love as universe and woman as microcosm was the subject of one debate; another was the trial of *Carolinus Asinus Bestia*, a discontented lover who was sentenced according to the fashion of the age, and with some accurate psychological analogy: '. . . because thou hast disdained to be true prisoner to Love, whose imprisonment is the sweetest Liberty, The Court doth therefore award, that [thou shalt be com-mitted] close prisoner . . . in the Fort of Fancy' (p. 76). The jury included characters such as *Innocentius Morio, Delirius Rusticus,* and *Simplicans Credulus*:[89] all types of fool, styled in the French *sottie* manner. The mottoes on the prince's arms were *Chaperon male advise* and *hodie mihi, cras tibi*. And his personal motto, *Plena*

---

[86] Ibid. 20. [87] Ibid. 42. [88] BL E. 1836(1), p. 76.
[89] Ibid. 50.

52   Kings of Winter Festive Groups

sunt omnia, was an abbreviation of Cicero's well-known dictum, *stultorum plena sunt omnia*. The encapsulating theme of this sophisticated and bawdy comedy was again a compliment to Elizabeth. The first entertainment was a challenge from her champion, outraged that the title had been usurped from her, and the Twelfth Night celebration was a masque of love performed at court for her.

The imaginative range of entertainments at all the inns was influenced, in part, by the contemplation of old and new scientific theories. The lord or prince became a creator and magician in control of a fantasy world and the theme of inversion was raised into a subject fit for a Renaissance monarch.

In the universities there was more emphasis on the drama, and between 1598 and 1601 St John's, Cambridge, achieved the three-part production, the *Parnassus* plays. But in 1607, at St John's, Oxford, there was a revival of the Christmas prince ceremonial after a lapse of thirty years. Interestingly, the reason for his inauguration was to prevent disputes breaking out between poulderings and punies—rival student years organizing the Christmas festivities. The election of Thomas Tucker took place at Allhallows, and his reign ended on Shrove Tuesday. The account of the proceedings does not attempt to conceal the constant disorder which threatened to break out between the groups of people involved. On the one hand there was the uproar of the election itself, which prompted Tucker to conceal himself when he first heard the hue and cry of 'Tucker, Tucker, Viuat, Viuat, &ct'. Once found he was 'more by violence then any will of his owne taken vpp, and wth continuall and ioyfull outcries, carried about ye Hall'.[90] And, as well, there were disorders created by the audience, very similar to those at Gray's Inn. The chronicler reported that their Christmas Day entertainment was particularly pleasing 'because there were no straungers to trouble vs'.[91] The determination to maintain dignity and decorum included the election of a government. Tucker chose a council of nine for 'graue and learned assistance',[92] and to prevent his reign becoming a personal tyranny. Each man, including the prince, was given the arms or insignia of his particular office. And when, towards the end of January, the prince was 'solemnly invited' by Christ Church to be honoured by an entertainment there called *Yuletide*, the chronicler relates in disgust that what in fact happened were the crude mocking

---

[90] *The Christmas Prince*, p. 5.   [91] Ibid. 55.   [92] Ibid. 32.

Kings of Winter Festive Groups

jests originally rejected by the college (see n. 30). Throughout the account there appears the struggle to maintain an image of an ideal lord presiding over a mixture of Latin and English satires, despite 'headstrong persons' and 'turbulent spirits', and though the prince's personality was not a developed part of the entertainments. Yet he had his penal system, the stocks, to which he arbitrarily sent those who had failed in their contribution.

In the reformed customs of the latter half of the sixteenth century, the title of prince virtually ousted that of misrule and this reflected the ethos behind the reconstituted festivities. The prince could be larger than life and his costume quixotic, but the mock court developed into a close copy of real government. The fellowship within the court aimed at Arthurian chivalry and a Utopian perfection of rule,[93] replacing the reductive reflection of kingship with a visionary one. The king and his court displayed the graces of dancing, singing, masking, debating, wit, and feasting. Honours were devised which exalted the ordinary man playing the prince far above his station. It was, for example, argued that Thomas Tucker's genealogy descended from the gods. Mockery was implicit in the exaggeration yet the romantic, larger-than-life characters were claimed to be all-powerful, and events for the season were placed under their infallible control, so that a perfect world in miniature of amity and brotherhood was maintained.

Such fantastic lords created a new type which could be used for play characterization, and the satiric possibilities were borrowed by Thomas Nashe. In 1599 he thanked Yarmouth for having harboured him, after the *Isle of Dogs* scandal in 1597, by writing the absurdist, prose eulogy, *Nashe's Lenten Stuffe*. According to the title-page, this contains 'a new Play neuer played before, of the praise of the Red Herring' (and whose sources elude the editor).[94] It seems that the content is further parodic adaptation of the courtly, carnival lord, with the herring in the role of prince. In Nashe's work the disparity between the intrinsic worth of the subject and the honours given is even more extreme. The herring was the least valued food item, symbolic of fasting not feasting, but as it dominated man's life during

[93] 'Utopus . . . brought the rude and rustic people to such a perfection of culture and humanity as makes them now superior to almost all other mortals . . .', T. More, *Utopia*, ed. C. Surtz, S. J. Hexter, and J. H. Hexter, iv (New Haven, 1965), p. 113.
[94] 'The only part of the work for which we need expect to find a source is the historical description of Yarmouth', T. Nashe, *Lenten Stuffe*, *The Works of Thomas Nashe*, ed. R. B. McKerrow (London, 1904–8), iv. 372.

Lent Nashe revalued it as 'king of the fishes'. Eulogy and inflation of its image took on burlesqued heroic proportions, with great attention paid to its lineage: 'Stately borne, stately sprung he is, the best bloud of the Ptolomies no statelier', and its entrance into, and rule of, man's life during Lent was said to be as joyful as the return of the sun in the sky.[95] Included in the narrated drama is conflict between the herring and kings of the rival food, meat. The contest is governed according to the tradition of acclamation: one supporter calls for 'Beife, Beife, Beife', another for 'Porke, Porke, Porke', a third for 'mitton, mitton, mitton', and the fourth for 'veale, veale, veale'. These contestants are swept aside by support for the herring: 'al their clamorous suffrages saluted with *Viue le roy* . . . and the Herring euer since weares a coronet on his head'.[96] The mock elevation of the anti-festive figure combines ideas from summer and winter games: competitive king games, and the more stately excesses of the winter court.

The main area of the drama influenced by the last was the Romances such as *Pericles* and *The Tempest*, where the reformed customs seem to have been used to overcome the problems of presenting a real and good king on stage. Pericles, in particular, is an exemplary ruler who strives to maintain order, and there are in the powers of Prospero, and in the actions of Pericles, similarities with courtly Christmas princes. It is also possible that the imaginative freedom in the devising of mock courts provided a stimulus. The limitless vision of Tamburlaine as well as of Dr Faustus could be related to courtly fantasies. Also, the debates could have been a model for presenting government in history plays. Dramatists were excluded from real council chambers, whereas the dramatized form of publicly debated government, at the inns of court and in chronicle plays from *Gorboduc* on, can be seen to have much in common.

[95] T. Nashe, *Lenten Stuffe*, iii. 189.   [96] Ibid. 190–203.

3

Summer Kings and Queens, and Kings of Fortune

Gather ye rosebuds while ye may,
Old Time is still a-flying:

Robert Herrick

Records and pejorative comment show that lords of misrule were popular in provincial towns and houses throughout the sixteenth century.[1] Yet the evidence of the winter king's activities frequently lacks detail, and tends only to exist as a record if it witnesses a patron's expenses or generous spirit.[2] By contrast, summer games were also mentioned for romantic or, alternatively, disapproving reasons by men unconnected with the events. And a third source of evidence is church records, since most parishes became involved with summer customs as a means of increasing their revenues.[3] As a result, the evidence for summer kings is surprisingly full and it is possible to identify some of their major features, and to assess how they influenced the later drama. However, the larger amount of evidence does also lead to greater problems of coherence, since variations in seasonal customs also become that much more evident, and while accounting for them it becomes crucial to remember that what was traditional in one place might in fact have been quite different from what customarily took place a few miles away.

Theoretically speaking, the season can be divided into three

---

[1] See *REED, Chester*, ed. L. M. Clopper (Toronto and Manchester, 1979); *Cumberland, Westmorland; Gloucestershire*, ed. A. Douglas (Toronto, 1986); *Devon; Coventry*, ed. R. W. Ingram (Toronto and Manchester, 1981); *Cambridge*, ed. A. Nelson (Toronto, 1989); and *Oxford*, ed. J. Elliott (forthcoming). Cf. Harwich Deposition 1535, PRO SP 1. 99, fo. 200.

[2] 'Mr mayor kepte a verye worthy howse, for all Comers dureinge all the tyme of Christmas, with a lorde of misrule and other pastymes in his cittye, as the witson plays' (1567–8), *REED, Chester*, p. 80.

[3] In about 1220 Thomas of Chobham acknowledged that the involvement was initially forced on parishes 'for many men would not otherwise come to [church] feasts if they could not play games', S. Billington, *A Social History of the Fool* (Brighton, 1984), p. 2.

56   *Summer Kings and Queens*

sections. The first games were those for St George's day, usually devised by the Guilds of St George, as at Norwich in the fifteenth century.[4] The second took place between 1 May and midsummer and played various combinations of king and queen, lord and lady, or (later) Robin Hood and Maid Marion, in a mixture of ritualistic wooing games and/or imitations of courtly behaviour (possibly including a Whitsuntide imitation of the heavenly court). The third were all male king games, begun at midsummer and sometimes continued until the end of August. The midsummer location was a hilltop which had metaphoric significance. Evidence from the late fifteenth and early sixteenth centuries shows that the most popular leading character from all the various games might change and might come to rule the whole season. Differences in domination can be seen in the Croscombe churchwardens' accounts between the years 1474 and 1516. To begin with, in 1474, money was donated in the name of the 'king's revel'; in 1476, 'xls. of Roben Hod's recones' was delivered, and in 1516 the aegis for the 'xijs' brought in was that of St George.[5] A similar pattern can be found in the less detailed accounts from St Laurence, Reading, between the years 1501 and 1504, and ending with the ascendancy of Robin Hood.[6] It is easy to visualize Robin Hood's and St George's roles, but the earlier title of 'king' can appear too unspecific to convey much character, for in many wooing games, particularly in early summer, the king was part of a seasonal ritual in which the queen might be the more dominant role. The election of the young man and woman symbolized reverence to the season:

> Tho to the greene Wood they speeden hem all,
> To fetchen home May with their musicall:
> And home they bringen in a royall throne,
> Crowned as king: and his Queene attone
> Was Lady Flora . . .[7]

[4] The Norwich Guild of St George (*c.*1400) used 'a garment steyned for the George at the riding', 'a sword covered with velvett with gilt harneys for the George', and 'a dragon', W. Hudson and U. J. C. Tingey (eds.), *Selected Records of the City of Norwich* (Norwich, 1906), ii. 396–7.

[5] E. Hobhouse (ed.), *Churchwardens' Accounts* (London, 1890), pp. 3–15.

[6] *Churchwardens' Account Book* of the Parish of St Laurence, Reading, 1498 –1626, Berkshire Record Office D/P 97/5/2, pp. 2–14. Robin Hood's greatest success was, perhaps, in 1510 when the young Henry VIII played the mock king and combined archery games with a separate wooing of his queen. See R. Holinshed, *Chronicles of England, Scotland and Ireland*, ed. J. Hooker *et al.* (London, 1867), iii. 554.

[7] E. Spenser, 'May', in 'The Shepheardes Calendar', ll. 27–31, in *Spenser: Poetical*

Summer Kings and Queens

Illustrations from the continent of Europe suggest that the queen became the focal point in play between rival suitors,[8] as found in Lyndsay's *Cupar Banns*.[9] By contrast, competition between rival queens seems to have been part of the English play. In Robert of Brunne's *Handlyng Synne*, young men were warned that inviting groups of young women to gather together and compete for a garland crown was an invitation to lechery.[10] The fifteenth-century theologian, Fabritius Carpenter, also denigrated the elected queen,[11] but in English games of the early sixteenth century the male lead regained his domination and this seems to have resulted in a combination of Robin Hood combat drama with wooing play. Gradual assimilation can be traced through some of the fuller records from Kingston upon Thames. On 27 June 1506, a king game only was recorded, and Joan Whytebred was queen to Wyliam Kempe's king.[12] In 1508 costs were recorded 'at ye Kyngham & Robyn Hood',[13] with receipts brought in separately from Robin Hood's gathering and from a 'kynges gatherynge ye sametyme'.[14] Proper accounting began in 1509 when larger festivities took place, probably to celebrate Henry VIII's accession. A king game and Robin Hood's gathering again took place separately. Only 8*d.* was spent on 'a goun for ye lady',[15] while a 'huke' of four yards of kendal for the Maid Marion cost 3*s.* and 4*d.*, and she was paid the large sum of 2*s.* 'for hir labor for ij yere'.[16] Robin Hood was also accompanied by the Friar, Little John, and a morris dance.[17] Maid Marion was the only person apart from the minstrel who was paid, and it is quite extraordinary that one of the game's participants should have been

---

Works, ed. J. C. Smith and E. de Selincourt (Oxford, 1912; repr. 1969). Cf. *Annalia Dubrensia* for a more dominant Flora, who 'Queene of May, | Doth re-install [Dover] into her holy-day', fo. B. 3ᵛ.

[8] See the illustrations in B. Lowe's 'Early Records of the Morris in England', *Journal of the English Folk Dance and Song Society*, 8 (1957), pp. 61–83.

[9] *The Works of Sir David Lyndsay*, ed. D. Hamer, STS 2 (Edinburgh, 1931), pp. 10–35.

[10] 'ȝyf þou euer yn felde, eyþer in toune, | Dedyst floure-gerland or coroune | To make wommen to gadyr þere, | To se whych þat feyrer were;—. . . | Hyt ys a gaderyng for lecherye, | And ful grete pryde, & herte hye' (ll. 997–1004).

[11] *Destructiorum Vitiorum* (1582), pt. 6, cap. II, 16, fo. 249r. N. M. Davis, 'The Playing of Miracles in England', Ph.D. thesis (Cambridge, 1977), p. 33. See Ch. 4, p. 97.

[12] Kingston upon Thames, *Churchwardens' Account Book*, KG 2/2/1, p. 40.
[13] Ibid. 60.   [14] Ibid. 51–2.   [15] Ibid. 54.   [16] Ibid. 66.
[17] Ibid. 19–20. Disordered entries.

paid at all. Therefore, it would seem hers was an important role and had probably changed from that of female beauty to a Dame character played by a man, as in Henry VIII's 1515 masque, in which there was a lady, while Mr Villiers played Maid Marion.[18] The Robin Hood game of 1509 travelled to Leatherhead and to the Walton king game, and after these two years the king game dropped out of the Kingston records. Evidence from dramatic texts follows a similar pattern. Whereas the 1475 Robin Hood play fragment is wholly combat drama, the 1562 text has in it Maid Marion whom Robin bestows on the Friar. The decorous image of the queen of the May is jokingly recalled when Robin calls her 'a Lady free',[19] but texts show that the Marion was outwardly a more bawdy character which argues for male impersonation.

In 1469, before Robin Hood became the dominant leader, the fullest account that we have of a late-summer king and queen game found its way into the legal records for Wistow, near York. One Thomas Hird gave evidence that on the Sunday before midsummer day:

... following the custom of the land, the young people of the town of Wistow came together to conduct a summer *ludus*, commonly called the Somergame. . On the preceeding Sunday they chose Margaret More to be Queen of the aforesaid game, in readiness for the Sunday when the game was to be held in a certain barn belonging to John Dudman and adjoining the churchyard. The said Margaret went there before the twelfth hour on Sunday—which is to say, before midday—and was in attendance from then until after sunset, all that time a Queen who held court in the upper storey of the barn. The witness said that he himself was Steward and serving man in the game . . . And once Margaret More was installed in the barn where the game was held, commonly called *Somerhouse*, she and the witness remained present, hour in hour out and continuously, until after sunset . . . as did those who carried on the game with them—Thomas Barker of Wistow, King

[18] A gown was made for Lady May in the traditional 14th-cent. style, with wide sleeves and tippets or streamers (see S. Billington, 'Routs and Reyes', *Folklore*, 89 (1978), pp. 187–8), and Mr Villiers wore a red and green kirtle and huke plus frontlet, neckerchief, and headkerchief, SPD, *1515–18*, vol. 2, pt. 2, ed. J. S. Brewer (London, 1864), p. 1504. There were female Maid Marions. A stalwart female spectator at William Kempe's morris dance to Norwich, 1599, danced a mile with him. He lent her bells and called her Maid Marion. See Kempe's *Nine Daies Morris* (London, 1600).

[19] D. Wiles, *The Early Plays of Robin Hood* (Woodbridge, 1981), app. 4, p. 76. The role of May queen seems to have fallen between the two extremes of unattainable ideal and fertility queen: the Virgin Mary and Eve dichotomy which bedevilled many female roles in the Middle Ages.

for the duration of the game, Robert Gafare, also from Wistow, and William Dawson, who were called Soldiers in the same game, and many more people in a copious multitude.[20]

The Sunday before midsummer is too late for this to be called a Whitsun game. Its name of Somergame and late selection of the leaders show that it was not just the final performance of something begun much earlier in the season, but rather a custom which was Wistow's usual midsummer game. Payments and receipts at Kingston, in 1508, mention May day, Fair day, and Whitsunday but earlier, in 1505 and 1506, the king and queen game was also a June event and, in 1506, might have had similarities with the Wistow game.[21] We have no details of what went on at Wistow, but N. M. Davis draws from Adam de la Halle's play of *Robin and Marion*, present-day children's games, and seventeenth-century customs to suggest that the multitude at Wistow might have engaged in a game of tasks designed to bring into the open romantic feelings which in normal life would remain hidden.[22] A further possibility, suggested by the evidence that the queen at Wistow was a decorous person (see n. 20), and supported by other evidence which I shall come to, is that the character of the king could have been a boastful figure and that his queen was a model of virtue.

But, firstly, C. R. Baskervill made the perceptive observation that the generic impulse behind all folk elections of kings and queens could well have been the imitation of medieval courts, particularly of the great public festivals sometimes held at Whitsuntide: 'feasts in which kings and queens participated'.[23] The magnificent celebrations from William the Conqueror to Edward III could have provided the models for fantasy king and queen games among the people

[20] Trans. N. M. Davis, 'The Playing of Miracles', Ph.D. thesis (Cambridge, 1977), p. 29. He continues: 'According to further depositions, a group of villagers led the King and Queen in procession, with a mime or minstrel going before, to the site of the game. When the court had been set up, the role of its members was not merely passive: the King and his Soldiers . . . presumably helped to keep the playing in motion, and the Queen for her part "continue permansit ludo ipso ascultando et jocundam se faciendo in eodem honeste," a description which would accord with the "Whitsun playing" of Perdita. The domain of the King and Queen seems to have been limited to the space in front of the "Somerhouse" . . . entry to this area must have implied willingness to submit to their rule' (pp. 29–30). Cf. J. S. Purvis (ed.), *Tudor Parish Documents* (Cambridge, 1948), pp. 160–1.

[21] In 1505 the money was brought in on 2 June, and in 1506 on 27 June. Kingston upon Thames, KG 2/2/1, p. 40.   [22] Davis, 'The Playing of Miracles', p. 30.

[23] 'Dramatic Aspects of Medieval Folk Festivals', *SP* 17 (1920), p. 49.

which, in some parts of the country, survived the Reformation. The possibility that there was conscious imitation finds support in the evidence in Chapter 2 that winter kings were often received in their cities with the ceremonies usually reserved for real kings. The icon of king and queen in a staged setting, originating either from real or mock courts, became a symbol of achievement and happiness—ultimately heaven—and was used for moral and other symbolic messages. One example is found in the fifteenth-century popular moral tract, *The Desert of Religion*. In this, an illustration of the familiar monster's mouth from Mystery plays depicts the descent into hell. The alternative choice of heaven is shown by a king and queen in a rough depiction of a castle pageant with a cloth backdrop, and a soldier and child with them (Fig. 3). Although they clearly indicate Christ and Mary, they are not formally depicted. In the Wistow game the king and queen held court in the upper storey of a barn. They too had servants and soldiers, and it would seem that the barn's upper storey provided the elevation of a castle. The illustration in the moral tract seems to have been modelled on such games, rather than on an idealized image. However, a more idealized or aristocratic picture of such games comes from the unlikely source of the Statutes of 1562 of St John's, Oxford. Permission for the college was granted on 1 May 1555,[24] and the Statutes drawn up later have on the first page a drawing of a king and queen pageant with St John as king and Elizabeth as queen (Fig. 4). In the sixteenth-century ballad, 'Bessy come over the Bourn to me', there is a similar borrowing. The marriage of Henry of Richmond to Elizabeth of York, in 1485, is recalled as a Robin and Marion romance.[25]

The possibility that king and queen games could provide allegorical readings leads on to the third section of summer sports which have so far largely lain in oblivion,[26] but which can be detected mainly through the use of allegory. These are midsummer competitions, games of physical prowess on a hilltop to decide a king title. There appears to have been no role for a queen and no church connection. Contests were included by one fifteenth-century monk in

[24] W. H. Stevenson and H. E. Salter, *The Early History of St. John's College* (Oxford, 1939), p. 114.
[25] J. O. Halliwell (ed.), *The Song of Lady Bessy*, Percy Society (London, 1847).
[26] Apart from the opening chapter of Davis's thesis.

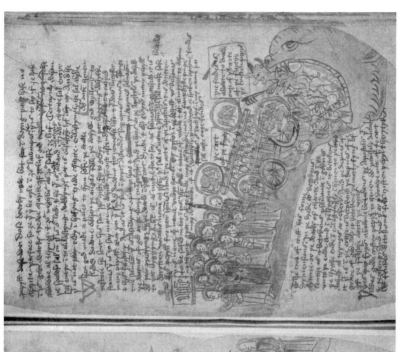

3 *Desert of Religion*, c.1450

4 Statutes, St John's College, Oxford, 1562

Summer Kings and Queens 63

his general denunciation of midsummer games,[27] and this appears to be the only medieval record of them. But the choosing of a king by such competitive games, and the symbolic importance of the hilltop and a castle, are explicit in the seventeenth-century restoration of such customs, Robert Dover's Cotswold games. *Annalia Dubrensia* (1636), commemorating his initiative, confirms the fragmented medieval evidence by explicitly describing the content and purpose of the games. There were competitive sports on the Cotswold hills, close to midsummer, and the winner was acclaimed king with a laurel crown at Dover's castle, built at the top of Dover's Hill. I will return to these in detail in due chronological order. Medieval observations on such sports, in literature and drama, show that the hill was seen as the equivalent of Fortune's wheel, and the achievement of the winner held subtle and harsh implications for the life of man. The one complete medieval example of sophisticated interpretation of such sports comes from the *Chester Mystery Cycle* 'Shepherds' Play'.

In this the boy, Trowle, rebels against the other shepherds who treat him well. At the opening, he rejects their offers of food and friendship, and insults the cleanliness of their kitchens and their virility. He sits apart from them on a small hill, 'one this hill I hold mee here',[28] ostensibly guarding the sheep, but berating the shepherds quite unjustly. Richard Axton has noted that Trowle's rebellion 'leads to the enthronement of a fool-king . . . who rules the watch',[29] and Trowle draws the analogy in the line 'I pippe [drink] at this pott like a pope'.[30] In his monologue Trowle says he will spend his time fighting with his fellows which, the editors observe, suggests there are other youths on stage.[31] If so, then Trowle vaunts his superiority over the shepherds, in front of his followers, and the

---

[27] 'Dico ejus [S. Johannis] Nativitatem cum gaudio; non illo tamen gaudio quo Stulti vani, & prophani amatores mundi huius, accensis Ignibus per plateas (Anglice, Bone-fires) turpibus & illicitis Ludis, Commessationibus, [contests] & Ebrietatibus, Cubilibus, & Impudicitijs intendentes, eam celebrare solent', C. R. Baskervill, 'Dramatic Aspects of Medieval Folk Festivals in England', *SP* 17 (1920), pp. 51–2 n. 117.

[28] *The Chester Mystery Cycle*, ed. R. M. Lumiansky and D. Mills (Oxford, 1974–86), i. 'Shepherds' Play', l. 206.

[29] R. Axton, *European Drama of the Early Middle Ages* (London, 1974), p. 190.

[30] *Chester Mystery Cycle*, 'Shepherds' Play', l. 189.

[31] 'Since his fellows seem to be distinct from the three shepherds, the reference is presumably to his companions, the other boys who . . . appear to give gifts to the Infant Christ', *Chester Mystery Cycle*, ii. 112, n. to l. 208.

64 Summer Kings and Queens

humiliation which the shepherds undergo is increased. Eventually, they challenge him to a wrestling match to restore their honour. This prompts the boy to give himself the boastful, sporting title of 'Trowle the Trewe',[32] and the wrestling only brings the shepherds more shame. Trowle scorns to fight with one of them and throws the other two. Only then does he eat the food they had previously offered him, still mocking them. This unsociable behaviour is quite contrary to May game festivity and 'holiday mood' in which harmony and reconciliation dominate, and on examination the Trowle play appears to be an allegory on the injustice of Fortune who, without God's control, overcomes all the reasonable strivings of men. In the Harley 2124 manuscript, Trowle's monologue contains a remark which indicates he is playing a persona not a character:

> At me all men learne mon [must]
> This Golgatha grimly to grope.
>
> ll. 192–3

He does not include himself in the scheme, but is the force which carries it out. Like the goddess, Fortuna, he stands elevated and ready to dispense buffets indiscriminately. The hill's name, Golgotha, connects the shepherds' overthrow with the apparent defeat of Christ on the hill of the crucifixion,[33] and the shepherds themselves link their defeat to Fortune belief. Tude says:

> Ofte wee may bee in thought wee be now under
> God amend hit with his makinge.
>
> ll. 298–9

The first line can be interpreted as 'often we think ourselves at the lowest point of Fortune's wheel', as the word 'under' suggests. The idea is supported visually, for Trowle is in possession of the higher ground. The wrestling match results in the shepherds being cast down from a height: a visual analogy for being thrown from ✓ Fortune's wheel. As Thomas Combe's later motto on Fortune was to put it: 'They that follow fortune's guiding | Blindly fall with often sliding'.[34] When the star of Bethlehem appears, it is Trowle who

[32] *Chester Mystery Cycle*, i. 135 l. 234.

[33] Cf. P. Gringore, *Les Fantasies de Mere Sote*, ed. R. L. Frautschi (Chapel Hill, NC, 1962), p. 109, for a hilltop story about Christ 'qui fut crucifie sur la montaigne de Calvaire'.

[34] Thomas Combe's own motto above his trans. of Guillaume de la Perrière, *The Theater of Fine Devices*, emblem 20, fo. B. 8ʳ.

responds first, and this might appear a contradiction since one would expect the humble to recognize Christ first. However, the point made is that renegade Fortune *is* subservient once God intervenes. Golgotha loses its power and, in the Christian context, the audience sees how God does amend Fortune with the 'making' of Christ.

It is likely that the Chester plays were performed at midsummer rather than on Corpus Christi day,[35] and the theme of a young man's pride in his superior vigour was appropriate to the longest day of the year. As midsummer was the pinnacle of the year's vigour, after which it declined towards winter, so it was likened to the peak of man's power and upward growth before growth turned to decay. The *Kalendar & Compost of Shepherds* decreed:

Then cometh June, and then is the Sun highest in his meridional, he may ascend no higher in his station, his glimmering golden beams ripeth the corn; and then is man thirty-six year, he may ascend no more. For then hath nature given him beauty and strength at the full, and ripeth the seeds of perfect understanding.[36]

Games on the ascent and superiority of a man at his physical peak were appropriately played at midsummer, and the hilltop summit provided a geographical extension to the metaphor of the height of youthful vigour.

Mountains were also the most popular residence for Fortune, or Lady Fame, in medieval literature and in illustrations where a hill figures as often as, if not more frequently than, the wheel. Numerous illustrations show Fortune's locale high up in mountainous country (Fig. 5).[37] Jean Cousin's sixteenth-century *Le Livre de fortune* contains about two hundred illustrations of Lady Fame in various influential positions. The wheel occurs rarely but the hilltop setting appears in nearly every drawing. As H. R. Patch wrote in 1927, 'the conception of a mountain as a figure of inaccessibility and adversity is common enough. One speaks of "scaling" one's difficulties or "surmounting an obstacle", and it is the mountain of Purgatory . . . which one has to climb on the way to paradise'. He concluded, 'the

[35] See Axton, *European Drama*, pp. 182–4. Corpus Christi was earlier in the summer on the Thursday after Trinity Sunday.

[36] p. 4. The theme is echoed by R. Herrick in the 2nd verse of 'To Virgins, to make much of Time': 'The glorious lamp of heaven, the sun, | The higher he's a-getting, | The sooner will his race be run, | And nearer he's to setting.'

[37] Cf. the illustrations in H. R. Patch's *The Goddess Fortuna in Medieval Literature* (Cambridge, Mass. 1927), *passim*.

5 *Le Roman de la rose*, early 15th century

Summer Kings and Queens

mountain obviously can also symbolize degrees of exaltation and humiliation in worldly dignity'.[38]

In order to prove superiority in games, similar difficulties and obstacles were scaled and surmounted. Yet one man's personal elevation and 'strength at the full' was inevitably followed by a fall, either because of his own physical decline or because his kingship was only temporary, and the whole basis of competitive games invited a comparison with Fortune. Subsequent decline or fall was implicit even in the crowning of a king at midsummer and in such a setting. The thought is retained today in the expression that a person is 'over the hill'.

Christianization of hilltops turned the palace of the Roman goddess into Christ's, as in *The Desert of Religion* and in Gavin Douglas's *The Palace of Honor*. In secular works, pagan and Christian themes interwound.[39] Spenser's proudly elevated, midsummer shepherd declares, 'Hereto, the hills bene nigher heaven' (Fig. 6).[40] And Gawain's testing by the Green Knight's lady took place in a hilltop castle. (Arthur's opening feast is described as 'So hardy an here on hille', which seems to indicate that his round table is also placed on a mountain top.)[41] Stronger pagan influence is found in the works of French medieval romance writers, who placed the lover's hopes of attainment at a similar height. Yet even Dante, while climbing the hill of Purgatory to Paradise, was also inspired by hopes of discovering Beatrice at the summit, while John Donne mocked scientific progress in 'An Anatomie of the World' with a reversed image. Man no longer climbs upward, but drags the heavens down.[42]

In 'The Hous of Fame', Chaucer used the pagan romance tradition of Margival for a light-hearted satire on English festive games and on excessive belief in Fortune, and so he provides another early example of Lady Fame or Fortune combined with mock kings and hills: one which is of particular relevance to Shakespeare's *Timon of Athens* (see Chapter 7). Geoffrey, the narrator, climbs a high perilous mountain to discover his native traditions and, at the top, discovers men and women taking part in a variety of pastimes. Musicians,

---

[38] Ibid. 132. [39] Cf. Gringore, *Les Fantasies*.

[40] 'The Shepheardes Calendar', 'Iulye', l. 89.

[41] Arthur's court itself sometimes seems to be situated on the top of a very lofty mountain which protects it from mortal eyes, H. R. Patch, 'Some Elements in Medieval Descriptions of the Otherworld', *PMLA* 33 (1918), p. 611. *Gawain and the Green Knight* is another work where winter and summer games are combined.

[42] *Complete Poetry and Selected Prose*, ed. J. Hayward (London, 1949), p. 204.

6 'Iulye'—The Shepheardes Calendar', Edmund Spenser, 1579

Summer Kings and Queens

magicians, jugglers, dancers, and story-tellers fill the hilltop outside
the palace of Lady Fame. Inside were many calling on her for
liberality. Some of these were elaborately dressed up as kings:

> And somme corouned were as kynges,
> With corounes wroght ful of losenges;
> And many ryban and many frenges
> Were on her clothes trewely.[43]

Once the grotesque Lady Fame granted an audience the people
flooded in:

> ... ther come entrying into the halle
> A ryght gret companye withalle,
> And that of sondry regions,
> Of alleskynnes condicions
> That dwelle in erthe under the mone,[44]
> Pore and ryche. And also sone
> As they were come into the halle,
> They gonne doun on knees falle
> Before this ilke noble quene,
> And seyde, 'Graunte us, lady shene,
> Ech of us of thy grace, a bone!'
> And somme of hem she graunted sone,
> And somme she werned wel and faire,
> And some she graunted the contraire.

ll. 1527–40

The image is the classic example of Fortune's power as shown in
Cousin's *Le Livre de fortune*, plate 39, where Fortune, standing on
raised ground, grants her dubious favours to supplicants (Fig. 7). The
result of such superstition in Chaucer's unfinished work promises
precipitation into hell from the less favourable side of Fortune's
palace.

In Trowle's case, the youth is favoured by Fortune in his success
over his fellows and he becomes her surrogate, dispensing the less
favourable side of her justice to the rest of his society. His manner to
those beneath him is arrogant and downright rude. This is in the
character of Fortune but it is also appropriate to competitive games.
For winners were not chosen king by their peers but achieved the

---

[43] *The Works of Geoffery Chaucer*, ed. F. N. Robinson (2nd edn., London, 1957),
p. 294, ll. 1316–19.

[44] 'Mone' rather than sun indicates the changeability of Fortune.

7 Jean Cousin, *Le Livre de fortune*, 1568, plate 39

8 Jean Cousin, *Le Livre de fortune*, 1568, plate 181

Summer Kings and Queens

position through their own prowess against them. Therefore, there was more self-aggrandizement than fellowship in the position. The exaltation seems to have led to a traditional play of boasting, or a vaunting of skills and superiority.[45] The idea behind it could have been a parody of the behaviour of real kings; deliberate exaggeration of kingly arrogance into bombast and excess, which made for comedy and the relief of feelings against authority. Alternatively, it could have been a simple expression of the heady flush of success. Although Trowle's behaviour appears quarrelsome and even anti-festive, such vaunting was hugely relished. Boasting games were included in Brunne's *Handlying Synne* as a summer temptation to be avoided:

> Hem were leuer here of a daunce,
>   Of bost, and of olypraunce [pomp]
> Þan any gode of Gode of Heuene . . .
>
> ll. 4691–3

Two of the most famous medieval boasters are other characters from the Corpus Christi plays, Herod and Satan. They were popular dramatic figures and, in religious terms, they were of course mock kings, again fittingly given their dramatic voice near to midsummer. Boasting is a characteristic of other scripted medieval kings, such as Rex in *The Pride of Life*. In this play, games of a king and queen are set against the vaunting of the summer king. The Lady, Regina, speaks for the Virgin Mary and the man, Rex, is the King of Life. He boasts his energy, power, and his soldiers' strength and scorns the threat of death, while the Lady pleads in vain for him to accept the limitations of mortality. The symbol of his exaltation is a throne, not a hilltop, but the sharpness of his tongue against the Bishop, summoned to appeal to him to think better, is as scathing as Trowle's:

---

[45] Similar vaunting mockery survives in the children's group game, 'I'm the king of the castle | Come down you dirty rascal' and variants. See I. and P. Opie, *Children's Games in Street and Playground* (Oxford, 1969), pp. 233–4, and L. Daiken, *Children's Games throughout the Year* (London, 1949), pp. 12–14. Mockery may well have degenerated into violence at times. According to Brunne, after gatherings for wrestling: 'whan swyche bobaunce for þe ys wroȝt | Cuntek þere comyþ, or oþer bobaunce, | And sum man slayn, or lost þurȝe chaunce' (ll. 994–6). Cf. *REED, Devon*, ed. J. M. Wasson (Toronto, 1986), pp. 100–1, 'Exeter 1459–60', for 'dysporte on Midsomer nyght [leading to] manslaghter'.

Summer Kings and Queens

> Wat! bissop, byssop babler,
> Schold y of Det hau dred?
> Þou art bot a chagler [windbag]
> Go hom þi wey, i red [advise].[46]

The allegory which *Pride of Life* draws from summer games is that temporary strength can blind man to his mortality, decline, and eventual descent into hell if he ignores spiritual guidance. Later Morality plays, such as *Youth* and *Mundus et Infans*, retain the analogy.[47] And it appears that the moving of Exeter's Corpus Christi pageants to the earlier date of Whitsuntide in 1414 was met with a midsummer insult from some of the more reluctant participants.[48]

Mottoes for the four points of Fortune's wheel were *regnabo*, *regno*, *regnavi*, *non regno* or *sum sine regno*, which apply more to every man's physical progress from birth to death than to the life cycle of a monarch, who would not need to keep reminding himself. The fourth position, *non regno*, was either death or proximity to death, and medieval literature includes the view of life seen from Fortune's lowest point, bewailing the loss of strength and superiority. Some king games included the fall as the final drama. In 1601, when Talboys Dymoke of South Kyme in Lincolnshire found himself in Star Chamber for allegedly mocking the Earl of Lincoln in a play about the summer lord's death, he brought out the well-worn excuse that it was a traditional part of the games. At the end of August, he said, they played 'the death of the Lord of Kyme, because the same day should make an end of the summer lord game in South Kyme for that year'.[49] This explicitly makes the games extend from the summit to the nadir of the summer lord's fortune.[50] Some non-dramatic

---

[46] N. Davis (ed.), *Non-Cycle Plays and Fragments*, EETS (London, 1970), ll. 407–10.

[47] 'YOUTH: I am promoted to hye degree | By ryght I am kinge eternal', J. S. Farmer (ed.), *Youth*, fo. C. 1ᵛ, *Old English Drama*, students' facsimile edn., printed 1909. Manhode, in *Mundus et Infans*, ed. J. S. Farmer, *Tudor Facsimile Texts* (New York, 1910), boasts like a champion fighter: 'All [Europe] I haue conquered as a knyght | There is no emperour so kene | That dare my lyghtly tene | For lyues and lymmes I lene | So mykyll is my myght . . . | Bryguant Ernys I haue beten to backe & to bonys | And beten also many a grome to grounde . . . | For manhode myghty that is my name | Many a lorde haue I do lame . . . | And many a kynges crowne haue I crakyd' (fo. Bᵛ [wrongly marked]).

[48] *REED, Devon*, pp. 82–3, trans. pp. 357–8. One wonders whether 'dorsum' should be translated as backside rather than back. See Fig. 17.

[49] Barber, *Shakespeare's Festive Comedy*, p. 44.

[50] As e.g. the playing of the death of summer in Nashe's *Summer's Last Will and Testament*, C. L. Barber, *Shakespeare's Festive Comedy* (Princeton, 1959),

Summer Kings and Queens

customs carried the same meaning. It was customary to roll flaming wheels down hills on midsummer night to symbolize the sun's subsequent decline,[51] and Lear's fool picks up on the same image of a downward rolling wheel as man's decline from Fortune.

There also exists a genre of medieval poetry which rails against Fortune because of the loss. The reminder that *all* earthly crowns are only temporary, and that death will bring an end to worldly eminence, is succinctly given in the line, 'Erthe uppon erthe wold be a Kynge'.[52] In other verses, a young man hears an old man's warning while engaged in hilltop games. The old man's moral tale becomes the central feature of the young man's play:

> As I went one my playing,
>   Undure an holt [copse] uppone an hylle
> I sawe and [*sic*] ould mane hoore make mornyng,
>   With sykyng soure he sayd me tylle,
> Sum tyme this worde [world] was at my wylle,
>   With reches and with ryallte,
> And now hit layd done ful stylle;
>   This word is but a wannyte . . .[53]

This more ominous perspective introduces satire on the illusion of worldly success, which can focus in harsh scorn on those enjoying it and include an attack on their worth. Such features can be found in the poem beginning, 'King I sitte and lok aboute | To-morwow I mai bean withoute', in which the narrator then gloats on the inevitable physical decay of a successful enemy.[54] Similar, though less vicious, consolation is drawn by Thomas Wyatt in Psalm 37, 'Noli Emulare', in which he reconciles himself to his own reviled position in society, by comparing the worldly success of others to the vanity of a seasonal king's hilltop pomp:

pp. 79–84. And for a winter dramatization of the same point, in 1607 the elected Christmas prince at St John's, Oxford, retired on Shrove Tuesday after the play of *Ira Fortuna*.

[51] 'Some others get a rotten wheel, all worne and cast aside, | Which couered round about with strawe, and tow, they closely hide | And caryed to some mountaines top, being all with fire light, | They hurle it downe with violence, when darke appeares the night: | Resembling much the Sunne, that from the heauens downe should fal', T. Kirchmaier, '"The Popische Kingdom"', in P. Stubbes, *Anatomie of Abuses* (London, 1977–82), p. 339. Cf. Baskervill, 'Dramatic Aspects', pp. 50–1.

[52] J. O. Halliwell (ed.), *Early English Miscellanies* (London, 1855), p. 40. The man crowned by Fortune will be uncrowned by God—see Fig. 8 and frontispiece.

[53] Ibid. 9.

[54] J. Wright and J. O. Halliwell (eds.), *Reliquae Antiquae* (London, 1841–3), i. 64.

74   *Summer Kings and Queens*

> Altho thow se th'owtragius clime aloft,
>   Envie not thowe his blinde prosperitye . . .
> I have well seene the wycked sheene lyke goolde,
>   Lustie and grene as Lawrell lasting aye;
> But even anon and scantt his seate was colde:
> When I have paste agayne the self same waye,
>   Wheare he did raigne, he was not to be fownde;
>   Vanyshte he was for all his fresshe arraye.[55]

The energy expended and the pride in the ephemeral attainment
could well be seen as a vanity by a jaundiced spectator. Shakespeare
too, in Sonnet 60, laments the brutish short life of man who 'Crawls
to maturity, wherewith being crown'd, | Crooked eclipses 'gainst his
glory fight'. Finally, in Nashe's *Summers Last Will and Testament*,
the dying lord, Summer, asks for his demise to be heralded in a sung
complaint. And so it can be seen that two kinds of satire resulted
from the crowning of a midsummer mock king. One was the
scorning of the rest of humanity by the successful contestant and, the
other, the point of view of a man at the opposite extreme and
experiencing Fortune's buffets. The latter perspective could be extended to include real kings seen in relation to the perfection and
power of the king of heaven (see Chapter 4). This is, perhaps, the
meaning of another of Cousin's illustrations, where a dignified man
receives a hilltop coronation at the hands of Fortune (Fig. 8).

However, if the ups and downs of life for the common man were
subject for satire, for real kings they were more usually the stuff of
tragedy, since they had so much further to fall.[56] Imagery for the fall
of kings was also usually the wheel, probably because any association with a hilltop automatically cast doubts on any claim to
kingship. The Prologue to Chaucer's 'Monk's Tale' has provided the
classic, English, medieval definition,[57] and Bochas's *Fall of Princes*,
translated by Lydgate, gives a similar one: 'the fate of Princes . . . hou
Fortune hath her wheel reuersid | Be tragedies remembrid many

---

[55] *Collected Poems of Sir Thomas Wyatt*, ed. K. Muir (London, 1949), Psalm 37,
ll. 1–2, 97–102.

[56] 'The fall is greater from the first rank to the second, than from the second to the
undermost', *Aphorisms of Sir Philip Sidney* with notes by J. Porter, 2 vols. (London,
1807), i. 86.

[57] 'Tragedie is to seyn a certeyn storie, . . . | Of hym that stood in greet prosperitee,
| And is yfallen out of heigh degree | Into myserie, and endeth wrecchedly', G.
Chaucer, *The Canterbury Tales*, ed. F. N. Robinson (2nd edn., London, 1957),
ll. 3163–7.

Summer Kings and Queens   75

fold'.[58] The tales contain a contradictory mixture of blame directed
at Fortune for her arbitrary control of man's destiny, combined with
reproof of princes for their vicious living, and nearly all Bochas's
examples co-operate with Fortune through some form of pride.
Other mistakes include those of citizens who elect a low-born man as
king: 'Men sholde of resoun dreede a leoun lasse | Than the reudnesse
off a crownyd asse.'[59] And the tale of Macheus the Tyrant provides
the moral exemplum, repeated in *The Mirror for Magistrates*,[60] that
tyranny and other forms of misgovernment cause rebellion. The
example of Midas is a satire, rather than a tragedy, since he is said to
have acted 'in disdeyn' and 'Leffte his crowne . . . to keepe sheep
vpon a pleyn . . . Al worldli worshepe was to hym but veyn'.[61] This is
an interesting variant on pastoral make-believe. In the story, Midas
adopted the *non regno* position to scorn worldly success.

In Book VI, Fortune defends her image but then continues with
examples of men whom, she boasts, she did ruin. Despite the
ambiguity of blame, the difference which appears between the use of
wheel and hill imagery is that Fortune is more in control of the wheel;
she turns it and makes men both to rise and fall whereas, in hill
imagery, men have to gain the summit by themselves. There is more
of their own achievement in the moment of glory, which inflates their
pride, before they are subsequently cast down. The power of Fortune
over the wheel is vividly described in the *Morte Arthure* (c.1400),
and some hilltop analogy is also found in the combat between Arthur
and the giant. The insults which Arthur directs at the giant on the
mountain top, before the fight, seem out of character yet were
appropriate to the vaunting of combat games. Arthur's success is not
a moment for self-aggrandizement, instead he quickly attributes his
achievement to God. The moment when Arthur does fall into the
trap of vainglory, a warning dream of Fortune comes to him, in
which she descends on a cloud with her wheel, and six kings, all

---

[58] Book VIII, ll. 2318–21.   [59] Book VI, ll. 235–7.

[60] Speaking of rebels, Ferrers writes 'though the devyll rayse theim, yet God
alwayes vseth them to his glory, . . . For whan Kinges and chiefe rulers suffer theyr
vnder officers to mysuse theyr subiectes, and wil not heare nor remedye theyr peoples
wronges whan they complayne, than suffreth GOD the Rebell to rage . . . ,' G. Ferrers
and T. Sackville, *The Mirror for Magistrates*, ed. L. B. Campbell (2nd edn., New York,
1960), p. 178.

[61] D. Lydgate, *The Fall of Princes*, ed. H. Bergen (London, 1924–7), Book VI,
ll. 3482–4.

76   *Summer Kings and Queens*

lamenting their errors, fall off one by one. One confesses to sins very
like those of Richard II:

> Whene I rode in my rowte, roughte I noghte elles,
> Bot reuaye [fishing], and reuelle, and rawnsone the pople![62]

And 'rowte' is a term more frequently used to describe the retinue of
mock kings. King competition follows, as two try and fail to reach
Fortune's now empty, upwardly mobile seat. Arthur gains the chair
with Fortune's help, and is described in doll-like, manipulative
terms. Attention is given that he does not even become dishevelled. A
real king must look the part (see Chapter 4).

> 'Thow salle the chayere escheue, I chese the my selfene,
> Be-fore alle the cheftaynes chosene in this erthe.'
> Scho lifte me vp lightly with hir lene hondes,
> And sette me softely in the see, the septre me rechede;
> Craftely with a kambe cho kembede myne heuede,
> That the krispane kroke to my crownne raughte . . .
>
>   ll. 3347–52

After this auspicious beginning, Fortune changes at midday and
Arthur is suddenly destroyed under the wheel. The moral is drawn
that Arthur has passed his pinnacle and must prepare for death.

Renaissance optimism trimmed Fortune's Janus face. Greater
faith was expressed in Providence's power over her and it even
became possible to honour kings with Fortune pageants without that
honour containing ominous undertones. The persona of Lady Fame
became separate from Fortune and was the first to be recuperated.
Lydgate's *Temple of Glass* marks the beginning, and Charles the
Bold's wedding of 1468, which included 'two luminous Palaces of
Fame',[63] probably influenced later English courtly pageants.[64] In
1567 Fame could declare the opposite of Chaucer's Lady:

---

[62] *Morte Arthure*, ed. E. Brock (London, 1871), ll. 3274–5.

[63] G. Kipling, *The Triumph of Honour* (The Hague, 1977), p. 107.

[64] As e.g. the Masque of Fame at the Inner Temple in 1561 which used the
Christianized meaning of deserved honour found in Douglas's *Palace of Honour*.
Lines to Robert Dudley read: 'Wisedome the Guyde of Armed strength, | Vp rayse
your Knightly name. | By force of Prowes hawte, to clymbe | the lofty tower of Fame, |
Aduance your honours by your dedes, | to liue for euermore . . .', G. Legh, *The
Accedens of Armorie* (London, 1562), fo. 224ᵛ. The compliment, however, is not far
removed from Manhode's boast (see n. 47). Cf. S. Chew, *The Pilgrimage of Life* (New
York, 1962).

As eache man bendes him selfe, so I report his fame in dede:
Yf yll, then yll through iarne trump his fame doth [straight] prosede;
Yf good, then good through golden trump I blo . . .[65]

Fortune was more problematic, but the change is apparent in the following dedication made to the Queen of Navarre in 1539, and translated into English in 1593. The poet's happiness at greeting the queen is tempered by the lack of time he had to complete his emblem book for her:

Seneca . . . saith . . . that Fortune is never at rest: and . . . she vseth not to giue ioy without sadnesse, sweete without sowre . . . and generally no felicitie without his contrary . . . I attribute to Fortune that which (as a Christian writing to a Christian Princesse) I ought to attribute to Gods prouidence: I say therefore, that your said happy comming depeded not any whit vpon fortune, but . . . onely vpon God's prouidence . . . and that consequently your sayd coming hath not bene to me hastie, but for the best.[66]

And the title-page of Robert Recorde's introduction to astronomy, *The Castle of Knowledge* (1556), depicts Knowledge as an alternative hilltop power to that of Fortune, standing on a firm square base, not Fortune's unstable globe (Fig. 9). However, in Tudor politics, the threats of real reverses in religion and monarchy seem to have delayed the confident use of Fortune until the 1590s, when England's Protestant autonomy was rather more secure. The early part of Elizabeth's reign, in particular, was fraught with the possibility of disaster. In 1574 a farewell speech after her progress to Bristol included the line, 'good fortuen follow thee, O Queen . . .',[67] which rather emphasized Elizabeth's vulnerability, and it was the character of *Good* Fortune who played the *deus ex machina* in the 1578 entertainment in Norfolk. Once the dangers of Mary Stuart and the Armada were safely past and Elizabeth herself a legend, Fortune was reintroduced. The Mariner protagonist in a lottery entertainment, presented to her in 1601, very firmly placed all attributes of the pagan goddess beneath Elizabeth's heel:

---

[65] *Three Tudor Classical Interludes*, ed. M. Axton (Woodbridge, 1982), *Horestes*, ll. 839–41.
[66] Combe's trans. of Perrière, fo. A. 3[r–v]. For the long-standing theological debate see H. R. Patch, *The Tradition of the Goddess Fortuna in Mediaeval Philosophy and Literature* (Northampton, Mass., 1922).
[67] J. G. Nichols (ed.), *Progresses . . . of Queen Elizabeth* (London, 1788–1823), i. 407.

9 Robert Recorde, 1556

Summer Kings and Queens

Cynthia, Queene of seas and lands,
That Fortune euery where commands,
Sent forth Fortune to the sea,
To try her Fortune euery way.[68]

And the infamous wheel was presented to Elizabeth as one of the lotteries, now hers. The same broadly Machiavellian thinking is found in the Ditchley portrait in which Elizabeth, not Fortuna, stands on the globe of the earth; while the goddess myth was sustained after Elizabeth's death in the Elegy, 'On the Death of Delia'. Fama promised that through her Elizabeth would enjoy earthly as well as spiritual immortality.[69]

Complimentary interpretations of Fortune became almost commonplace in James's reign. On his coronation in London on 15 March 1603–4, London itself was James's House of Fame which the Genius Loci, at the first pageant, invited James to 'boldly enter'.[70] At a further device James was shown controlling Fortune's malicious tongue. Detraction and Oblivion woken by Fame's trumpet were, at the king's approach, 'suddenly daunted and sunk down'.[71] And a third pageant, a Triumphal Arch, in Conduit Street showed the degree of confidence with which the unstable character could be reintroduced into a prince's life. Fortune, 'treading on the Globe, that mooude beneath her', was an ingenious technical feat, but it suggests the Roman view of mutability in man's affairs. However, the recorder ignored this and instead understood the meaning to be that 'his Maiesties fortune was aboue the world'.[72] One other pageant included Fortune combined with hill symbolism. 'The fifth "pegme", or structure, entitled *Hortus Euphoniae* (Garden of Plenty), showed Fortune standing on top of a little temple or palace, which in turn was on top of a hill.' As has been noted, 'this hill lacked the allegory's slippery slope down which Fortune's rejects slide'.[73] In 1612, Thomas Dekker included a fortune device for the Mayor of London's inauguration. Inigo Jones used a House of Fame as the

---

[68] J. G. Nichols (ed.), *Progresses . . . of Queen Elizabeth*, iii. 570.   [69] Ibid. 635.
[70] J. G. Nichols (ed.), *The Progresses . . . of King James I* (London, 1828), i. 341.
[71] J. Somers, *A Third Collection of Scarce and Valuable Tracts (chiefly from the library of J. Somers)* (London, 1751), p. 147. Cf. Nichols, *Progresses . . . of King James I*, i. 355.
[72] Somers, *Third Collection*; Nichols, *Progresses . . . of King James I*, i. 370.
[73] R. Soellner, *Timon of Athens: Shakespeare's Pessimistic Tragedy* (Kent, Ohio, 1979), p. 145.

device to bring about the heroic climax to Ben Jonson's *Masque of Fame* (1606); the emblem book, *The Mirrour of Maiestie* (1618), plate 28, shows the dedicated scholar at a hilltop castle receiving the laurel crown of Wisdom from Time (Fig. 10). And it is difficult to imagine that the Fortune theatre would have been so called in 1600 had the term commonly meant anything other than good fortune.

Finally, there remain the all-important Cotswold summer games,[74] revived by Robert Dover, in which the combination of the reformed goddess, Fortune, with hilltop, competitive sports received one final full endorsement.[75] The frontispiece to *Annalia Dubrensia* shows the castle placed on a small hilltop (Fig. 11). It appears somewhat impractical, and could have been some artistic figment or icon only, but Anthony à Wood provides evidence that this was not so:

Before the said book of 'Annalia Dubrensia' is a cut representing the games and sports, as men playing at cudgels, wrestling, leaping, pitching the bar, throwing the iron hammer, handling the pyke, leaping over the heads of men kneeling, standing upon their hands, etc. Also the dancing of women, men hunting and coursing the hare with hounds and greyhounds, etc., with a castel built of boards on a hillock with guns therin.[76]

The poems further suggest that the castle was painted silver and that Dover conducted the games from inside.[77] Some events involved storming it, but it was the victor of the sports who was crowned and made king of the castle.[78] In the evening, and during the night, it was used for feasting, music, and other entertainments, with Dover host

[74] 'Bright *Phoebus* Carre | Hath runne from *Pisces*, to the watry Starre: | From thence to *Leo*', *Annalia Dubrensia*, ed. M. Walbancke (London, 1636; Menston, 1973), fo. B. 3ʳ.

[75] The exact date of Dover's revival is not known but 1618 was when King James issued *The Book of Sports*, declaring such games to be lawful recreation. It is generally thought that Dover took advantage of the king's support. He was e.g. given an old suit of James's to wear at the first games. See A. à Wood, *Athenae Oxonienses*, ed. P. Bliss (London, 1813–20), iv, col. 222.

[76] Ibid.

[77] 'Brave DOVER, from whose Ioviall hand, | Their yearely Life, these revells take | In midst whereof, doth shining stand, | Thy Castle . . . | Which is so well, with vertue man'd, | That Vice, dare no approaches make', *Annalia Dubrensia*, fo. F. 3ᵛ.

[78] Each competitor 'labureth more to win | The name of Victor, then hee doth the Castle | Though made of silver . . .' (fo. D. 2ᵛ), and 'TIME. What is each Victors prize? FAME. No small reward: A castle; Dover *Castle*' (fo. H. 1ʳ).

10 *Mirrour of Maiestie*, 1618, emblem 28

11 *Annalia Dubrensia*, 1636

Summer Kings and Queens
83

to the whole gathering.[79] Although one wonders how food and equipment for all his neighbours could have been transported to the summit of the Cotswolds, yet such elaborate lengths do justify the accolades Dover received. His revival was a full-blooded recreation of a House of Fame, but without any pejorative overtones. In these renascent games Fortune controlled events for good only and even pride had its place:

> Away, dame fortune bids the formost ride,
> Whose fleet-naggs heels, throw dust in scornful pride
> At those which follow . . .

> fo. C. 2ʳ

Fame's trumpet was no longer a trump of doom, instead with sweet breath she blew her 'sacred *Trump*', while the contestants were made noble and heroic, when thoughts of Fame filled their quickened souls with every glance they took of 'Cotswold hill'.[80] As in *Pericles*, the winner was crowned king and the honour of kingship, somewhat similar to the *Timon* comedy, passed from the host king,[81] to the winner,[82] and, in the poems, even to the mountain itself.[83] An analogy was drawn with the ancient Greeks. Dover was praised for reviving what 'those brave *Grecians* [had achieved in] their games Olimpick, and so nam'd | Of that great Mountaine'.[84] However, the Grecian games were held on the plain by the river estuary. The tradition Dover had revived was English and medieval, and the victor was crowned and dressed with ribbons like the figures in Chaucer's

---

[79] 'On *Cotswold-hills*, all day repast they might: | In *Dover-Castle*, take repose all night' (fo. F. 1ʳ), and 'For of all honours to thy sport | Tis not the least that thou did'st chuse, | To furnish thy renouned Fort, | With straines of every gentle Muse' (fo. F. 4ʳ), and 'When sports are ended, then appeare doe free | Tokens of DOVERS liberallitie, | His roome will *Xerxes* Armie [the competitors] all containe | His Tables nere are fill'd with guests . . . | His drinke from *Wickham*, reacheth to the *Hill*, | Hee spares no cost . . . | None ever hungry from these games come home' (fo. E. 3ᵛ).

[80] Fo. D. 1ʳ.

[81] In the poems Queen Flora is said to have chosen Dover as her king (see n. 7) saying: 'Goe maides, and Lillies get, | To make him up a glorious coronet' (fo. D. 1ᵛ). In the first year when Dover dressed as King James, the analogy with *Pericles*, where Simonides has Dover's role, would have been even greater.

[82] 'Last Evening . . . I met a noble *Swayne*, | That spurr'd his spright-full *Palfrey* ore the playne | [Plateau: see *King John*, II. i. 295] His head with Ribbands crown'd, and deck't as gay | As any Lasse upon her Bridal day . . . | I asked the cause, they tould me this was hee, | Whom this dayes Tryumph crown'd with victory (fo. C. 4ᵛ).

[83] 'Happy oh hil! . . . in dread, | The aged Alpes shall bow his snowie head: | *Flora* with all her store, thy Temples Crowne' (fo. D. 1ᵛ). [84] Fo. B. 1ʳ.

84 *Summer Kings and Queens*

poem. The difference from the medieval position was that although the winner's kingship was only temporary, the virtue was in the doing and the achieving without any thought for the future. Dover, as host king, was wholly praised for the good he did as Fortune's surrogate.[85]

In many of these celebratory verses can be read the pleasure at overturning those Puritan constraints which had prevented the games. Any double-edged vision of Fortune's influence was irrelevant to Dover's intentions and would have weakened the case for reinstituting the custom. As James I put it, popular plays at this time were no more superstitious than eating fish in Lent.[86]

However, from the medieval evidence, the most consistent picture which emerges is of an ultimately ominous view of Fortune, and a satirical approach towards her participants. Verbal abuse was the appropriate speech of, and about, the mock king.[87] The play on hills was a part of the satiric tradition, and traces of the games can be found in works already thought of as English, medieval satires. Chaucer's Miller is a quarrelsome, self-opinioned churl; 'a janglere and a goliardeys', who led the pilgrims out towards Canterbury playing his bagpipes and whose brawn always won him the prize in the wrestling. Owst argues that goliardic satire, full of 'undisguised fun, the impish delight in personal taunt and abuse, akin to the careless schoolboy spirit',[88] disappeared from English works by the fifteenth century. It was replaced by the more earnest model of Piers Plowman, a sober, moral, simple rustic who, instead of railing for fun, seriously pointed to vice in society. Both types of satire can be

[85] Dover's summer hospitality provides another example of the congruence between winter and summer traditions. Approval of an open house was very much part of the Elizabethan attitudes to lords of misrule, as at Chester 1567–8. See n. 2 above.

[86] 'I cannot see what greater superstition can be in making playes and lawfull games in Maie and good cheere at Christmas, then in eating fish in Lent . . . the Papists as well using the one as the other', James I, *Basilicon Doron* (Edinburgh, 1599), ed. J. Craigie (Edinburgh, 1944–50), p. 164. By 1600, in England, fish days were for economic not religious reasons. See Billington, 'Butchers and Fishmongers', *Folklore* 101 (1990), p. 98.

[87] A further summer/winter similarity is found here. See 16th-cent. treatment of declining Christmas kings, Ch. 2. Also scornful elevation to a parodic crown was included in some punishments which took the form of public humiliation. Machyn records that on 22 Mar. 1559–60 and 8 Mar. 1555–6 a fishwife and a butcher respectively did penance wearing crowns of the offending fish and meat. H. Machyn, *Diary of a Resident in London*, ed. J. G. Nichols (London, 1848), pp. 253, 101.

[88] G. R. Owst, *Literature and Pulpit in Mediaeval Literature* (Oxford, 1933), p. 216. Cf. A. Kernan, *The Cankered Muse* (New Haven, 1959), pp. 40–4.

Summer Kings and Queens

found in the summer king play and related literature. The mock king railed like a goliard, and the fallen figure like a critic.

The setting for *Piers Plowman* follows Romance tradition, similar to that in 'The Hous of Fame', but suggesting more strongly the ominous side of Fortune's tower. Langland says his vision came to him on a May morning on the Malvern hills, where he dreamed he was in a wilderness and could see against the sun a well-built tower on a small hill. Beneath was a deep dark valley which struck fear into him, and between the two, the 'field full of folk'; all humanity, as in Chaucer's poem, not playing but going about their daily work. Langland expresses thoughtful criticism through Piers, but greater aggression came into what is known as the Piers tradition and the rough language of a Colin Clout was adopted as appropriate to that of the unlettered, direct, and forceful rustic.

One further aspect of the midsummer king to take into consideration is his fantasizing. Whether it was Trowle pretending to be a drunken Pope, Talboys Dymoke imitating the arrogance of the Earl of Lincoln, or John Pym accused of assuming the monarch's authority, outrageous fantasy was an inevitable part of any low-born man's assumption of the role of king. Such boastful fantasies were part of the summer game's legacy to the drama. It also contributed a vigour of language and the rise and fall of a man in a two-part play structure and, later, within a single play unit. The leading male role as summer king occurs repeatedly throughout the Elizabethan period. There was more dramatic potential in the medieval than in the reformation Fortune myth, applied to them, though perhaps a tension between the two exists in *Timon of Athens*. And final confirmation that Renaissance drama did so draw from midsummer kings comes from *Annalia Dubrensia*, which was of course written after the drama's greatest years. An anonymous R.N. praises Dover for a return to basics:

> . . . things there done in fact,
> Which Poets did but fayne, and Players act.
>
> fo. I. 2^v

4

The Role of the Sovereign

No-one would think power worth gaining . . . if he seriously considered the burden that has to be shouldered.

Erasmus, *The Praise of Folly*, trans. Radice, p. 173

The king was not above the moral law of God but he was usually considered to be outside his own instituted laws. Augustine argued that if a king erred, retribution was to be left to God: the lack of perfect kingship was another example of the fallen state of the world after Adam. In the troubled years of the mid-sixteenth century, after the well-advertised Henrician changes and the consequences of religious divisions, this argument was nevertheless reasserted by Bishop Latimer and by William Tyndale, who wrote that if the people discovered they were ruled by evil men then it was a sign 'that God is angry with us'.[1] Others, such as Ponet, considered it lawful to depose the rule of Mary Tudor, and 'some Catholics like Parsons took a similar line against Elizabeth'.[2] Understandably, all monarchs before and after the Reformation propagated the view that they were primarily responsible to God, and that earthly opposition to their divine authority on earth was treason.

The divinity that hedged a king had emanated from the Holy Roman Empire. As J. N. Figgis wrote, the Christian empire on earth had 'Christ as its King and his two Vice gerents [Pope and Emperor] upon earth'.[3] Conflict was inevitable since, to maintain their individual authority, each needed to claim autonomy, supremacy in relation to the other, and the direct approval of God. The Pope had a natural advantage in that his authority carried with it 'the supremacy of spiritual power', and Figgis makes clear that the king's claim to divine right originated, not for its own sake, but out of the need for secular rulers to counter the Pope's assumption of sovereignty over them. As a result, a monarch in his turn might see himself as 'head of

---

[1] H. White, *Social Criticism in Popular Religious Literature of the Sixteenth Century* (New York, 1965), p. 138.

[2] D. M. Palliser, *The Age of Elizabeth* (London, 1983), p. 301.

[3] J. N. Figgis, *The Divine Right of Kings* (London, 1914), p. 39.

The Role of the Sovereign

something more than a temporal state [instead, the chosen captain] of the divine organization revealed by Christ as part of the eternal order of the universe' (p. 41), with his civil government an instrument of cosmic order.

An inescapable flaw in this argument was that no mortal, Pope or king, could hope to live up to the ideal. Their escalating claims were easily demonstrated to be the opposite of their practice, and the more absolute a king's assertion of divine authority, the more likely was he to overreach himself and to topple into the opposite of tyranny. King John and Richard II both asserted themselves against the Pope and both were remembered as tyrannic towards their countrymen. And, since the absolute monarch claimed to lead cosmic order on earth, failure to live up to the ideal led to the obvious comment that in fact the king was a governor over misrule, as in the description of Richard in *Richard the Redeles*. In the eyes of satirists a mock king was not necessarily an untitled man pretending to be king, but could also be a real one whose title did not match the reality.

The most graphic example of kings in general being likened to summer kings comes from a 1515 copy of Erasmus's *Moriae Encomium*, to which Holbein added marginal cartoons. In the passage on the chief folly of princes, Erasmus assesses the burdens on a king ruling according to the ideals of divine right—his responsibilities both to God and to his people—and concludes that no one would think absolute power worth gaining if the position were considered seriously. However, Erasmus continues, the reality is quite different.

Picture the prince, such as most of them are today: a man ignorant of the law, well-nigh an enemy to his people's advantage while intent on his personal convenience, a dedicated voluptuary, a hater of learning, freedom and truth, without a thought for the interests of his country, and measuring everything in terms of his own profit and desires. Then give him a gold chain, symbol of the concord between all the virtues, a crown studded with precious stones to remind him that he must exceed all others in every heroic quality. Add a sceptre to symbolize justice and a wholly uncorrupted heart, and finally, the purple as an emblem of his overwhelming devotion to his people. If the prince were to compare this insignia with his way of life I'm sure he would blush to be thus adorned, and fear that some malicious satirist would turn all these trappings into a subject for mockery and derision.[4]

---

[4] D. Erasmus, *The Praise of Folly*, trans. B. Radice and introd. A. H. T. Levi (Harmondsworth, 1971), p. 175.

88   *The Role of the Sovereign*

The satire was added by Holbein, who drew the figure of the king as a man with a rough, peasant's face. The figure stands on a mountain-side and wears a large, ill-fitting gown; as James I was later to describe the peasant's idea of fashionable dress, 'ouer sluggishly clothed like a country-clowne'.[5] The man has his mouth open —possibly vaunting pride in his power—and holds the sceptre before him like a club (see Fig. 12). This image is quite unlike that of David (Fig. 15) and instead conveys the image of peasant king play.[6] It can be inferred that the actual quality of kingship shown by the voluptuary prince is as crude as a peasant's game, and is only fit to be considered as such. In other marginal drawings Holbein added grass beneath the indoor setting of the cardinal and the courtier. One possible interpretation of this is that it conveyed a similar satiric meaning (see Fig. 16).[7] David is placed in the outdoors but in full relationship with God, on his knees praying, as conventionally shown in Psalters.

Caesar, Erasmus says, preferred drunken Antony to the clever Brutus, and Holbein shows him with a crown although Caesar was never made king. In this case tyranny is suggested. The crown was the symbol of true sovereignty and, in Caesar's case, it appears an ambiguous sign indicating the usurper's game of make-believe. The make-believe of the monarch with a hereditary title arose from the gap between claim and reality, though tyranny was also implicit in absolute monarchy. For example, George Buchanan saw, in the Stuart adoption of the claim to divine right of succession, the founding of a tyranny which God would expose through public mockery. Buchanan went one stage further than Erasmus by opposing any dynastic foundation, but the cure he suggests is the same:

---

[5] See n. 64 below.

[6] I am grateful to Marie Axton for pointing out that the sheep insignia round the man's neck was not originally pastoral but is the 15th-cent., Burgundian order of the Toison d'or (Fig. 13). Between then and the early 17th cent. it was copied, in England, as an inn sign and provides further evidence of the interrelation between high and low cultures. See Fig. 14 and Thomas Heywood's *Rape of Lucrece* (full text of 1630): 'The Gintry to the *King's Head*, | The Nobles to the *Crown*. | The Knights unto the *Golden Fleece*, | And to the *Plough*, the Clowne' (fo. E 1ʳ). Holbein's cartoon could have been original parody or taken from pastoralization of the sign.

[7] There was also the serious use of pastoral illustration, as in early church mosaics and *The Desert of Religion*. The parodic convention, however, seems the more likely for the Cardinal, in the context of the central part of the *Moriae Encomium*.

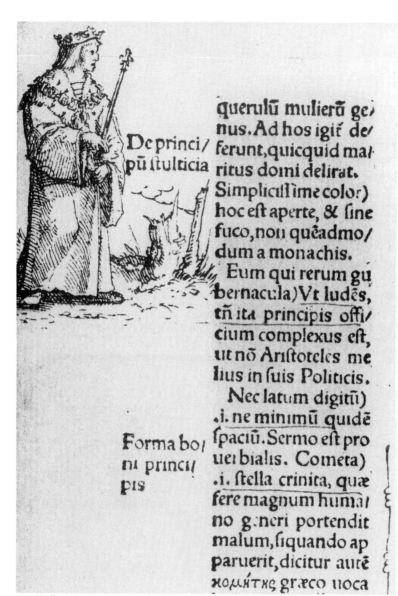

querulũ mulierũ ge/
nus. Ad hos igit̃ de/
De princi/ ferunt,quicquid ma/
pũ stulticia ritus domi delirat.
Simplicissime color)
hoc est aperte, & sine
fuco, non queadmo/
dum a monachis.
Eum qui rerum gu
bernacula)Vt ludēs,
tñ ita principis offi/
cium complexus est,
ut nõ Aristoteles me
lius in suis Politicis.
Nec latum digitũ)
.i. ne minimũ quidē
Forma bo/ spaciũ. Sermo est pro
ni princi/ uerbialis. Cometa)
pis .i. stella crinita, quæ
fere magnum huma/
no generi portendit
malum, siquando ap
paruerit, dicitur autẽ
κομήτης græco uoca

12 Holbein's cartoon to 'The chief folly
of Princes', *Moriae Encomium*, 1515

13 Claude Paradin's *Devises heroiques*, 1567

14 The Golden Fleece Inn, Thirsk, Yorkshire

The Role of the Sovereign 91

For what is less likely to be eternal than tyranny? . . . a tyrant is as a mark set up for the universal hatred of mankind, which cannot stand long . . . God sometimes seems to punish this foolish attempt . . . gently, and sometimes to expose it to public scorn.[8]

The political use of words such as 'tyrant' was constantly subject to changes but the errors of the men accused were rooted in an inflated belief in their abilities and power, which led either to usurpation or, if already king, to oppressive government. Medieval literature is full of stories of such mistakes and retribution. One of the most popular was of Robert of Sicily and the Angel. In the British redaction Robert was not depicted as a tyrant, but rather as a young Alexander, powerful yet compassionate to his subjects. However, his arrogance towards God led to God's most extreme mockery. Robert attended church 'on a nyght of seynt Johan'. He heard the text 'He hath put down the mighty from their seats and hath exalted the humble and meek', and interrupted the preacher to refute it in a boasting fashion:

> What man hath that powere
> To make me lowear and in dawngere?
> I am flowre of chevalrye,
> Alle myn enmyes y may dystroye!
> Ther levyth no man, in no lande,
> That my myght may withstande![9]

The service then lulled Robert asleep and an angel substituted himself, leaving the church in the king's place. All Robert's subsequent claims were taken as the ravings of a madman until he acknowledged that, in comparison with God, he was nothing more than a fool. The festival mentioned in the poem, Saint John's Eve, could have been either of the saint's two days in the calendar; one close to midsummer, on 2 July, and the other near Christmas, on 27 December. As in other literary and dramatic works, from Chaucer to Shakespeare,[10] customs from each solstice are combined, and the boasting of a midsummer mock king turns into the humiliation appropriate to the Christmas Feast of Fools, when the text Robert rejected was played out.

---

[8] G. Buchanan, *The History of Scotland*, ed. J. Aikman (Glasgow, 1827), i. 325.
[9] J. O. Halliwell (ed.), *Nugae Poeticae* (London, 1844), p. 51.
[10] For the midsummer activities of Chaucer's *Hous of Fame*, Book III, set on St Lucy's day, midwinter, see S. Billington, 'Suffer Fools Gladly', in P. V. A. Williams (ed.), *The Fool and the Trickster* (Ipswich, 1979), pp. 36–54. See Pt. 2 for Shakespeare's use.

15 Holbein's cartoon, 'David Praying', *Moriae Encomium*

16 Holbein's cartoon, 'Cardinals', *Moriae Encomium*

The Role of the Sovereign

The Christian justification for midwinter customs of inversion was Christ's humble birth, which was celebrated as the ultimate and Pauline example of the lowest in society as 'kyng of chrystmas'.[11] As mentioned earlier, Christ features throughout medieval drama as the apparent mock, fool king,[12] whose greater kingdom, not of this world, is misunderstood by men conscious only of their worldly power, and it would seem from the crown of thorns that this was how he was treated in his own time. The seasonal dethronement of kings at Christmas was a reminder to those in power of their relation to Christ and of the limitations of their human authority. The connecting of fools and kings was another way of keeping power in perspective. The custom was for kings to keep witless men to remind them of their own basic humanity,[13] and the two are frequently shown together to point a moral in medieval Psalter illumination.[14] It was a popular joke that those titles were the only ones to which a man had to be born, and could not otherwise achieve. Robert's growing understanding of his folly results in a moral story rather than a satiric one: a winter's tale develops from a midsummer mockery, as his position as fool becomes increasingly sympathetic. The *Romance of Alexander* was another popular medieval work about the most legendary and powerful ruler, and a cruder example than Holbein's of satiric visual mockery, based on king games rather than on fool symbolism, comes from the 1338 copy in the Bodleian Library. At the foot of the page relating one of Alexander's battles with Porus is one figure dressed up as a king and another man displaying his bare buttocks to him (Fig. 17).

Literature and illustration were one thing, public mockery of a living monarch another. For a time French *Sociétés joyeuses* ridiculed actual kings and popes with impunity in their carnival extravaganzas and the French court openly mocked Elizabeth in the

---

[11] 'Senek the sage that kyng ys of desert, | Regent and rewler of all wyldernesse, | Sendeth gretyng with all entier hert | Vnto yow hys brother, kyng of Christmas; | lettyng yow wete with hertly tendyrnes | What longeth now vnto youre astate royall | That ye be now so sodenly call', 'A Mumming of the Seven Philosophers', *Festum Natalis Domini*, in R. H. Robbins (ed.), *Secular Lyrics of the XIV and XV centuries* (Oxford, 1952), pp. 110–11.

[12] See Ch. 1 n. 60. The lowest in society were celebrated at the lowest seasonal point, in contrast with the emphasis on proud kings at midsummer.

[13] E. Welsford, *The Fool* (London, 1935), chs. 1–4.

[14] S. Billington, *Social History of the Fool* (Brighton, 1984), ch. 1.

17 *Romance of Alexander*, executed in England, c.1338

The Role of the Sovereign

1560s,[15] but in Britain only two such public satires are known and they were for a limited audience within the confines of the Stuart court. (We can only speculate about what went on in the privacy of mountain tops, but it is very likely that current grievances were sometimes played out; see Chapter 10.) The two extant examples are both satires of monarchs who claimed, or who encouraged others to claim for them, divine authority. In 1564 Mary, Queen of Scots, held a Twelfth Day celebration with her lady-in-waiting, Mary Beton, as queen of the bean. Beton's elaborate silver gown, covered with jewels, provided an image very like that of the portraits of Queen Elizabeth. Mary dressed simply in black and her only ornament was a ring Elizabeth had sent her. The icon presented was of the true queen waiting patiently while the mock queen flaunted herself during her temporary reign.[16] The second instance was during the 1580s, when George Buchanan was reported to have aped the young James VI. According to David Irving, Buchanan was appalled by James's freedom with his signature. As a lesson, he presented him with a paper which formally transferred regal authority to Buchanan for fifteen days. James signed without reading it, and was treated to Buchanan's imitation of himself.[17] In this case Buchanan was not attacking James's fundamental sovereignty but rather the foolish use he was making of it. Reported cruder mockery appears in the letters and papers of Henry VIII. After his marriage to Ann Boleyn, a Buckinghamshire man was reported to have said that Henry was 'but a knave and liveth in adultry, and is an heretic and liveth not after the laws of God . . . I set not by the king's crown, and if I had it here I would play at football with it'.[18]

A retrospective account of a usurper's make-believe is found in Holinshed's *Chronicle* of the crowning of Richard III. Holinshed likened the ceremony to a stage-play fantasy, or king game, of Richard's in which the people understood the truth but for their better safety went along with the fiction:

[15] '. . . two female dwarfs had been dressed up in the chamber of Catherine de Medici, and that the queen and her maids had excited them to mimic her [Queen Elizabeth] and ever and anon throwing in injurious words to prompt the vile little buffoons to a vein of greater derision and mockery', E. S. Clark, *Ralegh and Marlowe* (New York, 1965), p. 86.

[16] B. A. Henisch, *Cakes and Characters* (London, 1984), p. 28.

[17] G. Buchanan, *History of Scotland*, ed. J. Aikman, i. (Glasgow, 1827), pp. 174–5.

[18] M. H. Dodds and R. Dodds. *The Pilgrimage of grace, 1536–7 and the Exeter Conspiracy, 1538* (Cambridge, 1915), i. 69.

96 The Role of the Sovereign

... in a stage plaie, all the people know right well, that one plaieng the Soldan, is percase a sowter; yet if one should can so little good, to show out of season what acquaintance he hath with him, and cast him by his owne name while he standeth in his maiestie, one of his tormentors [executioners] might hap to break his head ... for marring of the plaie. And so they said, that these matters be kings games, as it were stage plaies, and for the more part plaied vpon scaffolds, in which poore men be but the lookers on. And they that wise be will meddle no further. For they that sometime step vp, and plaie with them, when they can not plaie their parts, they disorder the plaie, and doo themselues no good. (*Chronicle*, iii. 396)

Even a king who did not achieve absolute power could be subject to mock king analogy. Thomas Urquhart's comparison between real and temporary kings comes in a protest at the treatment of royalty in mid-seventeenth-century Scotland.[19] And, finally, as Anne Righter shows, the power of death, the antic in the crown, reduced all absolutism to the mockery of an insubstantial pageant:

In the moment of death, the king is parted from the role with which, since his coronation, he had seemed completely identified. It now appears plainly as a role, and his position becomes that of the Player King whose drama has come to an end. He lays aside his borrowed splendour, the grandeur which now reveals itself as mere illusion, and his entire life, in retrospect, acquires the quality of an empty show.[20]

A reminder of which was given by William Lauder in *The Office and Dewtie of Kyngis*:

Thir kyngs thai ar bot kyngs of bane (bean)
And schort wyl heir thare tyme be gane.[21]

It is perhaps not surprising, in a system dominated by the actions of kings and where it was impossible to conceive of a society without

---

[19] 'Verily, I think they make use of kings in their consistorian state ... as the French on Epiphany-day use their Roy de la febue, or king of the bean; whom, after they have honoured with drinking of his health, and shouting aloud, *Le Roy boit*, *le Roy boit*, they make pay for all the reckoning; not leasing him sometimes one penny, rather then that the exorbitance of their debauch should not be satisfied to the full. They may be likewise said to use their king, as the players at nine-pins do the middle kyle, which they call the king; at whose fall alone they aim ... or as about Christmas we do the King of misrule; whom we invest with that title to no other end, but to countenance the Bacchanalian riots and preposterous disorders of the family, where he is installed', *Tracts of the Learned and Celebrated Antiquarian Sir Thomas Urquhart* (Edinburgh, 1774), pp. 145–6.

[20] A. Righter, *Shakespeare and the Idea of the Play* (London, 1962), pp. 115–16.

[21] W. Lauder, *The Office and Dewtie of Kyngis*, ed. F. Hall, EETS, orig. ser. (Oxford, 1869), 'Hov Kyngis hes no Erthlie Permanence', pp. 4–5, ll. 29–30.

The Role of the Sovereign 97

one,[22] that an inverse image developed for every example, and that imitations of royal ceremonies were performed as popular custom. Any low-born leader invited comparison with the king if he came into effective conflict with him, and, even before death, the public nature of a king's role invited a pejorative comparison, as James I was well aware.[23] Any man who achieved a position of authorized power under the king and misused it was also open to the invidious comparison, as found in 'The Plowman's Complaint', Wyatt's 'Noli Emulare', and at the end of Fabritius Carpenter's sally against mock queens who, he says, forget their lowly origins and begin to despise them. May queens were not Carpenter's ultimate butt: the attack which follows is against men who have risen in society and who then behave outrageously in power against the poor, as though they were mock queens contemning their origins.[24]

The ideology surrounding kingship underwent a change at the Reformation, when there was greater need to assert the authority of the king over the Pope. Henry's Act of Supremacy made him and his heirs heretics and tyrants in the eyes of Rome, which persisted in trying to reclaim England either by reconversion or assassination. In the ideological conflict Henry VIII strengthened his position by adopting 'that of the French kings in the later Middle Ages, that every monarch *est in patria sua imperator*'.[25] This expressed a change in the concept of empire, from unification of all Christian states under religious leadership to each state as an inviolable entity connected to God through its independent emperor, and led to absolute monarchies on the continent of Europe.[26] It has been argued that Henry VIII came closer than the Stuarts to establishing an absolute monarchy in England, and it is still being debated whether what resulted under the Tudors was, or was not, despotism.[27] Certainly, the

---

[22] As in More's *Utopia*. Cf. 'The marveilous government of the King of the Bees', in T. Hill, *A Profitable Instruction in the Perfect Ordering of Bees* (London, 1608).

[23] See Introduction.

[24] N. M. Davis, 'The Playing of Miracles in England between *c.*1350 and the Reformation', Ph.D. thesis (Cambridge, 1977), p. 33.

[25] R. Strong, *Art and Power* (Woodbridge, 1984), p. 68.

[26] See R. Folz, *The Concept of Empire in Western Europe*, trans. S. A. Ogilvie (London, 1969), and M. Bloch, *The Royal Touch: Sacred Monarchy and Scrofula in England and France*, trans. J. E. Anderson (London, 1973).

[27] Even Henry remained 'dependent on the local administrative structures of the landed classes', J. E. Martin, *Feudalism to Capitalism* (London, 1983), p. 140, and 'all Tudor monarchs ruled under the constraints of law', Palliser, *The Age of Elizabeth*, p. 301. Alternatively, see J. Hurstfield, *Freedom and Corruption in Elizabethan England* (London, 1973), ch. 1, 'Was there a Tudor despotism after all?'.

98 *The Role of the Sovereign*

impression they strove for was godlike authority. Their strength and power 'were consciously heightened by all the devices of art, preaching and printing',[28] to present an image of inviolable command.[29]

Roy Strong has graphically reconstructed how the idea of kingship was propagated and sustained in festive pageantry, and he shows that the vocabulary of visual and verbal metaphor, through which the sacredness of the Reformation monarchy was maintained, came from pagan mythology:

The ideal prince was now one who had received both a Christian and a humanist education. The heroes and heroines whose virtues he should pattern himself upon figure in the classical tests . . . time and again figures representing the princely virtues were paraded for their contemplation, and examples of virtuous behaviour from antiquity were acted out, painted or sculpted.[30]

This description could apply equally to Reformation misrule lords, who also paraded princely virtues patterned on figures from classical texts. The change in conception of Christmas lords followed the same development, and it becomes logical that an idealized Christmas prince could be used as an exemplum for idealized kingship; for the inns of court entertainments had lost all traces of the original intention to subvert. The idea of monarchy was sustained by all forms of pageantry and the Christmas spectaculars at the inns produced further forms of supportive icons.

The power of festive iconography was most evident during Elizabeth's reign. She in particular needed all the emblematic support she could muster, since her right to succeed had been undermined by her father, she came to the throne of a country confused by religious upheavals and isolated in Europe, and it was the common opinion,

---

[28] Palliser, *The Age of Elizabeth*, p. 301.

[29] An early piece of Tudor pageantry, signalling the city of York's acceptance of Henry VII in 1486, suggests a king game played seriously to intimate that his crown came from the heavens, following which the native king yielded to him: 'Thirdly . . . shalbe craftelye conceyvid a place in maner of A heven or grete Ioy and Anglicall Armony vnder the heven shalbe a world desolaite . . . In the which shall spryng vp A rioall rich red rose convaide by viace vnto the which Rose shall appeyre an other Rich white rose . . . And yervpon shall come fro A cloude A crowne Couering the Roses after the which shall appeir A Citie with Citisyns with the begynner . . . called Ebrauk . . . the saide Ebrauk yelding his title and his Crowne vnto the king . . .', *REED, York*, A. F. Johnston and M. Rogerson (Toronto and Manchester, 1979), i. 139.   [30] Strong, *Art and Power*, p. 66.

The Role of the Sovereign

made painfully clear by John Knox, that any state governed by a woman was inherently weak. The remarkable history of Elizabeth's reign shows her transforming weakness into strength by using her femininity to obtain chivalric loyalty from her male court. At her accession she was not in a position to express pride in kingship; she spoke only of her love and duty to her people, and throughout her reign she maintained a populist point of view. However, the mythologies of Diana, Belphoebe, and Astraea, which she encouraged to grow up around her, stressed her uniqueness and sacredness to the point where she was accused of replacing the Virgin Mary.[31] The cult of Astraea in particular was quite other than previous English traditions associated with monarchs:[32] it was about Elizabeth herself, not about the position of queen she found herself in, and therefore lacked automatic connections with inversions. However, the mock king tradition continued through her favourites, notably Robert Dudley who, in the years 1558–64 when his barren name, devoid of title, was a stark contrast to the actual power he wielded, continually played mock king at court. After 1564 his ambition was partially rewarded in the title of Earl of Leicester: at the same time his ultimate ambition became less likely and the mock king references decreased. Dudley's family history had been full of serious and dangerous pretensions to power, and a brief summary will provide the background against which his contemporaries understood him.

His great-grandfather's claim to an ancient and decayed title had given him the name of Lord Quondam,[33] but he had his son, Edmund, educated into a position of power as lawyer to Henry VII. Edmund's ability to reason the king's right to other people's property earned him great hatred, great wealth, and marriage into the nobility. This came to an end with the succession of Henry VIII, when Edmund was executed by popular request. Edmund's eldest son, John, began the cycle once more, winning back his patrimony through prowess on the battlefield and in the tiltyard, until Henry 'designated him one of the sixteen regents who were to govern during

---

[31] R. Strong, *The Cult of Elizabeth* (London, 1977), p. 126. Cf. P. J. French, *John Dee* (London, 1972), pp. 185–6.

[32] See Palliser, *The Age of Elizabeth*, pp. 300–1; Strong, *The Cult of Elizabeth*, p. 126, and *Art and Power*, pp. 23–43, 65–97; F. Yates, 'Queen Elizabeth as Astraea', *The Imperial Theme in the Sixteenth Century* (London, 1975), pp. 29–87; and J. M. Levine (ed.), *Elizabeth I* (New Jersey, 1969), pp. 21–8.

[33] M. Waldman, *Elizabeth and Leicester* (2nd edn., London, 1945), p. 43.

100   *The Role of the Sovereign*

Edward VI's minority'.[34] Earl of Warwick by 1547, and Duke of Northumberland by his own nomination in 1549, his power over Edward succeeded that of Somerset. 'As an example of sheer unscrupulous genius to get on without popularity he stands alone in English history.'[35] The premature death of Edward and the hatred Northumberland had incurred in Norfolk when he put down Kett's rebellion were to be his downfall. Knowing he had no future were Mary Tudor to succeed, he seems to have kept Edward alive long enough to agree to his plans to maintain a Protestant monarchy. He 'lifted the king's sisters out of the order of succession and declared [the] rightful heir to be his cousin Lady Jane Grey',[36] at the same time marrying her to his eldest unmarried son, Guildford. 'On June 21st 1553 the King . . . signed the device and died.'[37]

Northumberland then needed to capture Mary Tudor before news of Edward's death leaked out, and it was his son, Robert, who went in pursuit of her, but she intelligently fled into Norfolk and was able to declare herself queen nine days after Lady Jane Grey had been declared. The puppet monarch had been called 'nothing but a Twelfth-day Queen' by de Noailles, the French Ambassador,[38] and Robert was brother to her consort, but Mary's unexpected leniency meant that he escaped the execution which fell on Guildford and their father. In 1558 he rode to court to offer his services to Elizabeth, and his abilities and charms threatened to repeat the family cycle for the third time. During the years 1559–61, when the possibility of Elizabeth's marriage to him threatened to return England to chaos, there were those who regretted that his life had been spared. However, Elizabeth did not marry him and Dudley remained an unofficial consort.

As one might expect, during the years of Dudley's pre-eminence his name is prominent in letters and in the extant court records. In the first year he appears to have gone in person to the Great Wardrobe in his capacity of Master of the Horse and freely helped himself. Fortescue records, 'Diuers gener de stuffur' were taken by him without noting the details which appear for material requisitioned by others.[39] And, in the near-illegible 1561–2 accounts of payments to courtiers to cover expenses, Dudley's title from the Inner Temple revels, 'Defender of the Queen',[40] is put by his untitled name

---

[34] Waldman, *Elizabeth and Leicester*, 46.   [35] Ibid. 47.   [36] Ibid. 49.   [37] Ibid.
[38] Henisch, *Cakes and Characters*, p. 31.   [39] PRO E.351/3033, fo. 3ʳ.
[40] 'Mro equore dne Regine defendo', PRO E.101/429/3, fo. 56ᵛ.

The Role of the Sovereign 101

showing that the fiction had continued into reality. The Arthurian chivalry of those revels was born out of the decorum Elizabeth herself instituted in the court immediately after her coronation, when two days were spent in jousts and tourneys with the noblemen of the court competing for the Queen's regard. By St George's day 1559, Dudley had ousted all rivals. Count de Feria reported on 18 April, 'lord Robert has come so much into favour that he does whatever he likes with affairs and it is even said that her majesty visits him in his chamber'.[41] On 23 April, Dudley was the only untitled courtier to be made a Knight of the Garter, defeating the Duke of Bedford to the place. His chivalric role had been formalized, and it was duly financed with a gift of £12,000 on 19 June. By the end of 1561, and once he had cleared himself of complicity in the death of his wife, he overcame most court and foreign antipathy to his suit of marriage to Elizabeth. This was the year he put most energy into wooing her, and it appears that it was at this point, when outside opposition to the marriage had faded, that Elizabeth herself became changeable. The closest to real power Dudley was to achieve was to be made a Privy Councillor in February 1561. The evidence for Dudley playing the mock prince mirrors his actual progress towards, and frustrations in, becoming prince of the realm.

The fullest account of his playing the prince is for his performance at the Inner Temple and at court at Christmas 1561–2 (see Chapter 2). The glorious image that he presented was nevertheless understood by the observer, Machyn, in the tradition of Ferrers. Machyn wrote of the progress through London to the Temple:

the xxvij day of Desember cam rydyng thrugh London a lord of mysrull, in clene complett harnes, gylt, with a hondered grett horse and gentyll-men rydyng gorgyously with chenes of gold, and there horses godly trapytt, unto the Tempull, for ther was grett cher all Cryustynmas ... and grett revels as ever was for the gentyllmen of the Tempull evere day, for mony of the [Privy] conselle was there.[42]

Though the suggestion was avoided by Legh, Dudley's Christmas performance was recognizably based on the lord of misrule tradition, wittily used to present the most likely candidate for the English throne. And, even more audaciously, he was a mock lord whose

---

[41] *Spanish State Papers—Elizabeth*, (London, 1892), i. 57–8.
[42] H. Machyn, *Diary of a Resident in London*, ed. J. G. Nichols (London, 1848), pp. 273–4.

The Role of the Sovereign

family had recently produced a usurping lord of misrule, yet the last line of Machyn's entry reveals the number of serious supporters Dudley had by then for his marriage suit.

A number of times Dudley acted as head of the court at festive seasons. In the years 1560–2 it was his company of players who provided Elizabeth's Christmas entertainment,[43] and in 1562 it was recorded that he maintained another kingly 'sport', bear-baiting.[44] In July 1559, Dudley led one half of a mock battle before Elizabeth,[45] and on midsummer's day, 24 June 1561, de Quadra wrote that Dudley feasted the court. It was also a day when Dudley proposed to marry Elizabeth. De Quadra reported:

> . . . they began joking, which she likes to do much better than talking about business. They went so far with their jokes that Lord Robert told her that, if she liked, I could be the minister to perform the act of marriage and she, nothing loath to hear it said that she was not sure whether I knew enough English.[46]

It would seem that summer king customs allowed for such liberties, and similarly it was rumoured that he had slept with her at another licensed time, New Year.[47] His social talents made him an excellent master of ceremonies, and in 1559–60 he was even made host to the Swedish prince, his rival for Elizabeth's hand. This control over his competitor in October 1559, outside the festive season, was a further indication of Dudley's real unofficial power, and de Quadra wrote that the mockery Elizabeth herself encouraged against the foreign suitor threatened to scandalize Europe. She and Dudley together flouted regal decorum.

Court Christmases were quiet in 1562 and 1563, and in 1564 Elizabeth was ill until after the New Year. However, Leicester was back in favour and hosted a feast and a joust on Twelfth Day (postponed until 7 January because of the weather). Again he was host at Shrovetide, though this was because he had lost a wager at the previous day's jousts and food was also served in Elizabeth's apartments. By July 1565 Elizabeth had started to play Leicester off

---

[43] E. K. Chambers, *The Elizabethan Stage* (Oxford, 1923), ii. 83.

[44] 'To the bearwards of Lord Robert Dudley iijs iiijd', J. C. Cox (ed.), *Churchwardens' Accounts from the Fourteenth to the close of the Seventeenth Century* (London, 1913), p. 269.

[45] Machyn, *Diary of a Resident in London*, p. 202.

[46] *Spanish State Papers—Elizabeth*, ed. M. A. S. Hulme (London, 1892), i. 208.

[47] Ibid. 520.

The Role of the Sovereign
103

against the new favourite, Thomas Heneage, and the following Christmas it was Heneage who was made twelfth day king, resulting in Leicester's humiliation,[48] and subsequent attempts to leave the court, and though Elizabeth kept calling him back, there was no further play-acting of the king by him. But during his most tantalizing years it was appropriate to his ambiguous status that at festive seasons the untitled Dudley hosted the court in the image of the man with most potential to the greatest place in the land. As said in Chapter 2, Dudley was suspended for five years as uncrowned king in the curious and finally unfulfilled position of 'king that is to be'.[49]

Literary works connected with his name further continue the Christmas king tradition: two as honours and a third as satire. At New Year, 1564–5, Arthur Golding presented Leicester with his translation of four books of Ovid's *Metamorphoses*: a promising title, and a work containing hopeful lines such as 'For Fortune ever favoreth such as boldly doo begin'.[50] Though, even before the full translation was published in 1567 with a more consoling dedication to Leicester, the early text also contained a moral caveat.[51] The second presentation to Leicester, Thomas Palmer's manuscript emblem book called *Two Hundred Poosees*, has a less specific seasonal dedication but, from internal evidence, John Manning concludes that 'its stylistic features bear such particular resemblances to the traditions of Saturnalia that we might suggest with some confidence that it was designed as a New Year's gift for either

[48] Reported by Giacomo Surian, the Venetian ambassador in France: 'It being the custom in England on the day of the Epiphany to name a King; a gentleman was chosen who had lately found favour with Queen Elizabeth, and a game of questions and answers being proposed, as usual amongst merry-makers, he commanded Lord Robert to ask the Queen . . . which was the most difficult to erase from the mind, an evil opinion created by a wicked informer, or jealousy? and Lord Robert, being unable to refuse, obeyed. The Queen replied courteously that both things were difficult to get rid of, but that, in her opinion, it was much more difficult to remove jealousy. The game being ended, Lord Robert, angry with that gentleman . . . and assigning perhaps a sense to this proceding other than jest, sent to threaten him . . . Her Majesty was very angry . . . and said that if by her favour he had become insolent he should soon reform, and that she would lower him just as she had at first raised him . . . Lord Robert was quite confused by the Queen's anger, and placing himself in one of the rooms of the palace in deep melancholy, remained there four consecutive days . . .', *Venetian State Papers*, vii. 1558–1580, ed. R. Brown and G. C. Bentinck (London, 1890), pp. 374–5.
[49] Waldman, *Elizabeth and Leicester*, p. 76.
[50] *Shakespeare's Ovid, being Arthur Golding's Translation of the Metamorphoses*, ed. W. H. D. Rouse (London, 1904), p. 4, ll. 145–6.
[51] 'We also learne by Icarus how good it is to bee | In meane estate and not to clymb too high too agree but | Too wholesome counsell . . .', ibid. 7, ll. 177–9.

104   *The Role of the Sovereign*

1564–65 or 1565–66'.[52] The term 'posies' was defined by Puttenham as 'Epigrammes that were sent usually for new yeares giftes'.[53] Emblem 5 is called 'Poosie for a Prince'. In it Palmer uses classical legend, after the manner described by Strong, to portray Atlas as the appropriate virtuous and legendary model for Leicester to emulate. The Titan is drawn supporting a planetarium, or world inside the cosmos, so combining tradition with North European interest in astronomy (Fig. 18). The verses beneath read:

> This Atlas was a valiannte man,
>   and kinge of manye landes
> Who, as theye fable, bare the worlde
>   wth shoulderes and withe handes.

The implication is that Leicester likewise carries or should seek to carry superhuman burdens of state, and the crown Atlas atypically wears might have related more to Leicester's seasonal status and aspirations than to Atlas's own title. It seems that the image of the crown and the style of prince, even if only in a festive context, was thought the way to Leicester's heart, either when Leicester was in the full confidence of his pre-eminence or, if the following year, just five days before festive signs turned against him. Finally, *Leycester's Commonwealth*, written in the 1580s and described by Elizabeth as scurrilous lies, attacks what it sees as his usurped position, in the form of a Christmas conversation, and ends with a piece of gloating over his foreseen decay as vindictive as any medieval verses.[54]

Dudley sweeps the board for mock king analogies during Elizabeth's reign, but in the first two years it appears from Machyn's *Diary* that city emulation of the new queen was also accepted as compliment. In 1559 London celebrated with a:

gyant, and drumes and gunes [and the] ix wordes [worthies], with spechys, and a goodly pagant with a quen . . . and . . . spechys; and then sant Gorge and the dragon, the mores dansse, and after Robyn Hode and lytell John, and M [Marion] and frere Tuke, and thay had spechys rond a-bowt London. (p. 201)

---

[52] *The Emblems of Thomas Palmer*, ed. J. Manning (New York, 1988), p. xxxi.

[53] *The Arte of English Poesie* (1585), Kent State University Press facsimile (1970), Book I, ch. 30, p. 72.

[54] 'His children shall bee worne out with beggary, and his owne hands shall returne upon him his sorrow. His (old) bones shall bee replenished with the vices of his youth etc. . . . .', 'A Godly and Profitable Meditation', *The History of Queen Elizabeth, Amy Robsart and The Earl of Leicester*, ed. F. J. Burgoyne (London, 1904), p. 245.

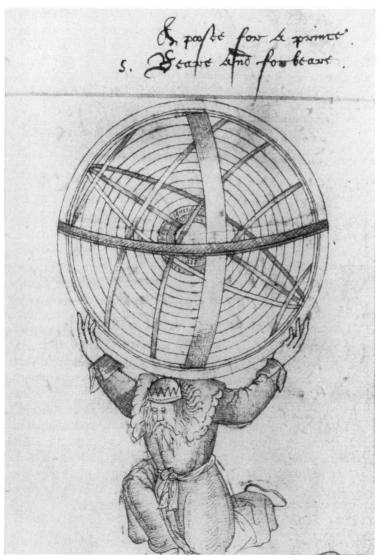

18 Thomas Palmer, *Two Hundred Poosees*, 1564–6, emblem 5

106 *The Role of the Sovereign*

The following day this celebration was repeated before Elizabeth. And on 1 July the Queen's own summer games began with Dudley leading the city's mock battle. As early as 10 April the following year the second mock queen processed through London with military pageantry probably in imitation of Elizabeth's celebration:

The x day of Aprell cam from sant Mare spytyll the Quen wyth a . . . M. men in harnes, boyth queners in shurth of malle and cosselet and mores pykes and a x gret pesses, cared thrugh London unto the court, with drumes and fluttes and trumpetes, and ij mores dansyng, in the cart wher ij quyke bers. (p. 230)

Though records are few, for most of her reign Elizabeth seems not to have taken any affront when such games, based on her own royal displays, were presented to her. In the 1580s Sir Philip Sidney's contest for the 'Lady of May', presented before Elizabeth at Wansted, contained a self-assertive rustic queen.[55] In the 1590s, however, records suggest that this changed. When, in September 1592, a bean king and queen play was presented to the then aged monarch out of season, in the Cotswold stronghold of such customs at Sudeley Castle, it was framed as a compliment to her, yet the performers ended with an abject apology.[56] The Queen's cult had reached its apogee by the 1590s, her temper had become famously uncertain, and the Sudeley performers did not rely on her tolerance. This is the sole record of any further mock king entertainment relating to Elizabeth, but during this last decade of the sixteenth century one of her youngest favourites, the Earl of Essex, fell into the rebellious role, and it could be that he provided a subject for Elizabethan drama.

He was 17 when his newly acquired stepfather, the Earl of Leicester, presented him at court in 1584, possibly as a bulwark against encroaching rivals for Elizabeth's favour. Essex's family was as long on pedigree as it was short of money, and Elizabeth's service

[55] '. . . *the Lady kneeling downe said in this manner:* Do not thinke (sweete and gallant Lady) that I do abase my selfe thus unto you because of your gay apparell . . . nor yet because of your great estate, since no estate can be copared to the Lady of the whole moneth of May as I am', *The Complete Works of Sir Philip Sidney*, ed. A. Feuillerat (Cambridge, 1922), iii. 332.

[56] 'Pardon, dread Sovereigne, poore Shepheards pastimes, and bolde Shepheards presumptions. We call ourselves Kings and Queenes, to make mirth; but when we see a King or Queene, we stand amazed . . . Kings names that fall upon Shepheards, loose no dignity, but breede more feare . . . In Theatres, artificers have plaide Emperours; yet the next day forgotten neither their duties not occupations', J. G. Nichols, *Progresses . . . Queen Elizabeth* (London, 1788–1823), iii. 143. Cf. Henisch, *Cakes and Characters*, p. 27.

The Role of the Sovereign 107

was the only way open to him to harmonize the imbalance, though, since his own ancestors included Edward II, his nobility was to become a threat. He had great charm and ease with all levels of society, which some thought ingratiating; he had proved a precocious scholar, and he was given an early chance to display his physical courage in the Netherlands war of 1585, while still in his teens. Yet, despite his charismatic qualities, he was temperamentally unsuited to the stress and inbuilt paranoia of late Tudor court life. The tantrums with which he often responded to rebuffs sometimes pleased Elizabeth, accustomed as she was to the calculated flattery which surrounded her and which she largely demanded. L. B. Smith gives a graphic description of the life for Elizabeth's later courtiers:

Her court, as her godson Sir John Harington sighed, had become a stage where there was 'no love but that of the lusty god of gallantry, Asmodeus', and Gloriana herself was forced to rely more and more upon deception and legerdemain to hold her audience. . . . the myth that Bess could do no wrong fitted ill with the sharpening image of a royal scold whose 'ireful speeches', tongue-lashings, ear-boxings, and prevarications left her servants and subjects hurt, frustrated, and angry. The enmity, back-biting, and emotional strain that were inherent within the Tudor political system were magnified tenfold when proud, impoverished and ambitious courtiers could lament that 'no man is rewarded to his desert'. The emotional atmosphere at court was electric with paranoia and the mirror of majesty shattered when an Essex could eventually be induced to cry out that his royal mistress 'was as crooked in her disposition as in her carcass'.[57]

The only way to dissent, without such disastrous expressions, was through the Tudor invention of evil counsellors. Since the monarch was divine and infallible, then any disunity must be caused by a fictional 'malignant *alter rex*'.[58] Essex cast both Raleigh and Sir Robert Cecil into this role, but eventually his paranoia trespassed on to the forbidden terrain of conceiving of Elizabeth herself as his enemy. In one of his many epistolary outbursts he wrote:

What, cannot princes err? Cannot subjects receive wrong? Is an earthly power or authority infinite? Pardon me, pardon me my good Lord, I can never subscribe to these principles.[59]

At his trial in 1601, after his abortive attempt to force his way into the palace, this statement was recalled as part of his treacherous plan

[57] L. B. Smith, *Treason in Tudor England* (London, 1986), p. 199.
[58] Ibid. 175.   [59] Ibid. 222.

The Role of the Sovereign

to cease being 'Robert the Last' of his earldom and become 'Robert the First' of the kingdom.[60] It was during the 1590s that, in the playhouse, the political statements critical of courts and kings bearing strong similarities with the English court of the 1590s, and even with its head, were carefully made in *Woodstock* and *Richard II*, and possibly affected *King John* and *Timon of Athens*. Although it was after 1603 that the deposition scene in *Richard II* was allowed to be printed, there was, it now appears, some recourse to king play methods of dissent during Elizabeth's reign. After 1603, such dissent proliferated, more from the contradictory image of kingship which James presented than from precise political grievances.

It has been argued that James was very vocal about his divine right on acceding to the English throne, 'because he had been kept short of it in his Native Country'.[61] In his childhood he had encountered the Presbyterian views of his tutor, Buchanan, and later complained that while on the throne of Scotland beardless boys had addressed him without reverence. In *Basilicon Doron* he articulated for Prince Henry his beliefs in monarchy, and this work has become a standard by which divine right has since been understood. The king's obligation, James wrote to Henry, was to God 'for that he made you a little God to sitte on his throne, and rule ouer other men'.[62] The king's morals therefore, must be impeccable, and shine and 'glister' before his people so that they can follow his example. But the king was not directly concerned with the people; his attention must be fixed on God. James nevertheless accepted that there should be a contract between him and his people: '. . . the true difference betwixt a lawfull good King, and an vsurping Tyran, [is that] the one acknowledgeth himselfe ordained for his people . . . the other thinketh his people ordayned for him, a pray to his passions & inordinate appetites.'[63] And, though rebellion was ever unlawful, the deposition of a tyrant by such means was 'not regretted' by other good kings. Therefore, despite the autocratic stance there was moral obligation behind his reasoning. James also accepted in theory the never-ceasing burdens which Erasmus had pointed out lay upon an all-powerful king. At no time might a king escape his responsibilities, including the physical

---

[60] Smith, *Treason in Tudor England*, 269.

[61] J. Welwood, *Memoirs of the most Material Transactions in England for the last Hundred Years* (London, 1702), p. 19.

[62] James I, *Basilicon Doron* (Edinburgh, 1599), ed. J. Craigie (Edinburgh, 1944–50), i. 25.   [63] Ibid. 55.

The Role of the Sovereign   109

impression he made on his people, and James advised Henry as to his dress, deportment, and gestures.[64] It is also worth mentioning that, in 1599, James said that a king should not take too much pleasure in performed comedies and tragedies, because tyrants such as Nero had delighted in them—seeing in them a reflection of their own power over life and death.[65] Later his views in this, and in other respects, changed.

One of his most famous statements came in a speech to the English House of Commons on 19 March 1603–4, arguing for political union between England and Scotland: a far-sighted idea lost beneath the paternalistic speech: 'I am the Husband, and all the whole Isle is my lawfull Wife; I am the Head, and it is my Body; I am the Shepherd, and it is my flocke.'[66] It was not long after this that James had further to assert himself against disaffected and disappointed Roman Catholics,[67] by reviving the Oath of Allegiance, which further enforced his public, autocratic image. Yet, despite such insistence on an imperial position, James found effusive allusions to his godlike majesty tedious, and stories about his rude responses became legion.[68] The masques of Ben Jonson and Inigo Jones, which were designed to deify him, were likewise subject to impatient interventions,[69] and to a royal preference for the comic antimasque, which could be described as the *mundus inversus* of the masque, and which Jonson developed partly to please him.

This dichotomy between outward show and spontaneous reaction had less superficial consequences. For example, while riding south from Edinburgh in 1603 and receiving the accolades his ears had

---

[64] 'Be also moderate in your rayment; neither ouer superfluous like a deboshed waister; nor yet ouer base, like a miserable wretche; not artificiallie trimmed & decked, like a Courtizane; nor yet ouer sluggishly clothed, like a country-clowne; not ouer lightly, like a Candie-souldier, or a vaine young Courtier; nor yet ouer grauelie, like a Minister', in 'Of a Kings Behaviovr in Indifferent Things', ibid. 171–3.

[65] Ibid. 197–9.

[66] *The Political Works of James I*, ed. C. H. McIlwain (Cambridge, Mass., 1918), p. 272. Plays of the Jacobean period frequently expressed an inverted reality: '. . . a prince's court | Is like a common fountain, whence should flow | Pure silver drops in general, but if't chance | Some curs'd example poison't near the head, | Death and diseases through the whole land spread', *The Duchess of Malfi*, i. i. 11–15.

[67] C. Bingham, *James I of England* (London, 1981), pp. 66–75.

[68] As e.g. one which is like game insult, '. . . sick and tired of the attention of a crowd which he was told desired to gaze upon his face, he exclaimed "God's wounds! I will pull down my breeches and they shall also see my arse!"', Bingham, *James I*, p. 15. Cf. R. Ashton, *James I by his contemporaries* (London, 1969), pp. 64–5.

[69] See S. Orgel, *The Jonsonian Masque* (2nd edn., New York, 1981), p. 70.

110   *The Role of the Sovereign*

been deprived of in the Scottish court: 'Hail, mortal god, England's true joy, great King',[70] James responded with the liberal gift of knighthoods to men brought forward in the cities he passed through. Gift quickly turned to sale, and in the first four months of his reign 906 were conferred,[71] as against the 878 during the whole of Elizabeth's reign. Elizabeth intended them as recognition of 'personal prowess or merit',[72] and James changed this motive into commodity and status symbol. As Smith shows, Elizabeth's parsimony stemmed from a barren purse and resulted in desperate tension in court, but the result of James's prodigality was that 'respect for the crown . . . was weakened'.[73] On the one hand the people accepted a deified image of kingship, and on the other there came from the court and into the public arena an increasing sense that the king was not necessarily 'the fount of honour'.[74]

The gap between image and reality was further widened after James decided that the succession was secure, began to follow his predilection for young men, and ceased to maintain the impeccable moral image that he had advocated to his son in 1599. The succession of favourites who resulted could never aim at the crown, but Sir Anthony Weldon's scathing retrospective comments include touches of summer king analogy. Hewme, who 'for all his great Honors, and Possessions, and stately Houses, he found no place but the top of a Mole-hill, near *Maleborough* to end his miserable life'.[75] Later, Villiers began '. . . to reign, without any controlement; now he rises in honour, as well as swells with pride, being broken out of the modest bounds . . . to the high-way of pride and scorn'.[76] And it has been argued that, in *The Masque of Gipsies*, Jonson's elevation of Villiers, then Duke of Buckingham, is a similarly dubious exaltation.[77] The final factors in this undermining of the kingly

---

[70] J. Savile, 'A Salutative Poem to the Majestie of King James I' (London, 1603).
[71] L. Stone, *The Crisis of the Aristocracy 1558–1641* (Oxford, 1965), p. 74.
[72] Bingham, *James I*, p. 18.
[73] Stone, *Crisis of the Aristocracy*, p. 82.
[74] 'Come all you farmers out of the countrey, | Carters, plowmen, hedgers and all. | . . . Honour invites you to delights, | Come all to court and be made knights. | . . . This is my counsell: think well upon it, | Knighthood and Honour are now put to saile. | Then quickly make haste and lett out your farmes, | And I will hereafter emblazon your armes', Stone, *Crisis of the Aristocracy*, p. 76.
[75] *The Court and Character of King James* (1650), in G. Smeeton, *Historical and Biographical Tracts*, 2 vols. (London, 1817), i. 5.
[76] Ibid. 39.
[77] See D. Randall, *Jonson's Gypsies Unmasked* (Durham, New Carolina, 1975).

The Role of the Sovereign

image were that James was susceptible to flattery, and that he preferred hunting to administering government: both of which were included by Erasmus as prime follies in a prince. His love of hunting provoked a retrospective portrait by Francis Osborne, intended to leave to readers a mock king image of the ruler:

I shall leave him dres'd to posterity in the colours I saw him in the next Progresse after his Inauguration, which was as *Greene* as the grasse he trod on, whith a *Fether* in his Cap, and a *Horne* instead of a Sword by his side: how sutable to his Age, Calling or Person, I leave to others to judge from his *Pictures*, he owning a Countenance not in the least regard semblable to any my eyes ever met with, besides an *Host* dwelling in *Anthill*, formerly a *Sheppherd*, and so metaphorically of the same profession.[78]

In the verbal portrait, grass is added beneath James's feet, as Holbein had done for the Cardinal.

However, the contrast between claim and reality had one redeeming feature. The autocratic figurehead was a more accessible and democratic man than might be expected. He stands out in this respect as ahead of his time for a seventeenth-century monarch. The only compliment offered by one of his detractors, was that the king 'was a peacable and merciful Prince',[79] one whom Dr Goodman might lecture while James retired to bed;[80] who himself argued that kings other than tyrants were happy to 'bind themselves within the limits of the law',[81] and whom lowly artists were not afraid to give advice. At the opening of the emblem book, *The Mirrour of Maiestie* (1618), the Bishop's mitre was placed on the same level as the king's crown and it was advocated that the 'mutuall hand | Of *King and Priest*' (emphasis added) were needed to bring wisdom to government. The idea of publishing advice to the monarch would have been unthinkable in Elizabeth's reign, who only suffered it obliquely in the privacy of court entertainments.[82] Other artists who criticized him during his

---

[78] F. Osborne, *Historical Memoires on the Reigns of Queen Elizabeth and King James* (London, 1658), Book II, p. 54.

[79] Sir A. Weldon, *The Court and Character of King James* (London, 1650).

[80] Dr S. Goodmen, *The Court of King James the First*, ed. J. S. Brewer (London, 1839), i. 199.

[81] Bingham, *James I*, pp. 149–50.

[82] At the end of the marriage debate in the Shrovetide celebrations, 1565, 'Jupiter gave a verdict in favour of matrimony . . . The Queen turned to me and said, "This is all against me"', Guzman de Silva to King Philip of Spain, *Spanish State Papers —Elizabeth*, i.404. Cf. M. Axton, *The Queen's Two Bodies* (London, 1977), *passim*.

The Role of the Sovereign

lifetime were the players he patronized. For even his moral warning against enjoying comedies and tragedies was fortunately laid by,[83] and he did nor react as forcefully as a seventeenth-century monarch might, when those he maintained bit the royal hand in public mockery of him. The most astonished comment came from the French Ambassador, Boderie, when he reported to the Marquis de Sillery his request for punishment of the playwright, Chapman, and players, who had in 1607–8 meddled in the current affairs of France. Within this complaint Boderie records that the King's Men had also 'depicted their king, his Scottish deportment and all his favourites in a strange way for after they had made him curse heaven at the theft of a bird and beat a gentleman for killing his dogs they showed him drunk at least once a day'.[84] Such public interpolations by Shakespeare's younger contemporaries, early in James's reign, were done directly, without the smoke-screen of mock king analogy. And the black societies depicted in Jacobean dramas could be said to have derived in part from the inverted example set by the court. However, one should not stress this too much, since it will appear that charges against the Elizabethan regime were also that the court was not the epitome of virtue it set out to be. Shakespeare's own approach appears to have been similar in both reigns, using well-known play structures to convey analogies, with greater edge in the 1590s than after 1603. The point repeated in his two Christmas plays, *Measure for Measure* and *King Lear*, was that a king must attend to government. Yet it is remarkable that, throughout the Renaissance, there were few depictions of perfect princes even by Shakespeare. The Duke, in *Measure for Measure*, is perhaps perfected by the end, and the romance hero, Pericles, retains a mythological perfection. But I shall be arguing that, on the whole, playwrights used the festive concept that, in play, a king was a leader of the opposite of an order which would only be restored once the play ended. The tradition was

---

[83] James's patronage was more generous than Elizabeth's. Performance fees doubled on his accession (Chambers, *The Elizabethan Stage*, iv, app. B) and he maintained the players when they were unable to work during outbreaks of plague (ibid.). Players now wore royal livery which also enhanced their status. See G. E. Bentley, *The Profession of Player in Shakespeare's Time 1590–1642* (Princeton, 1984), p. 18.

[84] 'Ils avoient dépêché leur Roy, sa mine d'Escosse et tous ses Favorits d'une estrange sorte; [*in cipher* []]—car apres luy avoir fait dépiter le ciel sur le vol d'un oyseau, et faict battre un gentilhomme pour avoir rompu ses chiens, ilz le dépeignoient ivre pour le moins une fois le jour]', Chambers, *The Elizabethan Stage*, iii. 257.

The Role of the Sovereign   113

suffered by Elizabeth, even when analogies could be read against her, and it was more largely accepted by James. Perhaps because James in particular held so strongly to the medieval tradition of divine right, he seems also to have appreciated the inverse tradition of mock kings in play, and allowed their subversive tendencies even in public. Yet he was surprisingly tolerant towards undisguised mockery,[85] and it is hard to know which, today, is the more startling: either the forbidden, dissenting comment in the last years of Elizabeth's reign, concealed in mock king patterns and other forms of fustian, or that of 1604–8, when liberties were directly taken with the king's image without recourse to concealment, in a way which was extraordinarily contradictory in view of the king's public, divine persona. Both aspects will be considered in Chapter 10.

[85] Letter written from Naples 8 Oct. 1621: 'As I remember som, years since, ther was a very abusive Satyr in Vers brought to our King: and as the passages were a reading before him, he often said, That if there were no more men in *England*, the rogue should hang for it: at last being com to the conclusion, which was (after all his railing) *Now God preserve the King, the Queen, the Peers* | *And great* [grant] *the Author long may were his Ears.* This pleas'd His Majestie so well, that he broke into a laughter, and said, *By my sol, so thou shalt for me*; Thou art a bitter, but thou art a witty Knave', J. Howell, *Epistolae* (4th edn., London, 1673), i, letter 40, p. 57.

PART II

A Critical Introduction

When one turns to Renaissance drama one finds that king games of various kinds are incorporated in a large proportion of them, as the anonymous poet in *Annalia Dubrensia* observed soon after their peak had passed.[1] It is even possible to suggest that, at the point where English playwrights successfully broke from Morality drama and from classical imitation into a freely interpreted, extended play structure, the achievement was through the use of summer king patterns. Their adoption makes sense from both commercial and, as analysis shows, critical points of view. Firstly, a strong rapport was needed between professional companies and audiences, since the ability to make or break a play lay in the reaction of the two or three thousand people who flocked to the Theatre, Curtain, and Rose. This is admitted at the end of *2 Henry IV*, where the Epilogue (ll. 30–1) promises that Falstaff will return in *Henry V* 'unless already a be killed with your hard opinions'. Whether *Merry Wives* did destroy audience interest in Falstaff,[2] this line acknowledges spectator power over playwrights. As Ben Jonson and John Fletcher also found, there was no prospect of audiences sitting quietly to be edified. Their work, particularly the stage history of *The Faithful Shepherdess*, tells of a failed battle to introduce new aesthetic ideas, and the published prefaces castigate audience resistence to innovation, and insistence on old familiar things.[3] One needs to take into account public pressure when the professional theatres first opened, before companies and playwrights developed any illusions of grandeur from royal patronage and knew that their success or failure lay in satisfying

---

[1] See Ch. 3 p. 85. Increased social disintegration in the 1630s led to fresh uses of mock kings, to which the poet might have been more immediately referring. See Conclusion and M. Butler, *Theatre and Crisis 1632–42* (Cambridge, 1984), chs. 8 and 9.

[2] H. Levin, 'Falstaff's Encore', *SQ* 32 (1981), p. 9.

[3] 'It is a pastorall Tragie-comedie, which the people seeing when it was plaid, having ever had a singular guift in defining, concluded to be a play of countrey hired Shepheards, in gray cloakes . . . sometimes laughing together, and sometimes killing one another: And missing whitsun ales, creame, wassel and morris-dances, began to be angry', J. Fletcher in *The Dramatic Works in the Beaumont and Fletcher Canon*, ed. F. Bowers (Cambridge, 1966–85), iii. 497.

118 *A Critical Introduction*

crowds of largely unprivileged people.[4] To some extent the use of popular structures helps account for the theatre's own popularity in the late 1580s. The dates of its first great successes correspond with those of the texts in which such patterns are widely incorporated. Even in history plays, or perhaps especially in history plays, the serious implications of failed and usurped kingship are conveyed by the familiar, staged iconography and, for example, one sees spectacularly revived, in *The Contention* and *The True Tragedy*, the mock king analogies which had declined in actual sixteenth-century rebellions. Part of the brilliance which today we find in Shakespeare's history plays is that they articulate, more profoundly, ideas on personal ambition, the deceptions of those in power, and the mutability of all power, which king games fundamentally explore; they portray them in a timeless way yet also without losing touch with the basic means of communication with the contemporary audience.

Accordingly, twentieth-century criticism needs to re-evaluate its conceptions of the Renaissance drama. C. L. Barber initiated this in 1959,[5] but a larger part of the corpus than he offers is altered by the new perspective; comedy other than Shakespeare's, histories based on the chronicles, Romance and satirical histories, and tragedies are all affected. I shall offer a reassessment of some well-known plays, and, in the case of others such as *Jack Drum's Entertainment*, an explanation as to why they had any popular appeal at all. It appears that audiences accepted cruder applications of the familiar, such as *An Humourous Day's Mirth*, while also greatly appreciating sophisticated extensions to their own fantasizing, as in *Tamburlaine*. For at best these traditions were more than an ancient rag-bag of motifs with which writers sprinkled their plays out of servility to the mass market. Together with the concept of opposites, they provided seminal and elastic structures for developing dramatic ideas and the variability of their reinterpretation becomes one of their most telling aspects. For example, the climb and descent of a summer king is

---

[4] My findings on the social status of Elizabethan playgoers at the public theatres accord with Butler's in *Theatre and Crisis*: app. 2, 'Shakespeare's unprivileged playgoers 1576–1642', rather than with those of A. J. Cook in *The Privileged Playgoers of Shakespeare's London, 1576–1642* (Princeton, 1981). Public theatres were not providing for an essentially élite audience.

[5] Cf. I. Donaldson, *The World Upside Down* (Oxford, 1970); R. Weimann, *Shakespeare and the Popular Tradition in the Theater* (Berlin, 1967; Baltimore, 1978); P. Womack, *Ben Jonson* (Oxford, 1986); and E. Berry, *Shakespeare's Comic Rites* (Cambridge, 1984).

A Critical Introduction   119

integral to two-part plays, all of which depict a rise and fall in ✓
fortune. The pattern is most obvious in the university satire, *The
Pilgrimage to Parnassus*, where, in Part 1, the protagonists en-
deavour to climb Mount Parnassus, hoping to return in Part 2
'triumphant with . . . laurell boughes'.[6] And, though one would not
immediately equate *Tamburlaine* with *The Troublesome Raigne of
King John*, in both plays the second part repeats much of the ground
covered in the first part, with greater satirical edge, and produces a
distorted mirror image of the first play. This technique can also be
found more subtly used in the two parts of *Henry IV*; while
Marlowe, in the second part of *Tamburlaine*, also constantly frus-
trates expectation of the fall. These three very different two-part
plays draw on the same concept, and single-text dramas also incorporate audience expectation of the pattern; the boldest reinterpretation, perhaps, being Richard's II's commentary on his own
mid-play descent from a castle elevation into the power of a usurper,
'Down, down, [to] the base court'.[7] The volatile form of the custom
was used creatively to produce a different structure per text.

One further aspect affects characterization. In many plays rival
kings or rival lords are opposite in character. In *The Tempest*,
Antonio has not only usurped Prospero, but his personality is also
antithetical to his brother's. In *King John* there is a similar division
between the Bastard, Philip, and his half-brother, Arthur, and in
Henry VI Henry is drawn as the opposite of both Richard, Duke of
Gloucester, and of Edward IV. The comedy, *As You Like It*, opens
with a similar gulf between the brothers Orlando and Oliver. The
obvious conclusion one might draw is that it is coincidence and, of
course, an author would differentiate his characters. However, after
studying the plays, I think that in *King John* and the *Henry VI* trilogy,
in particular, the impulse came the other way round and the author
thought in terms of opposites, for characters in opposition to each
other. Such use of clear-cut antitheses returned in Caroline drama.[8]

Other general observations relate to comedy, where two types of
saturnalia can be detected: one a creative and regenerative force, the
other evil and destructive. Sometimes a moral ending is pitted against
saturnalia, which then inevitably has vestiges of evil in it; sometimes
a creative saturnalia is pitted against an evil one, and occasionally, in

---

[6] *Three Parnassus Plays*, I. i. 107.   [7] *Richard II*, III. iii. 178–82.
[8] Butler, *Theatre and Crisis*, p. 221.

120   *A Critical Introduction*

Elizabethan plays, the saturnalia itself provides the moral. In comedy the examples of mock kings are possibly more promiscuously interchanged than in their ritualistic forebears and, along the lines suggested by the anonymous *Timon*, winter titles mix with those of summer and with other figures of inversion. The fullest example is George Peele's *Edward I* in which the rebel prince of Wales, Lluellen, adopts the name of Robin Hood, dresses his supporters in green, and takes to the woods. He also calls himself 'Master of Misrule' and uses Cicero's all-fool dictum, *Plena sunt omnia*. Later his Friar Tuck issues an outlaw's king-like proclamation in which the midsummer hilltop venue is included. Summer king, fool king, outlaw king, and misrule lord combine in a play more full of motifs than ideas. It is as often a professional fool as it is the king figure, or host, who is misrule lord for most of the play, since comedy concerns the reign of folly; and sometimes a suggestion of kinship between host and fool is found, similar to that in Ferrers's retinue.[9] The explicit exchange of leaders from host to fool and back, as found in *Timon*, is done with fewer signposts in *Jack Drum's Entertainment, An Humorous Day's Mirth, Friar Bacon and Friar Bungay,* and *The Shoemaker's Holiday.* While the final crowning of the greatest foolish contributor to the entertainment is also found in Marston's play, and suggested in the final, public humiliation of Shakespeare's Malvolio. In *Bacon and Bungay* fool-led misrule provides the moral touchstone for the two disorders in the play, but not all fools in comedies are given leadership. Touchstone, in *As You Like It*, is set apart from the romance disorder and Bessus, in *A King and No King*, reflects rather than controls social inversions. And since comedies are immersed in inversions of norms they are usually less concerned with the leaders than with the absurdities taking place under their aegis.

However, histories and tragedies *are* concerned with the leaders. It is self-evident that the irrational, excessive, and immoral acts of their protagonists instigate disorder and misrule. Richard III revels in it. Richard II experiences the results of his own abrogation of the order which maintains him. Macbeth traffics with the supernatural for a crown. In *Othello*, first performed at All Hallows,[10] the forces of disorder defeat the general while, in *Troilus and Cressida*, the disorders of war corrupt the protagonists. Claudius's murder of Old

---

⁹ See Ch. 2.
¹⁰ E. K. Chambers, *The Elizabethan Stage* (Oxford, 1923), iv. 171.

A Critical Introduction

Hamlet establishes misrule over which the wassailing usurper presides, the true king, Lear, turns himself into a mock king, and Antony's disorder is that of a near-absurd Prince d'Amour. Romeo and Juliet too, kingly in their youthful pride of life, fall into the error of worshipping love and the disorder of disobeying their parents. Family feuds make the parents 'rebellious subjects' and their children fall into the opposite extreme. The Roman plays have greater republican content. Caesar is murdered before we know whether he intends to accept the crown and Coriolanus perishes, ironically, because he refuses to play the king. While the aspirations of the commoner, Faustus, lead to his mock elevation and coronation at the hands of Mephistopheles.

The only ideal king that I can find, irrefutably accepted as such within the play, is Pericles. All the kings Shakespeare presents in the histories have feet of clay and this will deserve separate consideration in connection with the inherently subversive nature of the player king and the question of freedom for political dissent which he provided. My changed perspective on Renaissance drama sometimes contributes to bibliographic debate, such as the order of composition of *The Contention* and *1 Henry VI* and the dating of *Timon of Athens*, which I will consider as they arise. The latter may well be thought by some a contentious hiatus in the overall argument of the book.

In the Elizabethan period, use of unreformed games, particularly of the midsummer king, are most apparent while, in Jacobean dramas, the qualities attributed to reformed courtly Christmas lords might be added, sometimes to the point of their final domination of the play; or they might be open to further satire. Those plays under consideration here have been chosen for their telling mock king structures which, in a few cases, provide the only way to perceive the plays' appeal. For obvious reasons I have omitted well-known texts already interpreted by Barber, Donaldson, and Womack, but in no way does this claim to be an otherwise comprehensive survey. I concentrate largely on the extensive Elizabethan material and there is not space to explore the possibility of variations on the use of courtly lords which might well be perceived in works such as *The Faithful Shepherdess* and *Philaster*. Confirmation of the strength of the mock king tradition in the decade before the closing of the theatres in 1642 is found in Martin Butler's excellent analyses of Caroline drama, and I refer to the changes of this decade in the Conclusion. It has proved top heavy to try to include any Caroline texts in detail, therefore,

122   *A Critical Introduction*

regretfully, both those which fully adopt the tradition under consideration, and the subgenre of adaptations suggested by John Ford's *Love's Sacrifice* and *The Ladies Triall*,[11] have had to be omitted. I have considered the plays in chronological order, except in Chapter 5, where a need to start with the strongest evidence demands a consideration of *The Troublesome Raigne of King John* before *The Misfortunes of Arthur* (which was probably written a few months earlier). *The Troublesome Raigne* cannot then be divided from Shakespeare's *King John* and the valuable contribution of the *Misfortunes* is last in the chapter.

Criticism is always a selective exercise. While it opens up fresh horizons along its chosen route, it closes down alternatives for the duration of travel, whereas it is the multiplicity of simultaneous ideas in Shakespeare's greatest plays which can be absorbed in performance or in a reading of the text, and which strike us with the almost inestimable value of the work. However, not to apply the information critically to the Renaissance drama would be to ignore one fundamental value of it. The variety of mock king interpretations and analogies provides another kind of understanding of these texts to be added to our accumulated view of them. And, from the point of view of the games themselves, they could not have achieved a more complex realization of their varied potential before they were discouraged by Church disapproval and the aftermath of the execution of Charles I.

[11] See B. Opie, 'Ford's Analysis of Love and Friendship', in M. Neil (ed.), *John Ford: Critical Re-visions* (Cambridge, 1988), pp. 240–2.

5

Summer Kings in Conflict

The Popular Perspective in *The Troublesome Raigne of King John*, and *The Misfortunes of Arthur*

> Now *Lazarillo* thou art tumbl'd downe
> The hill of Fortune.
>
> F. Beaumont, *The Woman Hater*, v. i. 146–7

To begin with, it is necessary to establish the validity of claims for critical reassessment, and to demonstrate the ingenuity with which popular structures were absorbed and reinterpreted in the drama. One of the earliest popular Chronicle plays was *The Troublesome Raigne of King John*,[1] and it can be seen that this contains one of the most well-balanced and extended of summer game dramatizations. The complex politics of the plot are held together as an elaborate king game based on the fortunes of the main protagonist, John. As one might expect, in Part 1 he ascends, and in Part 2 falls, but the point is woven in organically rather than being left as an undramatic, literary allusion to Fortune's wheel.[2] The two-part story is told without act divisions, and it is the central hiatus between the two parts which is integral to its structure. Towards the end of Part 1 an aside by Peter the Prophet to a boy in the crowd provides a miniature of John's future:

---

[1] The earliest suggested date for the play, with which I agree, is late 1588. In the recent chronology debate begun by E. A. J. Honigmann (*King John*, Arden edn., preface), the evidence for *TR* preceding *KJ* is the securest. See S. Thomas, '"*Enter a Sheriffe*": Shakespeare's *King John* and *The Troublesome Raigne*', *SQ*, 37 (1986), pp. 98–100. Further, in the Folio edn. of *KJ*, Hubert in II. i. is called Citizen for the first half of the scene. In *TR* the same character is called Citizen throughout the scene. It is more likely that Shakespeare decided half-way through to tie this character in with the later plot than that the anonymous author reverted to the generic name for the character. Possibly, in Shakespeare's play, the actor playing Hubert doubled with the Citizen, until the 2 parts were identified with each other.

[2] There are many references to Fortune in the drama, but few to her wheel. The most effective is in *Tamburlaine*, 1. 1. ii. 174–81. Plays which less successfully attempt to develop the metaphor into plot structure are Greene's *Alfonsus* and Dekker's *Old Fortunatus*.

124   *Summer Kings in Conflict*

> Come hether boy, goe get thee home, and clime not ouerhie:
> For from aloft thy fortune stands in hazard thou shalt die.[3]

And, at the end of Part 1, Peter identifies John as a temporary, summer king:

> . . . ere Ascension day
> Haue brought the Sunne vnto his vsuall height,
> Of Crowne, Estate, and Royall dignitie,
> Thou shalt be cleane dispoyld and dipossest.

> fo. G. 3[r]

Ascension day usually falls in May, but the connection with the height of the sun and the name, Ascension, brings in overtones of man at the height of his powers as found in *Kalendar & Compost of Shepherds* (see Chapter 3). Peter implies that no sooner will John achieve the fullness of his powers than he will lose them, and Part 1 ends with John having successfully fought and tricked his way to the highest position of kingship, assuming divine right; and temporarily reassured that his position can be sustained because Arthur has not, after all, been murdered. Part 2 opens on Ascension day with Arthur hazarding and losing his life on the chance of surviving the leap from the castle walls. In the opening graphic action, the audience sees an aspiring king's fall from Fortune to death and, like dumb show, the fall further provides Part 2's argument regarding the ensuing fate of John. The leap today remains a good dramatic effect: in its time it had particular relevance to the audience. Immediately after, in scene ii, John enters carrying a clock and obsessed with the fact that it is midday. His preoccupation does not make any dramatic sense without summer king precedent, for John is aware that the sun is about to decline. Like Arthur in the *Morte Arthure*, he recognizes the turning of the tide on the day when his reign will end, and waits for his fate to be resolved. Peter repeats his prophecy with a subtle modification: 'King *Iohn* shall not be King as heeretofore',[4] and, before the day is out, John has agreed to send his crown in penance to Rome. Although he will be allowed to regain it, Peter's prophecy is fulfilled, for John has to forgo both his divine right and England's independence, and accept his restoration to the throne by the Pope as a puppet king only, which he sees as a disaster. The focus at the

---

[3] Printed 1591, *Old English Drama* facsimile (1911), pt. 1, fo. F. 2[r].
[4] Pt. 2, fo. B. 1[r].

Summer Kings in Conflict

midpoint of the two-part play structure on midsummer king customs and philosophy, through which to dramatize events, is striking. The mid-play change in fortune, for both Arthur and John, is performed through mid-year mock king traditions, and John's initial success was not bestowed on him by Fortune—he was not lifted in her wheel—he achieved his ambition through his own efforts. Critics have tended to argue that these and other events from English history had a peculiar but undecipherable fascination for the Elizabethans,[5] whereas the attraction was more likely to have been because the history was structured in familiar and popular patterns.

The battle for Angiers in Part 1 also looks more like a Cotswold game than political conflict—and this is even more true of Shakespeare's *King John*, where the battle is absurdly fought twice and, interestingly, on a hilltop. John orders his men, 'Up higher to the plain'.[6] The two battles resolve nothing, and the contestants even prepare for a third bout when the Bastard comments on the theatricality of their actions:

> By heaven, these scroyles of Angiers flout you, kings,
> And stand securely on their battlements,
> As in a theatre, whence they gape and point,
> At your industrious scenes and acts of death.[7]

The spectacle, for both stage and paying audiences to both plays, is of the royal figureheads vaunting their prowess, defying each other, and going off to fight, while, in the earlier play, the bastard, Philip, provides outright comedy, chasing Limoges round the stage and tearing his father's lion's skin from his shoulders. The fact that an untitled citizen insists on the battle, while he stands watching from the city walls, turns royalty into performers, and enlarges the anonymous citizen into Fortune's surrogate, in the fortress of a House of Fame, with power to determine the fortune of kings. In *TR* his failure to decide the winner is put in disrespectful terms, quite unrealistic in view of the actual historical relationship between citizens and their sovereigns; 'we care not which, if once we knew the right.'[8] And Constance's disappointment at the marriage of reconciliation confirms the game context:

---

[5] E. M. W. Tillyard, *Shakespeare's History Plays* (London, 1944), p. 158.
[6] II. i. 295.
[7] *KJ* II i. 373–6. Honigmann makes an interesting argument for a parallel between the battle for Angiers and Burbage's battle for the Theatre. Arden introd., p. l.   [8] Pt. 1, fo. D. 1ᵛ.

126   *Summer Kings in Conflict*

> Is all the bloud yspilt on either part,
> .   .   .   .   .   .
> Crowne to a louegame.
>
> Pt. 1, fo. D. 3^v

It is, however, more than a good commercial idea that these
sovereigns be presented as peasant game, it is also just. There is no
kingly integrity on either side, and this is reflected in the stalemate
outcome. In terms of the tournament adage that God defends the
right, both sides are equally matched since neither has such right.
And the later ceremony in *TR*, bestowing on John England's independent right, is a further fundamental sham. It takes place before
the people, one might say 'i'th'market place', where John excuses his
action and asserts:

> Now twice been crowned and applauded King:
> Your cheered action to install me so,
> Infers assured witnes of your loues.
>
> Pt. 1, fo. G. 2^r

In the play, the reason for the second crowning is the defeat of the
popish forces supporting Arthur, which John claims proves himself
to be the 'more than needfull [royal] braunch'.[9] Therefore, ostensibly
the repeated ceremony establishes his pre-eminence above both
Arthur and the Pope. However, if a coronation is symbolic of a king's
godhead, repetition devalues it and suggests that not even the king
believed in its original full majesty.

Shakespeare too uses the coronations to undermine John's position, but, in the earlier play, John's mock king role is further integral
to the two-part structure. His summer rise and fall is made explicit in
a way that Shakespeare does not attempt, and the sequence of events
is balanced in terms of John's ascent and descent. In Part 1 all the
battles, which John eventually wins, happen on French soil, while the
progress of his fall in Part 2 is charted by battles on his own territory,
with his own English Peers eventually in revolt and deserting to the
enemy. As the destiny of the State is tied up with that of the king, the
security of the throne of England is inevitably threatened as a
consequence of his decline. Also in Part 2, the Churchmen take
revenge on John for the plunder of their monasteries and the
Bastard's Part 1 mockery of themselves.

[9] Pt. I, fo. G. 1^r.

Summer Kings in Conflict 127

King games inform characterization as well as plot structure. John changes from opening aggressive confidence to mental and physical disintegration. At his entrance in Part 2 he becomes a railer on Fortune; an irascible satirist, who ironically perceives that his downfall 'must be',[10] while alternately cursing that inevitability and himself for the ruin of England. He perceives that disintegration of the realm is bound up with his personal decay, but is nevertheless redeemed from complete failure by his own prophecy of England's eventual release from the yoke of Rome, when he looks forward beyond the accession of Henry III to that of Henry VIII: 'A king shall raigne that shall suppresse [Pope and popery].'[11] The Bastard is, similarly, drawn from among game characters; a rebellious and ambitious 'boy',[12] Trowle-like with his mother, and who, in personal combat, overturns the triumph of his father's conqueror. This restorer of England's honour is nevertheless a popular iconoclast, not a gentleman; one who pits himself against the treachery of the Peers, and who combines individualistic self-assertion with the proper concept that allegiance to a crowned monarch cannot be broken. He provides an essential link between the experiences and fantasies of the audience and the politics of the play.

In view of the range of associations available to discredit staged kingship, it is worth considering young Arthur's presentation. In *TR* he is confident about his own claim, and is allowed a voice in the marriage peace proposals, which he prefers to the alternative of both countries being destroyed by war. To put national before personal interests is the behaviour of a true prince, and Arthur is the only contender for the crown who does this. He is the legitimate offspring of the House of Cordelion through Richard's brother, Geoffrey, and, in contrast to the headlong ambition of the false king, is content to rest his hopes in the future. When comforting his mother he paradoxically expresses his legitimate claim in play metaphor, with the thought that his midsummer is yet to arrive: 'seasons will change'.[13] This Arthur is not the pure, unworldly prince of Shakespeare's play, who conveys a paradox of his own. In the earlier play Arthur has a greater voice in the contest and uses it with dignity and reason. Once captured and put in Hubert's charge he places his faith in God rather than in his captor, and it is his moral reasoning which dissuades

---

[10] Pt. 2, fo. B. 2ʳ.   [11] Ibid., fo. B. 3ʳ.
[12] In Philip's words: 'My Sire a King, and I a landles Boy'. Pt. 1, fo. B. 4ᵛ.
[13] Ibid., fo. D. 3ᵛ.

128   *Summer Kings in Conflict*

Hubert from the murder. Arthur is here drawn as a young man with great objectivity and, potentially, an ideal prince, though inevitably conceived of in play terms.

The fact that Shakespeare's *King John* does not slavishly follow tradition is of course a plus rather than a minus, though it would appear that some of the critics' dissatisfaction with it relates to this. The end has been described as unstructured,[14] and to some extent the placing of all the Part 2 events into one and a half acts accounts for the hurly-burly of the disconnected action, though a positive purpose will also be considered. In contrast, criticism of King John as a colourless, neutral, or unheroic figure[15] can be attributed to an original and deliberate use of the pretend qualities inherent in a player king. The one aspect of John's sham majesty which Shakespeare plays to the hilt is, as I have said, the repeated coronation, in which John does not even show the dignity of the conviction of the earlier play. His opening lines are not only casual, but contain a 'here we are again' joke: 'Here once again we sit, once again crown'd',[16] which Pembroke and Salisbury rebuke him for, showing as little fear of him as do courtiers in other plays about mock kings, such as in the later *A King and No King*. At the opening of Act v, Shakespeare adds a further theatrical devaluation of the crown as John hands it to the Cardinal, who hands it back to him,[17] before attempting to catch up on events. The point that John is a player king only, and not a very convincing one at that, is made very strongly, but without the obvious signposts to tradition which appear throughout the earlier play. A further revelatory moment is his callous and playful manœuvring of Hubert to murder Arthur. He comes close to overacting his indecision, and there is near comedy in the final, staccato exchange: 'Death': 'My Lord?': 'A grave': 'He shall not live': 'Enough. | I could be merry now.'[18] John trivializes his order and wins Hubert by surprising him. In the same way as in his performance in the second coronation, the histrionic side of the player king is allowed to the fore to reveal the hollowness of his

---

[14] 'Shakespeare huddles together and fails to motivate properly the events of the last third of his play', Tillyard, *Shakespeare's History Plays*, p. 215.

[15] 'The few who accept John as hero condemn his colourlessness', Honigmann (ed.), *King John*, p. lxviii.

[16] *KJ* IV. ii. 1.

[17] 'KING JOHN. Thus have I yielded up into your hand | The circle of my glory. PAN. Take again' (V. i. 1–2).

[18] III. ii. 76–7.

Summer Kings in Conflict   129

kingly pretence. Hollowness and superficiality are John's hallmarks
and shiftiness can be read in his face:

> The colour of the king doth come and go
> Between his purpose and his conscience.

                                    IV. ii. 76–7

Lack of substance and integrity are inherent in the usurped position,
and it would appear that John's triviality and lack of heroic stature
may be problematic today, since our expectations are still for
historical personages to be presented as great men,[19] but at the time
these negative qualities could have been deliberately incorporated
into the pretence to kingship; which, in Shakespeare's version,
results in a villainy surprisingly greater than that of the Roman
Catholic Cardinal, Pandulph. Otherwise, the removal of explicit
popular patterns in Shakespeare's play means that language and
characterization can introduce wider psychological implications of a
world under a false leader. In his 'sceptical'[20] play of a proto-
Protestant king, satiric king comedy leads to alienation from reality,
and John's lack of integrity is superceded by a deception in events
outside his control.

In the shifting sands of his kingdom, Vaughan has pointed to a
conflict between 'majesty' and 'commodity',[21] summed up by Lewes
punning on his aim: 'To win this easy match play'd for a crown'.[22]
Like the rest he abandons political faith, essential to true kingship,
for expediency and tangible reward. In Philip's words:

> Bell, book, and candle shall not drive me back
> When gold and silver becks me to come on.

                                    III. ii. 22–3

And John, Pandulph, and the French leaders perform a base dance
of changing allegiances to maintain their immediate advantage.
England's wholeness or integrity is obviously broken when John, 'to
stop Arthur's title to the whole', willingly departs with a part,[23] and
the wholeness of innocent individuals becomes a casualty. In Act III
Blanche accuses Constance of speaking politically; 'not from her
faith | But from her need', and Constance counters that her need

---

[19] Honigmann (ed.), *King John*, p. lxviii.
[20] M. Axton, *The Queen's Two Bodies* (London, 1977), p. 108.
[21] V. M. Vaughan, 'Between Tetralogies: *King John* as Transition', *SQ* 35 (1984),
p. 413.   [22] V. ii. 106.   [23] II. i. 562–3.

130   *Summer Kings in Conflict*

results from the 'death of faith'.[24] Her alienation from the 'law' of
Pandulph, which is itself 'perfect wrong',[25] leads her to embrace a
different oxymoron, the 'sound rottenness'[26] appropriate to death
and so preferable for one who values integrity. Another victim is
Blanche, also alienated as kin prepare to fight kin, and her hysteria
records the dismembering of her emotions.

But treachery does not stem from John alone.[27] The marriage of
Lewes to Blanche was the anonymous citizen's plan, to counter the
Bastard's own idea of a temporary truce to defeat Angiers. Life in the
first part of the play is a game where the rules are made up and
changed according to the need of the moment. As a result, characters
are disposable, more innocent pawns than in *Troilus and Cressida*,
but there are faults, particularly in the male characters, and, surprisingly, even in Arthur. Despite being a true prince, of legitimate
descent,[28] without pride or self-seeking, and the proper alternative to
John, his pure unassertive nature fails to understand what kingship
entails. Like Henry VI, he aspires to being a shepherd and the son of
an ordinary citizen such as Hubert.[29] In Act II, he is pulled in two
directions between his mother and grandmother, and his protest, 'I
am not worth this coil',[30] shows that the politics of conflict are
beyond a child's strength and understanding. The psychological
insight also shows his vulnerability and the probability that he will be
destroyed. The Arthur of *TR* makes a more likely candidate for both
true and successful kingship, but Shakespeare did not choose his
practical virtues.

The other figure to consider is the Bastard. As already shown, he
engages in the unscrupulous action, particularly in the first half of the
play, although at the opening he apparently chooses the knightly and
ideal pursuit of glory instead of the base commodity of his estate.[31]

---

[24] III. i. 136–8.   [25] III. i. 110, 115.   [26] III. iii. 26.

[27] See J. Masefield for treachery dominating the play. *William Shakespeare*
(London, 1911), p. 81.

[28] Arthur's acceptance of Austria's help, 'God shall forgive you Coeur-de-lion's
death | The rather that you give his offspring life' (II. i. 12–13), suggests that Richard is
his father. Constance's subsequent lines to Eleanor: 'this boy | Liker in feature to his
father Geoffrey | Than thou and John in manners' (II. i. 125–7), reasserts the true
parentage and rebuts any illegitimacy charge. Arthur needs the conflicting attributes
of his uncle Richard's line, while being true-born to Geoffrey.

[29] Hubert's near killing of the innocent is similar to mystery plays of Abraham and
Isaac. Cf. H. Levin, 'Falstaff's Encore', *SQ* 32 (1981), p. 10.   [30] II. i. 165.

[31] And which is the argument of *TR*: 'Let land and liuing goe, tis honors fire | That
makes me sweare King *Richard* was my Sire', pt. 1 fo. B. 3ʳ.

Summer Kings in Conflict   131

Yet, paradoxically, the honour he seeks is itself corrupt. No sooner is
he dubbed knight than he shares with the audience the truth underlying the myth of chivalry. The world he has entered involves
breaking friendships, 'new-made honour doth forget men's
names',[32] and entails flattery, though in fact his outspoken satire is
the very opposite to this. And, most telling of all, in order to launch
himself on the supposed path of honour he has to dishonour his
mother. He shows no chivalric concern at all, as she says: 'What
means this scorn, thou most untoward knave?'[33] To which he
replies: 'Knight, knight, good mother.' Knave and knight are here
counterposed but in fact they are synonymous, as the Bastard's
preceding monologue had made clear. The honour of Philip is in
direct contrast to Arthur's sense of honour, which instinctively felt
for his mother before himself: 'O, this will make my mother die with
grief!'[34] On his first entrance, Philip is outrageously honest in his
claim of a kingly and *dis*honest birth. The sin that got him is the
epitome of kingly failure, and Philip literally embodies the falseness
at the head of the realm, even in England's saviour, Richard I.[35] In
the play Philip is, appropriately, the cynical spokesman against, as
well as participator in, the dishonesty at the heart of John's government; while, like a Vice, he remains faithful to his dishonest master.
And, like most satirists, he is possessed of the failings he
denounces.[36] Although, initially, he renounces wealth, later he too
becomes acquisitive.[37] Yet Philip's sense of England's honour does
remain and he is the best knave for the 'old world'.[38] In terms of the
play, even his puerile taunting of Austria, in the middle of Constance's passionate railing, serves to return us to satire when events
edge towards tragedy.

---

[32] I. i. 187. There is further mockery of the knight's martial prowess in Philip's
lines, 'Saint George, that . . . Sits on's horse-back at mine hostess' door' (II. i. 288–9).
St George of the Public House is the battle's dissipated emblem.
[33] I. i. 243.   [34] III. i. 15.
[35] M. Axton makes the interesting point that the personal failure was not necessarily a political one. The title, Duke of Normandy, bestowed on Philip reminds us
'that the founder of all these lines was himself illegitimate', *The Queen's Two Bodies*,
p. 109. However, this does also show the difficulty of representing the English
monarchy as true monarchy.
[36] '[The satirist's] reaction . . . is not self-examination but hatred and envy of the
more prosperous,' A. Kernan, *The Cankered Muse* (New Haven, 1959), p. 148.
[37] 'And why rail I on this commodity? | But for because he hath not woo'd me yet'
(II. i. 587–8).   [38] III. iii. 145.

132 *Summer Kings in Conflict*

After the betrayals and deceptions led by John, comes the deception of events. In Act v, when John accedes to Rome's demands, he shows no concern for England's resulting loss of independence. Instead of grief, we see relief for his own salvation, and this changes our reading of the plot. For, instead of a downward fortune as in *TR*, fortune itself appears deceptive, favouring the false king with the illusion of his fall only, yet, as the end of the play shows, his relief is itself a delusion. Prior to this, in Act iv, John casually breaks the news, as he thinks, of Arthur's death to his Peers, claiming natural causes. He misjudges their reaction and 'repents' his political mistake. But again it seems as though fortune is on his side for when he unfairly berates Hubert over the murder, and discovers that it never happened, it looks for a moment as though he will have another miraculous escape from disaster. The relief he expresses is consistently superficial, having in it no concern other than political expediency: 'Does Arthur live? O, haste thee to the peers.'[39] But deceptive events here work even more subtly against him. Morally speaking, he is guilty of Arthur's death, and he does not benefit from the integrity of the man outside the court. Hubert's humane saving of Arthur, and his kindly hopes to restore his sovereign as a whole person—'I'll make a peace between your soul and you'[40]—fail. The facts regarding Arthur's death are wrongly read, but in the mistake is an underlying truth. After trust betrayed in earlier promises, it is ironic but just that true facts should prove deceptive, and that John should be found guilty when, in point of fact, he is innocent. While fortune's inconsistencies appear on the one hand to favour him, on the other they produce random countertwists which defeat him. The lack of logical resolution to events then continues until the last scene of Act v, when they are suddenly brought to a halt with the death of John and the loss of Lewes's Armada. Though this may not appear dramatically satisfactory, the lack of structure follows the structureless pattern set by John. Having treated events as a game where the rules could be randomly changed, the random sequence continues with kinetic energy. The action during the play has been callous self-interest with near comic disregard for morality, resulting in a loss of consistent landmarks and the characters' own loss of identity, in a void where 'vast confusion waits'.[41] And the final irony is that John dies demoralized and deceived thinking that England has been

[39] IV. ii. 260.   [40] Ibid. 250.   [41] IV. iii. 152.

Summer Kings in Conflict

defeated, when a further chance event, the loss of Lewes's Armada,[42] changes the outcome.

The affirmative ending of *TR* puts the disorder and England's weakness in the past. In play terms, the chaos resulted from the reign of a mock king and, in social terms, from disunity and treachery by those same Peers the *Misfortunes of Arthur* had admonished a few months earlier. At the end of *TR* Lewes says:

> It bootes not me,
> Nor any Prince, nor power of Christendome
> To seeke to win this Iland *Albion*,
> Unles he haue a partie in the Realme
> By treason for to help him in his warres.
>
> E. 4ᵛ

The Peers' treachery was only a late event in the play, but it is picked out as the political message, contributing to a post-Armada assertion of national identity, and concluding with the Bastard's reinforcement of the crucial need for solidarity:

> Let *England* liue but true within it selfe,
> And all the world can neuer wrong her State.
>
> . . . . . .
>
> If *Englands* Peeres and people ioyne in one,
> Nor Pope, nor *Fraunce*, nor *Spaine* can doo them wrong.
>
> E. 4ᵛ

This quite clearly places *TR* in the genre of post-Armada patriotism: not so the ending of *KJ*.

Early on in the play the Bastard had embraced John's policies. On advising the temporary true to defeat Angier, he had said:

> How like you this wild counsel, mighty states?
> Smacks it not something of the policy?
>
> II. i. 395–6

One can accept this as satiric emulation, exposing misrule and inevitable in it. However, at the end, the Bastard's personal integrity remains as confused. At John's death, he makes a Kent-like pact to

---

[42] Pandulph's prophetic imagery to describe the support Lewes's forces will find in England is ambiguous: '. . . a little snow, tumbled about | Anon becomes a mountain' (III. iii. 176–7). Once Lewes's Armada is wrecked, his strength melts.

134   *Summer Kings in Conflict*

follow him, 'my soul shall wait on thee to heaven',[43] and a few lines later he swears his *eternal* allegiance to the young Prince Henry.[44] There was surely no need to include this contradictory language unless it was to show continued lack of faith. Also, at the end of *KJ*, it is the Cardinal who negotiates peace between Lewes and Henry, not the two kings face to face. The Machiavellian figure is still in charge of the old world with its pragmatism and duplicity, therefore there has been no significant improvement with the accession of Henry. Although the Bastard understands the need to keep faith with England's political destiny:

> Nought shall make us rue
> If England to itself do rest but true,
>
> v. vii. 117–18

a doubt remains as to whether he or anyone in the court understands what that means in terms of personal commitment. This makes the Shakespearian text rather more challenging and dissenting than one might expect. It would appear that the young playwright held some radical views, which will be considered further elsewhere. However, both versions are based on the concept of king as false king, and the possibility to be considered here is that, not just in comedy but in most plays, writers followed the popular saturnalian impulse. In history, satire, and tragedy, characters, or participants, experienced flawed situations and disorders, which ended, or were promised an ending, with the removal, usually by death, of the governing misrule lord, after his fall from the hill of Fortune.

The Misfortunes of Arthur demonstrates how extensive use of this tradition was, for, although it was put on privately by Gray's Inn men before Elizabeth's court at Greenwich (on 28 February 1587–8),[45] it too functions according to the popular pattern. Since the date of performance was between the execution of Mary, Queen of Scots, and Spain's anticipated retribution, it is not surprising that the character of the usurping king, Mordred (who is used to typify possible Roman Catholic sympathizers and would-be traitors in Elizabeth's court), is modelled on a Trowle-like, vaunting rebel.

---

[43] v. vii. 72.

[44] '. . . on my knee | I do bequeath my faithful services | And true subjection everlastingly (v. vii. 103–5).

[45] Eight contributors have been identified, one, Francis Bacon, and, final compiler, Thomas Hughes. See Axton, *Queen's Two Bodies*, p. 77 and app.

Summer Kings in Conflict

What is surprising is that Arthur, the figure who relates to Elizabeth, is also shown as having forfeited his right to kingship.

The play has an encapsulating theme of revenge, like that of the publicly performed *Spanish Tragedy*. But whereas Kyd's play contains the confident, nationalist message, the Gray's Inn play meditates on more ominous possibilities: being overcome by a foreign state and torn with civil war. Under the circumstances, the opening speech of the revenging ghost must have electrified the audience:

> Let *Bryttaine* rest a pray for forreine powers,
> ... let Ciuill warres
> And discorde swell till all the realme be torne.[46]

During the action all current perils are debated, particularly that of a ruinous internal war. No advice is given for any one policy, but the outcome of many is discussed and the leading protagonists had obvious contemporary parallels. Like a Protestant monarch, Arthur returns to England after triumphant battles against Rome only to find disorder at home. Guinevere had abandoned him in his absence for an incestuous marriage with his son, Mordred, and, Lady Macbeth-like, plots with Mordred Arthur's death. The sins of Phaedra and Clytemnestra combine to make as lurid a character as was contemporary opinion of the executed Scottish queen. And Mordred's open admissions express the basic sentiments of many courtiers, in the past even Leicester's in his frustration at Elizabeth's control over him: 'I hate a peere, | I loath, I yrke, I doe detest a head ... I loue to rule'.[47] Mordred cannot be tied to any one personality, rather he speaks for any in the audience who might also be tempted to take advantage of troubled times to execute personal advancement.[48]

King play is both a peripheral and integral feature. The dumb shows before Acts II and IV are simple plays, such as could have been staged at any Whitsun gathering, and Mordred's self-glorification eventually provokes the chorus's comment that 'the safest seate is not on highest hill'. Unlike Arthur, Mordred never claims he has the right to rule but simply affirms that he will. In Act II, Scene iii in particular,

---

[46] 1587. *Old English Drama*, facsimile, 1911, p. 3, fo. A. 2^r.
[47] Fo. B. 1^v.
[48] See Axton, *Queen's Two Bodies*, pp. 77–8, for the study of Mordred as representative of the Stuart claim to the English throne.

136   *Summer Kings in Conflict*

when Arthur proffers peace, Mordred's behaviour becomes most Trowle-like, mocking his father and inverting his messages. Whereas Arthur's love for his son 'descends too deepe to wish [his] death', Mordred's love for himself 'ascends to high to wish [Arthur's] life'.[49] At the end of the scene he dismisses his father's attempt at conciliation as 'boast', and himself brags that he will kill him. The intermediary's, Gawain's, final comment: 'Oh strange contempt . . . he reiects and scornes my words', points further to the outrageous summer king behaviour of the usurper,[50] which is continued in the next scene when he rashly divides the kingdom up between his followers, and creates kings before the outcome of battle is known. The Chorus concludes with a homily to watching Peers not to emulate him, bringing in the quotation already made:

> Ye Princely Peeres extold to seates of State,
> Seeke not the faire, that soone will turne to fowle:
>
> ·   ·   ·   ·   ·   ·   ·   ·
>
> The safest seate is not on highest hill . . .
>
> fo. C. 3ʳ

By contrast, Arthur's qualities at first establish him as a true king. Even when he reflects on the transitory nature of all kings, who are pawns to death, and calls his crown 'brittel . . . glasse',[51] paradoxically, and like the TR Arthur, his use of mock king imagery enhances his stature. He acknowledges his limitations and therefore, morally, appears a worthy ruler. However, in Act III, scene iv, it appears that his self-criticism was entirely justified. He muses on the vice which begot Mordred, an incestuous relationship with his sister:

---

[49] Fos. B. 4ᵛ and C. 1ʳ. There is in this a reminder of the near fatal consequences for Elizabeth of her hesitation to execute Mary. Approval of the eventual decision is included: 'A King ought alwaies to preferre his Realme, | Before the loue he beares to kin . . .' (fo. C. 4ʳ).

[50] Fo. C. 2ʳ. Arthur is stung by this mockery to respond, 'Goe: tell the boy that *Arthur* feares no brags' (fo. D. 3ʳ). Like the Chester shepherds, his attempts at appeasement fail and challenge follows. Touches of the same tradition are used inversely in *Henry V*. The French view of Henry is that he is a giddy youth, whose government can be safely mocked, and Henry uses the tennis ball gibe as his excuse to prove that he is not the upstart lord of games and disorder. However, a sceptical interpretation could be that Henry proves to be exactly that in France. The tennis ball insult would seem to be taken from *The Romance of Alexander*. Darius's mockeries include 'the ball, so that you might play with those of your own age'. Trans. A. M. Wolohojian (New York, 1969), p. 58.

[51] Fo. D. 1ᵛ.

All truth, all trust, all blood, all bands be broke,
The seedes are sowne that spring to future
    spoyle.

fo. D. 4ʳ

Like Gloucester, in Shakespeare's *Lear*, he realizes his sin has
rebounded on himself and, like Lear, he has caused not only his
personal but also his kingdom's ruin. It is not, after all, Mordred who
is the dominant mock king of this play, but Arthur himself, whose
claim to the kingship ideal was destroyed with the conception of
Mordred, and the grown result of the union now exists to make that
destruction a palpable reality. The mortal combat between him and
Arthur enacts in microcosm the fears of civil war in which fathers
and sons kill each other. In this case, the combatants are also rival
leaders of the realm: private and public tragedies combine to create
what is twice called a 'topsie turvie[52] kingdom. The festive basis to
Mordred's characterization is continued into the disastrous outcome
for the whole society. And, although Arthur is Mordred's opposite in
nature, philosophy,[53] and behaviour, he is only a different and greater
mock king. It is true that the conclusion, the destruction of Albion,
would have been even more devastating had Arthur been established
as a rightful king, in which case it would have appeared that God did
not defend the right. Yet one wonders whether the lurid history
behind his fault was a necessary incorporation from the legends
surrounding King Arthur, to avoid too close a similarity with
Elizabeth's own disputed right. And considering that Elizabeth was
in the audience, and that the play's purpose was largely to attack any
potential Mordred impulse in her courtiers, it would seem unneces-
sarily dangerous to be so explicit about Arthur's own failure,[54]

[52] 'There lay the chosen youths of *Mars*, there lay | The peerelesse Knights,
Bellona's brauest traine. | There lay the Mirrours rare of Martiall praise, | There lay
the hope and braunch of *Brute* supprest. | There *Fortune* laid the prime of *Brytaines*
pride, | There lay her pompe, all topsie turuie turnde' (fos. E. 3ᵛ–E. 4ʳ). Cf. fo. F. 4ʳ.
[53] Mordred's Calvinistic predetermination in: 'No *Fate* | But is foreset, The first
daie leades the last . . . | Let counsaile go: my purpose must proceede' (fo. C. 1ᵛ), is
matched by Arthur's Machiavellian attempt to control destiny described by the
Nuntius: 'He furious driues the Romaine troupes about: | He plies each place, least
Fates mought alter ought. | Pursuing hap, and vrging each successe' (fo. B. 2ᵛ). Each
motivation results in similar decisions.
[54] Particularly in view of the value given to the Arthurian legend by the Tudor
monarchy. The Worcester pageants welcoming Henry VII in 1485 concluded with
King Arthur, as 'Defence to England as a Walle' and made Henry VII the fulfilment of
Arthur's prophesied return. S. Anglo, *Spectacle, Pageantry, and Early Tudor Policy*
(Oxford, 1969), p. 31. Cf. pp. 44, 46, and 61.

Summer Kings in Conflict

unless it was scripted play tradition to incorporate from popular play the concept that kings in plays were customarily travesties. Such a reading continues throughout Shakespeare's history cycles, and helps explain the impossibility of portraying contemporary or near contemporary monarchs such as Henry VIII and even Henry VII, until after Elizabeth's death.

6

Kings, Princes, and Lords in Shakespeare's Plantagenet Plays

> The multitude of rulers destroyed the coutrey of Caria . . .
> whyle euery mā stroue to be a lord, it was brought at last to a
> thing of nought.
>
> Erasmus, *Adages*, trans. Tauerner

One might ask, how versatile and innovative could popular tradition be? Would not dramatists, particularly Shakespeare, find themselves in a strait-jacket which could only result in cliché? Other dramatists did fall into the trap of strict adherence to formula, and possibly Shakespeare did himself in *Timon*,[1] but a more discriminating use contributed to creative structures for large-scale works, such as the *Henry VI* trilogy and the two parts of *Henry IV*.

HENRY VI

In *Henry VI* the midsummer game pattern forms a matrix from one play to the next. Throughout the trilogy one mock government is repeatedly superseded by another in a progressive and enveloping mock king context. The process, established formally at the openings of Parts 1 and 2, increases in momentum from then on.

In Part 1 Charles is discredited as king because he gives away his power and authority to Joan:

> Let me thy servant and not sovereign be:
>
> . . . . . .
>
> Bright star of Venus, fall'n down on the earth,
> How may I reverent worship thee enough?
>
> I. I. ii. 111–45

Worship is deflected by him, the representative of Christ, to one of a pagan or devilish deity. The very fact that he, Christ's deputy on

---

[1] See Ch. 7 for the probability that Middleton's hand affected *Timon*.

140　　　　　　　　　　*Kings, Princes, and Lords*

earth, does submit, after defeat in single combat, to the manifestation
of a power above his own, discredits both him and Joan. The more
seriously and sincerely his homage, and the ensuing reversal of roles,
are played, the greater his discredit and her power.[2] The disorder
which ensues is governed by the supernatural and, from the English
point of view, it is excusable that even the upright warrior, Talbot,
should be powerless against it. Joan's power controls and distorts
true government and the subsequent course of events.

At the end of Part 1 Suffolk forecasts that England's king will
submit similarly:

> Margaret shall now be Queen, and rule the King;
> But I will rule both her, the King, and realm.

> > 1. v. v. 107–8

A French woman, a combination of La Pucelle and Helen of Troy,
will be brought inside the fortress island of England.[3] Out of
weakness, Henry in his turn will yield to a woman and so will allow
Suffolk's influence over her to pervert events. The destruction of the
social fabric moves from French to English soil as the disintegration
of the nation increases, and Henry displays his fatal tractability by
beggaring the kingdom to marry the wrong woman. The pattern of
moving from outside to inside the heart of the realm, and towards the
throne of England, is similar to that in the two parts of *TR* and looks
equally deliberate. It is true that the last speech of Part 1 is a contrived
link to Part 2, and could have been written at any time, but the
argument of progressive decay and of the pernicious influence of
warrior women starts in Part 1 and moves to Part 2 and, inevitably,
raises yet more questions in the debate on their order of composition.

Further, the difference in the way the conflict between Gloucester
and Winchester is expressed in the first two parts is comparable to
the obvious use of games in *TR*, and Shakespeare's subsequent, more
sophisticated approach in *KJ*. In *1 Henry VI*, games and formuli
crudely display the underlying argument. Gloucester and Winchester
vaunt themselves and berate each other with the mutual accusation
of being usurpers of the power they are each empowered to represent: the Lord Protector, 'but one imperious in another's throne',

---

[2] As in the 1987 English Shakespeare Company production.
[3] Talbot describes La Pucelle as an unnatural 'woman clad in armour' (1. 1. v. 3); a
martial quality which Suffolk admires in Margaret.

Kings, Princes, and Lords 141

and Winchester, prelate of the Church only 'as an outlaw in a castle keeps, | And useth it—to patronage his theft'.[4] Each accuses the other in mock lord terms, and in Part 1, Act 1, scene iii they are outrageously combative, their antagonisms extend into brawls, and the opposition between them is played out by their men in formalized or festive liveries of blue and red: all good horseplay in the spirit of Mordred's bravado in *The Misfortunes* and with a similarly obvious game structure. Whereas, in *The Contention*, the character of Gloucester is developed into a statesman of integrity, and the stature of the rest of the Peers is undermined through fuller characterization. One rather more subtle motif in Part 1, but a motif nevertheless, is the quarrel between rival lords (1. II. iv). This takes place in a garden at the inns of court, where Richard, Duke of York, is said to have rooms. The venue has no historical validity, but it was a place noted for its misrule traditions. Four men pick white roses and two red. Later, Henry takes a red rose. The quarrel between six men is exacerbated by their leader who attempts reconciliation, and the grouping can be compared with morality play technique in which an assembly of six men led by a seventh was frequently used as the motif for fool-led mayhem at the nadir of a moral decline.[5] This motif, in Part 1, divides the responsibility for the ensuing destruction of England's power equally between factious lords and Henry's innocent fool leadership.[6]

Also, the spectacle in Part 1 of the coronation of young Henry, with the Peers presenting a feigned picture of peace, amity, and allegiance is, in Part 2, played out for the sham which it is. In Part 1 the visual irony seems deliberate. The coronation on French soil is not performed until Act IV, by which time we have seen the discord between them, and so understand the falsity of the ceremonial image and, immediately after the coronation, Talbot is betrayed by the

---

[4] *1 Henry VI*, III. i. 44 and III. i. 47–8. One further insult suggests influence from *TR*. Gloucester calls Winchester 'Thou bastard of my grandfather' (1. III. i. 43) making them antithetical brethren. In the tavern scene, *2 Henry IV*, II. iv. 280, Falstaff calls Hal 'a bastard son of the King's'. Hal plays his own antithetical self and in the scene with his father says 'I shall hereafter . . . | Be more myself', 1. III. ii. 92–3.

[5] See S. Billington, 'The Fool and the Moral in English and Scottish Morality Plays', in F. S. Andersen *et al.* (eds.), *Popular Drama in Northern Europe in the Later Middle Ages* (Odense, 1988), pp. 121–2.

[6] In *2 Henry VI*, III. ii. 33, when Henry faints, hearing of Gloucester's death, Somerset says, 'Rear up his body; wring him by the nose'. There were more decorous means of revival; the insulting image seems to be a momentary incorporation of mocking a mock king.

142   *Kings, Princes, and Lords*

warring York and Somerset. This understanding of factions is taken
for granted in Part 2. In the opening scene, discord and treachery
follow in quick succession, which could presuppose a knowledge of
the background from Part 1.

Such evidence leads me to the conclusion that the writing of
Shakespeare's *Contention* was either contemporary with, or later
than, *1 Henry VI*.[7] It seems possible that collaboration for the trilogy
was intended and that this failed while Part 1 was being written. The
exact grievance Greene had against Shakespeare cannot be known,
but it might have had something to do with Shakespeare building
more successfully on those patterns which Greene and his co-writers
had more naïvely worked out for Part 1.[8] However, it still seems
likely that *The Contention* and *The True Tragedy* were performed
first. The 'ne[w]' that Henslowe added on 3 March to an entry of
'harey the vj', the large receipts that the performance brought in, and
Nashe's reference, later in 1592, to the overwhelming popularity of
the play of Talbot's death, do point to 3 March 1592 as the first
performance of Part 1,[9] while textual evidence, I would suggest,
points to its having been written before Parts 2 and 3. With this in
mind I will consider the plays further as a trilogy.

In Part 1, the focal point is Talbot and his unequal struggle to
preserve England's empire and the spirit of her nobility intact,
despite her spiritual and temporal lords being at each other's throats.
His strength and integrity make him an embodiment of the ideal
English spirit, but he is no match for the combined destructive forces
of evil and discord. The cameo of the deaths of Talbot and his son,
caused by the failure of England's honour, also symbolizes that
collapse. Later in the plays, the image of father and son dying bravely

---

[7] Dover Wilson's chronology places Parts 2 and 3 first under the titles *The Contention betwixt the Two Famous Houses of York and Lancaster* and *The True Tragedy of Richard Duke of York*, under which they were first printed. He argues that what we know as *1 Henry VI* was written in collaboration afterwards. I agree with Tillyard that internal textual evidence argues against this. To begin with, why would Shakespeare have felt it necessary to collaborate on a later and inferior preface play once he had 2 well-written plays to his own credit? Wilson cites the discrepancies between Parts 1 and 2 as evidence, yet logical answers do come to mind and factual consistency was not the strong point of these plays. Cf. Arden edn., pp. xiv–xv, for inconsistencies within the single text of Part 1.

[8] Malone's theory that the 3 parts became attributed to Shakespeare after he had appropriated initial drafts by Greene and others (Arden edn., p. xxx) seems relevant with regard to the way in which Part 1 came to be attributed to him.

[9] J. D. Wilson, *The First Part of King Henry VI* (Cambridge, 1952), p. xiv.

Kings, Princes, and Lords   143

and lovingly together is turned on its head as the disintegration
proceeds, and the bitter cameos of fathers and sons killing each other
are played out before Henry. Talbot's undaunted integrity transfers
in Part 2 to Gloucester and Lord Say; figures of upright honesty,
whose moral courage nevertheless does not save them. Gloucester is
trapped by his enemies and later, as the process of inversion gathers
momentum, Lord Say is killed simply because he is the representative
of order.

The decline progresses from problems of factious Lancastrian
Peers attempting to wrest the Protectorship from the proper hands of
Gloucester in an attempt to counter the Suffolk–Margaret alliance
—disputes which pay little attention to Henry himself—to the clear
setting up of an opposition to Henry, by Richard, Duke of York.
When York does detach himself as a rival for the throne, disintegration gathers momentum,[10] and festive aspects of king games start to
be incorporated as black comedy, portraying society's shift into
inversions. Firstly, Richard describes all the Lancastrian party as
wasteful, temporary lords:

> Still revelling like lords till all be gone;
> While as the silly owner of the goods
> Weeps over them, and wrings his hapless hands,
> And shakes his head, and trembling stands aloof,
> While all is shar'd and all is borne away.

> 2. I. i. 225–9

But in fact it is his own man, Cade, who literally carries this out, and
through whom York accidentally shows his own future responsibility for the final disintegration of the kingdom.

Cade has all the qualifications to be a misrule lord. He is a man of
low birth pretending a claim to the throne, and deliberately inverting
all normal values in his rebellion, including a use of the satiric
inversions of outlaws. Like James Beckwith, Cade intends his mouth
to be the parliament of England and, by coincidence, Beckwith and
Cade express the same aims: not simply subversion of the law, but,
more specifically, disinheriting the Duke of Lancaster and killing his
ministers. And though he offers complete freedom for the people,

---

[10] In Part 2 York is a sympathetic character who recognizes the virtues of Duke
Humphrey. Set against the factious Lancastrians and the absence of leadership from
Henry, he might appear the best choice for king. Not until he commits himself to
action does his ruthlessness emerge.

144   *Kings, Princes, and Lords*

Cade perpetrates the same oppressions the people had rebelled against. On the one hand he stirs them up with memories of being servile slaves to the nobility while, on the other, he has executed —almost in jest—a supporter who addresses him familiarly. Cade demonstrates the overweening pride of York, and the chaos to which he will reduce England. Like him he shows treachery in his promises and an arrogance which translates into murder. Though his entry into London at Act IV, scene vi, lines 1–4, is like Ferrers':

Now is Mortimer lord of this city. And here, sitting upon London Stone, I charge and command that, of the city's cost, the pissing-conduit run nothing but claret wine this first year of our reign—

yet his mock powers, applied to the fabric of society, destroy it. The killing of Lord Say, 'and it be but for pleading so well for his life',[11] is in the macabre vein of Richard III, with Cade's professional butcher playing executioner and prefiguring Richard's ultimate butchery. Iden, the independent and loyal yeoman, provides momentary relief. His brief scene overcoming and killing Cade promises that the English stock will none the less survive.

Before leaving for Ireland, York had described Cade as 'a wild Morisco',[12] who, in battle, capered and shook the arrows in his body like bells and had concluded: 'This devil . . . shall be my substitute.'[13] It would seem that Shakespeare here beautified himself with an inventive feather of Greene's,[14] devised for the play *Friar Bacon and Friar Bungay* (c.1589). For as the fool, Ralph, is there used as Edward's substitute to focus on the prince's moral depravity when absent from court (see Chapter 8), so too York's misrule lord provides a comment on his master's intentions. York's challenge to the crown will bring about all the inversions and corruptions we see in microcosm in the deputy. Henry, the foolishly peaceful king, is the antithesis of Cade,[15] and of his master, and the last scene in Part 2 shows the flight of the king and his forces before his powerful

---

[11] *2 Henry VI*, IV. vii. 101.

[12] A Morisco was an Elizabethan amalgam of the character from Moorish pageants, in the midsummer watches, and the morris dancer.

[13] *2 Henry VI*, III. i. 370.

[14] The borrowing could help explain Greene's antipathy to Shakespeare. See E. K. Chambers, *The Elizabethan Stage* (Oxford, 1923), iv. 241.

[15] 'HENRY. Was never subject long'd to be a king | As I do long and wish to be a subject', *2 Henry VI*, IV. ix. 5–6.

Kings, Princes, and Lords   145

opposite, throwing the country into a scramble for power, with its indiscriminate killings.

Part 3 opens with York and his men forcibly in possession of the parliament house, sitting in the chair of state: a classic mock king image, but not one open to harmless festive interpretation. York's pursuit of the crown cannot be contained by any law or order, and he gains his concession from Henry by threatening to turn the house, the symbol of civilized government and an alternative to war, into a 'bloody parliament'.[16] Subsequently, Edward adapts the convention that a king is above the law into an inverted reading to their own advantage: 'for a kingdom any oath may be broken.'[17] But, as the Yorkist party succeed, such topsy-turvy laws are proved true; the foresters consider their new oath to have superseded that to Henry. These ruthless dialectics result in the end of all humanitarian feelings, and a putting off of all qualities which distinguish men from beasts. Cade had licensed his butcher to kill men like 'sheep and oxen',[18] and was himself reduced to eating grass. Margaret and York, competing for power, give and receive similarly bestial treatment. Inversion of all norms is found in a society engaged in civil war, and festive games become further means for debased humanity to prove its bestiality. Mockery of the fallen, the dying, and the dead, in a spirit of inappropriate game, is adopted by both sides, beginning with the opening scene, when York's sons compete for their father's approval of the deaths they have caused among the Lancastrian Peers. Tamburlaine-like, York gives his judgment, and prophetically considers Richard to have done the greatest bloody deed by killing Somerset. York's concluding gesture, mockery of the dead duke's head, is repeated most tellingly against himself, once captured by Margaret, when the historical incident of the paper crown is extended into a vicious king game:

> Come make him stand upon this molehill here,
> That raught at mountains.
>
> 3. I. iv. 67–8

York's silence at the sight of the napkin stained with the blood of his youngest son provokes in Margaret a perverted, celebratory inversion of the proper feelings: 'Stamp, rave, and fret, that I may sing and

---

[16] 3 Henry VI, I. i. 39.   [17] Ibid. ii. 16.
[18] 2 Henry VI, IV. iii. 3.

146   *Kings, Princes, and Lords*

dance.'[19] When Margaret mockingly concludes that York 'cannot
speak unless he wear a crown', and places the paper crown on his
head, she not only performs a semblance of the historical incident
(see Chapter 1), but inevitably brings to mind Herod's mockery of
Christ. In the context of *Henry VI*, however, the parallel with Christ
is itself a travesty, contributing to the spectacle of the desecration of
all things sacred. For York is as debased a leader as is Margaret, and
his family continues the cycle of unchristian revenge when, in return
for the cruelty to him, Clifford's dead body is mocked. Continual
deterioration is also marked in repeated unequal, ignoble combats
between Old Clifford and the younger Richard, revenged by the
Young Clifford on York's child. All participants are in themselves
misruled and Margaret, with her foreign associations, continues the
specifically unnatural power of La Pucelle.[20]

   Henry does not participate, but cannot escape less than human
behaviour even while insisting on retaining his standards. He loses
the control he should exert because at every conflict he cannot lay
aside 'harmful pity'.[21] In Act I he will not 'make a shambles of the
parliament-house'.[22] Instead he concedes inheritance of the crown to
York, so behaving unnaturally towards his son, Prince Edward.
Clifford's oxymoron is correct, for Henry's misjudged attempts to
retain higher values feeds, rather than restrains, the downward
momentum, and Henry puts into Yorkist minds the promise that his
death brings them the crown by a dubious right. There is particular
irony in Part 3, Act II, scene v, by which time Henry is an irrelevance
to the battle, though ostensibly still the reason for it. Isolated,
detached, and sitting 'upon a hill',[23] he indulges in escapism, fantasizing on the pleasures of a subject's, rather than of a king's, life;
but immediately he witnesses the tragedies he, as king, has helped
force on his subjects. Not only are Plantagenets and Yorkists part of
one family (as Henry reminds York in Part 3, Act I, scene i, line 125,
'are we not both Plantagenets by birth'), but society too is a unit, and
once the murders are begun, no part can escape the inter-family
killing for the crown. Henry, like York enforced, places himself on a
'molehill'.[24] His uselessness as king is conveyed by the reductive
image, and the microcosmic tragedies enacted before him are parti-

---

[19] *3 Henry VI*, I. iv. 91.
[20] 'EDWARD. You that are *king* [emphasis added], though he do wear the crown',
ibid. II. ii. 90.   [21] Ibid. II. ii. 10.
[22] Ibid. I. i. 71.   [23] Ibid. II. v. 23.   [24] Ibid. II. v. 14.

Kings, Princes, and Lords   147

cularly pertinent king games. And, as has often been observed, in the
midst of total chaos, Shakespeare places one of his most profound
speeches extolling order.

After Richard, Duke of York's, death, the antithetical nature of
rival kings continues, with opposition shifting from the concept of
the martial to the moral. Once Edward, the womanizer, succeeds in
the Yorkist claim, Henry is further revealed, rather than disguised, as
a monk. With his fall confirmed, Henry's stature increases. He
prophetically perceives the hope in Richmond, the influence of
Warwick over the French court,[25] and identifies treachery in subjects. And, although in the chronicles Hall preferred Edward's to
Henry's reign, in the play no sooner is Edward installed than he
betrays his own mockery of state. Lady Grey's answers to his
interrogation define the love a true sovereign expects from a subject:
therefore, since Edward expects a different love, out of his own
mouth he reveals he is not a true king, while his brothers' bawdy
jokes complete the undermining of the seriousness of his court. The
respite from earlier carnage is in lust, frivolity, and further breaking
of pledges. The wedding is performed in a spirit of jest, with warring
revellers sent over from France to remove Edward from the throne.
Like Henry's marriage to Margaret, Edward's pursuit of desire,
rather than political expediency, proves no more virtuous than
pursuit of commodity, and Edward's outrageous levity towards the
French court would appear to be the greater mistake. However, in
this kingdom of inversions, his open insult is ultimately less disastrous for him than Henry's previous, unwitting mistake, and
Edward regains the throne. The kingdom, won by breaking any
and every oath, is, by the end of Part 3, a travesty of law, morality, and
seriousness. Success has gone to those with most animal energy, and
Richard finally surfaces as the most complete anti-king, combining
the callousness and frivolity prefigured by Jack Cade. The final series
of killings, especially those of Prince Edward and Henry, become an
automatic response, led by Richard and treated as sport, and when
Richard spars with Henry in prison before killing him the image is a

---

[25] He also questions the legitimacy of Henry V's French acquisitions: '. . . things
evil got had ever bad success? | And happy always was it for that son | Whose father for
his hoarding went to hell? | I'll leave my son my virtuous deeds behind; | And would
my father had left me no more!' (ibid. II. ii. 46–50). The Salic law, which Henry V used
to justify his pursuit of the French crown, made Mortimer's claim to the English
throne as good as his own.

148   *Kings, Princes, and Lords*

debased version of the icon of king and fool:[26] Henry is a fool-king and Richard a devil-fool.

The plot of *Richard III* exhausts all variations of inverted concepts, festive and serious. It becomes lawful to break sanctuary; Richard disguises himself as a monk while mockingly pretending reluctance to the crown. 'Poor . . . painted' queens 'in jest'[27] succeed one another; it is satirically upheld that Richard should have 'the garland of the realm',[28] and Christian mercy betrays Anne to Richard while Richard uses his own lack of mercy to joke himself out of the bestial insult.[29] If joking is the reversal of normality, allowing the disordered and unexpected to give relief and regenerate routine, the ultimate dominance of limitless inversions is even worse than Hal's prediction.[30] And, as in *King Lear* and *Measure for Measure*, it is shown how hard it is to replace the lid on Pandora's box. Only through the experience of degradation are the abandoned human values and norms rediscovered as the desired alternative, with the queens eventually uniting in sympathy. And, fittingly, Richard is finally defeated by the forces unleashed at All Soul's day. Although he is a misrule lord *par excellence*, combining evil and festive characteristics, and should dominate the season, the souls of his victims prove the stronger.[31]

HENRY IV

Henry VI reveals the serious consequences of inversions brought about by rivals to the crown and, like *Lear*, what should be temporary, festive inversions become a destructive norm. Yet, whatever Henry VI's political failings, he was a devout Christian with an inherited right to the throne.[32] In no way could one suggest that the kingdom under him must inevitably be a world controlled by the

---

[26] See p. 154.   [27] *Richard III*, IV. iv. 83, 91.

[28] Ibid. III. ii. 39.

[29] 'ANNE. No beast so fierce but knows some touch of pity. RICHARD. But I know none, and therefore am no beast' (ibid. I. ii. 71–2).

[30] 'If all the year were playing holidays, | To sport would be as tedious as to work' (*1 Henry IV*, I. ii. 199–200).

[31] All Souls day, 2 Nov., was created to strengthen the contest with the evil spirits abroad after Hallowe'en, 31 Oct.

[32] The Chronicles consider Henry VI's right to the throne indisputable and blame his disastrous reign on his youth and marriage to Margaret. While, in *The Mirror for Magistrates*, Henry's pure, princely character is seen as a dreadful irony in view of his tragic end.

Kings, Princes, and Lords

149

forces of misrule, as one can for the usurper, Bolingbroke. The two parts of *Henry IV* also employ multiple misrule lords; a king with no right of succession, nobles in revolt, and one robber baron living 'out of all order, out of all compass'.[33] Yet, though disorder is equally integrated into the fabric of life, there is less concentration on society's devastation. The issues are personalized and, in Part 1 in particular, we are invited to enjoy the rogue's view of life. In the earlier trilogy, expulsion of one mock king led to the inauguration of another while, in the two-part play *Henry IV*, we see the rise and fall of Falstaff, whose misrule fills the void of Bolingbroke's usurpation.

Breakdown of kingship begins in *Richard II*, at the end of which there is an impossible choice between one failed king,[34] and one good and upright soldier, who has no right of inheritance. Richard had forfeited his divine right when he broke his earthly contract by appropriating Bolingbroke's inheritance. As York unequivocally says:

> Take Herford's rights away, and take from time
> His charters, and his customary rights;
> Let not to-morrow then ensue to-day:
> Be not thyself. For how art thou a king
> But by fair sequence and succession?
>
> II. i. 195–9

On the other hand, York, perplexed spokesman for order, cannot approve Bolingbroke's reactions. He is equally severe towards the exiled Lord when he returns unbidden:

> Tut tut! . . . uncle me no uncle,
> I am no traitor's uncle.
>
> II. iii. 86–7

However, he realizes one old man cannot reforge a society, and capitulates with the weary line, 'things past redress are now with me past care'.[35] With the failure of the theoretically pure concept of divine right, which had produced a 'mockery king of snow',[36] had arisen its antithesis, the Machiavellian concept of a king by right of

[33] *1 Henry IV*, III. iii. 18–19.
[34] Shakespeare's introspective figure is neither that of the Chronicles, nor of myth. Chronicles, and *The Mirror for Magistrates*, stress Richard's tyranny, while tradition, as in *Richard the Redeles* and *Woodstock*, included a 'skipping king' attitude, resulting in a character more like Shakespeare's Richard III than II.
[35] *Richard II*, II. iii. 170.   [36] Ibid. IV. i. 260.

150   *Kings, Princes, and Lords*

popular support and winning battles. York's dilemma is allegorized in the gardener's scene. The unruly children which oppress the State are, on the one hand, parasitic weeds—Richard's retainers rather than Richard himself—and on the other, over-ambitious apricots, or Bolingbrokes, who need their heads trimmed.

Therefore, at the opening of *Henry IV*, where there should be an established king, there is a vacuum, which Henry later acknowledges to be because of his 'indirect crook'd ways [to the] crown'.[37] There is a more dramatic, spontaneous confession on the battlefield, when Douglas pursues the image of the king, killing those in his coats. Eventually he finds Bolingbroke and challenges him:

> What art thou
> That counterfeit'st the person of a king?
>
> I. V. iv. 26–7

The general rather than definitive article suggests Bolingbroke's usurpation, and Bolingbroke unwittingly corroborates this with an answer vibrant with double meaning:

> The King himself.
>
> I. V. iv. 28

Even when rebuking Hal and using his own past behaviour as an example, Henry likens himself to a comet, a sign of disorder and disaster, whereas, even while misbehaving, Hal explains himself in 'sun' imagery. The disorder in the kingdom is put into words by one of the Gadshill carriers: 'this house is turned upside down since Robin Ostler died',[38] and, in a country governed by such forces, Henry, Falstaff, and Hotspur are competing misrule lords.

Hotspur is another of Diana's squires who would 'leap | To pluck bright honour from the pale fac'd moon',[39] and whose unrestrained passions both exasperate and endear him to his companions. They call him a man of humours, and his unbridled tongue womanish. In his scenes with Kate he is very like an outrageous, uncontrollable pride of life king,[40] who sees the injustice done to Mortimer (rightful

---

[37] *2 Henry IV*, IV. v. 184–5.

[38] *1 Henry IV*, II. i. 9–10.   [39] Ibid. I. iii. 199–200. See Ch. 2.

[40] In the Folio his wife, Kate, whose role is largely to reason unsuccessfully with him, is identified as 'Lady'. Other plays also use pride of life confrontation between a virtuous 'lady' and a disordered lord, e.g. Tamburlaine and Zenocrate, and Richard II and Anne: see Chs. 7 and 10. Other such include Portia with Brutus, Desdemona with Othello, and Paulina's protest on behalf of Hermione, 'Good queen, my lord, good queen: I say good queen', *The Winter's Tale*, II. iii. 59.

Kings, Princes, and Lords   151

king in the rebels' eyes) in further terms of a true king turned into one
of the mock species, thrust out 'on the barren mountains'[41] to starve.
His aim is to restore the Yorkist claim, and therefore a kind of order,
yet his view of their possible success is a disordered one, like
Mordred's:

> If we without his help can make a head
> To push against a kingdom, with his help
> We shall o'erturn it topsy-turvy down.[42]

Henry's aim, to resolve the conflict according to his conception of
justice and order, is inevitably frustrated in the misrule environment
he himself has caused, whereas Falstaff, with his inverted values,
stands out as the natural lord already in possession when Part 1
opens. Henry and Hotspur are constantly subject to errors of
judgement. Their relationship to time seems faulty. Hotspur is
ahead, the firstlings of his heart are always the firstlings of his brain,
and Henry is always behind events. However, because of the *mundus
inversus*, it is time itself which is awry. The night-time reign of
misrule has usurped daytime governance. One could justifiably call
the events around Henry Bolingbroke the sub- and those around
Falstaff the main plot and, in this, the play stands out as the only
serious one in the canon in which the comic plot dominates, so
presenting a further inversion. From the point where Richard took
from Time 'his charters and customary rights', real government has
been slipping out of control of proper, sun-ruled authorities until, in
1 Henry IV, night-time power has become most potent.

There are many ways to approach the disorder of Falstaff. On the
one hand he leads a criminal band, intent on theft from the king's
officers; yet on the other, in Part 1 where this occurs, the author sets
the action within a licensed saturnalia. As Richard Levin puts it,
Shakespeare 'deliberately emphasizes Falstaff's saturnalian role, by
giving him a separate little world in the Boar's Head tavern which he
dominates in the manner of a festival Lord of Misrule, enforcing a
comic antidiscipline upon all who enter there, including the
Prince'.[43] Law is overturned more benignly than in the disorder of

---

[41] *1 Henry IV*, I. iii. 157.
[42] Ibid. IV. i. 80–2. Conquerors might also be seen as Fortune's surrogates, creating
a *mundus inversus* for their adversaries. See *The Mirror for Magistrates*, p. 93.
[43] R. Levin, *The Multiple Plot in English Renaissance Drama* (Chicago, 1971),
pp. 142–3.

Jack Cade,[44] and the prince acknowledges his role of jester to Falstaff during the time that he will uphold the 'unyoked humour of . . . idleness'.[45] C. L. Barber's analysis of the spirit in which retainers support mock kings is curiously apposite. Hal quite literally relishes Falstaff's bombast as a fleer against the authority of his father, while at the same time he enjoys turning on Falstaff and insulting 'his majesty'.[46] Falstaff's second rival, Hotspur, suffers eclipsing dishonour after his death at Falstaff's hands, which may provoke sympathy for him but is deserved. Hotspur is a deluded and misruled lord, no matter how valiant, and it is fitting that he is overcome, on the one hand by the disguised figure of order, the joker, the ambiguous Hal, and on the other, by his rival in disorder; a man more adept than Hotspur at depicting and surviving the world of misrule. The mock triumph over Hotspur is the highest point of Falstaff's fortunes, and, in a familiar pattern, Part 1 ends with the dominant lord at his zenith.[47] His unlimited licence, even criminality, is accepted in Part 1 as appropriate to the disorder in the kingdom. The spokesman for order, the Lord Chief Justice, retrospectively confirms this when he says in Part 2, of the Gadshill incident: 'You may thank the unquiet times for your quiet o'er posting of that action.'[48]

But in Part 2 comes the more critical view.[49] Disorder is less entertaining, and more subject to rumour, deception, revenge, and the imagery of disease, while Bolingbroke's forces win an ignoble victory. In Part 1 Worcester had pursued his treacherous, rebel role by concealing from his comrades the king's good offices, but in Part 2 the supposed royal order descends to similar tactics when Prince John betrays the rebels' terms of surrender. The Bishop of York had specifically accepted John's 'princely word',[50] and found no substance in it. And, after the Part 1 triumph, Falstaff also declines into

---

[44] However, there seems to be no real evidence that Falstaff is a holy fool. The biblical echoes remain on the level of parody. See R. Battenhouse's interesting article, 'Falstaff as Parodist and perhaps Holy Fool', *PMLA* 90 (1975), pp. 32–52.

[45] *1 Henry IV*, I. ii. 191.

[46] C. L. Barber, *Shakespeare's Festive Comedy* (Princeton, 1959), p. 37.

[47] On a lower parabola it is also Bolingbroke's zenith. As in other two-part plays, the sovereign appears to be made secure yet, in the 2nd part, disorder increases and only ends with the king's death.

[48] *2 Henry IV*, I. ii. 148–50. Falstaff here faces the man whose authority he still anticipates replacing.

[49] See N. Rhodes, *Elizabethan Grotesque* (London, 1980), for further discussion on the change at Part 2 from Carnival to Lent.

[50] *2 Henry IV*, IV. ii. 66.

Kings, Princes, and Lords   153

disease, gangsterism, and low cunning, in which it is his friends
rather than representatives of an opposing king, who are robbed by
him. Part 2 retreads the same ground as Part 1 with a more jaded,
satirical inflexion. Harry Levin has pointed out that, whereas in Part
1, Falstaff's opening call is for drink, in Part 2 it is about its diseased
end-product.[51] The Tavern in Part 1 presents the intoxicating beginning of holiday, and in Part 2 the hangover. High spirits are briefly
revived in the Justice Shallow scene when Silence is moved to
eloquence by Falstaff's presence and sings of merry Shrovetide. The
reference though anticipates the death-knell to festivity which at
Shrovetide was allowed a brief revival before the rigours of Lent, and
waiting in the wings is the lean figure of Hal, the starveling, elf-skin,
dried neat's-tongue or stockfish of Falstaff's abuse, waiting to act in
true Lenten manner towards the deteriorating Carnival figure.[52]
Falstaff's final exit at the end of Part 2, when he and his company are
carried off to the Fleet prison, illustrates the ambiguous boundary
between festive and real riot, and how much interpretation depended
on the governing attitude. With Henry's accession disorder ceases to
be endemic, and the forces of misrule are outlawed, yet Falstaff's last
line is irrepressible optimism. 'I shall be sent for soon at night'[53] is the
only conclusion for the lord of night's forces to come to regarding a
banishment pronounced during the day. However, Falstaff's death in
Henry V makes it decisively clear that his fortunes are over.[54] Hal has
extinguished the forces of misrule in his kingdom and, as has
frequently been observed, it is Hal who is the lesser person for his
success. In *Henry V* Fluellen's lines comparing Alexander and Henry
do nothing to lessen the impression: 'Alexander . . . did, in his ales
and his angers, look you, kill his best friend.'[55] Gower's blunt denial,
'our king is not like him in that: he never killed any of his friends',
provides time to recall the Hostess's line 'the King hath killed his
heart'.[56] And Fluellen's uncomfortable attempt to justify his remark

---

[51] H. Levin, 'Falstaff's Encore', *SQ* 32 (1981), p. 12.

[52] Falstaff's fate is prefigured by that of his 'lady', Doll, who is taken to prison by a
Lenten 'thin thing', 2 *Henry IV*, v. iv. 30. See N. Rhodes, *Elizabethan Grotesque*
(London, 1980), p. 117.

[53] 2 *Henry IV*, v. v. 89–90.

[54] If one takes the *Morte Arthure* and *TR* as precedents, Falstaff's death, 'between
twelve and one, ev'n at the turning o' th' tide' (*Henry V*, II. iii. 12–13) was between
noon and 1 p.m., though midnight to 1 a.m. would be appropriate to his night-time
orientation.

[55] *Henry V*, IV. vii. 40–1.   [56] Ibid. II. i. 88.

154   *Kings, Princes, and Lords*

returns us for a moment to the world of *Henry IV*: '. . . as Alexander killed his friend Cleitus, being in his ales and his cups, so also Harry Monmouth, being in his right wits and his good judgements, turned away the fat knight' (IV. vii. 47–50). The past master at such inverted logic was Falstaff himself.

Hal's behaviour towards his father is easier to justify, since he is to inherit the world disordered by Bolingbroke. It is clear, from his speech reported by Percy at the end of *Richard II*, that he is aware of the hollowness of his father's coronation. When bidden to Oxford for the ceremony his answer was:

> . . . he would unto the stews,
> And from the common'st creature pluck a glove,
> And wear it as a favour.
>
> v. iii. 16–18

The speech is understood simply as evidence of Hal's dissolute spirit, but his reaction can be seen as a comment on the coronation. The ceremony should embody all the highest ideals of kingship and courtliness, but in the circumstances the pomp is prostituted. And Hal's further dissolute behaviour in the two parts of *Henry IV* often casts an ironic reflection on his father's rule. His role in the Gadshill robbery can be seen as direct comment, in view of the fact that it is royal money which is stolen. Hal says to Poins: 'The thieves have bound the true men; now could thou and I rob the thieves . . . it would be . . . a good jest for ever' (*1 Henry IV*, II. ii. 88–91). In robbing Falstaff, Hal is in fact robbing his father, who stole the purse from Richard. Much more subtly than in *Friar Bacon* and *2 Henry VI*, Falstaff, as lord of misrule, stands in for the corrupt behaviour of a king figure. A second time he does this is in the tavern scene in Part 1, Act II, scene iv. The picture conjured up, when Falstaff plays Bolingbroke, is one known to all late medieval society from illustrations to Psalm 13,[57] beginning 'Dixit insipiens in corde suo', where king and fool were shown together, accusing each other and reflecting upon each other's folly. Falstaff takes the fool's role upon himself when he says: 'This chair shall be my state, this dagger my sceptre, and this cushion my crown.' The Prince's rebuff: 'Thy state is taken for a joined stool, thy golden sceptre for a leaden dagger, and thy precious rich crown for a pitiful bald crown', is, iconographically, a

---

[57] See S. Billington, *A Social History of the Fool* (Brighton, 1984), ch. 1.

Kings, Princes, and Lords   155

reading of the fool–king image in which it is the king not Falstaff under attack.[58]

But Hal is a more active character than a mere expression of disillusion. Bearing in mind that he has no sure traditions to rely on, the value of his wildness is that it allows him to find his own concept of order. In a milder way than Hamlet, there are times when he protects his true thoughts from those around him while he reorganizes his beliefs and allegiances, and, ironically, through studying his companions he develops into an even more pragmatic prince than his father.[59] When Poins tries to interest him in the Gadshill robbery, Hal presents every angle from which they could fail, and it is only when Poins has convinced him of the practicality of the plan that he agrees to it. The circumspect, political judgement over a doubtful venture is a foretaste of his behaviour in *Henry V* over the Salic laws. This can hardly be called a kingly virtue, except in the Machiavellian sense of making success the only criterion. Both Richard II and Bolingbroke were losers in terms of kingship, and in *Henry IV* there are several examples of how and how not to turn a losing game into a winning one. Hotspur tries to read nothing but good into events before his crucial battle. When he hears his father is too sick to attend he responds with bravado:

> I rather of his absence make this use:
> It lends a luster and more great opinion,
> A larger dare to our great enterprise.

> I. IV. i. 76–8

—a conviction he cannot maintain after Vernon's glowing account of Henry's forces. Governed by emotion, not reason, defiance becomes desperation: 'Doomsday is near; die all, die merrily.'[60] Hal himself shows a more truly merry and detached spirit, in response to Falstaff's jibes over fear of danger: 'Not a whit, I lack some of thy instinct.'[61] But it is Falstaff's ability to turn a losing game into a winning one, which appears to fascinate Hal most. Twice he corners the knight with facts which shame him, and each time Hal is eager to

---

[58] For a parallel argument see J. Winney, *The Player King* (London, 1968), pp. 106–14. Cf. N. Sanders, 'The True Prince and the False Thief', *SS* 30 (1977), pp. 29–34.

[59] The 'dark and disturbing' hypocrisy at the core of monarchy seen by S. Greenblatt in 'Invisible Bullets', in J. Dollimore and A. Sinfield (eds.), *Political Shakespeare* (Manchester, 1985), pp. 18–47.

[60] *I Henry IV*, IV. i. 134.   [61] Ibid. II. iv. 367.

156   *Kings, Princes, and Lords*

know how he will extricate himself. After the flight from Gadshill he insists: 'What trick, what device, what starting hole canst thou now find out, to hide thee from this open and apparent shame?'[62] In part 2, Act II, Scene iv, lines 303–5, in the second trap, Hal throws Falstaff's first excuse in Part 1, 'I knew ye as well as he that made ye',[63] back at the knight, defying him to play the same trick. Hal is engaged in a continuing battle of wits to defeat Falstaff publicly, but Falstaff almost always evades him.[64] He combines circumspection with flamboyance; his personality is of a size to see all angles of an argument and instantly pick the one he needs, reinterpreting the facts to put a public gloss on any shameful action, and Hal adopts Falstaff's tactics in the first scene with his father:

> So please your Majesty, I would I could
> Quit all offences with as clear excuse
> As well as I am doubtless I can purge
> Myself of many I am charg'd withal.
>
>   1. III. ii. 18–21

One does not doubt his sincerity. He is, as he said, preparing to 'pay the debt [he] never promised',[65] and he does it without losing face, by rearranging the facts to his own advantage. As, for example, turning defence into attack:

> . . . God forgive them that so much have sway'd
> Your Majesty's good thoughts away from me!
>
>   1. III. ii. 130–41

Though, according to Falstaff's testimony, Hal has committed enough crimes to hang an ordinary man. In the uncertain world Hal inherits, and which has led him to consort with thieves, there is a need to brave out the resulting adverse opinions of him by attributing them to jealous rumour.[66] Falstaff's courage of personality gives Hal

---

[62] *I Henry* IV, II. iv. 259–61.   [63] Ibid. II. iv. 263.

[64] An exception being ibid. I. ii, when Hal declares that in his own reign Falstaff will be hangman not judge. In Lyndsay's *Satire of the Thrie Estates* and Shakespeare's *Measure for Measure* the disreputable fool turns hangman to save his own neck. Falstaff is offered a demotion in the misruled world, which he wishes to impose on the dominant order and to be the controlling lord of, rather than fool in. In their public encounters, Falstaff, by winning, proves he can never be subject to order and perhaps confirms the necessity of his eventual banishment.

[65] *I Henry IV*, I. ii. 204.

[66] '. . . Rumour is a pipe | Blown by surmises, jealousies, conjectures', Induction to Part 2, ll. 15–16.

Kings, Princes, and Lords   157

examples to add to the basic self-assurance already in evidence at the opening of Part 1. Hal's use of sun imagery is quite different from that Bolingbroke used to describe Richard II. Richard appeared:

> As doth the blushing discontented sun
> From out the fiery portal of the East,
> When he perceives the envious clouds are bent
> To dim his glory and to stain the track
> Of his bright passage to the occident.[67]

This is an image of the sun seen from the earth round which it moves, a limited view depending on horizons. Any sun seen to rise will inevitably set. The clouds are active, and behave maliciously and, between horizons and clouds, the sun is helpless, suffering what is done to it. Whereas Hal says:

> Yet herin will I imitate the sun,
> Who doth permit the base contagious clouds
> To smother up his beauty from the world,
> That, when he please again to be himself,
> Being wanted he may be more wonder'd at
> By breaking through the foul and ugly mists
> Of vapours that did seem to strangle him.
>
> *1 Henry IV*, I. ii. 192–8.

The sun here is in control, and it is the earth which is seen from the sun's point of view. Any dimming of its glory is due only to the sun's own volition. Richard was a harassed, passive orb: Hal is an active one. One might suggest that touches of Copernican thinking are introduced into a Pythagorean cosmos, since Hal eliminates the dangerous horizon which will force him to set. This sun is permanent and would be there if the world were not. It is a world greater than our own which permits a dimming of his glory only to break through when he pleases. Were the world falling apart, which it is, yet Hal would remain, as he does, and become a centre of strength. And, as the sun shines not out of duty or remorse, but from generous free will, so Hal will repay his debt in the same spirit. It is also inevitable

---

[67] *Richard II*, III. iii. 63–7. Richard II made particular use of sun imagery in his heraldry; one was the 'sun-burst', the sun coming out from behind clouds, which 'derived from Edward III, and [the second] the "sun-in-splendour"—the full orb surrounded by rays', C. W. Scott-Giles, *Shakespeare's Heraldry* (London, 1950), p. 65.

158   *Kings, Princes, and Lords*

that when he does, squires of the moon will be banished from his orbit.

As James Winney said, the history plays need to be considered more as imaginative than moral and documentary works.[68] Shakespeare replays past events as a kaleidoscope of kingly failings, using the examples and philosophy of mock lords to convey character and catastrophe. This source provided as wide a range of reference as any literary tradition. It was not merely a primitive custom superseded; it was something a literary tradition could never be, the actual impulse behind the dramatic movement of experiencing and finally expelling disorder. And, in the history plays, the concept of the period of play equalling *dis*order is consistently retained. Henry IV's erroneous rule was common knowledge but, in their respective plays, both Henry V and VI also cast doubt on the legitimacy of their accession. Though Henry IV assured Hal he would be free of such qualms, before battle Henry V prays:

> Not to-day, O Lord!
> O not to-day, think not upon the fault
> My father made in compassing the crown!

> *Henry V*, IV. i. 298–300

And Henry VI, whose accession is doubly secure, responds when challenged:

> I know not what to say: my title's weak.

> *3 Henry VI*, I. i. 138

[68] J. Winney, *The Player King* (London, 1968), pp. 9–39.

7

Tamburlaine and *Timon*
Paradigm and Parable

[In the menippea] . . . the most daring and unfettered fantasies
(*fantastika*) and adventures are internally motivated, justified
and illuminated . . . by a purely ideological and philosophical
end, to create *extraordinary situations* in which to provoke and
test a philosophical idea.

Bakhtin, *Problems of Dostoevsky's Poetics*, trans. Rotsel

TAMBURLAINE THE GREAT

In 1587 and 1588, at the same time that political anxieties found
expression in *The Misfortunes of Arthur* and *The Troublesome
Raigne of King John*, the youthful Marlowe turned his back on
national issues to create instead a political situation of his own. On
leaving Cambridge, he invaded the theatre with the first part of
Tamburlaine the Great and, as Harry Levin put it, the confidence of
'the conqueror whose conquests he [had] chosen to dramatise'.[1]
Instead of looking at mythical and historical princes through a
reductive, critical lens, Marlowe magnified his hero unashamedly
and, for the two-part play to work in its entirety, audiences must
retain interest in Tamburlaine's persistent, soaring ambition which
repeatedly defies 'the accumulated wisdom of the ages'.[2] With
consistent boldness Marlowe not only freed English verse from
classical inhibition and jigging rhymes but, as I shall argue, he also
stretched the mock king tradition into a highly affirmative statement.

Tamburlaine was one of the most popular plays in Henslowe's
repertory, despite the unusually simple plot, and was still being
played at the Red Bull in the 1630s.[3] The reason usually given for its
success is the powerful blank verse, yet the play was also criticized for
this in its own time,[4] and equally relevant to its contemporary

---

[1] H. Levin, *The Overreacher* (London, 1954), p. 47.
[2] U. M. E. Fermor, *Christopher Marlowe* (London, 1926), p. 25.
[3] See A. Gurr, *Playgoing in Shakespeare's London* (Cambridge, 1987), pp. 183–4.
[4] Ibid. 137, 183–4.

160   Tamburlaine *and* Timon

popularity is the rather obvious point that its hero is a shepherd who
puts down kings. The subject for the great poetry is an ordinary
man's iconoclastic vision. The attraction of this basic ingredient was
evident in many of the sixteenth-century chronicle accounts of Timur
Khan's life. Not only did most European translators alter his high
birth to a humble one but, following Fregoso's 1518 *Dictis*, the
further fictional addition of Timur elected as a mock king usually
preceded his serious claims to kingship. In 1571 Thomas Fortescue
Anglicized the tradition and (as evidence shows appears in
medieval England) linked rebel with festive activity:

His first beginning was, as writeth *Baptista Fulgotius* [Fregoso], that beyng
the soonne of a poore manne, kepying cattle in the filde, liuyng there with
other boyes of his age, and condition, was chosen in sport by the others for
their kyng, and althought they had made in deede, this their election in plaie,
he whose spirites were rauished, with greate, and high matters, forst theim to
swere to him loialtie in al thinges, obeying hym as king, wher, or when it
should please hym ... After this othe ... he charged eache of theim
forthwith, to sell their troope and cattell ... seeking to serue in warre
accepting hym for capitaine: which indeed they did, beyng quickly
assembled of other worke men, and pastours, to the full number, at leaste, of
fiue hundred.[5]

The realization of his noble destiny here begins in king game and
progresses through outlawry to success, and this dimension needs to
be added to the study of Marlowe's dramatization where, similarly,
Tamburlaine has five hundred followers when he first prepares for
his outlaw defiance of Cosroe. Further evidence for connections with
mock king concepts appears in the 1590 Octavo where the editor
inserted a paragraph to say that he had purposely 'left out some fond
and frivolous gestures, digressing (and in my poor opinion) far
unmeet for the matter ... though (haply) they have been of some
vain, conceited fondlings greatly gaped at, what times they were
showed upon the stage in their graced deformities'.[6] Actual scenes
which also include comic gestures remain in the play, most notably
Tamburlaine's snatching of the crown from Mycetes in Part 1, Act II,
Scene iv, and the course of crowns served up at the banquet in Part 1,
Act IV, Scene iv, lines 108–12. It has been noted that both incidents
are written in prose, a form Marlowe did not usually adopt,[7] and

[5] U. M. E. Fermor (ed.), *Tamburlaine the Great* (London, 1930), p. 288.
[6] Ibid. 66.   [7] Ibid. 104, 154. Notes to ll. II. v. 28–35 and IV. iv. 125–7.

Tamburlaine *and* Timon   161

both can well be described as king game and king emblem jokes.
Bearing in mind the interpolated poor prose in which they are
written, it is possible that Marlowe did not write either. Also, an
interesting textual variant exists in the 1605 edition which suggests
further interpolation. In Part 1, Act 1, Scene ii, line 133 before the
threatened battle between Tamburlaine's five hundred and
Mycetes' two thousand men, Usumcasane urges Tamburlaine,
'Come, let us meet them at the mountain top', whereas the three
earlier printings, 1590, 1593, and 1597, place the projected battle at
the 'mountain foot'.[8] The earlier version avoids crude reliance on
popular tradition, and perhaps also makes more geographic sense,
but the 1605 alteration could well have happened through an actor's
alteration in performance, or because of the printer's familiarity with
popular customs. The changes and inconsistencies in the text suggest
that the fond and frivolous gestures were added touches of primitive
king play, while the mainspring of the action is the 'vulgar error'[9] or
rather popular preference to perceive Tamburlaine as a man of the
people.

   In the opening action, where Usumcasane's advice is found,
Tamburlaine has no need to fight; he wins Theridamas's support
with the bold arguments reiterated throughout the play, including
the assertion that he controls Fortune:

> I hold the Fates bound fast in iron chains,
> And with my hand turn Fortune's wheel about . . .
> . . . Jove himself will stretch his hand from heaven,
> To ward the blow, and shield me safe from harm.
>
>   I. I. ii. 174–81

In his vaunting he claims to be Fortune's surrogate, able to determine
the fates of, and immune to the attacks of, other men. It is a wheel he
claims to hold, though a hilltop setting for it seems not to have been
far from the contemporary mind. And the Jove image with which he
continues recalls the medieval icon of God's hand extending from
heaven and bringing judgment to the earth. This icon was to be used
in 1619 for the title-page of an undoubted king game play, *A King
and No King* (see Frontispiece) and in Marlowe's drama the concept

---

[8] Ibid. 83. Note to l. 1. 1. ii. 133.
[9] Sir Thomas Browne corrected this misconception. See *The Overreacher*, p. 49.
However, the error had been initiated by 16th cent. scholars and again illustrates the
interrelation between high and low cultures.

162   Tamburlaine *and* Timon

is developed into a highly innovative argument. Yet, like Fortescue's
shepherd, Marlowe's hero begins as a summer king. Possibly the
expectations of his audience would not let him depart too far from
popular themes.

When Tamburlaine steps into the sphere of upward action by
exchanging his rustic dress for a suit of armour and vowing chivalric
love to Zenocrate, he is neither proud nor ashamed of his humble
origins but states simply the contradictory combination:

> I am a lord, for so my deeds shall prove,
> And yet a shepherd by my parentage.

> I. I. ii. 34–5

His ambitions are like the extravagant fantasizing of any shepherd:

> . . . these that seem but silly country swains,
> May have the leading of so great an host,
> As with their weight shall make the mountains quake.

> I. I. ii. 47–9

Yet by the end of Part 1 this ambition, including making Zenocrate
his queen with her father's approval, is achieved.

From the point of view of Mycetes' men, Tamburlaine is a rebel
mock lord, providing a focal point for all disaffected outlaws:

> This country swarms with vile outrageous men,
> That live by rapine and by lawless spoil,
> Fit soldiers for the wicked Tamburlaine.

> I. II. ii. 22–4

But authorial sympathy is entirely for the overturning of order, and is
further expressed through the paradoxical character of Mycetes.
Despite his having undisputed right of succession, he is a figure of
fun. He frets about his inability to make speeches, and provokes the
contempt to which he then reacts petulantly.[10] His foolish behaviour
undermines his legitimacy, and at one point his brother, Cosroe,
mocks him with the most primitive of insults, ambiguously telling
him to kiss his 'royal seat'.[11] The implication that in fact Mycetes has
only temporary, waning power appears in the use of moon rather
than sun imagery for him. Theridamas promises to bring him
Tamburlaine, dead or captive, 'Before the moon renew her borrowed

---

[10] See the behaviour of Arbaces, Ch. 8.   [11] I. I. i. 97–8.

A very standard insult: see bare
buttocks in martyrdom of Apollonia miniature etc.

Tamburlaine *and* Timon   163

light'.[12] By contrast, the successful usurper continually appropriates sun imagery. Therefore, at the opening, the examples of achieved and aspiring kingship include polarized opposites: one idiot king with right of succession treated as a mock king, and a man of lowest birth with Titanic attributes, plus Cosroe with ordinary abilities and aspirations of his own. The only other Renaissance play to make rebellion heroic was to be Ford's Caroline drama, *Perkin Warbeck*,[13] and Marlowe's earlier play exceeds in iconoclasm through endorsement of the most grandiose inversions. As J. W. Harper says, Tamburlaine has the eloquence and heroism of Hercules, but the essential difference is that he is not a god.[14] His birth was into the opposite and lowliest section of society yet he does attain, temporarily, the status of a god over his fellow men.

For, in Part 1, Act 1, Scene ii, Tamburlaine claims Jove's protection, yet it proves to be Tamburlaine's arm, not Jove's, which stretches out to remove or protect kings. Before the battle with Mycetes, Cosroe says:

> . . . lift thy lofty arm into the clouds,
> That it may reach the king of Persia's crown.

> 1. II. iii. 52–3

And when Tamburlaine scorns to rob Mycetes of the crown, he foretells that in battle he will 'pull it from thy head'.[15] Afterwards, on stage, Tamburlaine's arm crowns Cosroe. Therefore, not only does he supplant Fortune, turning her wheel, he also supplants Jove even before he has likened himself to him. And, with success, Tamburlaine's behaviour becomes inflexible like the god, rather than fickle like the goddess. The death of the Damascus virgins must take place because the flags have changed to his unforgiving phase, and all men who acknowledge him their superior are supported by him, while those who do not are destroyed. This last characteristic is the opposite to the arbitrary nature of Fortune.

Throughout the play, the men who pit themselves against him are legitimate kings, more outraged by his origins than by his deeds. Despite the fact that Tamburlaine continually proves his godlike power over them, all they perceive is his humble birth. As the Soldan says:

---

[12] Ibid. 69.   [13] See Ch. 1 n. 46.

[14] J. W. Harper, *Tamburlaine, The New Mermaids* (London, 1984), p. xx.

[15] 1. II. iv. 39.

164 Tamburlaine *and* Timon

> That such a base usurping vagabond
> Should brave a king . . .
>
> 1. IV. iii. 21–2

Cosroe too had exclaimed against such disturbance of the cosmic order:

> What means this devilish shepherd to aspire
> With such a giantly presumption,
> To cast up hills against the face of heaven:
> And dare the force of angry Jupiter?
>
> 1. II. vi. 1–4

But the imagery consistently makes the usurper's success inevitable. For example, the opposites, shepherd and lord, which Tamburlaine admitted to at the beginning of the play, are astrologically reconciled, making his success pre-ordained:

> . . . at whose birth
> Heaven did afford a gracious aspect,
> And joined those stars that shall be opposite.
>
> 2. III. v. 79–81

The moral Manichaean view of the world is turned inside out,[16] replacing all rightful lords in the dominant society with the outsider and his cohorts. The kings have no sense of dualism; they cannot reconcile the antitheses of shepherd and king, and they suffer for it. In particular, the cruel punishment inflicted on Bajazeth is that which he himself said was appropriate for Tamburlaine *because* of his origins. A man born as a base slave must be imprisoned like a base slave, but it is Tamburlaine who makes the lord of Africa the slave. And, in a further conjunction of lowest with highest, Tamburlaine realistically acknowledges that before he can rival the gods he has to have popular support; while he behaves to others with invincible strength from above, he admits that his own strength nevertheless comes from those below:

> Though Mars himself the angry god of arms,
> And all the earthly potentates conspire,
> To disposses me of this diadem:

---

[16] See Harper, *Tamburlaine*, p. xxiii.

Tamburlaine *and* Timon 165

Yet will I wear it in despite of them . . .
If you but say that Tamburlaine shall reign.
ALL. Long live Tamburlaine and reign in Asia!

1. II. vii. 58–64

And this appeal to his subordinates recalls the opening suggestion of a mock election. In view of the shepherd's realism, the legitimate kings' reliance on right of succession becomes the greater fantasy.

The plots of Parts 1 and 2 show Tamburlaine facing different challenges which should overcome him, yet continually reversing expectation. According to the two-part play formula, the errors and injustices committed in Part 1 should undermine his position, and Fortune should prove her fickleness by deserting him. Part 2 opens with an event which promises the predictable pattern. Callapine, Bajazeth's son, escapes with the help of his gaoler, Amydas: he is crowned his father's heir and leads the forces against Tamburlaine, secure in the thought that inconstant Fortune will now revert to him:

> We shall not need to nourish any doubt,
> But that proud Fortune, who hath followed long
> The martial sword of mighty Tamburlaine,
> Will not retain her old inconstancy,
> And raise our honours to as high a pitch . . .

2. III. i. 26–30

But this does not happen. Tamburlaine defeats them, despite being personally weakened, mourning the death of Zenocrate, and though Callapine escapes and is ready to conquer after Tamburlaine has died. Another frustrated expectation of defeat comes in the character of Tamburlaine's recalcitrant son, Calyphas. Initially, Calyphas's mockery of his father provides a fresh perspective which could diminish Tamburlaine's stature. It seems Calyphas will be the satirist to expose his father's excesses. Particularly telling is his awareness of the brutality of war:

> I know sir, what it is to kill a man,
> It works remorse of conscience in me,
> I take no pleasure to be murderous,
> Nor care for blood when wine will quench my thirst.

2. IV. i. 27–30

But Calyphas turns out to be a gambler and womanizer, not a moral standard bearer through whom we may judge his father, and it

166   Tamburlaine *and* Timon

becomes inevitable that such weak opposition will neither stir his
father's conscience nor escape the force of Tamburlaine's will. The
execution of Calyphas, by his father, provides another example of
Tamburlaine's godlike, ruthless impartiality. There is no one to
oppose him effectively and even his enemies' subjects bow to him; as,
for example, when Callapine defies Tamburlaine's mockery by
making the one-time gaoler, Amydas, a king. The gesture is like
Tamburlaine's own king-making, yet Amydas asks Tamburlaine's
permission before receiving the proffered crown. The expectation
that Fortune will desert the hero of Part 1 is repeatedly delayed, and
supports the conclusion that Tamburlaine enjoys, primarily, the
godhead of inflexible Jove above that of Fortune. Even as late as Act
v, the degradation of kings continues, with four kings taking turns to
pull his chariot, maintaining, without ironic reversal, the pattern of
Bajazeth's humiliation in Part 1. The description by Theridamas of
Tamburlaine as one who has taken God's place—'That treadeth
fortune underneath his feet, | And makes the mighty god of arms his
slave'[17]—looks like an immutable fact.

However, in Part 2, Act v, Scene iii, he suddenly dies, and the seeds
of the change have to be in Part 2, Act v, Scene i, in the scene of the
burning of the Koran. There are several ways one can interpret cause
and effect. It could be that his challenge to Mahomet, one uttered
many times earlier in the play, at last provokes Mahomet's God to
destroy his enemy. Or it could be that it is the Christian God, which
he at last acknowledges, who destroys him:

> There is a God full of revenging wrath,
> From whom the thunder and the lightening breaks,
> Whose scourge I am, and Him I will obey.
>
> 2. v. i. 181–3

> The God that sits in heaven, if any god,
> For he is god alone, and none but He.
>
> 2. v. i. 199–200

The text allows either reading. Callapine's ally, the king of Amasia,
has a vision of Mahomet supporting their forces as they approach
Tamburlaine, and it was a dramatic tradition for scourges and
revenging agents finally to be destroyed. There is, further, the third
possibility which also finds textual endorsement, that in acknowl-

[17] 2. III. iv. 52–3.

Tamburlaine *and* Timon 167

edging God Tamburlaine divests himself of his own godhead. While
he claimed immortality and invincibility, events supported him.
Once he admits there is someone greater, he becomes vulnerable.
Tamburlaine's own words remove his godlike invulnerability and he
dies. Support for this view can be found in the weight Marlowe
places on the power of words earlier in the play. In Part 1, when
Mycetes sought battle strategy, his adviser recalled the miraculous
Greek myrmidon army, and Mycetes asked if the story were true.
The reply: 'So poets say, my lord', prompted Mycetes to observe:
'And 'tis a pretty toy to be a poet.'[18] Poets make fiction believed for
fact, they make their own realities, and can turn a shepherd into a
king with limitless power. Tamburlaine's power began with the
power of words. He won his first two battles with eloquence, pointed
out to Cosroe by Theridamas: 'You see my lord, what working
words he hath.'[19] These words are, of course, ultimately Marlowe's,
and his poetic fiction ends with an artistic coup when the author
makes his hero undermine his own position, again through the
power of words. Similarly, there is conscious fictionalizing of events
within the play, as for example when Tamburlaine concludes his
moving speech to Zenocrate with the aside: 'Women must be
flattered.'[20] This changes audience perception of events to a more
detached, ironic view, and reduces the serious intention of the play.
As T. S. Eliot said, it is not that the result is comedy, but that the play
'hesitates on the edge of caricature at the right moment'.[21] Conscious
authorial control is inevitably close to parody.

It would be wrong to leave the play without considering further
negative, or moral, judgements on Tamburlaine.[22] His successes
prove to be hollow, and Zenocrate's embalmed body accompanying
him through Part 2 provides a visual symbol of the futility of his
power to conquer, when he is powerless to create.[23] And, even
during Part 1, Zenocrate provided a moral commentary on all his
cruelties. She acted as the good queen opposed to his pride of life.
Despite the play's endorsement of Tamburlaine, we do not lose sight
of humane considerations. And yet the balance ends in Tamburlaine's favour. Commenting on the tournament pattern of the plot,

---

[18] I. II. ii. 53–4.   [19] I. II. iii. 25.   [20] I. I. ii. 107.
[21] Harper, *Tamburlaine*, p. xxiii.
[22] The title-page of the 1590 edn. calls the play 'Two tragicall Discourses'.
[23] Harper, *Tamburlaine*, p. xiv.

168   Tamburlaine *and* Timon

Levin wrote that the 'unseasoned challenger, by defeating the champion, acquires his standing'.[24] No one gains such glory from Tamburlaine; instead his deathbed is 'surrounded with trophies of
conquest', and Zenocrate's body can also be so interpreted in the last
scene.[25] Death's conquest of him is sudden and painless, allowing
him to escape all the moral expectations of suffering and repentance.
Tamburlaine even interprets his death as a transformation to a
heavenly throne. As previous images had suggested, his lowly and
great stars, conjoined, at least take him into the immortality of fame.
Unambiguous admission of defeat is never forthcoming. His last line,
'Tamburlaine, the Scourge of God must die', is preceded by, 'my soul
doth weep to see | Your sweet desires deprived my company':[26] the
tragedy is for those he leaves behind, not for himself. Saturnalian
moral ambiguity even includes such Christ-like echoes from the
anti-Christ. The audience, familiar with the moralizing and repentance of other two-part plays on Fortune, sees instead the reaffirma-
tion of the uniqueness of another kind of shepherd king, who falls so
fast it can be interpreted as a continued triumph: an artistic sleight of
hand to continue the iconoclasms by avoiding the painful decline,
and also sleight of hand consciously confirming the fiction.

   Marlowe's later king play, *Edward II*, is, as Bevington says, more
realistic, with more emphasis on historical accuracy and less 'generic
personification'.[27] Edward does not raise Gaveston above himself,
but only to his own level, creating the king and fool image in Act I,
scene iv, when Gaveston is seated with Edward on the throne. The
strength and realism of the play comes from a resistance to char-
acterize according to expected type. Both Edward and Gaveston are
powerful and believable; neither are ciphers. Gaveston's arrogance is
dangerous, not comic: he is a destructive opposite to order who must
be eliminated. Lancaster's remark in Act I, Scene iv, line 249, 'In no
respect can contraries be true', rejects dualism and supports the
exclusive philosophy found in moral comedies. But, in *Tamburlaine*,
Marlowe allowed the subversive to succeed. He dramatized Renaissance confidence in the reformed concept of Fortune, through the
man who finally overcomes her by interpreting his death as the

---

[24] Levin, *The Overreacher*, p. 52.
[25] 'The conquest of beauty . . . is preserved unwithered in her hearse' (ibid. 72).
[26] 2. v. iii. 247–8.
[27] D. Bevington, *From Mankind to Marlowe* (Cambridge, 1962), pp. 234–5.

Tamburlaine *and* Timon 169

ultimate exaltation by powers who 'mean t'invest [him] in a higher throne'.[28]

THE LIFE OF TIMON OF ATHENS

This later play returns us to the angst of social problems, expressed through the full cycle of Fortune's hill: though, as I shall argue, with a more original twist than at first appears; for instead of the fall reflecting on the main protagonist, larger questions are asked involving communal responsibility. Both Tamburlaine and Timon are untitled men who achieve elevation above their ruling classes, and both characters are written so as to avoid authorial censure in their falls, but Timon, in both his rise and fall, could not provide a greater contrast to the indomitable self-fulfilment of Tamburlaine. The contemporary success of the two plays was similarly different. Whereas *Tamburlaine* features in Henslowe's *Diary* as an audience magnet, it is still debated today whether *Timon* was in fact performed in Shakespeare's lifetime. To this argument I shall be presenting new evidence which argues that it was.

The initial debate to engage with is, however, that of authorship. Until recently, the means of coming to terms with the unevenness of the extant text has been through Chambers's theory that it is Shakespeare's 'unfinished'[29] work. However, it would appear from recent, rigorous analysis[30] that the play was, instead, a collaboration between Shakespeare and Middleton, and it is the addition of Middleton's hand which 'gives the play its irregularity of style'.[31] I shall be working with an acceptance of the evidence that Middleton wrote Act I, Scene ii; Act III, Scenes i–v; Act IV, Scene ii, lines 30–50, and Act IV, Scene iii, lines 458–536.[32] The one major critical study, Rolf Soellner's *Timon of Athens: Shakespeare's Pessimistic Tragedy*, perceptively analyses the play's remorseless, negative vision. He

---

[28] 2. v. iii. 121.

[29] E. K. Chambers, *William Shakespeare* (Oxford, 1930), i. 482. Cf. U. M. E. Fermor, '*Timon of Athens*: An Unfinished Play', *RES* 18 (1942), pp. 270–83.

[30] See D. J. Lake, *The Canon of Thomas Middleton's Plays* (London, 1975); P. J. Macdonald, *Studies in Attribution* (Salzburg, 1979); and R. V. Holdsworth, 'Middleton and Shakespeare', Ph.D. thesis (Manchester, 1982). Cf. W. Wells, 'Timon of Athens', *NQ* 12th ser., 6 (1920), pp. 266–9; H. D. Sykes, *Sidelights on Elizabethan Drama* (London, 1924); and C. Hinman, *The Printing and Proof-Reading of the First Folio of Shakespeare* (Oxford, 1963), ii. 285.

[31] S. Wells and G. Taylor, *William Shakespeare: A Textual Companion* (Oxford, 1987), p. 501.

[32] Holdsworth, 'Middleton and Shakespeare', p. 65.

170   Tamburlaine *and* Timon

comments, however, that the author had a difficult task in making a
tragic hero out of a mysogynist,[33] and I would suggest that the
category of 'tragedy', under which the play was included in the First
Folio,[34] is misleading. Timon's death is an incidental, rather than a
tragic, inevitability: it is his scathing intensity towards Athens's
duplicity which remains memorable, and Alvin Kernan's definition
of 'moral satire'[35] seems closer to the authors' intention.

Like *The Life and Death of King John*, *Timon of Athens* is set in an
age which has travelled far from its ideological source. In *KJ* the
Cardinal initiates Lewis into this fact mid-play: 'How green you are
and fresh in this old world.'[36] In *Timon* the perspective introduces
the play:

POET. . . . how goes the world?
PAINTER. It wears, sir, as it grows.[37]

                                                          I. i. 2–3

At the opening, the two artists are among Timon's followers waiting
to earn his patronage, and the Poet articulates the forthcoming plot
as he relates the tale of his own play offering to Timon. His story
establishes Timon as a summer king, in hilltop terms very similar to
those of Chaucer's *Hous of Fame*:

> I have upon a high and pleasant hill
> Feign'd Fortune to be thron'd. The base o' th' mount
> Is rank'd with all deserts, all kind of natures
> That labour on the bosom of this sphere
> To propagate their states. Amongst them all,
> Whose eyes are on this sovereign lady fix'd,
> One do I personate of Lord Timon's frame,
> Whom Fortune with her ivory hand wafts to her.

                                                          I. i. 65–72

Timon's liberality in Act I can be seen as the wasteful indulgence of a
seasonal king, in his case a citizen raised by his wealth to a status

---

[33] R. Soellner, *Timon of Athens: Shakespeare's Pessimistic Tragedy* (Kent, Ohio, 1979), p. 10.
[34] S. Wells and G. Taylor, *William Shakespeare: A Textual Companion* (Oxford, 1987), p. 501.
[35] A. Kernan, *The Cankered Muse* (New Haven, 1959), p. 203.
[36] III. iii. 145.
[37] At the opening to the *Return from Parnassus*, I. ii. 124, is a similar perspective. The world is 'bald pated': both old and pox ridden.

Tamburlaine *and* Timon   171

beyond his birthright and lasting until his wealth is gone. A lord of misrule or Christmas prince image is inevitable in Act I, Scene ii, when he hosts a banquet which is followed by a masque in his honour. Middleton's stage directions stress obsequious civility to him from men of higher station. When general dancing begins: 'The Lords rise from table with much adoring of Timon.' Such exaggerated courtesies are the mockeries given to a mock king. And, as Fortune's established favourite, Timon becomes her surrogate, dispensing favours to those climbing behind him and who woo him; as, for example, those artists waiting for him at the opening of the play. In Scene i, the Painter points out that the throne, Fortune, and hill of the Poet's creation apply equally to them, Timon's followers:

> . . . one man beckon'd from the rest below,
> Bowing his head against the steepy mount
> To climb his happiness, would be well express'd
> In our condition.
>
> I. i. 75–9

Therefore, the two are there at the beginning to improve their fortunes through Timon, and when the Poet describes his work with a self-deprecating and obsequious simile, 'a gum which oozes | From whence 'tis nourish'd',[38] he indicates what his attitude will be towards any patron. The Painter responds more cynically. After the Poet's effusive praise of his own portrait of Timon, he comments: 'It is a pretty mocking of the life.'[39] The Poet embraces his role as follower, while the Painter ironically concedes. The design of the subsequent plot has the *trompe-l'œil* quality of M. C. Escher's drawings, and can be understood as the traditional work the Poet offers to his benefactor,[40] with its conventional fall in the second half:

> When Fortune in her shift and change of mood
> Spurns down her late beloved, all his dependants
> Which labour'd after him to the mountain's top
> Even on their knees and hands, let him sit down,
> Not one accompanying his declining foot.
>
> I. i. 86–90

---

[38] I. i. 21–2.   [39] Ibid. 35.
[40] Ibid. 244–5. Timon says: 'When dinner's done | Show me this piece.'

172   Tamburlaine *and* Timon

The play which follows is, nevertheless, an original development on this 'common'[41] theme, for it is the followers who prove to be the greater mockeries through their servile and treacherous natures.

Timon's opening bounty, rescuing Ventidius from a paltry debt and providing a dowry so that the young lovers can marry with consent, are socially beneficial acts. He honourably plays out the part that Fortune has blessed him with, helping to raise the weak, patronizing the arts, and giving business to merchants. He is not initially over-credulous: he rebuffs the Jeweller's flattery, and expresses greater faith in painting than does the Painter himself, for surprisingly sceptical reasons. Once drawn, he says, a portrait does not change. It has an integrity which man lacks, for 'dishonour traffics with man's nature'.[42] Here he voices the later opinion of the cynic, Apemantus, who also finds an innocence in the portrait lacking in its maker. Once Apemantus enters, he acts as Timon's sceptical *alter ego*. Timon becomes more credulous in his relationship with society, but he invites Apemantus to comment. And, because of Timon's initial perception, one seeks justification for his later reckless acts, since they must be done with full consciousness of the possible outcome. Is his bounty a test of society to give it the chance to prove the adage wrong, or could Timon be trying to cure man's mercenary nature by providing a different example to follow, or is he, as others later call him, simply a fool?

There is a theory that the wealth brought by trade with the New World produced a changed concept of society.[43] The old pressures of survival were removed, and Utopia seemed within reach for all, if all behaved with equal generosity; if men could sustain the Arthurian brotherhood advocated in inns of court Christmas entertainments, and presented to the court as an example to follow. The idea

---

[41] I. i. 91.

[42] Ibid. 161. Authorial control, as in *Tamburlaine*, here makes Timon a commentator outside his character.

[43] '. . . one is . . . tempted to think that Shakespeare's Timon is modelled on Plutarch's Cimon. Here, for example, is Plutarch's description of the generosity of Cimon: "[it] surpassed even the hospitality and philanthropy of the Athenians of olden time . . . [for] he made his home in the city a general public residence for his fellow-citizens, and on his estates in the country allowed even the stranger to take and use the choicest of the ripened fruits, with all the fair things which the seasons bring. Thus, in a certain fashion, he restored to human life the fabled communism of the age of Chronus—the golden age." ' L. P. S. de Alvarez, '*Timon of Athens*', in J. Alvis and T. G. West (eds.), *Shakespeare as Political Thinker* (Durham, NC, 1981), pp. 161–2. Cf. Kernan, *The Cankered Muse*, p. 199.

Tamburlaine *and* Timon   173

complements the optimism of reformed Fortune pageants which expressed a belief that progress and success could triumph without a fall; a more Utopian interpretation of man's control over Fortune than found in the demagogic success of *Tamburlaine*. And the setting is, ironically, the home of the democratic ideal, Athens, where the idealized, seasonal lord, Timon, tries to bring in a golden age of brotherhood. In Act I, Scene ii, he anticipates with pleasure a time when he will need help, and his friends can repay brotherly love in kind. Although it looks imprudent when he refuses Ventidius's repayment of the debt, he proves that his bounty comes from love and faith, and not commodity; it is fraternal generosity and not a business transaction. His liberality is like Bassanio's in *The Merchant of Venice*, extended to all men, but, in *Timon*, it is shown to be a mistake to confuse the material with the ideal. Apemantus gives the treacherous alternative to Timon's vision. Not only will men consume his goods, but also himself; a thought unconsciously echoed by Timon to Alcibiades: 'You had rather be at a breakfast of enemies than a dinner of friends.'[44] For the world worn with age is far from paradisal, and once the courtly lord of misrule's season is over he is cast out to penury. As Alcibiades jokes, the world is, after all, 'defil'd land'.[45]

The ideals of Act I are set against the reality of Act II, with Apemantus's fool briefly embodying Timon's folly and making the point that, as in *King Lear*, it is better to be fool than knave. Timon is not a peer who falls short morally, but a citizen who loses his wealth foolishly and it is the men of higher birth, who have courted Timon, who are knaves to the point of Jonsonian caricatures. Lucullus grossly rejects the generous philosophy they were only too happy to endorse in Timon: '. . . this is no time to lend money, especially upon bare friendship, without security.'[46] Lucius gives a flattering, obsequious denial and Sempronius pretends affront at not being asked first. One cannot even believe the stranger's outrage at such two-faced behaviour. His assertion that, though not beholden to Timon, he would have supported him, 'so much I love his heart',[47] is not of course borne out.

As Timon begins to fall, post-midsummer analogies are drawn. His fair-weather friends depart,[48] the 'days are wax'd shorter with

---

[44] I. ii. 75.   [45] Ibid. 225.   [46] III. i. 41–3.   [47] III. ii. 81–7.
[48] 'SECOND LORD. The swallow follows not summer more willing than we your lordship. TIMON. [*Aside*] Nor more willingly leaves winter; such summer birds are men' (III. vi. 28–31).

174   Tamburlaine *and* Timon

him', and 'Tis deepest winter in [his] purse'.[49] Timon's ensuing rage
still focuses on the opposition of commodity and faith. His money,
given from the heart, has, after all, been treated materially. Now all
he can do is to mockingly treat that heart in a similar way, and offer it
in payment: 'Cut my heart in sums.'[50] The arguments between
Alcibiades and the Athenians mirror the sàme grievance. Alcibiades
had made Athens wealthy through giving his blood,[51] and now he is
told to suffer the slight he is given as something external to him:

> And ne'er prefer his injuries to his heart,
> To bring it into danger.

III. v. 35–6

Both men, though, do react according to their heart-felt grievances
and Timon mockingly welcomes the Athenian brotherhood of
knaves to the second feast with the line, 'with all my heart'.[52] The
surprise entertainment at this 'banquet' is Timon's attack on them.
The ideal of godlike harmony which the Act I masque had conveyed
is irrelevant, since Timon finds that, instead of this higher pattern,
man follows the lower, bestial model, and in his speech to them he
calls them wolves, bears, and flies. The medieval face of Fortune had
been a grotesque composite of beauty and bestiality and, in *Timon*,
this two-sided image is transferred to man. In Act IV, on leaving
Athens, Timon looks back at his House of Fame and its brutish
inhabitants; 'thou wall | That girdles in those wolves'.[52] It is not
Fortune who is at fault, since Timon, as Fortune, had smiled on
Athens, and had tried to raise her to a new level of social behaviour
where no one need fall, but all be mutually supported. It was the
suppliants who had been Janus-faced and treacherous. In this play it
is man, not Fortune, who is proved to be fickle and, ironically, it is
only those servants who had followed Timon for employment or
commodity, rather than professed friendship, who prove faithful.
After Timon's departure, his servants, like followers of a lord of
misrule, still wear his livery and still show some of his qualities. The
Steward shares out what money he has among the rest before leaving
to serve Timon in his exile. Whatever role Apemantus's fool was
intended to have, the Steward as fool makes a fuller point.

---

[49] III. iv. 11 and 15.   [50] Ibid. 91.
[51] Alcibiades says Timon had also protected Athens with 'sword' as well as
'fortune' (IV. iii. 96).   [52] III. vi. 25.   [52] IV. i. 1–2.

Tamburlaine *and* Timon   175

As an outcast, descending in fortune, Timon's attention is directed downwards, towards roots, a cave, and a grave. But he still has suppliants over whom he retains his own Fortune capability. Instead of being sought in a high palace, it is on the bare earth, as in many of Cousin's illustrations, where he now dispenses ill-fortune, and he uses the gold he finds in the low earth for destructive ends, having discovered that it was the gold and not the giving which was the idol rather than ideal. There is considerable irony in the exposure of each suitor. One of the most interesting is Timon's approval of the 'honest thieves', which cures them of their thievery.[53] As in *Two Gentlemen of Verona*, and some later Jacobean and Caroline dramas,[54] the honest disorder of the outcasts contrasts with the pretence to order within society, and the super-subtle, hypocritical Athenians are beyond cure. The artists, curiously, are the worst. In the same way that their work counterfeits nature, so do the men themselves counterfeit the higher natural instincts of men. And even the satirist, Apemantus, is a part of his society rather than apart from it.[55]

Society in this play is irredeemable, and the final threat which, were it carried out, would make the play a complete satire, is that Athens will fall with Timon. At Act III, Scene vi, line 100 he had called on Athens to sink as well as his own house to burn. Since the city had denied the beneficent gods, Timon leaves it more outlawed than himself, in the hands of the 'prosperous gods, | As thieves to keepers'.[56] However, it was perhaps beyond the dramatic privileges of the time to show Alcibiades razing a city out of private revenge, whether or not Timon and Alcibiades represented Essex,[57] and this fate is averted when Alcibiades is won over by the fair-sounding words of its Senators. The most pessimistic suggestion is that a new cycle of deception is beginning, with Alcibiades taking Timon's place, since no change has taken place in the Athenian outlook. Alcibiades is, perhaps, not so naïve, although in the text there is only the one line, 'Descend, and keep your words',[58] to show it. Finally, the lesson Timon tried to give the world goes unregarded even after his death. The soldier who reads the first epitaph comments that Timon's 'fall the mark of his ambition is':[59] a conventional and inaccurate gloss on events. Timon's ambitions had not been for

---

[53] An example of 'the moral and regenerative purpose of satire', Kernan, *The Cankered Muse*, p. 156.
[54] See Conclusion.   [55] Kernan, *The Cankered Muse*, pp. 202–3.
[56] v. i. 182–3.   [57] See n. 71.   [58] v. iv. 64.   [59] v. iii. 10.

176   Tamburlaine *and* Timon

himself but for humanity, and his fall is a mark of mankind's failure rather than of his own.

Curiously, Marston's satire of 1600, *Jack Drum's Entertainment*, contains one direct and two indirect references to Timon. If one believes his Prologue's promise not to make Ben Jonson's mistake[60] of giving his audience anything archaic:

> [He] vowes not to torment your listning eares
> With mouldy fopperies of stale Poetry,
> Vnpossible drie musty Fictions—

the allusions cannot have been to Lucian's dialogue, but rather to something the audience was familiar with. This raises the possibility that Marston was playing off audience knowledge of a recent production of *Timon*. Marston's play is known to contain satire of his contemporary, Ben Jonson. The character, Brabant Signior, was a savage caricature of him, and another, Planet, is a send-up of the stage satirist, prevalent at the time largely through Jonson's influence. However, Planet ends one eruption of bad temper with a reference to the character not in Jonson's work: 'Come, come, now I'le be as sociable as *Timon* of *Athens*' (B. 4[r]). Since Planet's speech ends here, the only way to give meaning to the line is if it were followed by a grimace or a howl in imitation of Timon which, it was assumed, the audience would recognize and appreciate. Brabant Junior follows Planet's line by calling him a droning sackbutt, and the observation that, since Planet was going to be like Timon, he will take him to an assembly of knaves at his elder brother's house.[61] Planet continues with a thrust at Brabant Signior, or Jonson, for behaving in a way opposite to Timon; putting down his guests in a superior manner:

> ... [who] makes costly suppers to trie wits ...
> That leades his Corkie Iests to make them sinke
> Into the eares of his Deryders.
>
> B. 4[r]

Brabant Signior is host of the off-stage subplot, and hardly appears until the end. In the main plot, the host is Sir John Fortune who oversees events from his, i.e. Fortune's, house. The house stands at the top of Highgate Hill; all the characters are his guests, and his

---

[60] See App. 2.

[61] 'Along with me *then* [emphasis added], you droming *sagbutt*, I'le bring thee to a Crewe' (fo. B. 4[r]).

Tamburlaine *and* Timon 177

bizarre liberality enables the comic resolution of the play. He is a deliberate and obvious surrogate of Fortune in her beneficent mood or reformed style, behaving generously to those depending on him from a hilltop house of Fortune. It seems clear that he is a parody of someone's staging of Timon. The character as seasonal host would have been well enough recognized without references to another variation on it, yet there are Timon allusions. It might be argued that Marston's butt could have been the character in the anonymous *Timon* who, like the hero under consideration, is also conceived of as a seasonal lord. Dyce dated the hand of the extant text as about 1600, and Bulman has more recently argued for 1602.[62] But there are some very academic qualities in the farce, such as lines written in Greek, which go beyond the archaisms any author would offer a public audience. Further features, such as rustic speech and the entirely conventional pattern in it of a rise and fall from Fortune, are strongly indicative of the 1580s. Finally, I doubt that an anonymous author would have provided a sufficiently interesting target for Marston's wit. Rather, the academic play might have provided the later playwrights with a model, and general interest in satires in the late 1590s could have led to a scholarly revival of it.[63]

The final and most conclusive piece of evidence that Marston was satirizing the play which ended up in the Shakespeare Folio of 1623 comes from the Usurer who criticizes Sir John's largesse and implies that he risks Timon's fate:

> . . . you keep too great a house . . .
> Go too you do, yon same dry throated huskes
> Will suck you vp, and you are ignorant
> What frostie fortunes may benumme your age,
> Pouertie, the Princes frowne, a ciuile warre.
>
> A. 4[4]

The first part of this is the message Apemantus dins into Timon's ears, and is not in the anonymous text, while the last part is a

---

[62] A. Dyce (ed.), *Timon* (London, 1842), p. v. J. C. Bulman, in 'The Date and Production of "Timon" Reconsidered', *Shakespeare Survey*, 27 (1974), pp. 111–27, points to an allusion to a tavern not opened until 1602.

[63] Dyce notes that the stage direction at the opening of v. ii for 2 spades was changed to 3, indicating that in performance 3 were found necessary, *Timon*, p. vi. The contemporary allusion Bulman discovers could have been part of the text's updating. I find it hard to believe that an author in 1602 would return to an archaic style without any innovations; see e.g. Ford's *The Queen*, Ch. 8.

178   Tamburlaine *and* Timon

summary of the end of the Middleton–Shakespeare play: civil war
also does not come into the *Timon* farce. And, to return to Planet's
line, the name of the character he imitates is 'Timon of Athens',
which suggests the Middleton–Shakespeare text rather than the
farce, whose title is *Timon* and where the text only incidentally
names the city.

   This evidence, which it is difficult to ignore, does however introduce problems of its own, though some are alleviated by the identification of dual authorship. Firstly, the uneven mixture of prose and
verse is accounted for by the evidence that Middleton wrote the
sections in which they occur. No longer need one conclude that the
text was not finished, and therefore probably not performed. As
Wells and Taylor say, the conclusion that *Timon* 'was abandoned
unperformed is mere speculation', particularly as a similarly uneven
work of collaboration, *1 Henry VI*, 'clearly did reach the stage'.[64]
Further textual objections, which may be raised to an earlier date for
the play, are the free verse in those parts written in Shakespeare's
hand, and similarities which have been found between *Timon* and
King Lear. With regard to the first point, it is true that *Timon* is very
much freer than *Julius Caesar*, but it is in fact very similar to the style
of *As You Like It*. Agnes Latham notes that the free verse in *As You
Like It* has itself sometimes been found a problem: 'The blank verse
shows considerable metrical freedom. It has puzzled early editors,
who demanded more regularity than they found. Some of the lines
can be smoothed by a slight rearrangement but there is no reason to
suppose that Shakespeare wanted a high polish.'[65] But there is no
doubt that *As You Like It* was written about 1600. With regard to
the second point, it is reasonable to point out that in all his work
Shakespeare constantly reinterpreted themes. *Timon* has aspects in
common with *Lear, John, Two Gentlemen*, and *Merchant of Venice*,
and probably with others, while *Merchant* has mercy in common
with *Lear*. In the past, similarity with *Lear* has dominated criticism,
but I cannot dismiss very telling similarities with *John*. Satire is a
large part of both, and the strongest criticism of their leading
protagonists is the same: Timon and John have both been said to be
'colourless and neutral'.[66] I would argue that both are play-acting

   [64] Wells and Taylor, *William Shakespeare*, p. 501.
   [65] Arden edn., p. xviii.
   [66] Fermor, 'Timon of Athens', p. 283. See Ch. 5 n. 15 for similar criticism of King
John.

being king or lord, and that the theme behind each rather than their characters was uppermost in the authors' minds. And, because themes constantly reappear throughout Shakespeare's work, such similarity cannot be used as evidence for dating either way.

It might be further questioned whether Shakespeare would have collaborated with Marston in 1601 after Marston had ridiculed his work. However, it is generally agreed that Marston attacked Shakespeare's 'Rape of Lucrece' in his *Scourge of Villany*, and this did not prevent the later collaboration. Jonson himself was to collaborate with Marston in 1605 for *Eastward Ho*. Leishman also tells us that the Chamberlain's Men might have been constrained by circumstances to co-produce *Satiromastix*.[67]

The argument that Middleton wrote this in collaboration removes, I think, the objection that 1600 is too early for him. In 1599, he published his verse satire, *Micro-Cynicon: Six Snarling Satyres*,[68] which shows his involvement with the genre at this time, and even suggests the final mood of Timon. Middleton left Oxford, without completing his degree, between 28 June 1600 and February 1600–1,[69] and the scenario I am left with is of his racing hotfoot to London at the end of June 1600 with his play sketch in his pocket, which is not impossible. Nor is it impossible that he had already made contact with the Chamberlain's Men before breaking off his studies.[70] Similar preparatory moves are made by undergraduates today. For, despite the problems, one has to take Marston's play into account. This indicates that there was a public and failed performance of a *Timon* play close enough to the appearance of *Jack Drum's Entertainment* for Marston's allusions to make sense to the audience, and the text of *The Life of Timon of Athens* best matches those allusions. 1600 was the period of political ferment surrounding Essex,[71] and of theatrical ferment surrounding Jonson's departure from the Chamberlain's Men; either or both of which could have enticed Middleton

---

[67] *Three Parnassus Plays*, ed. Leishman, pp. 56, 370.

[68] Holdsworth, 'Middleton and Shakespeare', p. iii, and A. H. Bullen, *The Works of Middleton* (London, 1886), viii. 28 June is near midsummer.

[69] Lake, *Canon of Thomas Middleton's Plays*, p. 22.

[70] See Ch. 10 p. 221 for the possibility it was Apr.–May 1600 when Middleton's idea was bought by the Chamberlain's Men.

[71] H. J. Oliver, ed. of the Arden edn., p. xxiii, reasonably finds D. Wecter's theory that Shakespeare wrote a full 5-act drama about the 'crying injustice of the Essex affair'—which was later mutilated because of its dangerous politics—implausible. Yet there are parallels with Essex's situation. See Ch. 10.

into throwing his own fortune upon an idea based on current events. The result was a not too successful contribution to the satiric trends of the time, in competition with, or stimulated by, Ben Jonson.

This satire is conceived of in popular English, rather than in classical or urban form and, unlike Shakespeare's adept use of tradition in other plays, the plot follows a strict summer king formula. The result is an under-characterized and over-schematized scathing view of the principle of court patronage. Middleton as a young man, like Marlowe as a young man, appears to have first exercised his dramatic talents by adapting a popular play concept. Though Middleton was less successful, both *Tamburlaine* and *Timon* stand out as unique experiments in daring and unfettered fantasies, such as Bakhtin described, to express the validity of a mock king above his fallible society, and even world.

8

Comedy

> In short ... the multitude ... love nothing that is right and
> proper. The farther [comedy] runs from reason or possibility
> with them, the better it is ... This is truly leaping from the stage
> to the tumbril again.
>
> B. Jonson, *Timber*

Comedy springs from the festive celebration of disorder, and there
are two alternative comic attitudes one might take towards it.
Inversion of order might be seen to be morally dangerous and,
though entertaining, be finally expelled with a sense of relief, or, as
John Stow first suggested regarding midsummer shows, it might be
seen as a temporary, necessary relaxation of laws to enable social
regeneration.[1] However, perhaps comic disorder is most telling
when a mixture of the two. Although, in Shakespeare's most saturnalian play, *A Midsummer Night's Dream*,[2] the hidebound, legalistic
attitude of Hermia's father is finally overruled by Theseus, and the
lovers' confusion in the forest is a necessary part of their maturation,
yet the betrayals and quarrels of the night-time flight are not in
themselves the stuff of social improvement. They are only the means
of obtaining self-knowledge upon which to build that improvement.
The lovers' own sense of relief on waking in Act IV is palpable, and
though it is stressed that the fairies can appear in daylight, and so are
not evil, yet the dangerous possibilities of the night-time world they
govern give a stronger quality to the eventual comic resolution.
Whereas, in *The Shoemakers' Holiday*, the actions of the misrule
lord, Simon Eyre, are divested of any danger, and it is necessary for
him to be elevated into a position of authority in order to intervene
and bring about a harmonious ending for the lovers. And, in *Twelfth
Night*, the order figure, Malvolio, is as dangerous as his disordered
opponents.

---

[1] 'Neighbours ... being before at controuersie were there by the labour of others,
reconciled and made of bitter enemies, louing friendes ...', J. Stow, *A Survey of
London*, ed. C. L. Kingsford (Oxford, 1908; repr. 1971), 101.

[2] See C. L. Barber, *Shakespeare's Festive Comedy* (Princeton, 1959), pp. 119–62.

182   *Comedy*

Within each saturnalia, leaders continually change, as in the anonymous *Timon*. The host of *A Midsummer Night's Dream*, Theseus, gives way to his wilder double or opposite, Oberon, and in Acts III–IV the clown, Bottom, becomes temporary king.[3] In *The Shoemakers' Holiday*, Eyre's rise in the outside world leaves the fool, Firk, to instigate further comic action, and, in *Twelfth Night*, Sir Toby gives way to the fool, Feste, for the Act IV punishment and rescue of Malvolio. The reign of folly naturally invites the rule of fools, though the plays are less concerned with the leaders than with the absurdities taking place under their aegis.

In overtly moral pieces there is less shape-shifting. The early Elizabethan, political morality, William Wager's *The Longer Thou Livest the More Fool Thou Art*, shows a recalcitrant fool, Moros, progressing through life. For a Protestant play it contains an interestingly unreformed and medieval figure of Fortune, who enters at the height of Moros's physical powers, or pride of life. Angered by Reformation disbelief in her, and to prove she still has arbitrary control, she raises him to the position of lord. Like the bad fairy she punishes mankind for ignoring her, by placing 'a popish fool . . . in a wiseman's seat',[4] so making the festive inversion a social threat. Moros's brief reign, with Wrath, Cruelty, Impiety, and Ignorance, is ended when the hand of God removes him. The stage directions read with the graphic simplicity of play: 'Strike *Moros* and let him fall down.'[5] Saturnalia in this play is an unregenerative and devilish alternative to order which has to be dismissed to the nether regions. Here, and, more humorously, in Morality plays for festive occasions, such as *Mankind* (*c.*1466) and the Elizabethan *Misogonus*, the moral runs counter to the leaders of inversion in it and works to expel them.[6] *Misogonus* was written for the Christmas season, and the fool, Cacurgus, has a largely licensed role. He plays master of ceremonies, presiding over the actual play's performance and, within it, works to prolong the period of misrule in the house over which he has control. The moral characters work in opposition to him to restore harmony and order, and when they succeed Cacurgus is expelled from the house.

---

[3] See E. Rickert, 'Political Propaganda and Satire in *A Midsummer Night's Dream*', *MP* 21 (1923), pp. 67–87.   [4] Ed. M. Benbow (London, 1967), p. 46, l. 1065.
[5] Ibid. 71.
[6] For a fuller study of their leaders, see S. Billington 'The Fool and the Moral in English and Scottish Morality Plays', in F. S. Andersen *et al.* (eds.), *Popular Drama in Northern Europe in the Later Middle Ages* (Odense, 1988), pp. 123–7.

Comedy 183

By contrast (and as I have already suggested), *moral* fool–lord leadership seems to have been devised by Robert Greene for his romance, *The Honorable Historie of Frier Bacon, and Frier Bongay* (*c.*1589). Greene's play is full of intellectual interrelations between the disorders of love, knowledge, and power. The fool, Ralph, begins by epitomizing the lack of moral order in Prince Edward but, eventually, he also points to the controlling dangers of necromancy in the main plot.

The play opens with the subplot where the Prince of Wales is 'malecontent', dishonourably in love with the country girl, Margaret. Ralph speaks familiarly and disrespectfully to him, and offers an Erasmian[7] solution: 'Marrie sirha Ned, thou shalt put on my cap, and my coat and my dagger, and I will put on thy clothes, and thy sword, and so thou shalt be my foole.'[8] Ralph is there to embody and play upon the folly of his master who is, morally, the greater fool. Edward takes his advice and while he, in disguise, pursues Margaret using Bacon's necromancy to help him, he orders Ralph to masquerade as himself at court.[9] While he negotiates with Bacon, Ralph leads the rest in a riot in Oxford, explicitly on Edward's orders: 'Ermsbie, take the foole, | Let him be maister and go reuell it.'[10] It is quite obvious that Ralph is Edward's substitute, or lord of misrule, playing out the disorder of Edward's behaviour, particularly the public repercussions of his private folly for, as well as threatening the ruin of Margaret, he has turned his back on the arrangements for his own marriage. When challenged by the masters of Brazenose College, Ralph's claim to be the Prince of Wales is upheld rather than discredited in the interrogation, since the 'braue and wise gentleman'[11] the Masters expect has nothing in common with the prince we have seen.

The second lord of misrule, in relation to Edward, is Friar Bacon, who is promised 'liuing and lands to strength thy colledge state'[12] if he succeeds in winning Margaret to Edward's lawless love. Further, Bacon also takes over the rule of Brazenose. The Masters come to

---

[7] 'Quid igitur postulas, ut princeps, qui ridet morione[m], commutet cum illo uestem?', D. Erasmus, *Familiarum Colloquorum* (Basle, 1543), p. 336.

[8] *The Honorable Historie of frier Bacon and frier Bongay* (London, 1594), Malone Society Reprints, ed. W. W. Greg (Oxford, 1926), fo. A. 3ᵛ.

[9] Though in fact they are next seen together at Oxford where Edward plays the fool to Ralph's Edward.

[10] Fo. C. 4ʳ.   [11] Fo. D. 3ᵛ.

[12] Fo. C. 3ᵛ.

184 Comedy

confirm his ambitious plans for England and despite Bacon's greeting, 'maisters of our Academicke state | That rule in Oxford',[13] by the end of the scene Bacon combines a similar phrase with his own assumption of authority:

> Thus rulers of our Accademicke state,
> You haue seene the Frier frame his art by proofe:
> And as the colledge called Brazennose,
> Is vnder him and he the maister there:
>
> fo. B. 4[r]

Brazenose College, as well as the prince, has put itself under the control of devilish powers, therefore Ralph's disrespect to the learned Doctors who arrest him is as appropriate a reflection on them as it is on Edward, for the greatest threat to order lies in Bacon's attempt to usurp God's power, even though for patriotic purposes, by securing England with a wall of brass. Not only is Bacon his college's, but he even threatens to become England's, lord of misrule. If his necromancy succeeds, then his actual power would be greater than that of the ordained King Henry, who draws audience attention to the fact that England is fortressed by the natural protection of the sea.[14] Bacon aims at creating an unnatural and unnecessary fortress, supplanting God's natural organization. Power over devils is repeatedly claimed by him as, for example, when he shows Edward his cell or study and calls it his 'consistorie court, | Wherein the diuels pleads homage to his words',[15] and where the disguised king's son is himself another suitor. The black arts practised at his court comprise all immorality, subsuming Edward's disordered behaviour under Bacon's own. The public riot in Oxford is joined by Miles, Bacon's comic servant, thus making explicit the connection between lesser and greater threat to moral and universal order. Yet since Miles lets Bacon down, the dangerous possibilities of the tricks shown on stage are reduced to entertaining displays appropriate for a university seasonal lord (as skilled as the accused magician John Dee), and of course all that it is humanly possible to stage.

The festive fluidity of leadership takes on a moral meaning.

[13] Fo. B. 1[v].
[14] 'Speaking to his Spanish and German guests: | Great men of Europe, monarks of the West, | Ringd with the wals of old *Oceanus*, | Whose loftie surges like the battelments, | That compast high built Babell in with towers, | Welcome my lords . . . | To Englands shore, whose promontorie cleeues, | Shewes Albion is another little world . . .' (fo. C. 1[v]). [15] Fo. C. 4[r].

Comedy

Princely power is usurped by the more entertaining black arts, which are then exposed as riotous folly. And, as well as multiple misrule lords, there are direct competitors for Bacon's dominant role. Bungay is an ineffectual one, while the more formidable Vandermast is, in sport, offered a 'coronet of choicest gold'[16] by King Henry, if he proves successful in competition against Bacon. Even the king has unintentionally acknowledged the power of the magic arts, and the contest proves Bacon's superiority without his even engaging in it. Comic though the interlude is, it confirms that Bacon is powerful, and were Miles not to let him down, England would be placed under the opposite power to God's, resulting in a devilishly inverted nation.

In the romantic subplot is a separate competition, for Margaret, between Edward in Robin Hood green, and Lacy, the Earl of Lincoln, dressed in rustic grey, who is sent by Edward to woo Margaret for him. Bungay works on behalf of the true lovers, and he tests Lacy with a moral allegory, pretending that his leaving court in disguise has been interpreted by Henry as rebellion:

> *Lacie* the Earle of Lincolne is late fled
> From Windsor court disguised like a swaine,
> And lurkes about the countrie heere vnknowne.
> Henrie suspects him of some trecherie,
> And therefore doth proclaime in euery way.
> That who can take the Lincolne earle, shall haue
> Paid in the Exchequer twentie thousand crownes.
>
> fo. D. i^v

But Lacy's love is honourable, and it is the rebel, Edward, who, like a medieval outlaw, accuses Lacy of betraying him. Allusions to the treacherous disorder of rebellion complement the riotous disorder of Ralph to exemplify forbidden, destructive, and inverted values.

The central, spectacular and comic scene, of Miles underestimating the significance of the brazen head's words, causes the loss of all Bacon's powers, and the moral resolution of both plots instantly begins with the prince returning to court for his bethrothal. Bacon, however, speaks of his own good fortune being over:

> My life, my fame, my glorie, all are past:
> Bacon, the turrets of thy hope are ruind downe.
>
> fo. G. 3^r

---

[16] Fo. C. 2^r.

186   Comedy

His *Ira Fortuna*, however, allows the fortunate happy ending, with a restitution of natural order in which Bacon himself repents and is regenerated, and where the only person finally raised in fortune is the pure and virtuous Margaret.[17] She had resisted all but the innocent fair-day participation in saturnalia. Since her progress from there, in reaction to Lacy's test of her, had been towards a convent life, it is her abstention from disorder which is rewarded. This comedy quite consciously uses the principle of tension between morally irreconcilable, rather than interdependent, opposites, and once disorder is defeated an almost neo-classic happy ending can ensue. While using comic disorder as entertainment, the ethics are strongly anti-comic.

Chapman's *An Humorous Day's Mirth* (1597) and Marston's *Jack Drum's Entertainment* (1600) function entirely on the affirmative but somewhat trivial use of mock lords. In *An Humorous Day's Mirth*, the fool, Lemot, who has a humour for words, spins the tale and manipulates the plot. He says he will 'sit and point out all his humorous companions . . . like an old King in an old fashion play, having his wife, his counsel, his children, and his foole aboute him, to whome he will sit and point very learnedly'.[18] Although it is he who presides over the action in such a way that other characters are mere ciphers to his will, the end is resolved by the intervention of an explicit king, with the excuse that Lemot caused quarrels and discord; 'but to make you mery in the end'.[19] The last scene of reconciliation and marriage includes a coda of reformed Fortune. The maid, Jaquena, is asked to impersonate the goddess, and her persona is one whose power is entirely beneficent, handing out gifts and unambiguous promises of good fortune to the other characters. By 1597, two years before Elizabeth's masque, this figure had been fully recuperated, within the context of a permissive and optimistic attitude to festive disorder.

Marston's *Jack Drums Entertainment: or the Comedie of Pasquill and Katherine* is a little more subtle, though, as already said, the Prologue also promises the audience something easy to watch. The play opens with a morris dance coming up the hill to Highgate, where

---

[17] After Lacy's test of her steadfastness—choosing a convent when he pretends that after all he is unable to marry below him—she is proved worthy to rise to his level.
[18] Malone Society Reprint, ed. W. W. Greg (Oxford, 1937), fo. A. 2ᵛ.
[19] Ibid. fo. G. 2ᵛ. The play concludes (fo. H. 2ʳ) with 'KING. . . . here I solemnly invite you all *home* to my court.' My emphasis indicates a conscious pretence to kingship.

Comedy 187

stand Sir Edward Fortune's house and its owner, to receive the dancers and their followers. Before the morris enters, there is the offstage cry '*A Lord, a Lord, a Lord, who!*',[20] and it becomes clear in the subsequent action that Sir Edward is this lord, to whom the dancers are travelling. The whole play which follows is his entertainment, and, as well as the contemporary satire, including some opening satire of court satire,[21] it contains a conflict between Sir Edward's positive saturnalia, and the evil disorder of the covetous, antifestive, Shylock-like[22] Mammon, as he tries to murder and enchant his way to one of Sir Edward's daughters. Though he expresses explicit antifestive sentiments, his magical tricks necessarily contribute most to the comic effects of this absurdist play, until his devilish powers are pantomimically destroyed at the end of Act III, after which he runs mad and exits to Bedlam. The effects of his spells are not countered until Act V, and the eventual happy resolution comes about arbitrarily, under the auspices of the joke-playing, sack-swilling, Sir Edward. Unlike Wager's and Greene's plays, saturnalian disorder is approved and, once the devilish disorder of Mammon is expelled, even the satirist, Planet, thaws and joins in the search for a wife.[23] The final trick is against the second antifestive figure, the parody of Jonson, Brabant Signior, who tries to make a fool of a Frenchman which results in his being cuckolded by him. Brabant is crowned at the end, with a horn bound on to a coronet, for giving the participants in the play the best entertainment: 'Now you Censurer | Be the ridiculous subiect of our mirth.'[24] The non-participating character turns himself into chief fool, like Malvolio, and is here made final king. Neither this play nor Chapman's add up to great theatre, but their popular patterns, used toward comic ends, seem to have guaranteed them some success.

In a period which saw continual innovation, playwrights increasingly departed from bucolic patterns. For example, the city

---

[20] Old English Drama, students' facsimile (London, 1912), fo. A. 3ᵛ. See Ch. 2 n. 78.

[21] 'SIR EDWARD. What newes at court; ha, ha, now Iesu God . . . what newes at court? | Reprobate fashion, when each ragged clowt, | Each Coblers spawne and yeastie bowzing bench, | Reekes in the face of sacred maiestie | His stinking breath of censure . . .' (fo. A. 3ʳ).

[22] The tearing of his usurer's bonds results in the parodic: 'Alas my Obligations, my Bonds, my Obligations, my Bonds, Alas, alas, alas' (fo. F. 3ʳ).

[23] This, rather more than *An Humorous Day's Mirth*, combines summer kings and wooing play.   [24] Fo. I. 3ʳ.

188   Comedy

comedies of Dekker, apart from *The Shoemakers' Holiday*, are based
on more naturalistic and less metaphoric actions, although *The
Honest Whore* retains in its second part the satiric retreading of
ground optimistically covered in Part 1. Middleton, too, was to
introduce greater realism in his work, but mock lord patterns were a
mode to which he returned in *A Game at Chess*, and which other
playwrights also used when relevant. It is even possible that Ben
Jonson, in his early satires, intended an English rusticated *vetus
comoedia*, rather than the classical Greek. Jonson's own description
of *Every Man Out of his Humour*,[25] and other contemporary uses of
the Latin phrase, suggest a domestic modification through 'older
forms of English drama', as C. R. Baskervill first observed.[26] Complementary to this is Peter Womack's description of Volpone's
bedroom as a 'travesty court', which also points to an ingenious
redeployment of native satiric patterns.[27] In *The Alchemist*, contend-
ing leaders misrule the house in the master's absence, playing out
each gull's fantasy, including Mammon's to become lord of the
philosopher's stone with Doll, his lady. And, as Ian Donaldson has
ably shown, *Epicoene* and *Bartholomew Fair* are also conceived of as
mundi inversi.[28] *Bartholomew Fair* in particular presents the fair as a
microcosmic inverted world where would-be authorities in law,
education, and religion compete for the most ridicule. The conclusion, 'we'll ha' the rest o' the play at home',[29] with Justice Overdo
placed in the role of host, connects the failed authority shown in the
play with that of the outside world. The frailities of Adam are to be
continued, despite the end of the disordered interlude, and neither
audience nor reader can escape association with them. *Bartholomew
Fair* is at one and the same time the most forgiving, and the most
inclusive of Jonson's satires.

The great Renaissance comedies combine so many strands of
thought that the loss of one does not necessarily impair the plays'
impact on a later audience. However, one casualty of lost mock king
traditions, which is worth recuperating, is Beaumont and Fletcher's
A King and No King. Without the completed patterns, the play's

---

[25] See App. 3.   [26] See App. 3.

[27] 'The king wears a nightcap instead of a crown; the courtiers wish him, not long
life, but immediate death; the most favoured suitors are chosen for their exceptional
avarice and stupidity; the court masque is a freak show in praise of folly; and so on',
P. Womack, *Ben Jonson* (Oxford, 1986), p. 73.

[28] I. Donaldson, *The World Upside Down* (Oxford, 1970), chs. 1–3.

[29] v. vi. 110–11.

Comedy   189

combination of positive saturnalia and evil disorder does not make
sense, and historical accident has helped further distort our understanding of it.

When it was entered in the Stationers's Register in 1618, it was
simply called 'A play', which recalls the precedent set by Beaumont in
the Prologue to his first and solo work, *The Woman-Hater*:

> I dare not call it Comedie or Tragedie; 'tis perfectly neyther;
> A Play it is, which was meant to make you laugh.[30]

And no indication of genre was made in the Revels' Office entry of
the first performance at court on St Stephen's Night 1611,[31] nor on
the title-page of editions from 1619 to 1676.[32] But, increasingly,
during the early seventeenth century, it became associated with
England's social tragedy. The printer of the 1631 edition inserted the
couplet,

> A Play and no Play, who this Booke shall reade,
> Will judge and weepe, as if 'twere done indeed.[33]

This refrain was included in all editions up to and including the
interregnum, and was omitted at the Restoration, showing that it
sprang from the title's evocative connection with the fortunes of the ✓
House of Stuart. Yet, though the title was flaunted for political
reasons in the decade prior to Charles I's execution,[34] it did not
evoke the same tragic sense in the victim's mind (nor in that of his
wife[35]). The sole pre-Restoration, generic comment comes from the
Monarch's hand who, in 1642, called it 'a Comedie'.[36] However, a
near-tragic interpretation of it has persisted ever since, with aesthetic
perception replacing the social.

The plot concerns the resolution of an action begun before the play

---

[30] *The Woman-Hater*, ed. G. W. Williams, p. 157, ll. 10–12, in *Dramatic Works*, i.

[31] *The Works of Francis Beaumont and John Fletcher: Variorum Edition* (London,
1904), i. *A King and No King*, ed. R. W. Bond, pp. 245, 247.

[32] Ibid. 244.   [33] Ibid.

[34] L. Hotson, *The Commonwealth and Restoration Stage* (New York, 1962),
pp. 6, 26, 29.

[35] In a remarkable letter from Queen Henrietta Maria to Charles in 1642–3,
regarding the bombardment of her ship by parliamentarian forces, she prefaces the
account of her personal adventures with the jocular sentence 'il fault vn peu que je
fasse le capitaine bassies [Bessus] et parle de moy mesme'. M. R. Toynbee, 'Le
Capitaine Bessus', *Times Literary Supplement*, 14 July 1950.

[36] See P. Simpson, 'King Charles the First as Dramatic Critic', *Bodleian Quarterly
Record*, 8: 92 (1936–7), pp. 257–62.

190   *Comedy*

begins. Arane, Queen Mother of Arragonia, having despaired of children of her own, pretends to give birth to a child, Arbaces. A long war with Armenia ensues, during which Arbaces grows up and leads Arragonia's forces. The play opens with Arbaces' victorious return, leading the noble prince of Armenia, Tigranes, as his captive. Arbaces then falls in love with his supposed sister, Panthea, and, although he has promised her to Tigranes, has them both imprisoned while he attempts incest. The resolution of the play comes about with the discovery that Arbaces is neither king, nor Panthea's brother. Like other saturnalian plays the resolution has less to do with linear plot development than with character reaction to situation,[37] and one quotation shows how far from comedy critical evaluation has gone.

> The horror felt by Mardonius [the honorable captain], Panthea and Arbaces himself at the passions which have engulfed him creates an atmosphere of evil, scarcely relieved by the clowning of the despicable Bessus [the dishonourable captain]. When Arbaces first appears on stage he is like a man possessed by some evil spirit which is counter-acting his native goodness. By the time of his fatal [or near-fatal] interview with Panthea he is tortured by the sense of an almost intangible power forcing him towards sin—a power which he describes as flame and venom and plague. And yet, miraculously, he remains unconsumed by the evil atmosphere . . . Despite its terrifying imminence, it is never truly manifested in his actions, and in the end it vanishes, leaving no trace.[38]

This is a profound perception of the dramatic strength of Arbaces' personal disorder, but of course, if Arbaces is not rightful king, he is unwitting usurper, countenancing bacchanalian disorders. This makes the plot from the very opening a series of 'twists and surprises' such as Donaldson finds in *Epicoene*;[39] a mystery thriller, not so much a whodunit as a why-is-he-doing-it? The fact that Arbaces feels tormented with unnatural and secret sins *before* he has seen Panthea suggests the unknown factor controlling events which the saturnalian course of the play will unfold.

[37] Barber notes, in relation to Shakespeare's early comedies, that 'so much of the action . . . is random when looked at as intrigue, so many of the characters are neutral when regarded as character, so much of the wit is inapplicable when assessed as satire, that critics have fallen back on . . . exclamations about poetry and mood', *Shakespeare's Festive Comedies*, p. 4. *AKANK* has caused a similar response.

[38] E. M. Waith, *The Pattern of Tragicomedy in Beaumont and Fletcher* (Yale, 1952), p. 38.

[39] Donaldson, *The World Upside Down*, p. 28.

Comedy   191

The frontispiece to the first edition makes clear the governing context of temporary, hilltop king uncrowned by God (see Frontispiece). And, in performance, the opening scenes establish Arbaces' mock king qualities. Firstly, Mardonius comments to Bessus on the king's split personality. Confiding in such an unreliable character would seem dangerous to Mardonius's own security, yet he concludes:

Doe not thinke mee thy friend for this, for if I car'd who knew it, thou shouldst not heare it. (I. i. 84–5)

Mardonius does not fear the king's wrath, as his subsequent behaviour shows. When Arbaces humbly observes that his captive, Tigranes, epitomizes 'wisdom, valour, all the graces | Man can receive', Mardonius remarks, 'And yet you conquered him'. Arbaces then reverts to arrogance, 'Puff! Did not I take him nobly?' and Mardonius puts him down: 'Why you did | And you have talked enough on't.'[40] Now enraged, the king threatens Mardonius's life, but serious threat is dispelled when he turns to Bessus for support, and Bessus gives the fool's reply of loud laughter. At this Arbaces takes up the theme of himself as the subject of mocking games, such as those the Gray's Inn men objected to at the end of the 1594–5 celebrations:

> By all the world, Ime growne ridiculous
> To my owne subjects. Tye me to a chaire
> And jest at mee.[41]
>
> I. i. 239–41

His excessive behaviour then takes another turn. He petulantly insists on knowing whether he was bragging and, as each tries to reply, adopts the comedian's trick of outrage at the interruption. All these absurd attributes, combined with his courtiers' lack of fear, establish Arbaces for the audience as a mock king. Further, the form of proclamation with which his arrival from war is announced is the one which acclaimed the Inner Temple lord in 1561, and other festive kings:

> Enter one [Man] running
> MAN. The King, the King, the King, the King: Now, now, now now.
>
> II. ii. 75–6

[40] I. i. 211–38.   [41] See the insult to Henry VI, Ch. 6 n. 6.

192   *Comedy*

Although the audience would not know until the end why Arbaces was a mock king, they would understand the basic falsity of his role, particularly at the first recorded performance in the Christmas season, and so would understand the context behind the grotesque, bacchanalian passions.

The patterns which misrule takes are ingeniously thought out. Unnatural disturbance within Arragonia cannot become apparent until Arbaces' return from war, since intially he is outside the kingdom, and war is the one situation in which personal instability can be interpreted as valour. As Mardonius says as a comment on Arbaces' peacetime mania:

. . . would he were well cur'd of this raging folly: Give me the warres where men are mad, and may talke what they list, and held the bravest Fellowes.[42]
(IV. ii. 108–9)

The transition from war to peace contains a fundamental flaw, for the vainglorious Arbaces captures the good prince, Tigranes. The pairs of princes and captains are wise and foolish opposites, and for the course of the saturnalia, as one might expect, wisdom is made subject to folly. This becomes apparent in several ways. Firstly, Arbaces declares that Tigranes will be more free as his captive than in his own freedom, unintentionally pointing to the fact that his freedom is licence. For he offers Tigranes the 'ransom' of marriage with his sister, Panthea. His seeming generosity would make Tigranes truly bound to folly, since he is already betrothed to Spaconia, as he forcefully asserts. However, Tigranes demonstrates that he has become subject to folly, for Arbaces gives him the liberty to refuse Panthea, but Tigranes falls in love with her of his own free will. The tables then revolve once more for, by this time, Arbaces is himself in love with Panthea, and the wisdom of Tigranes, first defeated by folly, is now imprisoned by its jealous lord. The physical incarceration does not immediately cure him. His opening speech:

> Foole that I am, I have undone my selfe,
> And with mine owne hand turnd my fortune round,
> That was a faire one,
>
> IV. ii. 1–3

might sound like regret for his moment of betrayal. One is prepared

---

[42] Other plays using a soldier valiant in war and disordered in peace include *Othello*, Claudius in *Much Ado*, and Beaumont and Fletcher's *The Mad Lover*.

Comedy 193

by Richard II, and Lear, for characters to find wisdom in prison. But Tigranes reproaches himself for his commitment to Spaconia, and it takes her fierce chastisement to restore him to sanity. Once this pair are reconciled, one would expect their freedom to ensue, since Tigranes is no longer a threat to Arbaces. But to have wisdom at large would upset the dominance of misrule, and this seems to be the underlying reason why Arbaces forms the wrong conclusion regarding Spaconia's presence, and why he has them both imprisoned. As with Lear and Cordelia the imprisonment ensures the outlawing of order, and its submission to alternative forces. Tigranes says: 'Well, I am subject to you, and must endure these passions',[43] and Spaconia adds in an aside: 'This is th'imprisonment I have look'd for always'.[44] In an ordered world, imprisonment would be a marriage contract, but the honourable resolution must wait. The theme of order outlawed is made more specific when Gobrius enters pleading for the release of a third prisoner, Panthea. Arbaces replies:

> She is in prison *Gobrius*, is shee not?
>
> . . . . .
>
> Alas she would be at libertie,
> And there be thousand reasons, *Gobrius*,
> Thousands that will denie it:
> Which if she knew, she would contentedly
> Be where she is, and blesse her virtue for it.

IV. ii. 196, 228–32

The thousand reasons are, as Arbaces reveals to Panthea in their subsequent interview, that he has lost his reason, and virtue would gladly be cast off from such misgovernment.

One original development is the plight into which Bessus falls. In his monologue in Act III, he shows that his true role is that of parasitical fool, or satirist, who had earned his bread by railing on his fellow men: '. . . what I said, was remembred in mirth, but never in anger'.[45] A well-meaning relative had thrust on him the army captaincy, from which he had fled with unforeseen, happy consequences for Arragonia. His flight helped win the war.

MARDONIUS. . . . thy feare making thee mistake, thou ranst upon the enemie, and a hot charge thou gav'st, as Ile doe thee right, thou art furious in running away, and I thinke we owe thy feare for our victorie.

I. i. 69–71

---

[43] IV. ii. 159–60.   [44] Ibid. 159.   [45] III. ii. 18–19.

194   *Comedy*

Bessus's behaviour complements that of Arbaces. His dishonourable actions led to victory, and Arbaces' graver attempts at dishonour will similarly result in good fortune. Without the upheaval of the saturnalia the truth about his birth would never come to light, and the disorder, which is extreme and apparently evil, is nevertheless proved to be a force for regeneration. However, Bessus's cowardly action does not immediately have fortunate repercussions for himself. Instead of his mistaken valour bringing him glory, it removes his immunity from recrimination, and in one of the best comic scenes we see him carrying 212 challenges from men whom he had insulted in the past, but who only now feel him to be a man from whom satisfaction must be demanded. In this particular world of misrule one of the errors is to take the fool seriously.

Since Bessus has received opprobrium in the past, it may be worth considering his positive role further. The most difficult scene to justify is his unblushing agreement to win Panthea for Arbaces. It is this which many find despicable, but what he does, by casually putting into explicit words Arbaces' corrupt intentions, is to ventilate the conscience of the king who recoils in horror from the amoral acceptance of his perversion, whereas Mardonius's own revulsion had only increased the king's determination. To adapt Kernan's phrase, one could call this the 'moral and sanative purpose' of fooling. Also, despite his total lack of honour, Bessus is proved right. In Act III, Scene i, when Arbaces first falls in love, he refuses to accept that Panthea is his sister. Mardonius is appalled but Bessus agrees:

> No, marry, is shee is not an't please your Majestie:
> I never thought shee was, shees nothing like you.
>
> III. i. 170–1

The fool speaks the truth while wiser men are proved wrong, and Bessus draws attention to this at the end of the play. Speaking familiarly to Arbaces now that he is a commoner below the rank of Captain, he says: 'Why if you remember, fellow subject *Arbaces*, I tolde you once she was not your sister, I and said she look't nothing like you.' Arbaces replies, humorously deferential: 'I thinke you did, good Captaine *Bessus*.'[46] Once the facts regarding Arbaces' birth come to light, his determined passion becomes proof of a true and unchangeable love. Since he and Panthea are able to marry, order is

[46] v. iv. 293–5.

Comedy

restored on personal and public levels. Not even the structure of society is changed, for Arbaces achieves the position of real king, now wise and virtuous in view of his harmony with natural order. This play is one of the most affirmative saturnalian texts for, almost as with antimasque and masque, the potential evil destruction is converted into good at the turn of a device. And the last line, 'Loud thanks for me, that I am proved no King', is the comic resolution to an Agatha Christie of disorder.

Another play, which fits Jonson's barbed definition of running 'from reason or possibility', is the 1620s comedy, usually attributed to John Ford, *The Queen, or the Excellency of her Sex*. This contains a further variation on gross absurdities arbitrarily happening under a summer king's rule, and patterned according to opposites and oppositions. The opening of the play is in the aftermath of a defeated rebellion in Arragon, seen from the point of view of three freed followers of the new captive rebel leader, General Alphonso. They brawl among themselves, in imitation, perhaps, of Jonson's opening trio in *The Alchemist*, and comment on their general's impending execution. On the scaffold, impervious to the jests of his henchman, Bufo, Alphonso declares his reason for the rebellion:

> I sought to free wrack'd Arragon from ruin,
> Which a fond woman's government must bring.[47]

To this crude political prejudice is added a strong personal misogyny, which includes railing against the queen as she approaches the scaffold:

> I hate your sex in general, not you
> As y'are a Queen, but as y'are a woman.
>
> 1, ll. 386–7

The subsequent confusions in the plot are deliberate, for Ford here reverses the Fortune pattern, and, instead of losing his head, Alphonso improbably gains the crown, through the queen's extraordinary love for him. When personally handing him down from the scaffold, the good queen attributes his difficult nature to his summertime pride of life:

---

[47] W. Bang (ed.), *Materialien zur Kunde des alteren Englischen Dramas*, xiii (Louvain, 1906), Act i, ll. 246–7, p. 3.

196　　　　　　　　　　　　*Comedy*

> . . . 'twas thy hight of youth, not hate of us
> Drew thee to those attempts.
>
> 　　　　　　　　　　　　　　　I. ll. 482–3

The wedding, which takes place at the end of Act I, Scene i, is not the reconciliation and regeneration usual at the end of comedies, but the start of a series of intrigues, battles between the sexes, tricks, and tests of love, with Alphonso established in a court separate from that of his queen. Not only are she and Alphonso opposite in nature, but a second pair, the good General Velasco and his mistress, the widow, Salassa, set a reversed pattern, with Velasco suffering from Salassa's female tyranny. The trials which he undergoes help resolve those of the queen, until at the end all partners are brought into harmony. Specific borrowings from king games include Alphonso as tyrannic ruler, liberally threatening death to everything that moves, and mocked and encouraged by his three followers for speaking 'like a king | That hath the whole World for his proper Monarchy'.[48] There is a drunken revel, led by him, which leads to further frustrated tyranny, and, in Act IV, the queen is seated in a chair as 'the subject of [Alphonso's] mirth'.[49] The play ends with a comic sequence of champions in armour coming to the aid of the queen for, suggestive of Ford's preoccupation with death, this comedy includes further close escapes from execution for her and for the widow, during the play's resolution.

The continual shift from one improbable situation to another is achieved with some dexterity; the play is at least better than the *Timon* farce, and can be classed as an absurd and positive saturnalia, like those of Marston and Chapman, but without the psychological tension of *AKANK*. If Ford did write this, then, like Marlowe and Middleton, he appears to have first exercised his talents with a familiar structure, in which he innovated an abrupt upward reversal of fortune at the opening, and gave himself a new set of plotting problems.

Jonson scorned the trivial uses of popular concepts found in this play and in most of the other comedies looked at here but, in *Bartholomew Fair* and *Volpone*, he himself created classics out of ideas from the same stable; using an evil saturnalia in *Volpone*, and the more regenerative concept in *The Alchemist* and *Bartholomew Fair*. The two alternative saturnalias allowed for complexities in

---

[48] Act I, l. 1120, p. 12.　　　[49] Act IV, l. 2557, p. 26.

Comedy

other plays. For example, the combination of rebellion and riot, briefly suggested in *Friar Bacon and Friar Bungay*, are a part of Falstaff's multifaceted disorders. From a moral perspective, Falstaff's misrule is another destructive saturnalia which has to be expelled, though this also destroys the regenerative aspect. The two are twinned even more closely than in *AKANK*: they are in the character of Falstaff rather than in the plot, therefore one cannot exist without the other. As well as providing kaleidoscopic possibilities for comic invention, mock king leadership could also pose serious questions. In *The Shoemakers' Holiday*, Eyre's saturnalia *is* the moral resolution, and the alliance between king and commoner at the end overrules but, unlike Stowe's optimistic recollection, does not reconcile city–court factions. The middle-ranking classes are still at fault at the end and, like Malvolio, do not accept the regenerated conclusion. And, finally, as already suggested in the study of the history plays, saturnalia need not be comic; the evil inversions of *Richard III* and in *Lear* destroy the fabric of their societies.

Conflicts between saturnalia and a moral resolution, and the possibilities arising from an evil saturnalia itself in opposition to a regenerative one, propagated varieties and hybrids from the 1580s to the closure of the theatres. While one concept, that of order outlawed, became increasingly attractive as society lost its cohesion, and beggar, or gypsy, leaders were portrayed as carrying the secret of social reconstruction.

9

Festive Tragedy

Troilus and Cressida, King Lear, and Antony and Cleopatra

> Men are continually in competition for honour and dignity . . .
> and consequently amongst men there ariseth . . . envy, and
> hatred, and finally war.
>
> Hobbes, *Leviathan*, chapter 17

TROILUS AND CRESSIDA

Peter Alexander, in 1928,[1] first suggested that *Troilus and Cressida*
might have been written for an Inner Temple seasonal entertainment; a view sensitively pursued by W. W. Greg in 1955, when he put
forward the further possibility of 'the habitual All Saints or Candle-
mas festivities of the Inner Temple'. Although he acknowledges 'no
shred of external evidence',[2] internal evidence from the printer's
Prefaces and the text makes it very likely that the Chamberlain's Men
performed the play for lawyers in the last Christmas season of
Elizabeth's reign, 1602–3. The recent editor of the Arden edition
asks a further question which points specifically to Twelfth Night.
Why, he asks, should Pandarus say in the Epilogue that 'some two
months hence my will shall here be made', when he has already made
it clear that he is dying, unless he means his final re-emergence on
Shrove Tuesday before being extinguished by Lent?[3] In which case
Pandarus would be referring to himself as the lord of misrule who
had presided over the now ended Christmas entertainment. Another
enigmatic line in the Epilogue also suggests Pandarus's exit from
temporary, seasonal eminence. He asks the audience to 'weep out at
Pandar's fall' which cannot relate to the plot of the play, since, in
that, Pandarus had neither risen nor fallen. Instead, the fall connects
with the previous line, 'as many as be here of Pandar's hall'. A double

---

[1] P. Alexander, '*Troilus and Cressida*, 1609', *Transactions of the Bibliographical
Society*, 9 (1928–9), p. 278.

[2] W. W. Greg, *The First Folio of Shakespeare* (Oxford, 1955), p. 340.

[3] K. Palmer (ed.), *Troilus and Cressida*, Arden edn. (London, 1982), introd. p. 21.

Festive Tragedy
199

association is raised between a Hall of Fame, Pandarus's house, and
the Lawyers' Temple. At one level of the joke, Pandarus calls himself
Fortune's surrogate lord, who has hosted the play and influenced the
destiny of others under his control, and now, at the seasonal and
satirical conclusion, comes his own fall and death. On another level,
his joke includes the suggestion that the lawyers, lords, and ladies
present will suffer the same fate as himself through the same
indulgence in the flesh.[4]

However, in the play, it is the war itself, as much as Pandarus,
which presides over events. The Prologue's appearance in armour
establishes the military condition under which the protagonists act,
and the disorders emerge as the corruptions of a long-drawn-out
offensive. The armour that he wears was, by 1603, only used for
ceremonial occasions, such as Inner Temple Christmas entertainments, and, since in the play its glamour is revealed as superficial and
deceptive, ideals past and present are undermined. The splendid
image of the Prologue is immediately contrasted by his lines of
careless indifference to audience response: 'Now good, or bad, 'tis
but the chance of war' (l. 31). The symbol itself is revealed as a
delusion in the last battle, when Hector fights and kills what is
described as a 'sumptuous armour'. He calls the anonymous man
inside a 'most putrified core, so fair without', and Adamson points
out that this conventional perspective is imbued with fresh life, since
Hector pursues the man purely because he desires his armour: what
was intended to protect becomes the cause of the soldier's
destruction.[5] Further, it shows that Hector, too, has only external
signs of chivalry, and his exposure precedes his own ignoble murder
at Achilles' hands, thereby preventing any appearance that Greek
villainy is set against an innocent. Ulysses' concept of honour is,
appropriately, a suit of armour kept bright by engagement:[6] an
exterior garment and nothing to do with the inner quality of the man.

The combination of a noble exterior concealing a debased reality is
contained at the heart of the play, the brief love of Troilus and
Cressida. It has often been observed that there is a sexual double

---

[4] Palmer asks, regarding the line 'brethren and *sisters* [emphasis added] of the hold
door trade', 'are we to assume that there were also women in the audience?' (ibid.). See
Ch. 2 n. 86.

[5] J. Adamson, *Troilus and Cressida* (Brighton, 1988), p. 160.

[6] 'Perseverance, dear my lord, | Keeps honour bright: to have done is to hang |
Quite out of fashion, like a rusty mail | In monumental mockery' (III. iii. 150–3).

200   *Festive Tragedy*

meaning in Troilus's comfort to her over the 'monstruosity in love' and in her reply:

> This is the monstruosity in love, lady: that the will is infinite, and the execution confined: that the desire is boundless, and the act a slave to limit.
> CRESS. They say all lovers swear more performance than they are able, and yet reserve an ability that they never perform: vowing more than the perfection of ten, and discharging less than the tenth part of one.

III. ii. 79–87

Instead of trying to separate out one meaning from the other, and perhaps allowing to Troilus the noble, and to Cressida the debased only, the ambiguity is there in both speeches, becoming explicit in Troilus's last and Cressida's first lines. His chivalric declaration, wishing to perform Herculean tasks as proof of his love, has sexual prowess at its core.

The pragmatic Greeks have little outward chivalry to provide a misleading exterior, instead it is their martial reputation which has led to delusions of grandeur, whereby their actual strength is reduced: their reputation as warriors is belied by what they have become. Achilles began this when his fame led him to aspire to the false nobility of a position beyond his true station:

> Achilles, the most popular warrior, refuses to fight. His immense prestige has made him so 'plaguy proud' that he finds it intolerable not to be first in all respects. Under his tent, with his mignon, Patroclus, he mocks Agamemnon, whom he wants to replace as commander-in chief.[7]

Ajax, likewise, aspires to being Achilles and in imitation of him withdraws from battle. He

> . . . bears his head
> In such a rein, in full as proud a place
> As broad Achilles; keeps his tent like him.

I. iii. 188–90

And much of the camp has ceased to function suffering from the same disease of emulation: '. . . in the imitation of these twain . . . many are infect.'[8] Their over-inflated self-esteem, based on Achilles'

---

[7] R. Girard, 'The Politics of Desire in *Troilus and Cressida*', in P. Parker and G. Hartman (eds.), *Shakespeare: The Question of Theory* (London, 1985), p. 201.
[8] I. iii. 185–7.

Festive Tragedy 201

example, has in fact turned them into a series of arrogant and useless imitation, or mock, lords—not greater men—which has given the Trojans the military advantage. Ulysses considers that Achilles' pride, which needs to be levelled first, results from the image bestowed on him by others' praise. He 'mistakes himself for a god because everybody worships him'.[9] Just as Ulysses understands honour in terms of external armour, so too he considers man's self-esteem a belief other men's opinions dress him in, and his second plan to remove this superfluous garment from Achilles' ego is direct and pointed mockery. Even the cuckold, Menelaus, the natural fool of the Greek camp, whom every one else derides, is given the chance to scorn the great man. Mockery of the mock lord, such as was lamented at the end of the 1594 Grays Inn entertainments, is here used to cure the soldier's aspiration to Agamemnon's kingship. However, Achilles survives the public humiliation. His self-assurance is more than superficial, and it consoles him with the thought that men whose honours *are* external to themselves, 'prizes of accident', chance, or Fortune, do decline when men's favours grow cold. But he is different, 'Fortune and I are friends':

> I do enjoy
> At ample point all that I did possess,
> Save these men's looks.

III. iii. 88–90

His opinion of himself is an imaginative fantasy, in direct descent from the exaggerated reputations credited to inns of court Christmas lords. Though he does waver in subsequent conversation with Ulysses, realizing his 'fame is shrewdly gored', he turns out not to be dressed in arrogance only, but rather to be conceited to the core, and it is a further deception in the play[10] that his return to battle is unexpected, even to himself. His desire to see his great rival, Hector, 'in his weeds of peace | To talk with him, and to behold his visage',[11] turns to a desire to kill him the moment his wish is fulfilled.[12] Noble and ignoble desires are again interrelated. For all the jokes and amicality of the truce in Act IV, the scene is electric with the knowledge that the following day they will be killing each other.

[9] Girard, 'The Politics of Desire', p. 204.
[10] See Adamson's chapter 'Changeful Potency', in *Troilus and Cressida*, pp. 132–6.   [11] III. iii. 238–9.
[12] Adamson, *Troilus and Cressida*, p. 132.

202   *Festive Tragedy*

The first person to show an awareness of the sham of chivalry is Cressida who, to some extent, plays Thersites' role in the Trojan camp. Girard notes that she is an outsider, without access to the beautiful people, and eager to gossip about them.[13] Her domestic anecdotes, such as Hector chiding his wife, and Helen sleeping while the flower of Troy risks its life on her behalf, help diminish any mythologically inflated admiration we may have for them. The Trojan court is not to be mistaken for an Arthurian or Utopian ideal, such as was usually presented at this time of the year in courtly circles. Her mocking responses in Act I, Scene ii also undermine the heroic picture presented by Troy's choicest warriors, as they file back into the city in all the glory of their armour. And, to deflate Pandarus further, she adds her own admiration to Achilles' already inflated reputation.

Recent criticism has ceased to accept automatic vilification of Cressida, and in this light I would like to consider further her contribution to the social disorder. How, one may ask, can the satire be perceived as tragedy, since the context lacks standards from which to fall, and Troilus and Cressida do not even die? Part of the answer seems to lie in a brief metamorphosis in Cressida, despite the acquisitive standards by which she is judged and judges herself.[14]

There is a considerable amount of posing by both central characters. Troilus considers himself a type of idealized lover, without realizing that his actions might in fact belie him. And Cressida begins with cynical detachment: her line to Pandarus, 'to say truth, true and not true',[15] being the defence mechanism necessary in their world of political and emotional betrayal. This defensive reaction operates even with Troilus, clouding any specific point at which one could say she had become a changed person. However, there is gradual change at their meeting between the first 'will you walk in, my lord?' and its repeat.[16] In that section Troilus tries to calm her fears of the 'monstruosity in love', and there is a disarming naïvety in his complete absorption in the abstract concept of the perfect lover—so total that he talks of himself in the plural. Cressida's repeated line gives the actress a chance to change a worldly invitation into one with deeper meaning. What had been her desire for the outward

---

[13] Girard, 'The Politics of Desire', p. 199.
[14] G. Greene, 'Shakespeare's Cressida "a kind of self"', in G. Green and C. Weeley (eds.), *The Woman's Part* (Chicago, 1980), pp. 135–7.
[15] I. ii. 98.   [16] III. ii. 60, 98.

Festive Tragedy

show of Troilus, seen only at a distance, has to become something deeper on meeting, for her passionate protest in Act IV, Scene ii to make any sense:

> Time, force, and death,
> Do to this body what extremes you can;
> But the strong base and building of my love
> Is as the very centre of the earth,
> Drawing all things to it.
>
> ll. 104–8

This is not the speech of the sophisticate in Act I. For her to understand the concepts she uses here she must speak from conviction. The relation of outward to inner is momentarily reversed and her physical being is informed by an inner sense of value. Yet she is from here on isolated by both Pandarus and Troilus. It is curious that Pandarus not only feels no sympathy for her, but also blames her for a situation which he, not she, brought about: '. . . would thou hadst ne'er been born! I knew thou wouldst be his death. O poor gentleman . . .'[17] And Troilus, who in Act III had exhausted all 'truth' similes to express his devotion to her, lets her go without a word of protest. In Act IV, Scene iv, he even appears content to let her go. One has to take into account the irony that he is on the Trojan inner council, and in Act II, Scene ii had changed Hector's mind over whether or not to return Helen. Then, his romantic idealism, appropriate to an Arthurian knight, had swayed the council into keeping her; but he makes no attempt to intervene on behalf of his own supposed love.[18] On Troilus's behalf, it should be said that because he was with Cressida that night he was, ironically, absent from the council which decided her fate. However, the monstrosity in love which Cressida feared is proved true. Troilus makes no last-minute intervention on her behalf, which would at least be evidence of his love even if it failed. The night has satisfied him, and her earlier line to Pandarus, 'to say truth, true and not true' could apply equally to Troilus. The exchange between them in Act IV, Scene iv is revealing:

TROIL. Cressid, I love thee in so strain'd a purity
  That the blest gods, as angry with my fancy,

---

[17] IV. ii. 88–9.
[18] See Girard for Troilus's underlying attitude to Cressida.

204 *Festive Tragedy*

> More bright in zeal than the devotion which
> Cold lips blow to their deities, take thee from me.
> CRESS. Have the gods envy?
> PAND. Ay, ay, ay, ay, 'tis too plain a case.
> CRESS. And is it true that I must go from Troy?
> TROIL. A hateful truth.
> CRESS.   What, and from Troilus too?
> TROIL. From Troy and Troilus.
> CRESS.   Is't possible?

IV. iv. 23–32

Cressida's line, 'Have the gods envy?', makes most sense as incredulous rejection of Troilus's blaming the gods for what is in fact man's pragmatic bartering.[19] As Adamson says, the play is 'entirely a matter of human actions, not godly interventions',[20] and, for some reason, Troilus, cannot reply to her at this point. Likewise, Cressida's subsequent questions are not to discover her fate, which Pandarus has already made clear to her, but to discover whether Troilus will be the rock he promised by opposing the decision. On 'Is't possible?' she is forced to accept that he will not. His idealization of chivalric love proves to be another glittering external which has no substance to it. Rather than proving himself an Arthurian knight, he turns out to be a Prince d'Amour.

The tragedy for Troilus is given him in words. His ideals are destroyed. What is not put into precise words is the part he unwittingly plays in the destruction. Cressida begins without ideals, and her tragedy is that she briefly loses her cynical defence, yet that cynicism is proved right. She progresses from desire to love, and from betrayal to whoredom. For one night there is apparent unity and harmony between herself and Troilus (as between Greeks and Trojans) before the war reimposes man's lower behaviour. And, as Girard has shown, the romantic hero falls off even before he hears of Cressida's exchange for Antenor. Thersites' view, and Cressida's opening view, of this society is the accurate one, all chivalry in love and war is a sham, and the achievement of the play is that it provokes a counter-response in the audience.[21] The moral and sanative effect of satire works on the audience not on characters, who continue to plunge further into the maelstrom.

Twelfth Night celebrations in the inns of court kept in mind the

---

[19] As in Richard Cottrell's 1973 Cambridge Marlowe Society production.
[20] Adamson, *Trolus and Cressida*, p. 164.   [21] Ibid. 165.

Festive Tragedy 205

force of *Ira Fortuna* on them and on the presiding Christmas prince, or misrule lord. This aspect, brought into Pandarus's final speech, informs the whole play. Tension is maintained throughout between idealization and ridicule of such dignitaries, through the false symbolic use of armour, and in the pose of great worth struck by most of the princes in it. Troy is used as one of the humanist exempla from the ancient world to set before modern princes, and in keeping with a satiric denouement to Christmas, the city and the lords in both camps are revealed as hollow poseurs.

KING LEAR

The first known performance of *King Lear* can be said with certainty to have been at Christmas, before King James on St Stephen's night (26 December) 1606,[22] when, traditionally, the mighty were put down from their seats. The year was one when the question of union between England and Scotland was being fiercely debated in Parliament.[23] However, the questions of union and abdication seem not to have been Shakespeare's main concern. Although these issues are still sometimes raised by critics as a continuing subject for debate,[24] today they serve rather more as aunt sallies. The real issue is one which leads naturally into the seasonal inversions. For Lear's error is to divide the power of kingship from the title *to* kingship. In 1948, Heilman had glanced at this in passing,[25] and in 1977 Marie Axton focused more closely on it: 'Lear makes an utter travesty of kingship by not only . . . giving away the power of his office and sundering the crown, but by retaining the name of king and thus the responsibility for all the ensuing disasters.'[26] Although Kent accepts the opening political propositions of division and abdication, which had caused the tragedy in *Gorboduc*, he breaks out when Lear demands to keep his title of king.[27] Shakespeare has, as it were,

[22] Arden edn., ed. K. Muir (London, 1972), p. xviii.
[23] M. Axton, *The Queen's Two Bodies* (London, 1977), p. 135.
[24] R. L. Levin, 'Shakespeare or the Ideas of his Time', in R. B. Heilman (ed.), *Twentieth Century Views of Shakespeare: The Tragedies—New Perspectives* (New Jersey, 1984), p. 16. Cf. Muir, Arden edn., p. xxii.
[25] Lear fails 'to perceive that a king cannot be a king without a crown and cannot maintain his perquisites by a kind of oral recipe . . . [the status] involves responsibilities as well as rights . . .', R. B. Heilman, *This Great Stage* (Washington, DC, 1963), pp. 161–2.
[26] Axton, *Queen's Two Bodies*, p. 139. [27] Ibid.

206   *Festive Tragedy*

moved the goalposts, but Lear still achieves an own goal, reacting from disappointment in Cordelia. At the opening, his purpose was to 'shake all cares and business' from his age and 'crawl toward death'.[28] However, having alienated himself from Cordelia's kind nursery, he changes his mind and demonstrates incipient second childhood by suddenly expecting to retain 'the name and all th'addition to a king'.[29] His private folly in mistaking Cordelia's inhibition for the pride he himself suffers from, produces the public folly. He also expects to retain a hundred knights who are to be maintained by Cornwall and Albany, although their allegiance will be to Lear, which is clearly an untenable proposition. The power he gives away:

> . . . the sway,
> Revenue, execution of the rest,
> Beloved sons be yours.
>
> I. i. 135–7

Therefore Lear demands a kingly nucleus for himself, with all its reverence and trappings, but none of the responsibility,[30] within the organized state. Kent and Cordelia perceive the fault, and because they retain standards of order, both are banished from the disordered world. The fool's apparent inversion of the facts, that Lear '. . . banish'd two on's daughters, and did the third a blessing against his will',[31] takes Lear's inverted world into account, and the powerless king follows his banished kin into what becomes his own internal exile. As Bradbrook says, Lear moves out of the world of real events, and into that of a mock king.[32]

The mistake Lear commits against himself is the one that Fabritius Carpenter found in the pride of a summer queen, who values the appearance of royalty without its substance. In reality, since the change from poverty to title is *without power and dignity* (my emphasis), she remains a poor and naked creature.[33] And Lear descends through the play to the similar realization that 'unaccommodated man' is only a 'poor bare forked animal'.[34] In Act IV his fantastic costume of flowers is an ironic figurative equivalent for

---

[28] I. i. 38–40.   [29] Ibid. 135.

[30] Another failure of kings identified by Erasmus. See Ch. 4.

[31] I. iv. 100–1.

[32] M. Bradbrook, *Shakespeare: The Poet in his World* (London, 1978), p. 190.

[33] 'Quae ab illo mutuauerit sine potentia, & dignitate nudi & pauperes remanebunt', N. F. Davis, 'The Playing of Miracles in England', Ph. D. Thesis (Cambridge, 1977), p. 33. See Ch. 4 n. 24.   [34] III. iv. 104–6.

Festive Tragedy

the trappings of kingship he had insisted upon; the superfluities of a mock king. As he exits from Act IV, Scene vi, he issues a Cotswold-like challenge for his title to the courtiers:

LEAR. Come, come; I am a king, masters, know you that?
GENT. You are a royal one, and we obey you.
LEAR. Then there's life in't. Come and you get it, you shall get it by running.
Sa, sa, sa, sa.

Exit running

IV. vi. 197–200

In his madness Lear not only behaves like a mock king, but appears to recognize that his claim to kingship can now only be expressed in such terms. The scene is particularly moving since the Gentleman means what he says in terms of the real and respected title.

As in the poem, 'Robert of Sicily',[35] analogies are drawn from both summer and winter seasons. The 'mad king of summer', at whose court Gloucester can find forgiveness,[36] is also a fool king in the winter of his fortunes. According to the fool, in Act II, Scene iv when Kent is set in the stocks: 'Winter's not gone yet, if the wild-geese fly that way.'[37] And he mockingly chides Kent for following a leader whose fortunes are now at their lowest, since 'there's no labouring i'th'winter'. He then continues with the midsummer metaphor: 'Let go thy hold when a great wheel runs down a hill, lest it break thy neck with following;[38] but the great one that goes upward, let him draw thee after . . . I would have none but knaves follow it, since a fool gives it.'[39] He gives the knavish advice of Timon's courtiers and dismisses it as such.[40]

Lear's madness is *sottie*-like, both a profound means of expressing man's frailty and, more satirically, a way of dissecting the corruption of power. In Act III, Scene vi, the mock arraignment of Goneril and Regan reveals his impotence. He can do no more than lead parodic debate on political misrule in the manner of a seasonal, Temple lord. But only accidentally, as in Act IV, Scene vi, does he come near to expressing, through madness and self-mockery, his own responsibility.

---

[35] For a comparison between the two kings see M. Mack, *King Lear in our Time* (Berkeley, 1965), pp. 49–50.
[36] '. . . in total licence of midsummer revelry, he pardons Gloucester's adultery', Bradbrook, *Shakespeare*, p. 192.
[37] II. iv. 45.   [38] See Ch. 3 n. 51.   [39] II. iv. 69–74.
[40] See E. Welsford's analysis of the fool's inversions in II. iv. 72–82, *The Fool* (London, 1935), pp. 254–6.

208   *Festive Tragedy*

Consciously, he thinks of himself as: 'The natural fool of Fortune';[41] 'More sinn'd against than sinning';[42] and not the man responsible for setting the downward course of events in motion. He perceives the wrong done to Cordelia, but not the public wrong to the State, which Kent's line after his death points to: 'He but usurp'd his life.'[43] Lear dies self-deceived and, most movingly, in the Folio text, deceived as to whether Cordelia has survived. It is the joyful and mistaken impression that she is alive which finally kills him. Although Lear learns many potent truths, he does not lose his basic human imperfections and inability to judge correctly.

The hardest result to accept is Cordelia's death. The deaths of Goneril, Regan, and Edmund have already been brought about, and hope is momentarily restored that she will be saved. The fact that, after this anticipation, she is not saved confirms that the waste begun in Act I, Scene i must be total. Her death is the lowest point, after which order can, perhaps, be restored. Kenneth Muir points to the sacrificial nature of her death,[44] and Elton finds in her the medicinal qualities of her name. She 'prays for a "cure" in "this great breech" in Lear's abused "nature", and her love would "repair those harms"'.[45] In the context of the play, nature is a deity abused by the scientific reasoning of Edmund, for whom nature provides a rationale for immorality at every level. According to the Gentleman's speech:

> Thou hast one daughter,
> Who redeems nature from the general curse
> Which twain have brought her.
>
> IV. vi. 202–4

Cordelia has the power to restore the higher values to the debased concept. While her sisters promise 'all' and give nothing, reducing civilization to nothing, Cordelia promises 'nothing' and gives all. In her death is the promise that it is her last cure, redeeming abused nature and, by demonstration, providing the basis for renewed social order. It matters to see compassion and love surviving in the engulfing soulless destruction. Despite its apparent failure, it provides

---

[41] IV. vi. 189.   [42] III. ii. 60.
[43] V. iii. 316. In retrospect, Shakespeare does include a suggestion of error in the abdication.
[44] Arden edn., p. lii.
[45] W. R. Elton, *King Lear and the Gods* (San Marino, Calif., 1966), p. 77.

Festive Tragedy 209

the hope, lacking in *Troilus and Cressida*, that positive values have survived. One need not, as Colie says, stretch her selflessness into an example of Pauline charity,[46] yet contemporary audiences may well have done, bearing in mind that they were very familiar with the ethics of St Paul and not with the mores of pagan theology.[47] Social order, in *King Lear*, is integrated with the universal and, through Cordelia, we see the price to be paid to regenerate both, once kingship fails.

ANTONY AND CLEOPATRA

If, in *Lear* and *Troilus and Cressida*, festive inversions are used to reveal a travesty in the ideal of kingship, and the travesty of idealizing its festive equivalent, *Antony and Cleopatra* reverses the process. To begin with, as Markels has observed, the movement of the play is one towards the success of disorder.[48] Antony and Cleopatra turn a fault into a virtue, and their ribald behaviour triumphs over the time-serving hierarchies asserted by Caesar. It can further be said that Antony's form of misrule follows the precepts of the Gray's Inn Prince d'Amour. On one level he is a more complete, amorous fool than the Falstaff of *The Merry Wives of Windsor*: an 'old ruffian', living in perpetual sensual gratification with the queen of the gypsies.[49] In Act I, Scene i he says:

> There's not a minute of our lives should stretch
> Without some pleasure now.
>
> ll. 46–7

---

[46] For a Christian interpretation see G. W. Knight, *The Wheel of Fire* (London, 1930); L. Danby, *Shakespeare's Doctrine of Nature* (London, 1949), and V. K. Whitaker, *The Mirror up to Nature* (San Marino, Calif., 1965) and, for what I find the more convincing pagan context, see R. Colie, 'Biblical Echo', *Some Facets of King Lear* (London, 1974), pp. 120, 139; L. C. Knights, *Some Shakespearean Themes* (London, 1959); Elton, *King Lear and the Gods*; and R. M. Frye, *Shakespeare and Christian Doctrine* (Princeton, 1963).

[47] In the earlier *Leir*, Cordelia sees her exile with the disguised king of France in terms of a holy May game: 'Ile hold thy Palmers staffe within my hand, | And thinke it is the Scepter of a Queene, | Sometimes ile set thy Bonnet on my head, | And thinke I weare a rich imperiall Crowne. | Sometimes ile helpe thee in thy holy prayers, | And thinke I am with thee in Paradise. | Thus ile mock fortune, as she mocketh me.' *The Historie of King Leir*, ed. W. W. Greg, Malone Society Reprints (London, 1908), fo. C. 3ʳ.

[48] J. Markels, *The Pillar of the World* (Columbus, Ohio, 1968), *passim*.

[49] Abbreviated from Egyptians.

210   *Festive Tragedy*

But, by the end of the play, both turn this into an ideal by pursuing it through death into the afterlife. The reductive concept is finally transformed into an exemplary one.

Mock king and queen images are directly used twice about Antony and Cleopatra: once by Enobarbus describing their first meeting and, more fully, by Caesar in Act III, Scene vi, marking Antony's provocative severing of relations with Octavia and himself. Caesar reports that, on Antony's return to Egypt, he and Cleopatra were publicly enthroned 'i' the market place'. The public setting causes Caesar some disgust, and he emphasizes the play-acting nature of the ceremony, which was performed 'i' the common show place where they exercise', with specious pomp and all their bastards around them.[50] Antony's public assertion of power over Egypt, Lower Syria, Cyprus, and Lydia from his market dais is the idle boasting of a powerless man.

Other typical inversions occur. Night is as appropriate to Alexandria as day is to Rome. Enobarbus recalls, 'we did sleep day out of countenance; and made the night light with drinking',[51] whereas Caesar cannot drink and dislikes feasting. He becomes irritable as a result of Pompey's shipboard revel and, before the final battle, calls the feast for his army, a 'waste' 'they have deserved',[52] whereas Antony warmly hosts his own army's supper.

As well as the basic misrule associations for the renegade from order, is a larger Ptolemaic backdrop which conveys idealization of both lords, as seen from Caesar's point of view, and which presents the god of the Roman Empire as sun to Antony's moon. Caesar sees himself and Antony as two planets, encircling the earth, which should be hooped together like contemporary drawings of the orbits of sun and moon. That way, he concludes, they would be 'staunch from edge to edge o' the world'.[53] However, the soothsayer provides a different aspect of the same relationship in his advice to Antony to leave Rome:

> Thy lustre thickens,
> When he shines by . . .
> But he away, 'tis noble.
>
> II. iii. 26–8

The moon's light can only be seen when at the opposite side of the world, not in the sun's presence. There is some humour when the two

[50] III. vi. 3–15.   [51] II. ii. 177–8.   [52] IV. i. 16.   [53] II. ii. 115.

Festive Tragedy

orbs meet in Act II, Scene ii. By asking Antony to sit first, Caesar gives the other man precedence, while assuming the authority which can bestow that honour, therefore asserting his own precedence. Finally, Caesar concedes to sit first so accepting that he is marginally the greater figure.

Beneath Caesar and Antony, the globe of the earth lies divided up and subject to their dual control,[54] in which Antony's power serves Caesar's, his conquests having enlarged the Roman Empire. Yet there is nothing ideal about either's means of control and maintenance of their public positions. Antony's marriage to Octavia is as pragmatic a trick as that Caesar tries to play on Cleopatra in Act V. Even the truce between them is a calculated, mutual playing for time. Enobarbus puts into precise words, like Bastard Philip before Angier, the game both are playing: 'Or if you borrow one another's love for the instant, you may, when you hear no more words of Pompey, return it again: you shall have time to wrangle in, when you have nothing else to do.'[55] Further, their dividing up the globe between them is not the beneficent relationship of sun and moon, but predation. Conquest is shown to be as lustful as Antony's and Cleopatra's carnal love. Again, it is Enobarbus who coins the telling phrase. He, representative of the masters of the land, shakes the hand of Pompey, master of the sea, and calls it 'thieves kissing'.[56] Conquest, which Caesar holds up to Antony as the noble life he has abandoned, is wilful robbery, and the pretence of peace between competitors, an unholy affair. The frequent use of banquet analogy shows further that conquest is at least as bestial an appetite, if not more so, than the 'monstrous banquets' of Antony's present dotage. In Act II, Scene i, Pompey wishes that Cleopatra might continue to bewitch Antony away from the ensuing conflict; that enchanted foods might increase his various desires for flesh. Yet, none of the 'Egyptian dish' imagery is as repulsive as Caesar's own praise for Antony's past ability to survive and even thrive in the arduous circumstances brought about by campaigns of war. Like the beasts he lived on bark and berries, but further:

> Thou didst drink
> The stale of horses, and the gilded puddle
> Which beasts would cough at: . . . On the Alps

---

[54] The third member of the Triumvirate, Lepidus, is more of a sleeping partner.
[55] II. ii. 103–6.   [56] II. vi. 96.

It is reported thou didst eat strange flesh,
Which some did die to look on.

I. iv. 61–8

His superhuman ability to survive and even feast, so that his 'cheek
lank'd not', was because of a lower than bestial appetite, which
Caesar calls nobility.

The ordered world is further out of joint. Characters frequently
describe each other through idealized, pageant-like imagery, which,
in attempting to display their superhuman nobility, results in a
picture which is not quite human. Enobarbus's description of
Cleopatra in her barge, adds to a royal triumph the qualities of
Venus's eroticism and supernatural enchantment. Caesar's appalled
reaction to Octavia's humble entry into Rome is likewise because her
rank demands a super natural pageant:

. . . the wife of Antony
Should have an army for an usher, and
The neighs of horse to tell of her approach,
Long ere she did appear. The trees by the way
Should have borne men, and expectation fainted,
Longing for what it had not. Nay, the dust
Should have ascended to the roof of heaven,
Rais'd by your populous troops . . .

III. vi. 43–50

Octavia's gentle character is at odds with the image conveyed by this
Marlovian triumph. And, although Enobarbus's speech of Cleopatra
records an event he saw, and Cleopatra's character is more equal to
such splendour, yet even in the speech is the affirmation that it does
not relate to the woman herself:

In her pavilion—cloth of gold, of tissue—
O'er-picturing that Venus where we see
The fancy outwork nature [emphasis
    added].

II. ii. 199–201

As does Shakespeare's description of Cleopatra. And it is Cleopatra
who confirms this. After Antony's death she denies regal ostentation:

No more but e'en a woman, and commanded
By such poor passion as the maid that milks.

IV. xv. 73–4

Festive Tragedy
213

There is a conflict between reality and the fame which surrounds them. Cleopatra faces up to the clash when she immortalizes Antony after his death. She describes him as a Colossus encompassing the earth: 'His legs bestrid the ocean, his rear'd arm | Crested the world.'[57] This image is also of a microcosm, a fitting analogy for Antony who was not only larger than life, but who also contained both highest and lowest attributes. The godly aspect of him, his face, she here sees as a cosmos of its own which contained 'a sun and moon' but, in conclusion, she asks Dolabella:

> Think you there was, or might be such a man
> As this I dreamt of ?
> DOL. Gentle madam, no.
>
> v. ii. 93–4

Yet Cleopatra continues that the power of imagination is greater than the insubstantial substance which mortal life in stark reality is. This is the only play of Shakespeare's which, while exposing artistic pretence, nevertheless allows it qualities above those of nature and even the final word.[58]

The seeds for Antony and Cleopatra's recuperation are set at the opening. The ideal cosmos for Antony and Cleopatra is defined by each other. She is his 'space',[59] and their love creates 'new heaven, new earth'.[60] In Antony's absence, Cleopatra experiences a 'great gap in time'.[61] Their private universe supersedes the public and, while falling from the public, Antony loses his immutable imagery until, in terms of worldly power, he is but a 'mangled shadow'.[62] He sues to Caesar to let him 'breathe between the heavens and earth'.[63] But Caesar, like Henry V, cannot admit a flaw in his own concept of order. Although Antony is not a political threat to him, as Antony points out in Act II, Scene ii, he is a personal insult. Hooped to Cleopatra rather than to himself, Antony diminishes Caesar's dominion. In Act III, Scene xi, after the flight from Actium, Cleopatra too admits that her realm can only subsist in tributary status to Rome, but both discover that there is no temporizing with Caesar: both must be made to contribute to a pageant glorifying him,[64] for him to recoup the fame they have stolen from him by visually adding

---

[57] v. ii. 82–3.
[58] To some extent, Hamlet's 'report me aright' conveys the same bias.
[59] I. i. 34.   [60] Ibid. 17.   [61] I. v. 5.   [62] IV. ii. 27.
[63] III. xii. 14.   [64] Caesar's plan is to take Antony, as well as Cleopatra, alive.

214   *Festive Tragedy*

it to his own. Cleopatra perceives that further humiliations will
follow, with actors debasing the story of their love, with portrayals
not too far removed from Enobarbus's descriptions of them in Act II,
Scene ii. Instead they defeat Caesar's plan with their own pageant
which turns carnal love into sublimity.

For Antony, confidence in love alternates with fury at the way it
destroys his worldly power. His reason is said to be subject to both
Cleopatra and Caesar,[65] and his reactions are governed entirely by
emotion. He veers from insane jealousy and mistrust, to an ability to
sustain breathtaking generosity in the face of defeat, which shames
the rational Enobarbus into death. But his emotions persistently
undermine the heroic, Herculean metaphors others use to describe
him. Whipping Caesar's envoy is unjustifiable brutality. His flight
from Actium, on the point of unexpected success, makes the tie with
Cleopatra the most foolish and destructive kind, as Enobarbus
accurately observes, and leaves Antony with nothing but her. The
device of Eros to replace Enobarbus brings in pure Prince d'Amour
moments, such as Eros buckling on his master's armour while
Cleopatra calls Antony back to bed. Antony calls Eros the 'armourer
of [his] heart',[66] and battle, 'a business that we love'.[67] Celebration
of the one success he has, fought in the spirit of love rather than
enmity, continues similarly. His soldiers' gashes will be kissed whole,
and he jokingly asks that the queen should 'know of our gests'.[68]
Even more than in the relationship between Falstaff and Hal, the
warmth of Antony's personality eclipses the calculated worldliness
of Caesar. But none the less it is not heroic. As Mason says, we never
see the Colossus that the other characters tell of.[69] Most telling is his
pursuit of death, which Antony seeks at first in terms of a woman's
passion, 'with a wound I must be cur'd',[70] and which Eros will not
give. Antony has to be compelled into the role of bridegroom, not
bride, in death;[71] then in classic, anti-heroic act, and as one student
wrote, 'Antony tries to kill himself but only succeeds in inflicting a
fatal wound'. Antony's last thoughts are for Cleopatra's safety, yet

---

[65] 'Caesar, thou hast subdued | His judgement too' (III. xiii. 36–7).

[66] IV. iv. 7.   [67] Ibid. 20.   [68] IV. viii. 2.

[69] H. A. Mason, '*Antony and Cleopatra*: Telling versus Showing', Casebook
Series, ed. J. R. Brown (London, 1968), p. 206.

[70] IV. xiv. 78.

[71] He reminds us as he dies that he has finally controlled his destiny: 'Not Caesar's
valour hath o'erthrown Antony, | But Antony's hath triumph'd on itself' (IV. xv.
14–15). Cf. IV. xv. 55–8.

Festive Tragedy

his advice to trust none 'but Proculeius',[72] is wrong; the only trustworthy man proves to be Dolabella, who loves. Dolabella provides the final endorsement that for Antony and Cleopatra trust in love is their only option, while Antony continues his generosity and, like Lear, his fallibility into his death.

The festive and the sorrowful are combined throughout. To begin with, their juxtaposition is part of Cleopatra's wiles. If Antony is 'sad, | Say I am dancing; if in mirth, report | That I am sudden sick'.[73] In his absence she learns he is 'nor sad nor merry', 'heavenly mingle'.[74] Moments in the 1987 National Theatre production were inspired in combining the two opposite emotions, particularly at the moment when, after his attempted suicide, Antony learns that Cleopatra is alive. The information comes to him indirectly. Diomedes enters and Antony, still intent on having his task completed for him, urges:

> Draw thy sword, and give me
> Sufficing strokes for death.
> DIOMED.   Most absolute lord,
> My mistress Cleopatra sent me to thee.

IV. xiv. 116–18

The momentary gasp of laughter which preceded Antony's 'When did she send thee?' contained superhuman generosity. Even before speaking, he had understood and accepted Cleopatra's trick to save herself from his wrath, even though it had resulted in his own end. The apparent undercutting of the tragic with a comic response enlarged his final nobility, and gave to the last demonstration of their love a mutual understanding of godlike proportions, which dared continue the festive spirit in death. At the same time, however, heroism continues to be undermined, particularly for Antony. Shakespeare could hardly go further in anti-heroic extremes than to have Antony hoisted up to the monument, inert and passive: a quite deliberate dramatization of Cleopatra's earlier metaphor about catching him like a fish:

>   I will betray
> Tawny-finn'd fishes, my bended hook shall pierce
> Their slimy jaws; and as I draw them up,

---

[72] IV. xv. 48.   [73] I. iii. 3–5.   [74] I. v. 52, 59.

216   *Festive Tragedy*

> I'll think them every one an Antony,
> And say 'Ah, ha! y'are caught.'

                                                    II. V. 11–15

And in Act IV, when exerting herself like a fishwife, Cleopatra still
cannot resist joking, 'here's sport indeed'.[75] Macho deeds and
feminine elegance belong to Caesar's world. Antony and Cleopatra
embrace the anti-heroic with humorous commitment.

For Cleopatra, the pattern of her triumph is set by what we know
of her from the beginning. Her godlike reactions when angry, 'some
innocents 'scape not the thunderbolt',[76] convey her absolutism. She
is further described as a goddess who combines opposites, subsumes
faults, and even vices, making 'defect perfection'[77] and 'vilest things |
Become themselves in her'.[78] Her ultimate triumph is in showing that
she does *contain* opposites. Rather than being simply changeable like
the moon, she proves to be both changeable and steadfast, to appear
to be faithless while being faithful, to contain the qualities of the sun
and the moon, as in her own description of Antony. When dealing on
the level of the outside, ordered world of Caesar she employs the
same pragmatic deceptions, such as attempting to conceal from
Caesar the extent of her treasure. Exposure of the deceit is her lowest
degradation, and evidence that she too cannot compete and win on
Caesar's terms. But the private cosmos of Antony and Cleopatra is
beyond and alternate to such petty trafficking. Their choice of the
private lifts them out of Caesar's reach. As already said, his intention
to restore his fame by having them parade in his pageant is overturned by the pageant of their deaths, which instead makes his army
attenders 'in solemn show'[79] at their funeral. As many have
observed, it is the nobility of their characters which triumphs over
Caesar's time-serving world, and the means of presenting their
qualities is through a display which is more forceful than all the
preceding descriptions and eulogies. Other characters become actors
in the spectacle of their final apotheosis. Charmian straightens
Cleopatra's crown which metaphorically had been 'awry'[80] all her
life, and Caesar's last lines pay them both tribute. And, since their
deaths provide the play's last image, there is no dramatic space for
the new heaven and new earth of the now idealized misrule lord and

---

[75] IV. XV. 32. Fishwives had one of the lowest reputations which contributed to
festive flytings.   [76] II. V. 77.   [77] II. ii. 231.
[78] Ibid. 238–9.   [79] V. ii. 362.   [80] Ibid. 317.

Festive Tragedy

his lady to be subsequently tarnished. In contrast to *Lear*, where the king's opening actions destroy his royal claim, and he is later shown reduced to pastoral king conventions, in *Antony and Cleopatra* the renegades' closing actions bestow on them royal deification, through the splendour of their Christmas king pageantry. This is one tragedy which does end on a note of poetic justice.[81]

---

[81] In contrast to Welsford's observation on *King Lear*; *The Fool*, p. 265.

10

Political Dissent and Drama

> Think not the king did banish thee,
> But thou the king.
>
> *Richard II*, I. iii. 279–80

Sixteenth-century drama is redolent with the unease characteristic of Tudor courts, and this was perhaps first translated by John Skelton into the Morality play Vice as an evil *alter rex* of cosmic proportions. Debate continues as to whether Magnyfycence was intended to represent Wolsey misled by his own material nature, or Henry beguiled by Wolsey.[1] But, as W. G. Glassco says, 'one cannot escape the impression that the play is an indictment of all the Cardinal represents'.[2] It might be thought surprising that Wolsey's sensitivity about such matters, which caused John Roo's imprisonment after his similar play in Gray's Inn, at Christmas 1526–7,[3] did not react immediately against Skelton, for it was only at the end of his life that the poet was in real danger from the prelate.[4] In the upheavals of the Reformation, a decade later, further dramatic satires on affairs of state can be detected, through the authorities' reaction to them. In 1537, it was alleged that seditious comment was added to the Suffolk May games, when the mock king was found to be advising how to rule a realm, and, in performance, the actor who played Husbandry 'said many things against gentlemen more than was in the book of the play'. The possibility that there might be other 'light persons, especially at games and plays', resulted in the banning of all such gatherings in Suffolk for the year.[5] In 1539 an ex-priest, Spenser, who had become an interlude player, went too far in mocking religion, and was burned at Salisbury for 'matter concerning the

---

[1] See P. Neuss (ed.), *Magnifycence*, The Revels Plays (Manchester, 1980), introd., pp. 35–6. [2] Ibid. 61 n. 90.

[3] E. Hall, *The Triumphant Reigne*, ed. C. Whibley (London, 1904), ii. 79.

[4] When Wolsey's influence over Henry replaced that of Skelton, the poet was forced to take sanctuary in Westminster, where he died. I. A. Gordon, *John Skelton; Poet Laureate* (Melbourne, 1943), pp. 18–44.

[5] SPD *Henry VIII*, vol. xii, pt. 1, ed. J. Gairdner (London, 1890), p. 557. Cf. p. 585.

Political Dissent and Drama

sacrament of the altar'.[6] And, similarly, at London 'a man was "presented for procuring an interlude to be openly played, wherein priests were railed on and called knaves"'.[7] It is possible that many more such escaped the eye of authority, and that those which were discovered indicate the bold statements which could be made with greater safety in 'uplandish'[8] or hillside privacy. Today, the best-known festive satire is the summer game led by Talboys Dymoke, in 1601: not against the state, but one pillar of it, the Earl of Lincoln, and which again found its way into the records because of legal action the earl took against the Dymoke family, resulting in their financial ruin.[9] One other event, previously mentioned, is the 1592 suppression of the midsummer games, on account of potential riot rather than satire. The bulk of extant records and all surviving play texts show instead those attacks directed into approved channels, with the anti-Protestant *Respublica* (Christmas 1553) celebrating Mary Tudor's accession, and Wager's *The Longer thou Livest the More Fool thou Art*, in 1559, marking the return to Protestantism.

Officially, in Elizabethan England, popular drama was not allowed to concern itself with contemporary matters. The 1559 proclamation, that all play texts be submitted to a local authority before performance, stated that none should be permitted '. . . wherein either matters of religion or of the governaunce of the estate of the common weale shalbe handled or treated . . .', though the continuation shows that, within the privacy of the court, there would be greater freedom: '. . . beyng no meete matters to be wrytten or treated vpon, but by menne of aucthoritie, learning and wisedome, nor to be handled before any audience, but of graue and discreete persons'.[10] *The Misfortunes of Arthur* is one example of serious political debate before such an audience.[11] Earlier in the

---

[6] V. C. Gildersleeve, *Government Regulation of the Elizabethan Drama* (3rd edn., Westport, Conn., 1975), p. 7.

[7] Ibid. 7. Such cases led to the first legislation concerning the content of plays; the Statute of 1543 dealing incidentally with them. 'Seditious people, the act states, have tried to subvert the true doctrine not only by sermons, "but also by prynted bokes, prynted balades, playes, rymes, songes, and other fantasies"' (ibid.).

[8] The name given to describe rough, uncontrollable rustics. See the Prologue to Lydgate's 'Mumming at Hertford', *The Minor Poems of John Lydgate*, ed. H. N. MacCracken, EETS (London, 1934), p. 675.

[9] C. L. Barber, *Shakespeare's Festive Comedy* (Princeton, 1959), pp. 36–51.

[10] E. K. Chambers, *The Elizabethan Stage* (Oxford, 1923), iv. 263.

[11] The only censored line was Mordred's rejection of the code by which all nobility served queen and country: 'Must I for Countrie's ease disease myselfe, | Or for their loue dispise my owne estate' (fo. B. 4ʳ).

220   *Political Dissent and Drama*

reign, at Elizabeth's second Christmas, there was another interesting event; outside players touching on sensitive matters. Machyn notes: '. . . ther was a play a-for her grace, the wyche the plaers plad suche matter that they wher commandyd to llyff off, and continent [immediately] the maske cam in dansyng.'[12] However, Sir John Mason's Accounts record that this same Christmas the players were not only generously rewarded by Elizabeth, but their maintenance from the royal purse was agreed for the next twenty-one months.[13] This would suggest that, though publicly embarrassing, the subject was one which privately pleased her. One wonders whether it could have been more about the unfortunate Swedish suitor, who was present.[14] (It is also possible that the players were those Dudley had already supported in June 1559.)[15] The players would have known their matter, whatever it was, would be controversial, but in general it appears that the concept of play as a legitimate time of anarchy, endorsed by those who came to watch, provided some immunity within the law; particularly when arguments employed the fustian analogies of king games and, outside the court, the convention was deliberately used from 1588 to 1600 as a means of evading restrictions.

Unfavourable remarks about government could be made through historical analogy, which might sometimes glance at the current head of state. For example, King John, as a character, raised issues similar to those of Arthur. Like him, John was part precursor and part disappointment to Protestant England for opposing the Pope but finally failing to advance England's interests. In *TR* and *KJ* John bears obvious similarities to Elizabeth, while at the same time he is the villain of the piece, yet the combination clearly did not inhibit the authors. As well as being accused of usurpation, defying the Pope, and asserting divine right, John is excommunicated and imprisons a rival who is barred from the crown by a will. In the plays, the Pope offers pardon to his murderer,[16] and invites another king to invade

---

[12] H. Machyn, *Diary of a Resident in London from 1550 to 1563*, ed. J. G. Nichols (London, 1848), p. 221.

[13] '. . . payed by vertue of the quenes Mati warr . . . Westm the xxvth daye of Decembre dmo scdo Eliz. Regina to her highnes Entrelude playeres . . . to John Brown, Edwarde Strowdewrke, John Smythe, and William Readinge eu[r]ye of them at lxvij sh. viijd . . . and xxiijsh iiijd for theire Lyu[ng]e yerly to be payd qrterlye. done vnto them for one fole yeare and [three-quarters] ending at the feaste of Mas [Michaelmas] Ao iij [1561]'. *Declared Accounts, Treasurer of the Chamber*, PRO AO 1/380.2.

[14] See Ch. 4.   [15] Chambers, *Elizabethan Stage*, ii. 86.

[16] Canonization in *KJ*: see Honigmann for the list of similarities, introd., Arden edn., p. xxix.

Political Dissent and Drama   221

England. The invaders intend to kill the Englishmen, who help them, and their navy is providentially wrecked. Finally, English unity is achieved at the point of the invasion's failure. In *TR*, since all troubles were associated with John's false reign, the ending is of strong regenerative hope. The historical analogies accentuate the perils recently overcome in order to give greater relief, optimism, and desire to maintain unity in the future. In Shakespeare's play there are additional negative parallels between John and Elizabeth. The king urges the murder of his rival and then uses the murderer as a scapegoat. These touch on more sensitive royal involvement in Mary's execution: a point of comparison which returns in *Richard II*. Further, Shakespeare's ending suggests that the demise of the mock king has not necessarily cured the disorder in court, and that corruption will continue. This means that the analogies between the historical John and contemporary England are finally brought to focus on corrupt government as a current possibility.

The inherent treachery of the impoverished Tudor court system is fully excoriated in *Timon of Athens*, and if 1600 is the right date for the play, then an Essex analogy for Timon becomes likely.[17] Essex was noted for a combination of extravagant benevolence when all seemed well, and virulent melancholy when frustrated. His letter to Elizabeth of 12 May 1600, when under house arrest, is a vivid example of the latter and its Timon-like bittterness includes the line 'and shortly they will play me upon the stage'.[18] The date of the letter coincides with the probable time that Middleton planned his play with the Chamberlain's Men. Looked at from Essex's point of view, a Timon comparison is not entirely complimentary to him. Though his supporters are shown to be despicable, the man wafted to the top of the hill was frequently an invidious metaphor for royal favourites. At the very least, since Timon is portrayed as a summer king and not an idealized Christmas prince, the suggestion is of a figure of mockery rather than the hero Essex felt himself to be.

However, as has often been observed, the dominant analogy of the period was between Richard II and Elizabeth.[19] As early as 1578, the

---

[17] J. Hurstfield's assessment of Essex's predicament is almost a summary of Timon's. 'When he was deprived of his powers of rewarding his followers, his system and his authority collapsed with them', *Freedom, Corruption and Government in Elizabethan England* (London, 1973), p. 151.

[18] SPD, *Elizabeth 1598–1601*, ed. M. A. E. Green (London, 1869), p. 435.

[19] E. G. Clark, *Ralegh and Marlowe* (New York, 1965), p. 116, and below n. 39.

222   *Political Dissent and Drama*

dangers of Elizabeth heeding only flattery were expressed by Sir Francis Knollys:

For who woll persiste in gyvinge of safe counsayle, if her Majestie woll persiste in myslykyng of safe counsayle? Nay who woll not rather shrynkingly (that I may say no worse) play the partes of King Richard the Second's men, then to enter into the odious office of crossing her Majesties' wylle?

With the subsequent danger:

. . . up startes the pryde and practice of the papists and downe declyneth the comforte and strengthe of her Majesties safety.[20]

The received view of Richard II, by birth a rightful and legitimate king, was even more critical than that of the usurper King John. Holinshed details his extravagancies and injustices, calling him dissolute, prodigal, ambitious, and, according to the Duke of York, worthy only of the lowest and most ambiguous of leadership titles: 'it was the part of a wise man . . . to leave the following of such an unadvised capteine'.[21] Such a character combined kingship by divine right with all the sins of pride and luxury, listed by Erasmus, and opposed by commoners morally better than he. Used as an analogy for Elizabeth, it undermined the deified image of her at its peak in the 1590s. In *Jack Straw* (1592), which uses the peasants' revolt of Richard's reign against the poll tax as an analogy for contemporary grievances, the unnamed king is depicted without mock king reverberations and, at the end, the rebels are put down in a theoretically proper manner. It reads more like a warning against rebellion than criticism of government.[22] By contrast, in the early *Richard II* or *Thomas of Woodstock*[23] (which for some reason was never printed) it appears that the inherently subversive nature of king play was successfully used as a stalking-horse, under cover of which the playwright shot his dissident wit. It begins as an anti-courtier, but

---

[20] T. Wright, *Queen Elizabeth and her Times* (London, 1838), i. 75.
[21] R. Holinshed, *Chronicles of England, Scotland and Ireland*, ed. J. Hooker *et al.* (London, 1807–8), ii. 849. During the peasants' revolt, after Tyler's death, Richard is reported to have won the crowd with words which sound as much like game fantasy as any rebel's promises, and which were possibly Holinshed's rather than Richard's. 'What is the matter my men, what meane you . . . I will be your king, capteine and leader, follow me into the fields, and you shall haue all things that you desire' (ibid. 741).
[22] The Lord Mayor's pageant by the Fishmongers' Guild, 1590, also concentrated on the defeat of Jack Straw and could have been another warning.
[23] Boas's name for the text, which lacks a title-page.

Political Dissent and Drama   223

quickly becomes an anti-king, play. Richard is drawn as mock king above his lords of misrule, similar to the image of him as Richard the Redeles, but also with the sinister characteristics of a Richard III, and possibly influenced by the earlier play, *The True Tragedy of Richard III*.[24] He countenances and ultimately leads the villainy against his moderate and right-minded critic, the Lord Protector, Sir Thomas Woodstock. In *Woodstock*, like no other play of the period, the king is presented until the end in mock king terms, as both true-born and an outright villain whose overthrow must ensue. And even more devastating is the connection with Elizabeth which is made in it.

The meticulous transcriber of the text from MS Egerton 1994, Wilhelmina Frijlinck, emphasizes the play's evident popularity. The manuscript contains numerous property and stage directions, written in different hands, and it shows the resulting wear and tear of repeated use. Yet, despite its subject-matter, the hand of the censor is only lightly shown. Tilney's cannot be identified at all, though that of his post-1603 successor, Sir George Buc, is, suggesting a later revival. The main correction Buc asked for was a change of Woodstock's address to the king, from 'cuss' to 'my lege'.[25] Yet this play was far more subversive than the unfortunate *Book of Sir Thomas More*, which Tilney censored probably to the point of keeping it off the stage.[26]

Act 1 opens with a black joke. Richard's minions attempt to murder four of his uncles by poisoning a cup intended to wish the king health. Greene, Bushey, and Bagot, led by the malevolent Tresilien, are the evil influences against whom the good lords, Lancaster, York, Arundel, and Surrey, led by Woodstock, must pit themselves with equal cunning. In Woodstock's words, they must 'be smooth awhile'.[27] Here, however, Woodstock himself fails. He is not knavish enough for guile, and undermines their attempts to regain influence over Richard by losing his temper, possibly influenced by his unusually sumptuous garments.[28] Richard responds by making Tresilien Lord Chief Justice, thereby setting up a parody of justice. As

---

[24] Printed 1594.

[25] Also a change to the phrase 'superior lord of Scotland'. W. Frijlinck (ed.), Malone Society Reprints (Oxford, 1929), pp. xxii–xxiii.

[26] See S. McMillin, *The Elizabethan Theatre and 'The Book of Sir Thomas More'* (Ithaca, 1987), for the possibility that it was performed after 1603.

[27] I. i. 176 *Woodstock: A Moral History*, ed. A. P. Rossiter (London, 1946).

[28] Under protest he replaces his frieze garments with 'brave' dress to avoid provoking his nephew.

224 *Political Dissent and Drama*

in many Jacobean dramas, Tresilien becomes the lord of inverted law for the duration of the play, profiting from the disorder he is empowered to create. He is chief knave, in the explicit belief that the lords are fools whom his greatness will keep in awe.[29] His comic servant, Nimble, both encourages and takes liberties with Tresilien's new-found dignity, and confirms the disordered world under his master, in the exit line, 'a fig for the rope'.[30] Yet it would be wrong to say that Tresilien is the most dominant misrule lord. Nothing he does is without Richard's initial decree and control:

> Young Henry Greene shall be Lord Chancellor,
> Bagot, Lord Keeper of our privy seal,
> Tresilien, learned in our kingdom's laws,
> Shall be Chief Justice: by them and their directions
> King Richard will uphold his government.
>
> I. iii. 184–8

Rossiter finds it a weakness in the play that there are no scenes of confrontation between Tresilien and Woodstock, whom he considers the chief antagonists.[31] However, there are very telling scenes of opposition between Richard and Woodstock, in which Woodstock's sense of justice forces him into traitorous denunciation:

KING. We let you know those gifts are given to them: We did it Woodstock . . .

WOODSTOCK. Ye have done ill, then.

KING   Ha, dare ye say so?

> I. iii. 165–7

Richard further places himself above Tresilien as ultimate mock king, when, like King John, he has himself crowned a second time, once he has wrested the final vestiges of authority from the hands of Lancaster and his supporters. He demonstrates publicly that the topsy-turvy world is ruled over by the true-born mock king.

The 'wild and antic habits' he and his cohorts next appear in not only reveal their moral, wasteful folly, but closely identify them with the professional fool, who adopted the 1380s fashion of parti-colouring, pointed toes, and peaked cap for his professional dress.

---

[29] I. ii. 70.   [30] Ibid. 131.
[31] Rossiter, *Woodstock*, introd., pp. 24–6, 40–1.

Political Dissent and Drama   225

The point is made by Nimble, who comments that his copying their dress has turned him into 'a morris dancer'.[32] Richard's next act is to divide England up into areas to be farmed, or misruled, by each of his four deputies (a parodic version of the action of *Gorboduc*, *King Leir*, and like Mordred in *King Arthur*). Since the division is done by the king, he shows that the misrule governance of his cohorts, over their respective areas, has the king as head and source. There is no other play in the whole of the Renaissance where a true king is so scathingly and repeatedly reduced to the image of mock king, and where one cannot sympathize at all with the legitimate ruler: one longs instead for the overthrow of his unscrupulous arrogance.[33]

Woodstock's own reactions are, to say the least, unorthodox. Hearing of the public discontent and defiance, he finds that 'Afore my God I cannot blame them . . . Can they be rebels called, that now turn head?'[34] The answer, of course, should be 'yes' in a society ruled by a little God. He himself defies Richard's summons to court, which could be considered treason, though Elizabeth forgave Essex a similar snub. And Woodstock finally makes his rejection of rebellion clear in his answer to the masque in Act IV, which he thinks a further invitation to lead opposition, though in fact the whole masque is Tresilien's ruse to trap and abduct him. The theme of the masque, announced by the goddess of the moon, Cynthia, is that she and her squires are hunting a 'cruel, tusked boar' who is destroying the kingdom, and, before they eliminate it, they wish to honour a faithful prince, adding, equivocally, that if such a one exists it must be Woodstock:

> That keeps a court of love and pity here.
> Reverend and mild his looks.

> IV. ii. 114–15

Before they dance Woodstock translates the singular wild boar into the safer plural, meaning Richard's followers rather than the king

---

[32] III. i. 114.
[33] Richard's Queen Anne is, like Zenocrate and the queen in *Pride of Life*, the moral antithesis to her lord; loving, obedient, and, although a foreigner, devoted to the people. At her death Richard's grief is expressed in Tamburlaine-like sentiments. He wishes to pull down the house at Sheen where she dies as a monument to her (see Holinshed, *Chronicles*, ii. 823) and his actions achieve this with regard to his family house.   [34] III. ii. 82, 85.

226   *Political Dissent and Drama*

himself, and declines the offer. Richard, in disguise, then reveals that
it is Woodstock who is their quarry, so demonstrating that Woodstock's understanding of the masque was nearer the truth. The king is
the uncontrolled will, who continues his acts of destruction by now
removing his opponent, the symbol of good government and whose
court is of love and pity.[35] The masque's presiding goddess, Cynthia,
was, of course, goddess of night-time and courtly misrule, but more
extraordinary is the fact that she was also one of the deities through
which Elizabeth was idealized.

At the end of the play the problems regarding Richard are perfunc-
torily resolved. Ancestral ghosts warn Woodstock of his impending
murder, and tell him that *his* family line is the legitimate one. The
masque's ironic compliment had been correct. Though Woodstock
never claims the throne, his right to it had been dammed up by
Richard, whose French birth is recalled as explanation for his evil
deeds. Within the fiction, it turns out that Richard is not a true-born
English prince after all, but more of a perfidious Frenchman. Seeds
for this reversal are set in the opening scene where Woodstock both
praises and criticizes Richard in front of his new queen.

> A youth unsettled; yet he's princely bred
> Descended from the royal'st bloods in Europe,
> The kingly stock of England and of France.
>
> .   .   .   .   .   .
>
> But his maturity I hope you'll find
> True English-bred . . .
> KING. I thank ye for your double praise, good uncle.

                                                    I. iii. 26–32

From Morality play precedent it might seem that Richard is placed in
the role of young, wild prince whose escapades can be forgiven.
However, it turns out that his renegade actions are, instead, obdurate
sin stemming from the taint of his mongrel ancestry. Therefore, the
political dangers in approving rebellion, defiance, and disrespect of
the king were, in the final act, greatly reduced. The technique was to
be used comically in Beaumont and Fletcher's *A King and No King*.
Also, in the eventual battle to overthrow Richard, the dangers of a
deposition scene are avoided, by using Tresilien as the chief lord to be

---

[35] His wife dreams of an angry lion, the forest king, leading a herd of wolves and
slaying both Woodstock and the sheep who try to rescue him. It is Richard himself, not
Tresilien, indicated here as instigator of the murder.

Political Dissent and Drama 227

vanquished. But the techniques to prevent immediate objections to the play do not rule out the likelihood that the evils of Cynthia's court related to contemporary England, and that the play should be seen as a dissenting political statement, with conventional enough plot devices for the allusion against the crown to escape the eye of Tilney.

The grossest injustice in the play is taxation, a particularly sore point in the 1590s. The farming out of direct and indirect taxation was a desperate resort of sixteenth-century heads of state to pay the salaries of their officers, the equally bankrupt nobility. The Tudors found it increasingly difficult to realize taxable income, the more that government was centralized in London and removed from the sources of revenue. Therefore the policy was adopted, by Elizabeth in the middle and end years of her reign, and continued by James I, of leasing out the rights to indirect taxation for set sums, which they could then be sure of, while the lessees were free to extort for themselves whatever they could. The choice of beneficiary declined from patronage to favouritism, the difference spelled out as follows: 'patronage was a system of rule appropriate and practical for its day . . . favouritism was merely the reward from the public resources for irrelevant personal qualities'.[36]

Direct taxes were also administered by her courtiers or officers, though Francis Bacon argued in 1593 that the right of deciding and administrating taxation was the exclusive right of the elected house,[37] which today we might find less than perfect, but an improvement on unelected tax-gatherers, conscious that their own income depended on the success of their endeavours, and still with residual influence in the courts of law. But the greatest and most recent burden was Elizabeth's double subsidy to pay for the country's defences in 1593. The extra tax was to be raised at twice the speed of any previous emergency measures, but not many in Parliament dared raise their voices against it: Peter Wentworth, who did, was sent to the Tower. Francis Bacon made a more careful plea to reconsider, while still suggesting that the monarch was slipping into

---

[36] Hurstfield, *Freedom, Corruption and Government*, pp. 304–5. Leicester began as a favourite but became a minister, whereas Essex began and ended his life as an impecunious courtier, relying on Elizabeth's favours, particularly the gift of the farm of sweet wines, to keep himself solvent. When she tried to curb him by withholding this, she helped propel him into desperate remedies.

[37] *The Works of Francis Bacon*, ed. J. Spedding, R. L. Ellis, and D. D. Heath, i. *The Life and Letters* (London, 1862), pp. 216–17.

228   *Political Dissent and Drama*

tyranny.[38] Resistance in the country to the new tax may have been the reason for the writing of the governmental warning, *Jack Straw*, and the reply, *Woodstock*.

Woodstock shows bitter resentment at the freedom of court favourites to fleece the populace, and one might wish to cast Essex, whose grandfather accused him of 'wasteful consumption' in the 1580s,[39] as the model for Richard's minions; with sober counsellors, such as Lord Burghley, the antithesis. However, the ancestral connection between Woodstock and Essex is the stronger, and Woodstock's fate, being abducted and murdered by his enemies, was the one which Essex's paranoia increasingly imagined from Raleigh's, or Burghley's, court factions. Also, Essex enjoyed great popularity, despite his reliance on farming, and his final downfall was to be partly due to his misconceived conviction that the people would rally behind him against his enemies. Finally, it was Essex whose open incivility to the queen enraged and amused her, and which was to culminate in the unforgivable challenge, 'Cannot princes err?' The dates of composition of this play, 1591–4, precede Essex's final suicidal act, and it is impossible to cast exact role models though, possibly, the play's own continued success was due in part to the way it somewhat foretold the inevitable end to Essex's permanent wrangle with the sovereign. All that can be said with any certainty is that the play does dramatize contemporary injustices and the popular conception of their cause. The play is more concerned with these injustices than with Woodstock's ill-treatment, and Woodstock takes on Bacon's role, pointing to the change from careful patronage to wanton extortion. He protests to Richard that Bagot and his fellows:

> . . . cut the columns that should prop thy house
> They tax the poor . . . those late oppressions rise
> To set the Commons in a mutiny.
>
> I.iii. 121–4

---

[38] '. . . the poor man's rent is such as they are not able to yield it, and the general commonality is not able to pay so much upon the present. The gentlemen must sell their plate and the farmers their brass pots ere this will be paid. And as for us, we are here to search the wounds of the realm and not to skin them over; wherefore we are not to persuade ourselves of their wealth more than it is . . . we shall thus breed discontentment in the people. And in a cause of jeopardy, her Majesty's safety must consist more in the love of her people than in their wealth' (ibid. 223).

[39] L. B. Smith, *Treason in Tudor England* (London, 1986), p. 200.

Political Dissent and Drama   229

Other grievances include wasteful court consumption in such matters as dress. Again Woodstock takes John Commonwealth's part
against this cause of inflation for the common people:

> Should this fashion last I must raise new rents,
> Undo my poor tenants, turn away my servants . . .
> But I'll build castles in my tother hose.

I. iii. 104–9

And rich prizes, taken at sea, are said to be squandered by Richard on
favourites, instead of being used to reimburse the people: an issue
completely irrelevant to Richard's historical situation, but a popular
contemporary conception of how Spanish plunder was wasted.

One other negative feature of Elizabethan society, which understandably rarely found expression, was the prohibition against
dissent. In the Parliament of 1593 only one man sacrificed his own
liberty in the cause of liberty, and Ben Jonson later recalled how, in
1597, when imprisoned for his contribution to *The Isle of Dogs*, men
were planted in his cell to draw him out, but he was warned by his
guard.[40] *Woodstock* contains one graphic scene of a police state,
where men are arrested on whims to instil fear and reduce resistance
to the tax; giving, as a result, the picture of an inverted world more
damning than in any other play of the period. The attacking humour
expressed through Bailiff Ignorance, a devastatingly colluding Dog-
berry, and through the man condemned to be hanged for whistling
treachery, provides stringent black satire of the kind one usually
associates with Brecht.

Taxation, wasteful fashions while the people went hungry, the
influence of mock king favourites at court, and the police state in the
country; all these suggest a critical reflection of the harsher side of
Elizabethan life and the reason for the play's popularity. But the most
extraordinary aspect of this political allegory is Cynthia presiding
over the masque and, therefore, in microcosm, leading the corrupt
court destroying good government.[41] Allusions to Elizabeth as
Cynthia in the 1590s were ubiquitous, and a parallel in the minds of

---

[40] 'In the tyme of his close imprissonment, under Queen Elisabeth, his judges could
gett nothing of him to all their demands bot I and No. They placed two damned
villains to catch advantage of him, with him, but he was advertised by his keeper.'
Ben Jonson's Conversations with William Drummond of Hawthornden, ed. R. F.
Patterson (London, 1924), pp. 24–5.
[41] The character enters separately from the rest of the masquers and much could
have been suggested by the way she was dressed.

230   *Political Dissent and Drama*

the audience could not be avoided. It is hard to understand how this play evaded the censor, except that Andrew Gurr tells us the Master of Revels noticed only superficial offences, such as insulting a Polish Ambassador in *The Isle of Dogs*; casting aspersions on the Scots in *Eastward Ho!*, and the disrespectful 'cuss' in *Woodstock*. Careful reading only took place when texts were published,[42] which may be why the authors of this play decided against publication.

   The Book of Sir Thomas More is the only extant play manuscript in which we can see heavy censorial objections. The play begins with a literal re-enactment of the 1517 London uprising against the privileged Flemish settlers, with Sir Thomas More's mythologized intervention to save the rioters. 1586 had seen further, threatened, anti-alien activity which, in the mind of the correspondent, would have been a repeat of 1517.[43] It would appear that the current danger of such disturbances (and which flared up again in 1592) caused Tilney to write:

Leaue out yᵉ insur wholy & yᵉ Cause ther off & ⟨b⟩egin wᵗ Sr Tho: Moore att yᵉ mayors sessions wᵗ a reportt afterwards off his good servicᵉ don being Shriue off Londō vppō a mutiny Agaynst ye Lūbards only by A shortt reportt & nott otherwise att your own perriles.[44]

Incitement to riot was a recognizable danger. *Sir Thomas More* expressed no anti-government sentiments, but might revive smouldering resentments in London's artisans. *Woodstock* would seem to show that clever satire might escape the censor. Provided the message was blurred, or revoked by a final twist, it was in fact possible to make incisive comments against the monarch. Therefore, since the play was so popular, why were there not others in which a contemporary dissenting voice could be detected? Possibly some of those lost plays listed by Harbage include other manuscript deviants from orthodoxy. It might also be worth while to look more closely at other minor dramas of the 1590s; as, for example, Thomas Heywood's *First and Second Partes of King Edward the Fourth*, printed in 1600, and chiefly remembered today for the Jane Shore episode. At the end of Part 1 Jane is obliged to accept her dubious rise in fortune with its subsequent catastrophic fall. However, under the

---

   [42] *King Richard II* (Cambridge, 1984, introd., pp. 9–10. Ben Jonson developed his stage satire in *Everyman Out* after prose satire had been banned in 1599.
   [43] Recorder Fleetwood to Lord Burghley, 6 Sept. 1586, in Wright, *Queen Elizabeth and her Times*, ii. 308.
   [44] Fo. A. 1ʳ. Malone Society Reprints, ed. W. W. Greg (Oxford, 1911), p. 1.

Political Dissent and Drama 231

cloak of moral tragedy, state tyranny is placed under scrutiny. The misrule lord of Part 1, Edward IV, is replaced in Part 2 by the greater mockery of Richard III; Jane is portrayed as defender of peoples' rights, and Haywood only allows moral condemnation of her when spoken by Jane herself. When, for example, her one-time confidante, Mistress Blague, changes from condoning immorality to a denunciation of the outcome, Jane points out her hypocrisy, and Mistress Blague's motives turn out to be self-interest rather than objective moral comment. The decree against Jane results in her lingering death and takes up the last two acts of Part 2, thus providing a sustained portrayal of state inhumanity, with its effects on the rest of society who are forbidden to help her. And Brackenbury's soliloquy of protest sounds more like general comment than reaction to Jane's situation:

> Oh, God! how full of dangers grow these times,
> And no assurance seen in any state
> No man can say that he is master now
> Of anything is his, such is the tide
> Of sharp disturbance running through the land!
>
> (Part 2, *King Edward IV*, IV. ii).

Observations on tyranny, and the enactment of its resulting corruption of society, provide as bitter an attack on government as does *Woodstock*.

The similarities in Shakespeare's *Richard II* between Richard and Elizabeth, and Bolingbroke and Essex, have already been thoroughly explored,[45] and the only evidence I will repeat is that which shows how such analogies were perceived during and immediately after Elizabeth's reign. In 1598, Edward Guilpin attacked Essex for deliberately wooing the people, to further his ambitions, in words which echo Richard's description of Bolingbroke's 'courtship to the common people'.[46]

---

[45] See E. A. Albright, 'Shakespeare's *Richard II* and the Essex Conspiracy', *PMLA* 42:3 (1927), pp. 686–720; V. C. Gildersleeve, *Government Regulation of the Elizabethan Drama* (3rd edn., Westport, Conn., 1975), ch. 3; Clark, *Ralegh and Marlowe*, pp. 125–32; and Gurr, *King Richard II*, introd., pp. 7–8.

[46] 'Ourself and Bushy | Observ'd his courtship to the common people, | How he did seem to dive into their hearts | With humble and familiar courtesy; | What reverence he did throw away on slaves . . . | Off goes his bonnet to an oyster-wench; | A brace of draymen bid God speed him well, | And had the tribute of his supple knee, | With "Thanks my countrymen, my loving friends"' (I. iv. 23–34).

Political Dissent and Drama

> For when great Foelix passing through the street,
> Vayleth his cap to each one he doth meet,
>
> .   .   .   .   .
>
> Who would not thinke him perfect curtesie?
> Or the honny-suckle of humilitie?
>
> .   .   .   .   .
>
> *Signior Machiauell*
> Taught him this mumming trick, with curtesie
> T'entrench himselfe in popularitie . . .[47]

And in 1603 an attack on Raleigh (who, rather, cultivated unpopularity) was contrasted with the greater civility of the then deceased Essex, borrowing even more obviously from *Richard II*.[48] Elizabeth's famous remark after Essex's execution, 'I am Richard II, know ye not that . . . this tragedy was played 40 times in open streets and houses',[49] shows her own consciousness of the invidious analogy between herself and the monarch who took away Bolingbroke's rights, and overtaxed the people.[50] Yet, despite the contemporary analogies, understood by others as well as by herself, she never intervened to ban the play or to punish the players, not even after the performance on the night before Essex's rebellion. 'The one aspect of the whole episode that is difficult to understand, is the complete exemption of the players from punishment. The Chamberlain's men actually played before the Queen on the night of Essex's execution.'[51] Whereas John Hayward's publication of *The Life and Raigne of Henry IIII* left him languishing in prison for several years.[52] And, Gurr argues, even the deposition scene, cut from the printed text until after her death, was probably included in performance.[53] Sidney's argument on behalf of tragedies, printed in 1595, that they 'openeth the greatest woundes, and sheweth forth the

---

[47] *Skialetheia*, Shakespeare Association Facsimiles, no. 2, ed. G. B. Harrison (Oxford, 1931), satyre 1, fo. C. 3ᵛ.

[48] 'Renowned Essex, as he past the streets | Woulde vaile his bonnett to an oyster wife, | And with a kinde of humble congie greete | The vulgar sort that did admire his life.' *Poetical Miscellanies*, ed. J. O. Halliwell, Percy Society: Early English Poetry, vol. 15 (London, 1845), p. 17, no. 1.

[49] In conversation with William Lambert. J. G. Nichols (ed.), *The Progresses . . . of Elizabeth* (London, 1788–1823), iii. 552.

[50] Intelligence-gatherers might not have discriminated between performances of *Richard II* and *Woodstock*.

[51] Clark, *Ralegh and Marlowe*, p. 132.

[52] Ibid. 128–30.

[53] *King Richard II*, introd., pp. 9–10.

Political Dissent and Drama   233

Vlcers that are couered with *Tissue*, that maketh Kings feare to be Tyrants',[54] found an echo in Bacon's words of 1593[55] and appears to have been respected. As long as the 1559 ban was observed, and no direct contemporary comment was made,[56] oblique, performed analogies might escape the censor. A large part of the metaphor in *Woodstock* is through mock king analogy, with which the mass of the people were familiar. *Richard II* is more subtle and complex, but the analogy is there when Richard, mid-play and looking like the setting sun, descends from the elevation of Flint Castle.

After the *Isle of Dogs* scandal in 1597, which resulted in Jonson's imprisonment and the threatened, but ignored, closure of the theatres, measures were again taken against authors in 1605, when an intelligencer reported to James that one speech imitating the king, and another wishing the Scots in Virginia,[57] had been interpolated into *Eastward Ho!*, played by the Children of the Queen's Revels at the Blackfriars. Jonson and Chapman were imprisoned for their involvement, threatened with losing their ears, and Chapman alleged that the real culprit, Marston, escaped. As is believed regarding *The Isle of Dogs*, the offending material was direct and incidental comment, not a considered parable on the new king's policies. Such direct comment, which had been attempted by foreign companies in the last years of Elizabeth's reign, became prevalent in the early years of James.

Chambers tells us that as early as June 1604 (three months after James's accession) the French ambassador wrote:

Consider for pity's sake . . . what must be the state and condition of a prince, whom the preachers publicly from the pulpit assail, whom the comedians of the metropolis bring upon the stage, whose wife attends these representations in order to enjoy the laugh against her husband.[58]

[54] *Defence of Poesie*, fo. E. 4ᵛ.   [55] See n. 38.
[56] In 1602 Italian comedians were prevented from playing in the street 'L'Histoire anglaise contre la royne d'Angleterre', possibly about post-1593 events. Other plot summaries of anti-Elizabeth plays performed on the Continent show direct mockery similar to that in English plays against Spain. Chambers, *Elizabethan Stage*, i. 323 n. 2.
[57] In Virginia will be found 'a few industrious Scots. But as for them there are not greater friends to Englishmen and *England*, when they are out an't, in the world, then they are. And for my part, I would a hundred thousand of 'hem were there, for wee are all one Countrey-men now, yee know; and wee shoulde finde ten times more comfort of them there then wee doe heere' (III. ii. 1382–7). *Eastward Ho!*, ed. J. H. Harris, Yale Studies in English (Yale, 1926), p. 46. Quarto, 1605, original fo. E. 3ᵃ⁻ᵇ.
[58] Chambers, *Elizabethan Stage*, i. 325.

Political Dissent and Drama

This evidence 'is confirmed by a letter of 28 march 1605 from Samuel Calvert . . . in which he writes that "the play[er]s do not forbear to represent upon their stage the whole course of this present time, not sparing either King, state, or religion, in so great absurdity, and with such liberty, that any would be afraid to hear them"'.[59] Chambers adds that it may well have been Queen Anne's approval which was in part 'responsible for the long-suffering'[60] with which the insolence of the Children of her Revels was met; particularly since she replaced the king's censor, Buc, with Samuel Daniel, who was responsible only to her. For eighteen months free and open criticism can be found in her company's extant texts, such as Marston's *The Fawn* and *Eastward Ho!*, John Day's *The Isle of Gulls*, and the anonymous *Nobody and Somebody*, while offence was also given by their censor's play, *Philotas*, and by Marston's *The Dutch Courtesan*.

The opening of *The Fawn* appears to include a comparison between the outward severity of Elizabeth's court in her later years, and the open laxness of James. Duke Hercules leaves the governing of his State to allow himself disguised liberty and disorder in a neighbouring State, and says, with some disregard of syntax:

> And now, thou ceremonious sovereignty—
> Ye proud, severer, stateful compliments,
> The secret arts of rule [*Basilicon Doron?*] I put you off;
> Nor ever shall those manacles of form
> Once more lock up the appetite of blood.
> 'Tis now an age of man whilst we, all strict,
> Have lived in awe of carriage regular
> Apted unto my place; nor hath my life
> Once tasted of exorbitant affects . . .
> But we must once be wild.[61]

Hercules' motives are beneficiently saturnalian, and the results only superficially immoral, but the concept of enormities caused by a prince's absence from government was more fully developed in other works through mock king play (see Chapter 11). In *The Isle of Gulls*, the division of characters into Scots and English caused some to be 'committed to Bridewell'.[62] And, despite the Induction's denial that

[59] Chambers, *Elizabethan Stage*, i. 325. [60] Ibid. 326.
[61] I. i. 40–50. *The Works of John Marston*, ed. A. H. Bullen, 3 vols. (London, 1887), ii. 119.
[62] Chambers, *Elizabethan Stage*, iii. 286. This suggests that some actors were now adult.

Political Dissent and Drama   235

'it figures anie certaine state or priuate gouernment',[63] much of the
play is a broadside against minions, 'up-start basenes crept into the
bedde of greatnesse',[64] exemplified by the absurdly dangerous and
potential usurper, Dametas, one of the 'Court spyders that weaue
their webbes of flatterie in the eares of greatnesse [and] in the end . . .
hauing lapt the sweet milk of greatnes, made themselues strong in
authoritie and friendes, they turne their stings of enuie into their
preseruers bosome'.[65] Marston's Mendoza could well be a more
fictionalized version of the same phenomenon.

Nobody and Somebody both inveighs against the king making
Britain unhappy with his lasciviousness, and also openly lists political grievances. Ironically, Nobody is a Mundus figure, dressed as ✓
such, a generous host and preserver of the poor. Nobody's

> Barnes are full, and when the Cormorants
> And wealthy Farmers hoord vp all the graine,
> He empties all his Garners to the poore
> Vnder the stretcht prise that the Market yeelds,—
> *Nobody* racks no rents, doth not oppresse
> His tenants with extortions. When the King
> Knighted the lustie gallants of the Land,
> *Nobody* then made daintie to be knighted,
> And indeede kept him in his knowne estate.[65]

The negative is of course doubly stressed and, though no complaint
was made against this play, possibly the author felt anonymity was
the better part of valour.

The two letters quoted by Chambers, however, suggest greater
liberties than even these texts reveal, and committed by several
companies. The most outrageous comments would have been more
safely made as unscripted interpolations, and possibly some of the
productions were for street corner gatherings.[67]

---

[63] *The Works of John Day*, ed. A. H. Bullen (London, 1881; repr. 1963), p. 211.
[64] Ibid. 219. Further described as a 'little hillock made great with others ruines'
(p. 220), similar imagery to that used for James's favourites.   [65] Ibid. 226.
[66] Fo. B. 4ʳ. Old English Drama, students' facsimile (London, 1911).
[67] See n. 56. One of J. Howell's letters, from Brussels 10 June 1622, indicates that
such plays were short drolls or comic gags: '. . . the last week I heard of a play the
Jesuits of *Antwerp* made, in derogation . . . of the proceedings of the Prince *Palsgrave*,
wher . . . they feign'd a Post to com puffing upon the stage, and being ask'd what news,
he answer'd how the *Palsgrave* was like to have shortly a huge formidable Army, for
the King of *Denmark* was to send him a hundred thousand, the *Hollanders* a hundred
thousand, and the King of great *Britaine* a hundred thousand; but being asked

236   *Political Dissent and Drama*

After *Eastward Ho!*, Queen Anne seems to have been induced
to withdraw her patronage, though the Children of the Revels
continued to perform at the Blackfriars. When Francis Beaumont
wrote *The Woman-Hater* for them in 1606, he warned hopeful
intelligencers, in the Prologue:

> . . . if there bee any lurking amongst you in corners, with Table bookes, who
> have some hope to find fit matter to feede his [Maiestie's?[68]] malice on, let
> them claspe them up and slinke away, or stay and be converted. For he that
> made this Play meanes to please Auditors so, as hee may bee an Auditor
> himselfe hereafter, and not purchase them with the deare losse of his eares.[69]

However, the title may have been a deliberate means of attracting his
audience. Like one of Jonson's later alchemists, Beaumont may well
have decided to lure spectators into his arena, by playing on their
vicarious vices, more than satisfying them. The one aspect of James's
character which possibly was parodied, was his love of learning.[70]

Finally, Chapman's two-part play, *The Conspiracy and Tragedie
of Charles Duke of Biron*, played at the Blackfriars by the Children
of the Revels, resulted in another momentary crisis, yet the author's
confidence in persisting with publication of the albeit censored text,
despite the antipathy the play had aroused, shows what little danger
was felt from James's wrath.[71] His courtiers did not fear him, and
could even present him with mockeries if they were softened with
wit, as Howell's letter illustrates.[72] After the Biron plays, James
banned all London performances, yet the other four London Companies were able to recover permission to play by offering him the
remarkable sum of the equivalent of 100,000 francs.[73] They were
forbidden to present recent history, yet as Chambers observed, the

---

thousands of what? he replied the first would send 100000 of *red Herrings* the second
100000 *Cheeses* and, the last 100000 *Ambassadors* [since six English gentlemen] have
all bin employ'd in quality of Ambassadors . . . since the beginning of these German
broils.' *Epistolae Ho-Elianae* (London, 1673), p. 89.

[68] A. W. Upton, 'Allusions to James I and his Court in Marston's *Fawn* and
Beaumont's *Woman-Hater*, *PMLA* 44 (1929), p. 1053.

[69] *The Dramatic Works*, ed. F. Bowers (Cambridge, 1966–85), i. 157.

[70] Upton, 'Allusions to James I', pp. 1049–53.

[71] J. B. Gabel, textual introd., *The Conspiracie*, *The Plays of George Chapman*,
The Tragedies, gen. ed. A. Holaday (Woodbridge, 1987), p. 265. For further evidence
of James's approachability see *The Commons Complaint* (1611) (BL 1651/1062)
addressed to James and complaining against the 'destruction and waste of Woods' and
'the extreme dearth of victuals'.

[72] See Ch. 4 n. 85.   [73] La Boderie, Chambers, *Elizabethan Stage*, iii. 258.

Political Dissent and Drama · 237

ban 'left the even more dangerous resources of allegory and of historical parallel still open to the "seditious" playwright'.[74] It is possible that *A King and No King* could be an example. Though a comedy and a fiction, the unnatural passions, and mock king associations, combined in Arbaces, could be interpreted as a king game allegory on James's own behaviour.[75] For sustained criticism, interpolated comment was less effective than allegory, where mock kings might be used to portray a fictionalized, corrupt court and to give thoughtful advice on the requirements of government.

---

[74] Ibid. i. 327.

[75] See Gildersleeve, *Government Regulation*, pp. 109–11, and Clark, *Ralegh and Marlowe*, pp. 169–70, for *The Second Maiden's Tragedy* as another thinly veiled play against the king.

11
Moral Political Criticism through Saturnalia in Jacobean Drama

> There is no goodnes of shepe, yf the
> Shepherde be awaye . . . That
> commonaltie is nothynge worth, tis not
> gouerned by thauthoritie of a prince.
>
> Erasmus, *Adages*, trans. Tauerner

Both before and after Chapman's skirmish of 1608 the mock king genre continued to be used for comment and criticism of courts and kings. Similar to the use in *Woodstock*, corruption in high places was shown as a *mundus inversus* dominant over order, and against which better forces pitted themselves. The king for the duration of the play led unredeemable disorder which might be finally eliminated, as in Webster's and Middleton's tragedies; expelled through theatrical device, as in *Pericles* and Marston's *The Malcontent*, or, more realistically, controlled, as in *Measure for Measure* and *The Tempest*. Within the context of disorder, plots frequently contain a contest between good and bad varieties of opposites to order, to determine the outcome. All such features are found in Elizabethan drama, but the difference with later plays is that the misrule has over it a gloss of authenticity. Hypocrisy and self-deception have to be combatted, as well as the inversions they maintain and, frequently, when defeated their potential remains a threat.

Possibly because the devil has the most dramatic plots, plays, other than *Pericles*, do not follow the fortunes of an incorruptibly virtuous prince. The protagonist of this one exception, however, is portrayed as an ideal courtly lord and effective prince, whose virtue does not waver despite the effects of the plot on it. The first two acts are controlled by a wayward medieval Fortune who, according to Gower, emanated from the corruption at Antioch,[1] and caused Pericles's initial fall, while in the final acts the ideal lord is restored by

---

[1] Antiochus's blatant passions, like those of Arbaces, could contain implied comment on the English court.

Saturnalia in Jacobean Drama

239

the deity of courtly entertainments, the goddess Diana. And, in the tradition of Christmas princes, Pericles provides a model for princely behaviour, in an otherwise largely corrupted world.

The evidence that Pericles is a perfect prince comes in the opening scenes. He is the first man pure enough to divine Antiochus's riddle and in Act I, Scene ii, when he perceives that Antiochus's revenge will destroy Tyre if necessary, Pericles leaves his kingdom for that kingdom's good. The counsellor, Helicanus, sees the flight as cowardice and like Kent speaks his mind yet Pericles, unlike Lear, approves the refusal to flatter. To leave his kingdom is in effect to abandon it to misrule, but the fault is not his; the stress laid on written instructions to Helicanus, and the letters which continue between them show that the absent king does not disregard his duties. Scenes and images, including the name, Marina, given to his child, assert that life is a hazardous voyage, controlled by Fortune, who may disrupt the best of intentions and may herself impose misrule. Yet Pericles's inherent virtue does not alter: even when a refugee at Tharsus his supplies save the city and turn him into a benefactor. The prince's Utopian qualities are eventually crowned at the nadir of his own misfortunes in Pentapolis. The victory in the festive games not only results in the laurel wreath making him 'king of this day's happiness',[2] but translates into more substantial honours, winning the hand of the heir to the throne, Thaisa, in a way that Dudley's attempts never could. The entire court at Pentapolis is an oasis in a turbulent world, functioning in mythical Arthurian harmony.

Pericles's words at the end of his travels, 'my twelve months are expir'd',[3] specifically recall the annual cycle of mock king election and, in the Epilogue, Gower connects all Pericles's misfortunes with the ill-fated trip to Antioch, which precipitated a time when Fortune imposed such Christmas prince status on him. The setting of the play in the mythological past, as a festive legend and example to courts, suggests a difference between fantasy and reality. The story was, as Gower explains, 'sung on ember-eves and holy-ales', and read by: '. . . lords and Ladies in their lives | . . . for restoratives';[4] not based on chronicled history, nor contemporary example from the latter age where, Gower continues ambiguously, wit is 'more ripe'. *Pericles*

---

[2] II. iii. 11.

[3] III. iii. 2. In fact the 12 months extend from the death of Antiochus.

[4] Prologue, ll. 6–8.

240 *Saturnalia in Jacobean Drama*

continues the humanist tradition of presenting an ideal prince from the ancient world as a model for contemporary society.

In Marston's *The Malcontent* (1602–4), the ideal lord, Altofront, acknowledges that undisguised good is powerless against evil, and so conceals himself in the supposed villainy of Malevole, who alludes to the possibility that Genoa's lord is also changed annually:

> Behold for ever banisht Altofront,
> This Genoa's last year's duke.[5]

The ruler has been treated as a courtly mock lord, expelled from society once his annual term of office expired. Malevole now scourges such inverted concepts to bring about a moral regeneration which will allow the ideal lord's return. His relationship to the puppet duke, Pietro, is that of court fool, able, as an outsider, to tell him the most painful truths.

PIETRO. I like him 'faith, he gives good intelligence to my spirit, makes me understand those weaknesses which others' flattery palliates.[6]

I. ii. 23–4

Like *Pericles*, Marston's play is also conceived of as a theatrical artifice in which varieties of mock lord participate. One of the most clearly specified roles is Biblioso. He represents law and order, but with added connotations for his title of Marshall relates to inns of court festivity, and Malevole calls him 'the father of maypoles',[7] or the man from whom travestied order was engendered. Yet appropriately, Mendoza, the dominant leader of the play's action, is the greatest knave who advances to the position of lord over the disorder he creates. Whereas Pietro is basically a weak, good man, placed in his usurper's role above his inclination or ability, Mendoza is a self-confessed perverter of order, delighting in being Pietro's favourite, while cuckolding him. Although Pietro makes Mendoza his heir and the Duchess plans to make him duke once Pietro is killed, Mendoza intends to instigate even greater treachery by being finally

---

[5] I. iv. 7–8. *Jacobean Tragedies*, ed. A. H. Gomme (Oxford, 1969), p. 18.

[6] 'The fact is, kings do dislike the truth, but the outcome is extraordinary for my fools. They can speak truth and even open insults and be heard with positive pleasure; indeed, the words which would cost a wise man his life are surprisingly enjoyable when uttered by a clown.' D. Erasmus, *Praise of Folly*, trans. B. Radice (Harmondsworth, 1971), p. 119.   [7] I. iv. 44.

Saturnalia in Jacobean Drama 241

rid of them both and marrying Altofront's wife. Mendoza's victims, those in power above him, conspire in his elevation and their own downfall. As chief knave Mendoza is natural leader and bound to succeed while society is governed by inversions. The structure of Mendoza and Malevole as rival mock lords, in conflict to determine the outcome of the play for either good or bad, is precisely articulated in Malevole's line, 'better to play the fool lord [Malevole] than be the fool lord [Mendoza]'.[8] Combined in the term 'fool' are the meanings of evil man who denies morality and festive character raised to the status of temporary leader.

Both express a cynical contempt for the world: Mendoza in accordance with his character; Malevole with his disguise and, paradoxically, Malevole wins Mendoza's trust because of his apparent untrustworthiness. For example, at Act II, Scene v, lines 103–8, he disconcerts Mendoza by uttering the sincere: 'God arrest thee.' Mendoza's challenge: 'At whose suit?' brings the response: 'At the devil's', suggesting there is treachery in heaven and even God is in league with evil. Considering that Malevole is aligning himself with Mendoza in order to bring him down, there is literal truth in the metaphor, but it is the duplicity in the wit which wins Mendoza's trust. Later, in admiration of his deviousness, Mendoza asks, 'why wert not thou an emperor?',[9] since he has even greater skill than Mendoza to rise to the top of the upside-down world. Again there is irony, for Malevole *is* using his wits to restore himself to power, though in so doing the world will be put to rights. The ideal lord uses the ambition of his opposite to restore his own rightful place. And the masque of Act v, called for by Mendoza to celebrate his accession, provides the moment when the immoral plot is used to bring about the happy ending. The spectral god, Mercury, calls from the 'gloomy shades', to bring on the four lords opposed to Mendoza, who have been concealed or in disguise for much of the play. All are men Mendoza plotted to kill, and their return from the shades confronts the evil usurper with his rival and restored court, from which he is now excluded. His disorder was that of a demonic and dangerous opposite which, in moral comic terms, is expelled not destroyed. The moral tripwires, with which Malevole defeats each aspect of Mendoza's plot, turns the demonic into a regenerative saturnalia. Chambers considers the play Marston's first for the Queen's Revels

---

[8] v. ii. 39–40.   [9] III. iii. 108.

242   *Saturnalia in Jacobean Drama*

after they were formed in 1604,[10] and though in the printed text
Marston denied any contemporary satire,[11] some remarks in the play
could be taken to mean James's court while others look like contemporary comments on the state of the reformed or 'deformed'
Church.[12]

Contemporary advice, rather than satire, can be found in the
development of the protagonists of *Measure for Measure* and *The
Tempest*, where the device of rightful duke, in disguise until the
moral resolution of the play, includes the message that kings must
actively govern if disaster is not to fall upon them and their kingdoms. A similar reading can be found in *King Lear*, and in view of
James's absences from court, it is, perhaps, more than coincidence
that these plays performed at court in the Christmas season bring
home the responsibility rightful kings have not to neglect their duties.

Measure for Measure was first performed on St Stephen's night
1604,[13] and bears several superficial resemblances to Marston's
satire. The Duke is concealed as a man of God; opposing lords
contest the outcome; a virtuous woman is a pawn, and both plays
incorporate an aspect of metaphoric oppositional use of 'day' and
'night'.[14]

At the opening, the state of Vienna is disordered before the Duke
leaves, on account of his own lax law enforcement. As he departs
totally from the seat of government he, like James, expresses a dislike
of the public ceremony which turns kings into players:

> I'll privily away. I love the people,
> But do not like to stage me to their eyes:
> Though it do well, I do not relish well

---

[10] E. K. Chambers, *The Elizabethan Stage*, iii. 432.

[11] 'To the Reader . . . it was my care to write so far from reasonable offence, that
even strangers, in whose state I laid my scene, should not from thence draw any
disgrace to any, dead or living. yet in despite of my endeavours, I understand, some
have been most unadvisedly over-cunning in mis-interpreting me, and with subtility
(as deep as hell) have maliciously spread ill rumours.'

[12] As in Day's *Isle of Gulls* the opening scenes, before the plot is under way, contain
comment against Church and king.

[13] Chambers, *Elizabethan Stage*, iv. 171.

[14] Evil rather than saturnalian disorder takes place, as Mendoza says, in the
'immodest waist of night' (II. v. 87). And when Malevole regains control dawn is
promised: 'The beauty of the day begins to rise, | From whose bright form night's
heavy shadow flies' (II v. 153–4). In *Measure for Measure* such dawn expectations are
ironically frustrated. The Duke waits at the prison in anticipation of Claudio's dawn
reprieve only to hear the execution reaffirmed.

Saturnalia in Jacobean Drama　　　　　243

Their loud applause and *Aves* vehement;
Nor do I think the man of safe discretion
That does effect it.

I. i. 67–72

Though the sentiment appears a good one, yet the resolution of the play is public and, I would suggest, conveys the message that justice must be seen to be done. Once the State is left in the hands of Angelo, the season of performance invites expectation that the law officer will in fact perpetrate a greater misrule than that left behind by the rightful prince. The ensuing disorder then revolves around the question of personal morality, with the two oppositional characters changing to Angelo and Claudio, both of whom exemplify types of moral failing. Angelo's extreme legality produces an inverted society, where what is legal replaces what is humane and humanly possible. Both he and Claudio had been engaged to their respective partners, Mariana and Julietta, under similar understandings. They were privately contracted without Church solemnization because of lack of agreement over the dowry.[15] Angelo had let his contract lapse when Mariana's dowry failed, which was legally correct if heartless, whereas Claudio and Julietta stepped beyond the bounds of their contract, consummating the agreement through mutual love. According to the law, which Angelo revives, this was an illegal act of immorality without distinction from outright prostitution. Yet Angelo's legally correct attitude to Mariana does not compare well with the sin of Claudio and Julietta, and there is less natural order in his upholding the law against Claudio than there was in Claudio breaking it. The lawlessness of the inverted world is, paradoxically, the arena in which to explore the results of unjust law enforcement, as well as those resulting from licence, and, within the dramatic fiction, reconciliation is brought about by change in Isabella and in the Duke, though not in Claudio who remains an example of the best that can be expected from sentient human nature.[16]

Angelo's misruled world is demonstrated in the court-room in Act II, Scene i, when Mistress Overdone's servant, Pompey, is tried for pimping. The prosecuting constable, Elbow, cannot distinguish between a 'respected' and a 'suspected' person.[17] His disordered interruptions, full of Dogberryisms, obscure the facts and, in disgust,

[15] See H. Hawkins, *Measure for Measure* (Brighton, 1987), pp. 21–2.
[16] Ibid. 54–7, 69–72.　　[17] II. i. 165.

Saturnalia in Jacobean Drama

Angelo passes authority to the further deputy, Escalus, and leaves the court. Yet Angelo's concept of justice at the opening of this scene, when he sentenced Claudio to death, was also a travesty, and, between Elbow and Escalus, the trial of Pompey is a parodic continuation of Angelo's misjudgement: in manner the opposite to the clarity and precision of Angelo's execution; in fact, a further confusion between a crime and its appropriate punishment. The judgment of letting Pompey (a greater offender than Claudio) off with a warning complements Angelo's inverted justice and introduces a problem. When later committed to prison, Pompey again has his sentence reduced for volunteering to help execute Claudio and Barnadine.[18] The anomalous treatment of him is never corrected and suggests the possibility (finally continued by Lucio) of a flaw within all systems of justice.

In Act II, Scene ii, the cold, compassionless, legal mind of Angelo meets the equally cold and pure novitiate, Isabella, who herself approves of his 'just but severe law'.[19] She would not persist in her suit after the first denial were it not for the intervention of Lucio, the most dissolute and lawless character in the play, whose encouragement is full of innuendo. The mercy she pleads for is the greatest of Christian virtues without which all fallen men would be lost, but ironically, when she uses this argument her passionate pleading rouses the fallen man in Angelo rather than his mercy. If Angelo is to be brought to a more humane understanding, it is his own fallen humanity which he must experience first, and his failing is not to make the connection between that and the need of mercy for it. Yet Lucio's bawdy comments are not without relevance to both Isabella's intervention as well as to Angelo's response. Emotion is one step removed from her opening, absolute virtue in which she too had rejected the temporizing world. In this scene both characters lose their absolute values, inducted into the world by the bawd. Isabella and Angelo are two of a kind, not only in their opening purist positions, but also in the change they undergo by the end of Act II, Scene ii. Isabella uses the metaphor of bribery, to make more persuasive the argument of her future prayers of thanks for him.[20]

---

[18] In the dramatic tradition of fools becoming executioners. See Ch. 6 n. 64 and S. Billington, 'The Fool and the Moral in English and Scottish Morality Plays', in F. S. Anderson *et al.*, *Popular Drama in Northern Europe in the Later Middle Ages* (Odense, 1988), pp. 130–1.
[19] II. ii. 42. [20] II. ii. 146–56.

Saturnalia in Jacobean Drama

Her motives are still pure, but she clearly understands the corrupt concept in order to transform it. And Angelo understands at least the paradox that it is her virtue which attracts him, and through which he has fallen:

> Never could the strumpet
> With all her double vigour, art and nature,
> Once stir my temper: but this virtuous maid
> Subdues me quite.
>
> II. ii. 183–6

Claudio had accidentally exposed the danger in Isabella's youth and innocence, using a suggestive vocabulary in his belief that it is precisely these qualities which could induce Angelo to change his mind:

> For in her youth
> There is a prone and speechless dialect
> Such as move men.
>
> I. ii. 172–4

In the next confrontation, at Act II, Scene iv, line 18, Isabella is introduced as 'one Isabel, a sister', which focuses on the conflict between natural, sisterly feelings and the pure life from which such feelings are excluded, and suggests that the natural has taken over from the ascetic. And if the passion with which she rejects Angelo might be said to be calculated to rouse him the more,[21] it also reveals an emotional character in herself, one which it is hard to imagine returning to the cloister once this incident is over. A further sign of her change from idealism to a more worldly point of view is her agreeing to the bed trick with Mariana after having at the opening held the purist view that such behaviour from Claudio was a sin worthy of death.[22]

Looked at schematically, the misrule reaches its apex in Act III, Scene i, when Claudio too finds himself electing for Isabella's dishonour and his own life. His sin is no longer 'accidental but a trade'.[23] The Duke is forced to work like a sleuth against the pressure of time for Claudio's execution, and to keep ahead of his adversary, the mock lord there to counter, but in fact exacerbating the results of

---

[21] Hawkins, *Measure for Measure*, pp. 27–8.
[22] Ibid. 16–29.   [23] III. i. 147.

246 *Saturnalia in Jacobean Drama*

the Duke's own failings. The aberrant shyness, which Lucio accuses the Duke of in Act III, was in evidence at the play's opening. Like Isabella, the Duke began as an unworldly character who retired from conflicts and from his own responsibilities. Inevitably, his dislike of playing the king prevented him from acting like one. And his change to public statesman comes about through his role as a more saturnalian and disordered figure. In Act IV the Duke is given godlike authority in his friar's robes, yet by 1604 the friar was a discredited role, usually comic and a symbol of misrule. In this imperfect disguise, the Duke has no choice but to exert his power to save Claudio through the immoral bed trick, appropriate to the character of a friar. In Act V he then displays his power, converting instantly from an imperfect to a perfect image of rule. The mendicant beggar, travesty of God's authority while Angelo ruled, is revealed as the truly Protestant and godly authority. Far from being shy, the Duke chooses the most public place in the city for the two denunciations of Angelo and the final revelation. Through the process of misrule and threatened injustice, caused by his previous evasion of his duties, the Duke learns to assert himself, to accept his public office, and to administer his God-given authority.

Though Angelo might seem to be beyond the pale, yet the whole of this society is a dark and difficult one to regenerate. The subplot introduces us to the range of humanity, beginning in a brothel and moving to the prison, where Pompey finds himself very much at home since it is full of Mistress Overdone's customers. Both resorts are stages in the rake's progress of man's life. At the beginning of Act III the prison can be interpreted as a Platonic microcosm of the world. The Duke's opening speech of comfort to Claudio contains the familiar argument that since baseness is the essence of life, death is preferable. Claudio's bitter acceptance of the paradox is a timely insertion in this riddling play:

> To sue to live, I find I seek to die,
> And seeking death, find life. Let it come on.

III. i. 42–3

Examples of humanity include Pompey, the natural fool for whom sin is his trade; Lucio, the artificial fool who makes it his profession, and Barnardine, the completely unregenerate man insensible to any alternative. The best this society can aspire to is Claudio and Julietta, the loving and unthinking sinners. Yet, in Act V, Barnadine's refusal

Saturnalia in Jacobean Drama

to die is rewarded by the Duke's forgiveness and precedes forgiveness of Angelo. One can sympathize with Barnadine since only his humanity and not his crime is shown, yet there is little difference between him and the law officer. Both are obdurate sinners, yet both are pardoned: Angelo receiving Cordelia-like charity from Isabella. No attempt, however, is made to reclaim Lucio. He is fitly matched with a whore for wife, but set free to his old ways. Disorder will be as much a part of the renewed world as it was of the inverted one, if not more so, since further reprobates will be engendered; suggesting perhaps a full interrelation between order and disorder which will continue once the play is over, though this conclusion could well be a refuge from paradox.

The problems remain largely because the characters are more than ciphers. One cannot write them off as theatrical stereotypes, as one can with Marston's devilish Mendoza. It is as though, on the one hand, one has the fiction or dramatic fantasy which is happily concluded, and on the other, an underlying reality or probability which is impossible to harmonize with the easy resolution. For example, there is the psychological reality of the characters' anguish —even Angelo's.[24] And there is an uneasy sense that the injustice of greater sinners, Pompey and Lucio, receiving lighter sentences is all too likely an occurrence, even in the ostensibly ordered world. The imposed denouement, dictated by the fantasy, only serves to strengthen the impression that the realistic outcome would be a continued miscarriage of justice, particularly in the case of Isabella claiming redress. The way that her accusation is so easily turned aside by those in power, and that punishment threatens to fall on her, the innocent party, as she is first led away to prison, has too convincing a reality in it to be easily disregarded. One is alerted to the uncomfortable probabilities by the apparent completeness of the resolution. And, like Lyndsay's *Satyre of the Three Estates*,[25] in which the final liberty given to the fool-vice is a comment on the failure of the apparent reformation in the play, Shakespeare could have intended a similar comment. On a simple level, riddles and the final escape of the artificial fool were fundamental to Christmas entertainments. If the problems are not finally resolved, they confirm the potency of the genre. On a more thoughtful level, the ending could be seen as a warning to the Duke, or to James, not to abandon

---

[24] Hawkins, *Measure for Measure*, pp. 57–9.
[25] Billington, 'The Fool and the Moral', pp. 130–3.

248   *Saturnalia in Jacobean Drama*

his State in future, nor to be slack about his duties, since justice on a permanently disordered planet is not easy to obtain: it needs the constant intervention of the hand of God's representative.

The Tempest, recorded to have been performed at court at Hallowmas, 1 November 1612,[26] is also not as resolved as might at first appear, though the sense of order in it is very strong. The island's wonders are reminiscent of the invention of a courtly Christmas prince, with Prospero the idealized lord ruling according to a strict concept of order, rather than overseeing disorder. The debased, inverted world which had expelled him exists off-stage, and for its recuperation enters into the supernaturally ordered one. Prospero's island, however, is not without evil, which had possession first through the witch Sycorax. Good even has aspects in common with evil. Prospero acknowledges Caliban as his own, and at the opening of the play he threatens to repeat Sycorax's punishment of Ariel for the same offence of refusing to obey orders. Both powers can inflict hurt, though Sycorax lacked the creative power to undo harm. More than in any other of Shakespeare's plays, the motor for the action is fired by a twin-like interrelation between good and evil, visualized in the comic scene of Trinculo and Caliban, beneath one gabardine, observed by Stephano as a single creature whose 'forward voice, now, is to speak well of his friend; his backward voice is to utter foul speeches and to detract.'[27]

A series of king plays focus on the central issue and unify the action. Every leading character who arrives on the island, apart from Ferdinand,[28] fancies himself a king. Prospero was landed 'upon this shore . . . To be lord on't',[29] before which Caliban had been 'mine own King'.[30] Gonzalo muses:

> Had I plantation of this isle . . .
> And were the King on't, what would I do?
>
>   II. i. 139–41

He wishes for a Utopian commonwealth: a paradoxical impossibility, as the mockery of Antonio and Sebastian is not slow to point out, and which is followed by the plot to make Sebastian king of Naples, expressed by Antonio in hand of Fortune imagery:

---

[26] Chambers, *Elizabethan Stage*, iv. 177.   [27] II. ii. 92–4.
[28] Ferdinand seeks to serve his 'goddess' and, hoping his father is still alive, wishes not to be a king (III. i. 60–1).
[29] v. i. 162.   [30] I. ii. 344.

Saturnalia in Jacobean Drama 249

> My strong imagination sees a crown
> Dropping upon thy head.
>
> II. i. 203–4

And Ferdinand and Miranda are discovered in Act v, Scene i playing the archetypal king game, chess. But the most vivid pageant is in Act IV, Scene i, when Stephano is trapped by fripperies into dressing up as king and bestowing clothes as favours before he has disposed of his rival. Although one's common sense knows that Prospero helped by Ariel would always defeat a Stephano, yet this scene plays as though, but for being tricked into revealing his true self, Stephano would have achieved a more murderous mockery of state.

For, as already said, the island like the world outside is not a Utopia. The moment Prospero relaxes with the celebratory masque he gives time for usurpation to be plotted. The danger of usurpation is a constant one on the island and off. Like King James, Prospero originally preferred books to government, with the result for Prospero of losing his throne. His books provided him with the skills to become an ideal lord, with power above his enemies for the duration of the play. Yet the point is to return finally to reality, and to sustain his legitimate rule in Milan without such recourse, and despite continued threats against him. The king plays throughout the play repeat the point that no prince, no matter how legitimate, is safe. Trinculo observes that, when god Stephano sleeps, his obsequious servant will also steal his power, or 'rob his bottle';[31] an attempt is made to murder Alonso as he sleeps, and Prospero nearly falls into his old error of intellectual distraction before rule. And Antonio's ominous silence, on being forced to concede victory to his brother, provides a threat of continued struggle on their return to Milan. Sebastian, too, on seeing one of his obstacles to the crown of Naples, Ferdinand, still alive, exclaims 'a most high miracle',[32] which better fits his character if not delivered as a reborn Christian. Though the evil of these men has been defeated, there is no more sign than for Angelo that they have undergone Alonso's sea change.

Nor does any voluntary support exist for Prospero from either the natural or supernatural world. In contrast with *A Midsummer Night's Dream*, where, although Puck adds confusion, Oberon and Titania are there to bless Theseus and Hippolyta, Ariel is as coerced a helper as is Caliban. The magician king is one of the most isolated of Shakespeare's rulers, and once divested of his magical powers he

---

[31] II. ii. 151.   [32] v. i. 177.

250   *Saturnalia in Jacobean Drama*

returns to a turbulent natural world which constantly threatens his
downfall. As the captain says of the storm at sea: 'What cares these
roarers for the name of King?'[33] Likewise, the men around him are
likely to be treacherous and remorseless. Gonzago's Utopian fantasy,
in Act II, scene i, of excelling the Golden Age is not a possibility,
unlike the romantic conclusion to *Pericles*. Antonio's and Sebastian's
ridicule of Utopia reveals that, while such men as *they* exist, it is a
concept fit only for ridicule. And Miranda's innocent belief that
Ferdinand cheated at chess, whether he did or not, encapsulates the
theme of treachery. Similar to the betrayal by the courtiers in *Timon*,
the idealistic inns of court lord will, in a political context, always be
threatened by his followers. And, unlike *Timon*, *The Tempest* is
concerned with issues of true kingship. As in *Measure for Measure*,
simply being king by virtue of right is not enough. To avoid disaster
the true-born king must continually attend to affairs of state. In
Antony and Cleopatra a cameo of the same dangers of kingly
relaxation occurs in the shipboard feasting with Pompey, who could
be said to combine Essex's genealogy with Raleigh's reputation: he
has a control over the sea which Rome's power base cannot dislodge
from him. The feast to conclude the peace between them takes place
on that element, with Pompey as host, when Menas feeds him with
fantasies: 'Wilt thou be lord of all the world?'[34] Pompey's
squeamishness prevents a deflection from the plot, but the scene
shows how mortal and vulnerable lords of the world are, no matter
what iconographic deification of absolute power the rest of the play
contains.

Even in Fletcher's and Shakespeare's *Henry VIII* (1613), the
message is similar. Affairs of state only progress towards the
apotheosis of Elizabeth's birth, and the consolidation of the Church
of England, once Henry assumes his proper role and ceases to lean on
Wolsey.[35] Initially, when Wolsey is in control, Henry is reduced to
leading masquer in the misrule overseen by the prelate. *Henry VIII*
functions largely through a succession of spectacles of power,[36] and
the masque is one which serves to blur Henry's culpability in the
change from Katherine to Anne. One might say that it is both an
anti-masque and masque, for it combines the threat of Katherine's

---

[33] I. i. 16–17.   [34] *Antony and Cleopatra*, II. vii. 60.
[35] *Henry VIII*, opening stage direction, I. ii.
[36] See M. E. Hazard, '"Order gave each thing view": "shows, pageants and sights
of honour" in *King Henry VIII*', *Word and Image*, 3:1 (1987), pp. 95–103.

Saturnalia in Jacobean Drama   251

unjust removal with the promise of the eventual order of Elizabeth. And it is Wolsey who hosts this entertainment where Henry in disguise first meets Elizabeth's mother, Anne Bullen. Even though the prelate recognizes the leading masquer as his king, and gives up his seat to him (as an Inner Temple Christmas lord did in respect of the Chancellor), Wolsey is here an unreformed lord of misrule overseeing, in the style of Pandarus, a bacchanal. While Wolsey is in control, all the pageants in the play are disordered. Henry is depicted as needing his support and as an actor in the honouring of him; the loyal Buckingham processes across the stage to his execution,[37] and, not only are Wolsey's entrances more splendid than Henry's, but he also has carried before him the symbols of power, the purse and, in Act II, Scene iv, the Great Seal. It is in the court scene, unjustly arraigning Katherine, that Wolsey's inverted law is most potent though, ironically, his actions here contribute to his own downfall. Through overreaching pride, he causes Katherine's fall from, and inadvertently the Lutheran, Anne's, rise to, fortune, without either queen becoming tainted. The masque and subsequent events up to the coronation of Anne begin a necessary and positive saturnalia, for the regeneration of England, which will expel the negative inversions of Wolsey. Like Mendoza's, Wolsey's plots contain the seeds of his own defeat, but Wolsey does not have a rival attempting to counter his plans. His own errors betray him; firstly in introducing Anne to Henry, and, more decisively, by accidentally sending him the wrong letters. This last reveals Wolsey's previous power to have been no more than that of a temporary fool lord, as Wolsey himself says.[38] Henry's role had been that of an imperfect youth, eventually guided by Reformation providence, not medieval fortune,[39] towards discovering the Vice nature of his erstwhile mentor. Henry's later decisive intervention, which foils treachery in the Church against the Protestant cause, is performed in full and solitary majesty. He

---

[37] Buckingham, like Katherine in II. iv, refuses to participate in Wolsey's shows. He rejects the decorating of his barge, which he says, 'now will but mock me' (II. i. 101). See Hazard, '"Order gave each thing view"', p. 101.

[38] 'O negligence! | Fit for a fool to fall by' (III. ii. 213–14).

[39] The inventory of Wolsey's goods and his letter to the Pope, which Wolsey sends the king, is attributed to Fortune by Wolsey: 'What's this? "To th'Pope"? | . . . Nay then, farewell: | I have touch'd the highest point of all my greatness, | And from that full meridian of my glory | I haste now to my setting. I shall fall | Like a bright exhalation in the evening, | And no man see me more' (III. ii. 220–7). Norfolk, however, attributes the accident to providence: 'It's heaven's will' (III. ii. 128).

becomes more than a figurehead relying solely on spectacle, but instead participates in person in the government of the Church, putting down Cranmer's opponents with direct and rough language. This is a king who, even more than the Duke in *Measure for Measure*, finally does not fear to spoil his deified image in the kitchen of politics. The need for strong government, repeatedly expressed in Shakespeare's Jacobean plays, suggests a political vacuum rather than the tyranny portrayed in *Woodstock*.

Conclusion

I have tried to show the variety of interpretations which playwrights were able to spin out of the complex philosophy and popular traditions surrounding the concept of kingship. Many scripted fantasies bore an organic relation to the games of pretence indulged in by the audiences who came to see them. The success which this helped bring the professional theatre is further clarified by the aesthetic rejection of the results. In the 1580s Sir Philip Sidney distinguished the fantastike from the eikastike, and rejected the former as a poetic aberration which should not deter a more judicious love of true poetic inspiration. In his examples, fantasia equates with crude methods such as tragicomedy and its mingling of clowns and kings. His neo-classic sense was to find agreement in the work of the Jacobean, John Fletcher: both preferred delight to laughter in comedy and 'well-raised admiration'[1] in tragedy. The result in *The Defence of Poesie* was that, while on the one hand theoretically defending the drama, Sidney's actual examples of current plays reveal that he found early Elizabethan theatre rather too lowbrow and fantastike for his taste. Similar criticisms were to be raised again during the Caroline period.[2]

Many Elizabethan plays also issued a challenge to the status quo. Even the conservative comedies of Greene and Dekker, *Friar Bacon and Friar Bungay* and *The Shoemakers' Holiday*, end with the crossing of social boundaries. In Greene's play, the country girl Margaret is raised to the aristocracy as a reward for her virtue, and in *The Shoemakers' Holiday* a poor but resourceful man becomes Lord Mayor of London. Other texts containing a strong element of satire in them, such as *Timon*, *King John*, and *Woodstock*, end negatively after stripping bare a society with similarities to the one in which they were written. Interesting though it is, there is no need for recourse to Freud[3] to account for the radical nature of such Renaissance drama; it sprang from use of a radical tradition. Graham Holderness writes:

---

[1] *Defence of Poesie*, fo. 1. 1ᵛ. Sidney's argument is sophistical, allowing to the eikastike an imaginative freedom found also in the fantastike, but arguing for an idealized rather than satiric expression of aspiration.

[2] A. Gurr, *Playgoing in Shakespeare's London* (Cambridge, 1987), p. 183.

[3] See R. Nevo, *Shakespeare's Other Language* (London, 1987).

Conclusion

It is of course an established fact that prior to Shakespeare's drama there existed a tradition of popular culture—a subculture, incorporated into yet intrinsically in tension with the official culture of the Tudor nation-state. This culture was democratic, imaginative and fantastic rather than realistic and historicist. It voiced the aspirations of sections of the common people —peasant, artisan, lower bourgeoisie . . . and above all, it was, to some degree *hostile* to the official culture which sanctioned it.[4]

I would not go so far as to say that the attitudes demonstrated in play were *necessarily* democratic. Holderness's perception here is based on Bakhtin's observation that carnival crowds mingled regardless of rank,[5] but the ceremonies within the festivity were modelled on the hierarchical structures of the society which they temporarily re-placed, and could be variously channelled and interpreted. It is true that festive liberties included mocking leaders and changing them whenever play initiative was wrested by, or awarded to, another member of the group, and perhaps levelling is a closer description for such organization: a primary process which might or might not also contain a democratic vision. As the True Leveller, Gerard Winstanley, put it in 1649, 'freedom comes clothed in a clownish garment . . . Freedom is the man that will turn the world upside down'.[6] There is here no statement of how that freedom is to be used, and the metaphor is, initially, most reminiscent of Caliban's response to Stephano.

In drawing from the anarchic and *un*democratic aspects of festive tradition, Shakespeare and others had at their disposal icons of *dis*unity,[7] already sceptical of the encompassing order of any state, and *Tamburlaine* is, perhaps, the most fully dramatized of such expressions.[8] English Renaissance playwrights were in the position which Dario Fo has recently discovered in Italy.[9] They had a subversive tradition, taken from the people, which could be used to express sophisticated criticism and dissent. When presenting a crowned man on stage it was possible to claim disassociation from

[4] G. Holderness, *Shakespeare's History* (Dublin, 1985), p. 130.
[5] M. Bakhtin, *Rabelais and his World*, trans. H. Iswolsky (Cambridge, Mass., 1965), pp. 10–13.
[6] C. Hill, *The World Turned Upside Down* (London, 1972), p. 86.
[7] See R. J. Sieman, *Shakespeare's Iconoclasm* (Berkeley, Calif., 1985).
[8] In Dekker's above-mentioned comedy a democratic resolution is, perhaps, reached.
[9] D. Fo, 'Some Aspects of Popular Theatre', *New Theatre Quarterly* 1 (1985), p. 135.

Conclusion   255

reality. The actor was an obvious sham, and a contrast to the power and glory of any real head of state, past or present. On the other hand, the sham of the actor could be seen as a satire on the reality. While pretending an aberrant fiction from which all would finally emerge into the perfectly ordered cosmos under Elizabeth, James, or Charles, philosophical ideas and contemporary allusions might maintain reference to the aberrations of those ordered worlds.

The volatility of the customs allowed for a variety of plots which could change to reflect current interests. In the Elizabethan period summer kings were the dominant models, especially in Chronicle and Morality plays, both of which rely on summer self-aggrandizement and its subsequent fall, while Nashe's *Svmmer's Last Will and Testament* is necessarily based on playing the death of the summer lord, and the character of Winter is presented, not as the rival host, Christmas, but the antifestive Backwinter. However, Shakespeare's *A Midsummer Night's Dream*, written a few years earlier, can be said to draw from both winter and summer customs. In terms of the whole play, all the disorders provide the entertainment Theseus asked for to fill in the time until his wedding, which might be at either season.[10] But the power which transfers from the daytime authority, Theseus, to his night-time opposite, plus Oberon's magical abilities, suggest connections between Theseus's *alter ego* and a courtly Christmas lord; while Titania's behaviour towards Oberon can be read as midsummer self-aggrandizement, which is humiliated and implicitly mocked when, from her elevated bower, she boasts to an ass:

> I am a spirit of no common rate;
> The summer still doth tend upon my state;
>
> III. i. 147–8

The crucial difference between Titania and most of the queens looked at in Chapter 8 is that she is a commanding figure, not a caricature; one could say that she also has the authority of the good queen. Suggestions of winter as well as of summer lords in *Timon of Athens* and *Troilus and Cressida* are also for mockery, but during the Jacobean and Caroline periods one finds serious consideration of the demands on divinely inspired, or empowered, princes through the

---

[10] The 2 court weddings which are likely contenders for the first performance, were celebrated in Jan. 1594–5 and Jan. 1595–6. H. R. Brooks, *A Midsummer Night's Dream*, Arden edn., p. lvi.

256   Conclusion

medium of Christmas lords. They helped present an idealized concept of monarchy, through which a flawed monarch could be
artistically converted into a head closer to the ideal. The fantastike
might be channelled into aspiration *for* rather than *against* the
monarch, as in *Pericles* and in Brome's apotheosis of a summer
queen, *The Queen and the Concubine*; while the idealization of a
Prince and Princess d'Amour provides the concluding triumph of
Antony and Cleopatra.

As indicated by the title of Brome's play above, there was, in
Caroline drama, greater interest in the mock queen; further exemplified in Shirley's *The Politician* and *The Sisters*. These plays
contain a more careful incorporation of seasonal play than that
found in Elizabethan drama; the inversions are used finally to
confirm a necessary inflexibility in the social order. Brome's text may
be in the romance tradition of *Friar Bacon and Friar Bungay*,[11] yet
what is wrong in his depicted society is that the proper order has been
displaced. Shirley's plays are even more assertive in supporting the
hierarchical status quo, and in neither playwright does one find a
country girl, such as Greene's Margaret, raised to the aristocracy as a
just reward for her purity. This is a curious paradox in view of the
fact that society was more mobile in the Caroline than in the
Elizabethan era. Later playwrights appear to have found such upward mobility a mistake.[12] Also, and in contrast to the Jacobean
development of conveying idealized kingship through a Christmas
lord, in *The Sisters* real royalty is perceived by its exclusion from such
analogies.

Although Ford verges on the iconoclastic, his plays also finally
confirm a hierarchical inflexibility, and his interest is rather in the
personal qualities of his disordered protagonists. Much of *The
Broken Heart* can be classed as theatrical fantasy, focusing on the
tyrannical behaviour of an ambitious summer lord and Prince
d'Amour,[13] yet Ford works towards the freeing of Ithocles's innate
nobility through death. The crown he wears when dead is not a
mockery, but the sign that he has achieved the pure royalty of his

[11] M. Butler, *Theatre and Crisis, 1632–42* (Cambridge, 1984), p. 35.
[12] See Gurr, *Playgoing in Shakespeare's London*, p. 180.
[13] On return from battle he receives a 'provincial garland' from the princess,
Calantha (I. ii. 66). Later his excessive behaviour in love prompts the remark, 'This
odd youth's pride turns heretic in loyalty' (IV. i. 97), and the instrument of his death is
called a 'throne of coronation [for a] 'fool of greatness' (IV. iv. 23–4).

Conclusion 257

princess, Calantha. In *Perkin Warbeck*, similar natural *virtú* in the pretender outfaces the petty nature of the king, and Warbeck's line on himself and his followers could be said to apply to Ithocles as well. Both ambitious men become heroic 'Kings o'er death'[14] instead of falsely achieving this status in life. In their final triumphs, the two characters might have been modelled to some extent on Shakespeare's Antony.

Playwrights changed their point of view in response to changing problems, but creatively engaged writing continued up to the closure of the theatres, and much Caroline drama shows the critical and regenerative attitude to society found in earlier plays. Martin Butler writes:

It seems to me that the parliamentary order closing the theatres in September 1642 makes much more sense in relation to . . . recent and repeated collisions between the authorities and the playhouses over the drama's political freedom . . . The theatres were dangerously volatile and articulate [and audiences] politically alert and involved.[15]

And the medium for expressing political ideas was the ubiquitous tradition of mock kings and queens. The turning of Queen Alinda, in *The Queen and the Concubine*, into a May queen highlights the problems inherent in 'the king's capacity to act without control'.[16] And Peregrine, mock king of *The Antipodes* (1638), rules over an inverted world which displays both the flaws of, and cures for, contemporary London.[17] Beggars, bandits, and outlaws also retained their capacity to reflect on supposed order. In *Two Gentlemen of Verona* and *Timon of Athens* outlaws are criminal only by the order of a State which is at least as corrupt as they. *Beggars Bush* (1622) includes an uneasy moment at the end when the beggars become aware that the final return to order, supposedly regenerated by them, nevertheless poses an unjust threat to their liberty, threatening to make them 'beat hempe, and be whipt twice a weeke'.[18] This is comfortably resolved by the play's Dutch context, and the beggars decide to leave for the land of the free, England. But *The Court Beggar* (1640) incurred Charles's wrath for its implicit argument

[14] *Perkin Warbeck*, v. iii. 207.
[15] Butler, *Theatre and Crisis*, p. 136.
[16] Ibid. 37.   [17] Ibid. 219.
[18] v. ii. 209. *The Dramatic Works in the Beaumont and Fletcher Canon*, ed. F. Bowers (Cambridge, 1966–85), iii. 329.

258 Conclusion

that Charles was king over a court of beggars who threatened to impoverish the entire commonwealth,[19] and a challenge, which appears more explicit today, is found in Massinger's earlier play *The Guardian* (1633), which includes proto-Brechtian thinking on the similarities between outlawed criminals and successful princes.[20]

An equally innovative inversion came from the aristocrat, William Cavendish, Earl of Newcastle, who protested against Charles's lax distribution of honours by calling *himself* a lord of misrule: 'I take that for an honour in these days rather than the other more common title.'[21] Increased social disintegration in the last years of Charles's reign found other festive forms of expression, as for example in those pamphlets either bewailing or advocating a social *mundus inversus*. And Charles's supporters, performing in a masque in Witney in May 1646, themselves contributed to the image the opposition had of them as riotous summer lords and fools. The title of masque was a euphemism for a drunken debauch, not far removed from the action in the *Timon* farce, during which the cavaliers were entertained by a morris dance and themselves joined in subsequent songs.[22] It might have been more than coincidence that in November of the same year a parliamentary pamphlet appeared presenting the cavalier as an overberibboned 'English Antic' modelled on the morris dancer.[23]

In *The Queen and the Concubine*, Brome had transformed a royal May queen into an example of true Protestant spirituality, but a similar apotheosis in *Eikon Basilike* (printed in 1648 when it was perceived by Charles's supporters that his earthly fortunes could not recover) showed the pitfalls inherent in the serious interpretation of a complex tradition. The frontispiece, by William Marshall, uses the mountain top and temple as religious icons, conferring an accolade on Charles for the Christian suffering imminent in his threatened execution. But after the king was dead, and when he was worshipped by some as a saint, Milton was able to attack the hilltop image in *Eikon Basilike* through its long-standing connections with play-

---

[19] Butler, *Theatre and Crisis*, p. 224.

[20] The claim that outlaws are as good as princes is replaced by one that princes are no better than outlaws. 'SEVERINO. All those Kingdoms | Subdu'd by *Alexander*, were by force extorted, | Though gilded ore with glorious stiles of conquest; | His victories but royal robberies, | And his true definition a Thief' (v. iv. 32–6). *The Plays and Poems of Philip Massinger* (Oxford, 1976), iv. 189.

[21] Butler, *Theatre and Crisis*, p. 195.

[22] Thomason Collection. BL, E. 336(14).

[23] Ibid. 669, fo. 10(99).

19 *Eikon Basilike*, 1649 edition, frontispiece

acting: '... for though the Picture sett in Front would Martyr him and Saint him to befool the people yet... quaint Emblems and devices begg'd from the old Pageantry of some Twelf-nights entertainment, at *Whitehall*, will doe but ill to make a Saint or Martyr' (see Fig. 19).[24]

When Charles was beheaded, the man elevated most firmly above his public was not merely killed by inter-family wrangles, but was executed in the name of the people. The event was 'deeply shocking... even for many of his opponents, and [it] reverberated through the following century'.[25] It would be logical to conclude that the trauma caused the end of all seasonal customs involving the rise, fall, and death of mock kings throughout the country, but some did survive in weakened forms and despite the stronger force militating against them, the reformed Church; not in institutions such as the universities, however, where Christmas lords of misrule were completely suppressed by presbyterians who 'looked upon such laudable and ingenious customs as popish, diabilical and antichristian'.[26] And the only winter custom to survive, and even flourish in society, was the French version of the Twelfth Night king of the bean, in which a king or queen was discovered by means of the bean concealed in a portion of cake, and ruled for one night only.[27]

However, remote from centres of power, some summer customs did continue; the fullest extant record being that made in 1792 of the Lammas (1 August) festival in Midlothian. The definition of a survival well describes the events, for it would appear that, although all the medieval games were performed, their full significance was lost. There were mock battles led by captains for possession of towers on elevations, but no significance was attached to the towers. Further, the games ended with a race run for no title, though the commentator, J. Anderson, cannot finally resist a kingship analogy:

All the herds[men] within a certain district, towards the beginning of summer, associated themselves into bands, sometimes to the number of a

---

[24] *Eikonoklastes* (2nd edn., London, 1650), fo. A. 4ʳ.
[25] P. Curry, *Prophecy and Power: Astrology in Early Modern England* (Oxford, 1989), p. 6.
[26] *Observations on the Popular Antiquities of Great Britain*, rev. and augmented by W. C. Hazlitt (London, 1870), i. 273.
[27] B. A. Henisch, *Cakes and Characters* (London, 1984), *passim*.

Conclusion   261

hundred or more. Each of these communities agreed to build a tower in some conspicuous place, near the centre of their district, which was to serve as their rendezvous on Lammas day. This tower was usually built of sods; for the most part square, about four feet in diameter at the bottom, and tapering to a point at the top, which was seldom above seven or eight feet from the ground.[28]

To prevent rival herdsmen from demolishing the towers during their construction, guards were set round them at night. And:

as the great day of Lammas approached, each community chose one from among themselves for their Captain, and they prepared a stand of colours to be ready to be then displayed [using napkins and ribbons]. Things being thus prepared, they marched forth early in the morning on Lammas day, dressed in their best apparel, each armed with a stout cudgel, and, repairing to their tower, there displayed their colours in triumph, blowing horns and making merry. (pp. 195–6)

The different gangs sent out sorties to discover which tower they might conquer most easily but, although blood might be spilled, Anderson saw only diplomacy at work, and the day usually culminated peacefully in a competitive race for a bonnet instead of a crown:

A bonnet ornamented with ribbons was displayed upon a pole, as the prize of the victor; and sometimes five or six started for it, and ran with as great eagerness as if they had been to gain a kingdom. (p. 197)

Nineteenth-century English historians record midsummer wrestling on hilltops in Cornwall, and suggest it for Northumberland and Cumberland.[29] There is no mention of metaphorical meanings nor of the title of king, but the omissions might have occurred in the selective minds of the observers, especially that of John Bourne, who abhorred superstition and undertook his 1775 collection of popular customs to advise on 'which may be retain'd, and which ought to be laid aside'.[30] Mention of summer kings *was* made in early nineteenth-century Cheshire and Shropshire records. One was the 'lord of the pit', elected by men who dug out top dressings for farms from the side of the road, and with whom they demanded money

---

[28] J. Anderson, 'An Account of the Manner in which the Lammas Festival used to be celebrated in Mid Lothian, about the Middle of the Eighteenth Century', *Archaeologica Scotica*, 1 (1792), pp. 193–7.

[29] *Popular Antiquities*, rev. H. Ellis (London, 1853), i. 318. His n. 1 ref. to Hutchinson should read Hodgson, John.

[30] *Antiquitates Vulgares* (Newcastle-upon-Tyne, 1775), title-page.

262   Conclusion

from any neighbouring landowners who passed by. At the end of each day the men made a ring, and proclaimed the gifts in a parodic manner, crying 'oyez, oyez, oyez, Mr——has been with us to day and given my lord and his men part of a hundred pounds', or 'part of a thousand pounds' if the figure was above sixpence.[31] Such seasonal highway robbery was similar to the coercive methods used on spectators during the Woodstock Whit Ale in the same century.[32] And, finally, a festive context was retained in the mythology surrounding the nineteenth-century rebellions of Ned Ludd and Captain Swing.[33] In more recent times, the principle of half-rebellious, half-comic kingship, in opposition to authority, appeared in 1960s–1970s youth cult graffiti proclaiming that some unknown teenager 'rules O.K.', a practice gangs immediately abandoned once the slogan was appropriated by the Establishment for advertising.

But the change in play content at the Restoration is striking. Neo-classicism in tragedy purified extraneous or complex plots, and social manners comedy, though working on the ancient principle of a *speculum* reflecting the follies of the age, similarly did not find use for king game confusions. Not even under the promising title of *The Country Wife* did Wycherley include any allusions to rustic kings and queens. During the interregnum the concept of plays as a period of disorder within a social order began to be lost, as was shown in the following 1653 protest on the prolonged closure of the theatres:

> How happens then this rigour o're the Stage
> In this restor'd, free and licentious age?[34]

And in 1676 Wycherley completed the reversal between artistic disorder and social order in the Prologue to *The Plain-Dealer*:

> . . . where else, but on stages, do we see
> Truth pleasing or rewarded honesty?[35]

---

[31] H. Green, *Knutsford, its Traditions and History* (Manchester, 1859; repr. 1969), p. 84.

[32] A. Howkins, *Whitsun in Nineteenth-Century Oxfordshire*, History Workshop Pamphlets 8 (Oxford, 1974), pp. 7–8.

[33] See N. Simms, 'Ned Ludd's Mummers Play', *Folklore*, 89 (1978), pp. 166–78, and E. J. Hobsbawm and G. Rude, *Captain Swing* (Harmondsworth, 1969), pp. 207–15 (cf. Introduction, n. 1).

[34] W. Bang (ed.), *Materialien* (Louvain, 1906), xiii. 7*.

[35] *The Plays of William Wycherley*, ed. P. Holland (Cambridge, 1981), p. 355.

Conclusion

Reversed reversals had been rife during the mid-seventeenth century, and the mock king tradition itself, as already said, made all kingly icons treacherously ambiguous. Joseph Jane completed the *mundus inversus* argument in his reply to Milton's attack on *Eikon Basilike*; this time saying the world of inversions had become a hellish reality:

> We have lived to see that sure evill, which the . . . wisest of men complained of, *to see Princes on foote, & Servants on horsebacke*, when the Licentious insolence of the meanest tramples vpon the Soveraigntie of the highest, and the basest of the people revile the King.[36]

As well as the impact of religious dislike of superstition in the games, some writers, perhaps, wished not to desecrate the royal image further. Charles II's divine right was circumscribed by events,[37] and authors turned their attention to concepts such as rationality and progress.

[36] *Eikon Aklastos* (1651), p. 7.
[37] A. Fraser, *King Charles II* (London, 1988), pp. 189–90.

Appendices

I. Timon, a play, *edited by Alexander Dyce for The Shakespeare Society (London, 1842)*

ACT II Scene v

Enter LOLLIO *at one dore; and* TIMON, HERMOGENES, GELASIMUS, PSEUDOCHEUS, EUTRALEPUS, *at another, with feathers in their hatts;* DEMEAS, LACHES, OBBA

LOL. Call they this Athenes? Lord, what vaire buildings!
HERM. See yee that clowne? how hee admires all things!
EUTR. I knowe him well: 'tis Lollio, the sonne
    Of couetous Philargurus, who ne're
    Permits his sonne to frequent the cittie,
    Least hee shoulde learne the citties luxurie;
    Hee liues at home, eates browne breade and butter,
    Sometimes fat bacon.
LOL. Good godds, good gods, what preparation!
    What a concourse of people! This zittie zunne
    Seemes brighter than our country zunne. Lord, Lord,
    How many starres see I! how nere they are!
               [*The* [*inn*] *signe of the* 7 *stars*]

   .   .   .   .   .   .

EUTR. Seest thou these young men?
    They are the prime men of this same cittie.
LOL. Will they not imprisonne mee?
EUTR. Feare nothing.
LOL. What daintie burds doe zitte vppon their hatts!
    I wonder much they doe not vlie away.
    Their eies are on mee; must I make a legge?
EUTR. They come to salute thee.
LOL. Prithee, hold my staffe.
TIM. Most welcome vnto Athenes!
LOL. Thanks, by Joue.
TIM. Wee longe haue look'd for such a one, whom wee
    Might substitute prince ore the whole country.
GELAS. Foh, how he stinks of garlicke!
LACH. All are not muskified.
TIM. Putte on thy hatte; thou shalt bee our fellow.

   .   .   .   .

266   *Appendix I*

This day shall bee a day of sporte and mirthe:
   Bring cuppes of wine; let's welcome our new prince.
LOL. I am afraid least my behauiour
   Bee to to rusticke. . . .
GELAS. Heare, youngest of youthes; I am betrothd
   Vnto thy sister, whom I meane to wedde.
LOL. Giue mee thy hande.
   How doth my father's seruant, Grunnio?
EUTR. Thee, Timon, wee electe as soueraigne,
   Prince and commaunder of these Bacchanales:
   What lawes dost thou ordaine?—Peace, ho, awhile!
TIM. That this our compotation may haue
   A prosp'rous euente, wee will and commaunde
   Whole hogsheades to bee empt'ed, platters fill'd;
   None to depart, vnles hee first obtayne
   Leaue of the prince; wee also doe enacte
   That all holde vp their heades, and laughe aloude,
   Drinke much at one draughte, breathe not in their drinke;
   That none goe out to pisse, that none doe spew
   In any corner. Hee that shall offende
   In any one of these shall weare infixt
   Vppon his hatte an asses eares, and drinke
   Nothing but soure wine lees for three daies space.
[*All*] This acte wee ratifie, confirme, allow.
LOL. I thinke my father hath transgress'd these lawes;
   Hee nothing drinks but lees.
TIM. What, thy father!
   Hee is not worthy to exchange old shoes;
   But thou art noble, and king of good fellowes.
LOL. Father! hee noe more shall bee my father:
   I am a prince; I scorne and renounce him.
TIM. Lollio, I drinke to thee this whole one.
LOL. Were it a whole hogsheade, I would pledge thee.
   What, if I drinke two? fill them to the brimme.
   Wher's hee that shall marry with my sister?
   I drinke this to thee super naculum.
DEM. This wee doe call at Athenes . . .
TIM. Sounde, musicke! wee will daunce.
                              [*Sounde musicke*]
EUTR. Weele celebrate the feaste of Bacchus.—
   To make thee prince, I crowne thee with this bole.

            ·   ·   ·   ·   ·   ·   ·   ·   ·

Appendix I 267

[*They daunce*]

EYTR. Why sleepes the cuppe? why doth it not walke rounde?
    Thou a commaunder and forget they place!
TIM. I will; and commaunde thee, Eutrapelus,
    To couer Lollios heade with thy hatte,—
    And thou, Hermogenes, lende him thy cloke.
HERM. I lende him my cloke!
TIM. Soe wee commaunde.
HERM. I care not much; my clothes, without my cloke,
    Are trimme enough to make the people gaze.—[*Aside*]
    Take heede thou soyle it not.
TIM. Gelasimus
    Gird Lollio with thy sworde.

   ·   ·   ·   ·   ·

LACH. Hee wants a coate.
LOL. O noble Lollio, O braue Lollio!
[*All*] Thrice noble, thrice resplendente Lollio!
TIM. Into thy handes my empire I resigne.
LOL. Am I a prince then?
TIM. What dost thou commaunde?
LOL. Bringe mee a cuppe; I am as dry as duste:
    Thou shalt my butler bee.
GELAS. What shall I bee?
LOL. My butler too; all shall bee my butlers.
    What, can yee sing? singe, sing; I, Lollio,
    Your prince wills and commaunds.
TIM. Wee must obey.
    Who doth beginne?

   ·   ·   ·

[*Bawdy song*]

EUTR. Lollio!
TIM. Prince!
LOL. A little more good ale!
GELAS. Bring the cuppe, Obba.
LOL. Where are yee all, my butlers? follow mee;
    I will conducte yee to my fathers house;
    Follow your prince, followe mee in order:
    Eutrapelus, thou shalt my ensigne beare;
    Display the flaggon as it were a flagge.
    I am Achilles, yee my Myrmidones:
    Follow Achilles; wee haue leuell'd Troy
    Down with the earthe. Hector? art thou Hector?

268   *Appendix I*

GELAS. I am Gelasimus, thy brother [in] lawe.
LOL. Hadst thou beene Hector, I protest by Joue,
  I woulde haue Bor'd thee thorough with this sworde.
                    [*Exit* LOLLIO, *the rest following*]

THE THIRDE ACTE, THE FIRST SCENE.
Enter LOLLIO, TIMON, HERMOGENES, EUTRAPELUS *aduancing his*
        flaggon, GELASIMUS, PSEUDOCHEUS, DEMEAS
LOL. Display the flagge-on.—Where are those Troians?
  What, doe they hide their heades?
TIM. Why dost thou reele, Achilles, to and fro,
  Like to a shippe that's tossed with the waues?

            .   .   .   .

                        Enter GRUNNIO
GRUN. Good gods, whom doe I see? what Lollio,
  My masters sonne!
LOL. Grunnio, art thou here?
  Thou wast not here at first.
GRUN. Art in thy witts?
LOL. Thou knowest not who I am, Grunnio.
GRUN. Why, thou art Lollio.
LOL. Why laughe yee not?
GELAS. Must wee laughe? ha, ha, he!
  What stratageme is to·bee effected?
LOL. This calls mee Lollio. I Achilles,
  Or otherwise am called Pelides;
GRUN. Art not thou Lollio, and hold'st the ploughe?
  Didst thou not cutte mee out this very morne
  A portion of cheese, when I was sent
  To call thee to thy sisters marriage.
LOL. I Lollio! I holde the ploughe! I cutte
  What did I cutte thee out this very morne
  A portion of cheese, when thou wast sent
  To call mee to my sisters marriage?
DEM. Anaphora or a repetition.
LOL. I yee to witnes call, my Mirmidones;
  What say yee?
[*All*] Hees Achilles, Achilles.
GRUN. O miracle!—Callimela, Blatte,
  Come hither! Lollio is Achilles.
                    Enter CALLIMELA *and* BLATTE
BLAT. O mee, what tumulte is before my dores?
GELAS. My lady mistris, Calimele, my queene,

Appendix I 269

Withdrawe not backe your feete.

BLAT. Saue yee, youngmen: what is't that yee would haue?

LOL. Yee Myrmidons, beholde olde Hecuba!
What shall wee stone her?

GELAS. My fellowe soldiers, this shall bee my wife:
Is shee not faire?—How does my Calimele?

.   .   .   .

EUTR. Timon, why are your eies fixt on the grounde?

TIM. I feele a wounde.
I subiecte am to Venus tyranny:
These eies betraide my hearte; these were the gate
And onely way where loue first entred in;
I saw and lou'd, and must my loue enioye.

EUTR. What sodaine metamorphosis is this?

TIM. I loue, extreamely loue.

EUTR. What, Callimele?

TIM. The very same.

[*Exeunt* CALLIMELA *and* BLATTE
Enter PHILARGURUS *at another dore*

.   .   .

EUTR. Lollio, thy father.

LOL. My father hange himselfe! I'me Achilles;
I haue this day three thousand Troians slayne.

PHIL. To ploughe, thou slaue! . . .

HERM. Giue mee my cloke, Achilles; it is colde.

EUTR. To bedde and sleepe.

DEM. This birde hath lost his borrowed feathers.

LOL. I pray yee also, O my Myrmidons,
Pull of my doublette; Ile goe sleepe awhile.

[*All*] Goodnight, braue generall; farewell.

LOL. This flaggon shall serue mee for a pillow.

PHIL. Thou drunken knaue, Ile wake thee with this staffe!

LOL. Hector, oppresse mee not, while I doe sleepe; . . .

PHIL. Beare him in, Grunnio.—Hath wine subdu'de
Thy heade and feete at once?

LOL. Prithee, Obba, one cuppe; but one cuppe more.

PHIL. Thou art drunke, thou theefe.

LOL. Thou li'st, thou rascall.—
Where art, Agamemnon? helpe Achilles!

[Callimele chooses Timon's wealth against Gelasimus's love. Once Timon is told his ships are lost she deserts him and Gelasimus mocks him.]

270   Appendix I

Actus Tertii Scena Quinta

.   .   .   .

GEL. Ha, ha, he!
   How melancholy walkes he to and fro!—
   Thou shalt, if that thou wilt, mende my olde shoes.

Actus Quarti Scena 1ma,
[Demeas mocks him]
   Ha, ha, he! how tragicall hee is!
[Timon rages]
   Fire, water, sworde confounde yee! let the crowes
   Feede on your peckt out entrailes, and your bones
   Wante a sepulchre! . . . Rushe on me heaun'n,
   Soe that on them it rushe! Mount Causasus
   Fall on my shoulders, soe on them it fall!

.   .   .   .   .   .

[Gelas becomes the next fool of the play. He rejects Callimele, sells his land
to sail to a mythical princess, is tricked out of his gold, and is left an ass's
head.]

Scena 3 Act. Quinti.
GELAS. O, yee good people, what will become of me?
   My land is sould, and all my gould is fledd,
   And nothing left mee but this asses heade.
[Which is passed to the philosopher]

[Scen. 4 Act. Quinti]
HERM. This philosopher is chainged into an asse.
[Timon discovers Philargurus's buried gold, which produces an instant
change.]
GELAS. Timon hath found a mightie heape of gould:
   See, see how many clyents follow him!

Scen vlt. Act. vlt.
TIM. What company is this that followes mee?
   What would yee haue?
CALL. My Timon, my husband!
PHIL. My sonne in lawe!
HERM. My Maecenas!
EUTR. My protector!
DEM. My sublunary Jupiter!

Appendix I

Timon *Epilogue*

I now am left alone; this rascall route
Hath left my side. What's this? I feele throughout
A sodeine change; my fury doth abate,
My hearte growes milde, and laies aside its hate.

. . . .

Timon doffs Timon, and with bended knee
Thus craues a fauour.

II.   Ben Jonson and 'The War of the Theatres'

Jonson claimed that Marston began the Poetomachia by representing him on stage in *Histriomastix* (1598), though Marston 'seems in part at least to have intended, not a rebuke but a compliment', *Three Parnassus Plays, 1598 –1601*, ed. J. B. Leishman (London, 1949), p. 85. Jonson's reply was in 1599, in *Every Man Out of His Humour*, put on by the Chamberlain's Men. Jonson 'assigned to Clove a speech ridiculing Marston's "fustian" language' (ibid.). Marston's further riposte was in *Jack Drum's Entertainment*. Jonson left the Chamberlain's Men in 1599 after his production of *Every Man Out*. Marston's and Dekker's continuation of the war, *Satiromastix*, put on jointly by the Chamberlain's and Paul's Companies in 1601, suggests that Jonson's departure 'may not have been altogether voluntary' (ibid. 369). In Jonson's next play, *Poetaster* (1601, Children of the Chapel) he appears to attack the Chamberlain's Men; and in the 1601–2 *Return from Parnassus*, 2. IV. iii, Shakespeare is included in the quarrel at the end of Will Kempe's claim that Shakespeare can 'put down' any university playwright. Kempe adds:

> And Ben Jonson too. O that Ben Jonson is a pestilent fellow, he brought vp Horace giuing the poets a pill [*Poetaster*], but our fellow Shakespeare have giuen him a purge that made him beray his credit.

Although it was Marston and Dekker who wrote the purge in *Satiromastix*, Leishman points out that by assisting in the production, Shakespeare was implicated (ibid. 370–1). A further possibility for Shakespeare's purge is Jonson's removal from the Chamberlain's Men.

III. *Ben Jonson and* Vetus Comoedia

Every Man Out of his Humour, Opening Chorus, ll. 226–40.

MITIS. You have seen his play, Cordatus? Pray you, how is't?

CORD. Faith, sir, I must refrain to judge; only this I can say of it, 'tis strange, and of a particular kind by itself, somewhat like *Vetus Comoedia*: a work that hath bounteously pleased me; how it will answer the general expectation, I know not.

MITIS. Does he observe all the laws of comedy in it?

CORD. What laws mean you?

MITIS. Why, the equal division of it into acts and scenes, according to the Terentian manner; his true number of actors; the furnishing of the scene with Grex or Chorus, and that the whole argument fall within compass of a day's business.

CORD. Oh no, these are too nice observations.

MITIS. They are such as must be received, by your favour, or it cannot be authentic.

CORD. Troth, I can discern no such necessity.

The Complete Plays of Ben Jonson, ed. G. A. Wilkes (Oxford, 1981), i. 292

C. R. Baskervill observed in 1911:

The phrase *Vetus Comoedia* would naturally be interpreted at once as referring to classic comedy, and the context seems to support this interpretation. I am tantalized, however, by the question whether the reference may not, after all, have been to the older forms of English drama. Nashe in *The Returne of Pasquill* twice uses the term in connection with old English plays (Vol. 1, pp. 92 and 100), and Drummond reports Jonson himself as saying that 'according to *Comedia Vetus*, in England the Divell ... carried away the Vice'. At any rate, there is little in the structure, the type of incident, or the method of characterization to connect *Every Man out* with classic comedy. (*English Elements in Jonson's Early Comedy* [Texas, 1911; 2nd edn., New York, 1967], pp. 212–13)

In Drummond's recollection, and as Baskervill concludes, *vetus comoedia* would appear to refer to Morality drama. However, there was also a Vice and a devil in the 1601 summer lord game in Lincolnshire (see Barber, *Shakespeare's Festive Comedy*, p. 43), and in Nashe's *The Returne of Pasquill*, vol. i, it is the May wooing game of Martin Marprelate, pp. 83 and 88, which is (on p. 92) given the 'old comedy' name. On p. 100 Martin further says, 'By her gate and her *Garland* [emphasis added] I knowe her well, it is *Vetus Comoedia*. She hath been so long in the country, that she is somewhat altered.' This appears to mean that the high or pure Greek

Appendix III

invention had developed into a rustic English form, whether Morality or seasonal play. In the opening of *Every Man Out*, Jonson appears to pose Cordatus's more rustic expectations against the classic demands of Mitis.

SELECT BIBLIOGRAPHY

I Manuscript Sources

Artickelles aȝenst Thomas Corthorp curate of harwiche, PRO SP 1. 99, fo. 203^v.

Berkshire Record Office D/P 97/5/2.

Declared Accounts of the Treasurer of the Chamber, 1559–60, PRO AO1/380.2.

Desert of Religion BM MS Add. 37049.

Kingston upon Thames, *Churchwardens' Account Book*, KG 2/2/1.

PALMER, T., *Two Hundred Poosees*, BM Sloane 4794.

SOTHERTON, N., 'the commoyson in Norfolk', BM Harley MS 1576.

Schönbartbuch, Fitzwilliam Museum 382.

Queen Elizabeth's Wardrobe Accounts 1559–60, PRO E. 351/3033, fo. 3^v.

—— 1561–2, PRO E. 101/429/14 fo. 56^v.

II Published Sources

ADAMSON, J., *Troilus and Cressida* (Brighton, 1988).

ANGLO, S., *Spectacle, Pageantry, and Early Tudor Policy* (Oxford, 1969).

Annalia Dubrensia, ed. M. Walbancke (London, 1636; Scolar Press facsimile, Menston, 1973).

ASHTON, R., *James I by his Contemporaries* (London, 1969).

AXTON, M., 'Robert Dudley and the Inner Temple Revels', *HJ* 13 (1970), 365–78.

—— *The Queen's Two Bodies* (London, 1977).

AXTON, R., *European Drama of the Early Middle Ages* (London, 1974).

BAKHTIN, M., *Rabelais and his World*, trans. H. Iswolsky (Cambridge, Mass., 1965).

—— *Problems of Dostoevsky's Poetics*, trans. R. W. Rotsel (Ann Arbor, 1973).

BALDWIN, A. P., *The Theme of Government in Piers Plowman* (Bury St Edmunds, 1981).

BARBER, C. L., *Shakespeare's Festive Comedy* (Princeton, 1959).

BARTON, A., 'He that plays the king', *English Drama: Forms and Development*, ed. M. Axton and R. Williams (Cambridge, 1977).

BASKERVILL, C. R., 'Dramatic Aspects of Medieval Folk Festivals in England', *SP* 17 (1920), 19–87.

—— *English Elements in Jonson's Early Comedy* (2nd edn., New York, 1967).

BEAUMONT, F., *The Dramatic Works in the Beaumont and Fletcher Canon*, ed. F. Bowers, 6 vols. (Cambridge, 1966–85).

276 Select Bibliography

BEER, B. L., *Rebellion and Riot: Popular Disorder in England during the Reign of Edward VI* (Kent, Ohio, 1982).

BELLAMY, J., *Crime and Public Order in England in the Later Middle Ages* (London, 1973).

BERCÉ, Y.-M., *Fête et révolte: des mentalités populaires du XVIeme au XVIIIeme siècle* (Paris, 1976).

BEVINGTON, D., *Tudor Drama and Politics* (Cambridge, Mass., 1968).

BILLINGTON, S., 'Sixteenth-Century Drama in St. John's College, Cambridge', *RES*, NS 29 (1978), 1–10.

—— *A Social History of the Fool* (Brighton, 1984).

—— 'The Fool and the Moral in English and Scottish Morality Plays', in F. G. Andersen *et al.* (eds.), *Popular Drama in Northern Europe in the Later Middle Ages* (Odense, 1988), 113–33.

—— 'Butchers and Fishmongers', *Folklore* 101 (1990), 97–103.

BINGHAM, C., *James I of England* (London, 1981).

BLOMEFIELD, F., *An Essay towards a Topographical History of the County of Norfolk* (Norwich, 1745).

BOAS, F. S., *University Drama in the Tudor Age* (Oxford, 1914).

BRADBROOK, M., *Shakespeare: The Poet in his World* (London, 1978).

BRIE, F. W. D., 'Wat Tyler and Jack Straw', *EHR* 21 (1906), 106–11.

BRUNNE, R. of, *Handlyng Synne*, ed. F. J. Furnivall, EETS (London, 1901).

BUCHANAN, G., *The History of Scotland*, ed. J. Aikman, i (Glasgow, 1827).

BURKE, P., *Popular Culture in Early Modern Europe* (London, 1978).

BUTLER, M., *Theatre and Crisis, 1632–42* (Cambridge, 1984).

CHAMBERS, E. K., *The Medieval Stage*, 2 vols. (Oxford, 1903).

—— *The Elizabethan Stage*, 4 vols. (Oxford, 1923).

CHAUCER, G., 'The Hous of Fame' and *The Canterbury Tales*, *The Works of Geoffrey Chaucer*, ed. F. N. Robinson (2nd edn., London, 1957).

Chester Mystery Cycle, The, ed. R. M. Lumiansky and D. Mills, EETS (Oxford, 1974–86).

Christmas Prince, The, ed. F. S. Boas, Malone Society Reprints (Oxford, 1923).

CLARK, E. G., *Ralegh and Marlowe* (New York, 1965).

COMBE, T., *The Theater of Fine Devices* (London, c.1593).

CORNWALL, J., *Revolt of the Peasantry, 1549* (London, 1977).

COX, J. C. (ed.), *Churchwardens' Accounts from the Fourteenth to the Close of the Seventeenth Century*, The Antiquary's Books (London, 1913).

COUSIN, J., *Le Livre de fortune*, ed. L. Lalanne (Paris, 1883).

DASENT, J. R. (ed.), *Acts of the Privy Council of England*, NS 21, 22, 1591–2 (London, 1900–1).

DAVIS, N. M., 'The Playing of Miracles in England between *c.* 1350 and the Reformation', Ph.D. thesis (Cambridge, 1977).

DAVIS, N. Z., *Society and Culture in Early Modern France* (London, 1975).

Select Bibliography

DEE, J., *Autobiographical Tracts of Dr John Dee*, ed. J. Crossley, Chetham Society, 24 (Manchester, 1851).

DOBSON, R. B., *The Peasants' Revolt of 1381* (London, 1970).

——and TAYLOR, J., *The Rhymes of Robin Hood: An Introduction to the English Outlaw* (London, 1976).

DODDS, M. H., and DODDS, R., *The Pilgrimage of Grace, 1536–7 and the Exeter Conspiracy, 1538* (Cambridge, 1915).

DONALDSON, I., *The World Upside Down* (Oxford, 1970).

DUGDALE, Sir W., *Originales Iuridiciales* (London, 1666).

DUNCAN, A. M., *Copernicus: On the Revolutions of the Heavenly Spheres* (Newton Abbot, 1976).

ELBOW, P., *Oppositions in Chaucer* (Middletown, Conn., 1975).

ELTON, W. R., *King Lear and the Gods* (San Marino, Calif., 1966).

ERASMUS, D., *The Praise of Folly*, trans. B. Radice and introd. A. H. T. Levi (Harmondsworth, 1971).

FABYAN, R. (attrib.), *The Great Chronicle of London*, ed. I. Thornley and A. H. Thomas (London, 1808).

FERRERS, G., and SACKVILLE, T., *The Mirror for Magistrates*, ed. L. B. Campbell (2nd edn., New York, 1960).

FEUILLERAT, A., and FEUILLERAT, G. (eds.), *Documents Relating to the Office of the Revels in the Time of Queen Elizabeth* (Louvain, 1908).

——and —— *Documents Relating to the Revels at Court in the Time of King Edward VI and Queen Mary* (Louvain, 1914).

FIGGIS, J. N., *The Divine Right of Kings* (London, 1914).

FLETCHER, A., *Tudor Rebellions: Seminar Studies in History* (London, 1968).

FLETCHER, J., *see* BEAUMONT, F.

FRENCH, P. J., *John Dee: The World of an Elizabethan Magus* (London, 1972).

Gesta Grayorum, The, ed. W. W. Greg, Malone Society Reprints (Oxford, 1915).

GILDERSLEEVE, V. C., *Government Regulation of the Elizabethan Drama* (3rd edn., Westport, Conn., 1975).

GIRARD, R. 'The Politics of Desire in *Troilus and Cressida*', in P. Parker and G. Hartman (eds.), *Shakespeare: The Question of Theory* (London, 1985).

GOODMAN, Dr G., *The Court of King James the First*, ed. J. S. Brewer (London, 1839).

GREENE, R. L. (ed.), *Early English Carols* (2nd edn., Oxford, 1977).

GRINGORE, P., *Les Fantasies de Mere Sote*, ed. R. L. Frautschi (Chapel Hill, NC, 1962).

GURR, A., *Playgoing in Shakespeare's London* (Cambridge, 1987).

278 Select Bibliography

HALL, E., *The Triumphant Reigne of Kyng Henry the VIII* (London, 1550), ed. C. Whibley, 2 vols. (London, 1904).

—— *Chronicle; Containing the History of England [from] the Reign of Henry IV . . . to the end of the Reign of Henry VIII* (London, 1548), ed. Sir H. Ellis (London, 1809).

HALLIWELL, J. O. (ed.), *Nugae Poeticae* (London, 1844).

—— *Early English Miscellanies* (London, 1855).

HAWKINS, H., *Measure for Measure* (Brighton, 1987).

HENINGER, S. K., *Touches of Sweet Harmony: Pythagorean Cosmology and Renaissance Poetics* (San Marino, Calif., 1974).

HENISCH, B. A., *Cakes and Characters: An English Christmas Tradition* (London, 1984).

HOBHOUSE, E. (ed.), *Churchwardens' Accounts of Croscombe, Pilton, Yatton, Tintinhull, Morebath, and St. Michael's; Bath, 1349–1560*, Somerset Record Society Publications (London, 1890).

HOBSBAWM, E. J., and RUDE, G., *Captain Swing* (Harmondsworth, 1969).

HOLDSWORTH, R. V., 'Middleton and Shakespeare: The Case for Middleton's Hand in *Timon of Athens*', Ph.D. thesis (Manchester, 1982).

HOLINSHED, R., *Chronicles of England, Scotland and Ireland*, ed. J. Hooker *et al.*, 5 vols. (London, 1807–8).

HOPWOOD, C. H. (ed.), *Middle Temple Records, Minutes of Parliament*, 4 vols. (London, 1904–5).

HUDSON, W., and Tingey, U. J. C. (eds.), *Selected Records of the City of Norwich*, 2 vols. (Norwich, 1906).

HURSTFIELD, J., *Freedom, Corruption and Government in Elizabethan England* (London, 1973).

INDERWICK, F. A. (ed.), *A Calendar of the Inner Temple Records*, i (London, 1896).

IRVING, D., *Memoirs of the Life and Writings of George Buchanan* (Edinburgh, 1817).

JAMES, I., *Basilicon Doron* (Edinburgh, 1599; London, 1603), STS, ed. J. Craigie, 2 vols. (Edinburgh, 1944–50).

JOHNSTON, A. F. (gen ed.), *Records of Early English Drama, Cambridge*, ed. A. Nelson, 3 vols. (Toronto, 1989).

—— *Chester*, ed. L. M. Clopper (Toronto and Manchester, 1979).

—— *Coventry*, ed. R. W. Ingram (Toronto and Manchester, 1981).

—— *Cumberland, Westmorland; Gloucestershire*, ed. A. Douglas (Toronto, 1986).

—— *Devon*, ed. J. M. Wasson (Toronto, 1986).

—— *Oxford*, ed. J. Elliott (forthcoming).

—— *York*, ed. A. F. Johnston and M. Rogerson, 2 vols. (Toronto and Manchester, 1979).

Select Bibliography 279

Kalendar & Compost of Shepherds, trans. R. Copland (1508), ed. G. C. Heseltine (London, 1930).

KERNAN, A., *The Cankered Muse* (New Haven, 1959).

KIPLING, G., *The Triumph of Honour: Burgundian Origins of the Elizabethan Renaissance* (The Hague, 1977).

KIRCHMAIER, T. (Neogeorgius), '"The Popishe Kingdom" 1553, Englisht by B. Googe', ed. F. J. Furnivall, in P. Stubbes, *Anatomie of Abuses* (London, 1877–82).

KNIGHTON, H., *Chronicon Henrici Knighton*, ed. J. R. Lumby, 2 vols. (London, 1889–95).

KNOX, J., 'The First Blast of the Trumpet against the Monstrous Regimen of Women, *The Works of John Knox*, ed. D. Laing (Edinburgh, 1895), iv. 349–422.

LADURIE, E. le R., *Carnival in Romans: A People's Uprising at Romans, 1579–80*, trans. M. Feeney (Harmondsworth, 1979).

LAKE, D. J., *The Canon of Thomas Middleton's Plays* (London, 1975).

LANGLAND, W., *The Vision of Piers the Plowman in three Parallel Texts together with Richard the Redeles*, ed. W. W. Skeat (Oxford, 1886).

LEGH, G., *The Accedens of Armorie* (London, 1562).

LEISHMAN, see *Three Parnassus Plays*.

LEVIN, H., *The Overreacher: A study of Christopher Marlowe* (London, 1954).

—— 'Falstaff's Encore', *SQ* 32 (1981), 5–17.

LEVIN, R., *The Multiple Plot in English Renaissance Drama* (Chicago, 1971).

LEVINE, J. M. (ed.), *Elizabeth I*, Great Lives Observed (New Jersey, 1969).

Loseley Manuscripts, The, ed. A. J. Kempe (London, 1836).

LYDGATE, D., *The Fall of Princes*, ed. H. Bergen, 4 vols., EETS (London, 1924–7).

LYLE, H., *The Rebellion of Jack Cade 1450*, Historical Association Pamphlet (London, 1950).

MACDONALD, P. J., *Studies in Attribution: Middleton and Shakespeare* (Salzburg, 1979).

MACHYN, H., *Diary of a Resident in London from 1550 to 1563*, ed. J. G. Nichols, Camden Society (London, 1848).

MARKELS, J., *The Pillar of the World: Antony and Cleopatra in Shakespeare's Development* (Columbus, Ohio, 1968).

Mirror for Magistrates, see FERRERS, G.

MORE, St T., *Utopia, The Complete Works of St. Thomas More*, ed. C. Surtz, S. J. Hexter, and J. H. Hexter, iv (New Haven, 1965).

Morte Arthure, ed. E. Brock, EETS (London, 1871).

NASHE, T., *The Return of Pasquill*, i (1903).

—— *Lenten Stuffe, The Works of Thomas Nashe*, ed. R. B. McKerrow, iii and iv (London, 1904–8).

280   *Select Bibliography*

NICHOLS, J. G. (ed.), *The Progresses and Public Processions of Queen Elizabeth*, 3 vols. (London, 1788–1823).
—— *The Progresses, Processions, and Magnificent Entertainments of King James I, his Royal Consort, Family and Court*, (London, 1828).
OWST, G. R., *Preaching in Mediaeval England* (Cambridge, 1926).
—— *Literature and Pulpit in Mediaeval Literature* (Oxford, 1933).
PALLISER, D. M., *The Age of Elizabeth: England under the late Tudors 1547–1603* (London, 1983).
PALMER, T., *The Emblems of Thomas Palmer: Two Hundred Poosies. Sloane MS 4794*, ed. J. Manning (New York, 1988).
PASTON, J., *The Paston Letters and Papers*, ed. N. Davis, 2 vols. (Oxford, 1971–6).
PATCH, H. R., 'Some Elements in Mediaeval Descriptions of the Otherworld', *PMLA* 33 (1918), 601–43.
—— *The Tradition of the Goddess Fortuna in Mediaeval Philosophy and Literature*, Smith College Studies in Modern Languages, vol. 3, no. 4 (Northampton, Mass., 1922).
—— *The Goddess Fortuna in Old French Literature*, Smith College Studies, vol. 4, no. 4 (Northampton, Mass., 1923).
—— *The Goddess Fortuna in Mediaeval Literature* (Cambridge, Mass., 1927).
PETTITT, T., 'Here Comes I, Jack Straw', *Folklore*, 95 (1984), 3–20.
POWELL, E., *The Rising in East Anglia in 1381* (Cambridge, 1895).
Prince d'Amour (1597–8) BL E. 1836(1).
PURVIS, J. S. (ed.), *Tudor Parish Documents of the Diocese of York* (Cambridge, 1948).
RAMSAY, J. H., *Lancaster and York: A Century of English History AD 1399–1485* (Oxford, 1892).
RHODES, N., *Elizabethan Grotesque* (London, 1980).
RIGHTER, A., *Shakespeare and the Idea of the Play* (London, 1962).
ROBBINS, R. H. (ed.), *Historical Poems of the XIV and XV Centuries* (New York, 1959).
—— *Secular Lyrics of the XIV and XV Centuries* (Oxford, 1952).
SIDNEY, Sir P., *Defence of Poesie* (London, 1595).
—— *The Complete Works of Sir Philip Sidney*, ed. A. Feuillerat, iii (Cambridge, 1922).
SIMMS, N., 'Ned Ludd's Mummers Play', *Folklore*, 89 (1978), 166–78.
SIMPSON, P., 'King Charles the First as Dramatic Critic', *Bodleian Quarterly Record*, 8: 92 (1936–7), 257–62.
SMITH, L. B., *Treason in Tudor England* (London, 1986).
SOELLNER, R., *Timon of Athens: Shakespeare's Pessimistic Tragedy* (Kent, Ohio, 1979).
Spanish State Papers—Elizabeth, vol. i, ed. M. A. S. Hulme (London, 1892).

Select Bibliography

SPENSER, E., 'The Shepheardes Calendar', Spenser, *Poetical Works*, ed. J. C. Smith and E. de Selincourt (Oxford, 1912; repr. 1969).

STONE, L., *The Crisis of the Aristocracy 1558–1641* (Oxford, 1965).

STONES, E. L. G., 'The Folvilles of Ashby-Folville, Leicestershire, and their Associates in Crime 1326–1347', *TRHS* 7 (1957), 117–36.

STOW, J., *A Survey of London*, ed. C. L. Kingsford, 2 vols. (Oxford, 1908; repr. 1971).

STRONG, R., *The Cult of Elizabeth* (London, 1977).

——*Art and Power: Renaissance Festivals 1450–1650* (Woodbridge, 1984).

STRUTT, J., *Sports and Pastimes of the People of England* (London, 1831).

STUBBES, P., *Anatomie of Abuses in the Kingdom of Ailgna*, ed. F. J. Furnivall (London, 1877–82).

TILLYARD, E. M. W., *Shakespeare's History Plays* (London, 1944).

Three Parnassus Plays, 1598–1601, ed. J. B. Leishman (London, 1949).

TOYNBEE, M. R., 'Le Capitaine Bessus', *Times Literary Supplement*, 14 July 1950.

WALDMAN, M., *Elizabeth and Leicester* (2nd edn., London, 1945).

WALKER, J. D. (ed.), *The Black Books of Lincoln's Inn*, 3 vols. (London, 1897).

WELLS, S., and TAYLOR, G., *William Shakespeare: A Textual Companion* (Oxford, 1987).

WELSFORD, E., *The Fool: His Social and Literary History* (London, 1935).

WHITE, H., *Social Criticism in Popular Religious Literature of the Sixteenth Century* (New York, 1965).

WILES, D., *The Early Plays of Robin Hood* (Woodbridge, 1981).

WILSON, J. D. (introd.), *The First Part of King Henry VI* (Cambridge, 1952), pp. ix–l.

WINNEY, J., *The Player King: A Theme of Shakespeare's Histories* (London, 1968).

WOMACK, P., *Ben Jonson* (Oxford, 1986).

WOOD, A. à, *Athenae Oxonienses*, ed. P. Bliss, 4 vols. (London, 1813–20).

Woodstock, A Moral History, ed. A. P. Rossiter (London, 1946).

WRIGHT, T., and HALLIWELL, J. O. (eds.), *Reliquae Antiquae*, 2 vols. (London, 1841–3).

Index

acclamation 47–8, 54, 191
Act of Supremacy 97
allhallows 3, 52
alter rex 107
alterae terrae 38
Annalia Dubrensia, see Cotswold
  games
antimasque 109, 250
Arthur, King 137, 220
  Gawain and the Green Knight 67
  Morte Arthure 75–6, 124
Arthurian chivalry 12, 53, 101,
  172–3, 202
Aske, Robert 25
Astraea 99
audiences 117–18, 125, 181
Augustine, Saint 86

Bacon, Francis 50, 227, 233
Balthazar 32
Beaumont, Francis, *The*
  Woman-Hater 123, 236
  and Fletcher, John, *A King and No*
  King 120, 128, 161, 188–95, 226,
  237
boast 71–2, 91, 136, 191, 201
Book of Sir Thomas More 223, 230
Brome, Richard, *The Antipodes* 257
  The Court Beggar 257
  The Queen and the Concubine 256,
  257
Buc, Sir George 223
Buchanan, George 88–9, 95, 108

Cade, John, *see* outlaws
captain 15–16, 18, 32, 222
Carpenter, Fabritius 57, 97, 206
Chapman, George, 44, *An Humorous*
  Day's Mirth 118, 120, 186
  Charles Duke of Biron 236
Charles I 23, 122, 189, 255, 257–60
Charles II 263
Chaucer, Geoffrey, 'The Hous of
  Fame' 67–9, 170
  'Monk's Tale' 74
  'Miller's Tale' 84
Christ 25, 60, 67, 93, 146, 168

Christmas 20–1, 30–5, 37, 40–3,
  46–53, 91, 93, 192, 205, 121, 218
Christmas Lords 20–1, 30–3, 34–7,
  38–43, 46–53, 93, 98, 101, 103,
  121, 171, 182, 184, 198–9, 219,
  220, 221, 239, 240, 248, 255
concordia discors 2, 43
Constable Marshall 46–8
Copernicus 43–4, 157
Corpus Christi, Feast of 65, 71, 72
Corthorpe, Thomas 34
cosmos 210, 213
  see also Dee, John; Pythagoras
Cotswold games 63, 80–4, 85, 106,
  117, 125
court entertainments 30–2, 37, 38–43,
  46, 50, 76, 77, 101–3, 106, 109,
  134, 205, 219–20, 242
courtiers 100–4, 107, 110, 130–1,
  171–2, 184, 223–4, 225, 227,
  229, 250
Cousin, Jean, *Le Livre de Fortune* 65,
  69
Croscombe games 56
Cynthia 225–6, 229–30

Day, John, *The Isle of Gulls* 234
Dee, John 43, 46 n. 71, 184
Dekker, Thomas, *The Shoemakers'*
  Holiday 120, 181, 188, 197, 253
  The Honest Whore 188
de Quadra, Bishop 102
Desert of Religion 60
Diana worship 45–6, 99
divine right 86–7, 108, 113
Dominus 37, 42
Dover, Robert 63, 80–4
Dudley, Guildford 100
Dudley, Robert 46, 48–50, 99–104,
  106, 220, 239
Dugdale, Sir William 46, 48
Dymoke, Talboys 72, 85, 219

Edward II 31
Edward III 31
Edward IV 21
Edward VI 22, 31, 40

Index

Elizabeth I 44–5, 48, 49, 50, 77–9, 93, 95, 98–9, 101–3, 104–8, 111, 113, 134, 137, 220, 226, 227, 255
Swedish suitor 102, 220
Emblem 23, 69, 74, 80, 103–4, 111
Erasmus, Desiderius, *Adages* 139, 238
Praise of Folly (*Moriae Encomium*) 50, 87–8, 108, 111
Essex Earl of 106–8, 175, 179, 221, 228

Falstaff 45, 46, 47, 149–56, 197, 209, 214
fantasy 23, 42, 52, 54, 59, 85, 118, 127, 146, 162, 180, 201, 219 n. 7, 239, 247, 250, 253, 256
Ferrers, George 31, 38–43, 47, 101
Festive iconography 19–20, 87
Fletcher, John, *The Faithful Shepherdess* 117, 121
and Beaumont, *A King and No King*, *see* Beaumont F.
and Massinger(?) *Beggars Bush* 257
Fo, Dario 254
fools 4, 42, 93, 182–3, 154–5, 172, 173, 174, 191, 193–4, 206, 241
fool-king 63, 91, 93, 141, 148, 154–5, 183, 192, 201, 206–7, 208
Ford, John *The Broken Heart* 256
The Ladies Triall 122
Love's Sacrifice 122
Perkin Warbeck 21, 163, 257
(attrib.) *The Queen or the Excellency of her Sex* 196
Fortuna (Fortune) 64–9, 72–85, 125, 161, 165, 172, 174, 195, 201, 208, 238–9
Fortune's hill 63, 64–9, 73, 79, 123, 124, 134, 136, 161, 169, 170–1, 207
Fortune theatre 80
Fortune's wheel 72, 74, 75–6, 79, 123, 125, 161, 163, 207

Gesta Grayorum 50–1
Gladman, John 19–20
Greene, Robert, *Friar Bacon and Friar Bungay* 120, 183–6, 197, 253, 256

Hall, Edward 21, 26, 218 n. 3
Heneage, Thomas 103
Henry VI 21

Henry VII 21, 138
Henry VIII 57, 58, 97, 138
Herod 71
Heywood, Thomas, *First and Second Partes of King Edward the Fourth* 230–1
hilltop games 60–5, 69, 73–4, 80–4, 88, 125, 135–6, 161, 170–1, 186–7, 219, 233, 255, 258–60, 260–1
see also Fortune's hill and king games
Holinshed, Raphael 95–6
Holy Roman Empire 86

iconography of kingship 87, 98
Inns of Court 98, 141
Gray's Inn 50–1, 134–5, 191, 201, 218
Inner Temple 46–50, 100, 191, 198–9
Lincoln's Inn 28, 35
Middle Temple 36, 51–2
Isle of Dogs 53, 229

James VI and I 6, 9, 79–80, 108–13, 233–7, 247–8
Basilicon Doron 6, 9, 108–9, 234
Jonson, Ben 117, 229, 272
The Alchemist 188, 195
Bartholomew Fair 188, 195
Eastward Ho! 179, 236
Epicoene 188, 190
Every Man Out of his Humour 188, 273
Timber 181
and *Vetus Comoedia* 273
Volpone 188, 196

Kalendar and Compost of Shepherds 65
Kett, Robert 20, 22, 25
king game 56–8, 60–5, 67, 69–72, 73–4, 95–6, 135, 145–7, 160–1, 180, 196, 222, 248–9
King Leir 209 n. 47
king of the bean 30–2, 35, 95, 96, 106, 260
king of the minstrels 30–1
Kingston-upon-Thames 56–7
Kirchmaier 4, 73 n. 51

Lady Fame 65–9, 76, 79, 83
Lady Jane Grey 100

Index

285

Langland, William 9
   Piers Plowman 2, 14, 85
   Richard the Redeles 13, 33
Lauder, William, *The Office and*
   Dewtie of Kings 96
Legh, Gerard, *Accidens of Armorie* 49
Leicester, Earl of, *see* Dudley, Robert
Leycester's Commonwealth 104
Lincoln, Earl of 72
Lodge, Thomas 35, 36
Lord of Kyme 72
lord of misrule 3, 30–2, 46–7
   etymology of 33
Lord Quondam 99
Lydgate, Dan, *Fall of Princes* 74–5
Lyndsay, David, *Cupar Banns* 57

Machyn, Henry, *Diary* 101–2, 104
Maid Marion 56–8, 104
Manichaeism 2, 164
Marlowe, Christopher, *Edward II* 168
   Dr. Faustus 54, 121
   Tamburlaine 54, 118, 119, 159–69,
     180, 254
Marston, John 179
   The Fawn 234
   Jack Drums Entertainment 118,
     120, 176–9, 186–7
   The Malcontent 238, 240–2
Mary Queen of Scots 95, 134
Mary Tudor 100
Massinger, Philip, *The Guardian* 258
may queens 56, 106, 257
microcosm 46 n. 71, 213, 246
midsummer 58–9, 60–3, 65, 71, 91,
   102, 121, 124, 125, 173, 207
midwinter 93, 207, 255
   see also Christmas
Milton, John *Eikonoklastes* 260
Mirrour of Maiestie 80, 111
Misfortunes of Arthur 122, 134–8,
   141, 159, 219
mockery 13, 35–6, 51, 53, 64, 87–8,
   91, 93, 95, 112–13, 126, 131,
   136, 145–6, 148, 149, 171, 172,
   174, 191, 201, 221, 255
moon worship 44–6
   see also Diana
Moriae Encomium, see Erasmus
mundus inversus 38, 42, 109, 188,
   258
Mystery Cycle, Chester 'Shepherds'
   Play' 63–5

Nashe, Thomas 53–4
   Lenten Stuff 53–4
   Summers Last Will and
     Testament 74, 255
New Year 102–4
   see also Yule
Nobody and Somebody 234–5
Norfolk, Duke of 17, 19
Norfolk, Sheriff of 17
Northumberland, Duke of, *see*
   Warwick, Earl of (1547–52)
Norwich 17, 18–19

oppositions 1–3, 6, 12, 28, 119,
   141, 144–5, 147, 163, 164,
   168, 182, 192, 193, 195, 196,
   208, 215–16, 224, 241, 242–3,
   255
Osborne, Francis 111
outlaws:
   Beckwith, William 15, 29, 143
   Chirche, Roger 16–17
   de Folville, Eustace 10, 13, 14–15
   de Vere, Robert 10, 13
   Venables, Piers 18
Ovid, *Metamorphoses* 103

Palmer, Thomas, *Two Hundred*
   Poosies 103
Parnassus Plays 119, 272–3
Paston, John 16–17, 33
Paston John II 18
patronage 102, 112, 220
Peele, George, *Edward I* 120
Prester John 32
Prince d'Amour 51–2, 121, 214
Prince of Purpoole 50–1
Pym, John 23, 85
Pythagoras 37–8, 43–4, 157

Raleigh, Sir Walter 43, 107, 232
Reading, St. Lawrence games 56
Rebellions 3
   Cornwall 25
   Evil May Day 25, 26–7, 33, 230
   Norfolk 22, 25
   Norwich 19–20
   Pilgrimage of Grace 23–5
Rebels
   Aske, Robert 25–6
   Cade, Jack 16
   Kett, Robert 20, 25–6
   Simnell, Lambert 21

Index

Rebels (*cont.*):
  Tyler, Wat 16, 28
  Warbeck, Perkin 21
reconciliation of opposites, *see*
  concordia discors
Recorde, Robert, *The Castle of*
  Knowledge 77
rex fabarum, *see* king of the bean
rex stultorum 30
Richard I 131
Richard II 13, 76
  as analogy for Elizabeth 221–2,
  231–2
Richard III 21, 95–6
Richard, Duke, of York 20–1
riot 3, 25 n. 61, 26, 28, 33–6, 230
Robert the Bruce 12
Robert of Brunne, *Handlyng*
  Synne 34 n. 20, 57
Robert of Sicily 91, 207
Robin Hood 13–15, 18, 28, 56–8, 60,
  104, 120

St George 56
St John's College, Cambridge 37, 52
St John's College, Oxford 35, 52–3, 60
satire 88, 112–13, 121, 170, 187, 204,
  218, 242
saturnalia, devilish 35, 140, 181, 185,
  195–7, 241, 263
saturnalia, regenerative 181, 186–7,
  195–7, 241
Schembart Festival 40
Shakespeare, *Antony and*
  Cleopatra 209–17, 250, 256
  As You Like It 119, 178
  Coriolanus 121
  Hamlet 121
  1 Henry IV 119, 148–58
  2 Henry IV 117, 119, 152–8
  Henry V 153, 158
  1 Henry VI 121, 139–42, 178
  2 Henry VI, or *The First Part of the*
  Contention between the Houses of
  Lancashire and Yorkshire 118,
  119, 121, 143–5
  3 Henry VI or *The True Tragedy of*
  Richard Duke of York 118, 119,
  145–8, 158
  Henry VIII 250–2
  Julius Caesar 121, 178
  King John 108, 119, 122, 125,
  126–34, 140, 170, 178, 220

King Lear 112, 121, 148, 178, 197,
  205–9, 217
Macbeth 120
Measure for Measure 112, 148, 238,
  242–8
Merchant of Venice 173, 178
Merry Wives of Windsor 117
Midsummer Night's Dream 181,
  249, 255
Othello 120
Pericles 54, 83 n. 81, 121, 238–40,
  250, 256
Richard II 108, 120, 231–2
Richard III 120, 148, 197
Romeo and Juliet 121
The Tempest 54, 119, 238, 248–50
Timon of Athens, *see* Shakespeare
  and Middleton
Troilus and Cressida 120, 130,
  198–205, 209, 255
Twelfth Night 120, 181
Two Gentlemen of Verona 175,
  178, 257
Shakespeare and Fletcher, *Henry*
  VIII 250–2
Shakespeare and Middleton, *Timon of*
  Athens 67, 85, 108, 121, 139,
  169–80, 221, 250, 253, 255, 257
Shirley, James, *The Politician* 256
  The Sisters 256
Shrovetide 3 n. 8, 5, 19, 52, 102, 153
Sidney, Sir Philip, *Defence of*
  Poesie 37–8, 232, 253
  'Lady of May' 106
Smith, John, court fool 42
Societes Joyeuses 93
Sotherton, Nicholas 22
sotties 30, 207
sovereignty 15, 86–8, 95, 96–9, 108–9
Stowe, John 3, 181 n. 1
Straw, Jack 15–16, 28

Thomas of Woodstock, *see* Woodstock
Timon farce 4, 36, 83, 120, 177, 196,
  265–71
Troublesome Raigne of King John,
  The 119, 122, 123–8, 130, 133,
  140, 159, 220
Trowle 63–4, 69–71, 85, 127, 136
True Tragedy of Richard III 223
Tucker, Thomas 52–3
Tyler, Wat 15–16, 28
tyranny 87–91, 108, 109, 196

Index

287

University entertainments 3, 36–7,
52–3, 73 n. 50, 177
Urquhart, Sir Thomas 35, 96, 239, 250
Utopia 53, 172–3, 202

Vetus Comoedia 273
Vice 131, 218, 247
Villiers, Duke of Buckingham 110
Virgin Mary 56, 60, 71, 99

Wager, William, *The Longer thou
Livest the more Fool thou art* 182,
219

War of the Theatres 272
Warwick, Earl of (1458) 21
Warwick, Earl of (1547–52) 20,
99–100
Webster, John, *The Duchess of
Malfi* 46
Whitsuntide 56, 59
Wistow summergame 58–9
Woodstock 108, 222–31, 253
Wolsey, Cardinal 218
Wyatt, Thomas 73–4

Yule 4, 34, 52

in fitting clothes - 88-89